Architectural Intelligence

Architectural Intelligence

How Designers and Architects Created the Digital Landscape

Molly Wright Steenson

The MIT Press
Cambridge, Massachusetts
London, England

This book was set in Stone Serif Std by Westchester Publishing Services. Printed and bound in the United States of America.

Graham Foundation

This book is supported by a grant from the Graham Foundation for Advanced Studies in the Fine Arts. Founded in 1956, the Graham Foundation fosters the development and exchange of diverse and challenging ideas about architecture and its role in the arts, culture, and society.

Publication is made possible in part by a grant from the Barr Ferree Foundation Publication Fund, Department of Art and Archaeology, Princeton University.

Library of Congress Cataloging-in-Publication Data is available.

ISBN: 978-0-262-03706-8

10 9 8 7 6 5 4 3 2 1

To Simon and our tiny family

Contents

Acknowledgments

This book is a map of the questions that won't leave me alone. Maybe that's what all books are. But it's also a diagram of people—of people who helped bring it into being, and there are people (and places) I'd like to thank.

Architectural Intelligence initially took shape as a dissertation at Princeton University in the School of Architecture with my adviser, M. Christine Boyer, secondary adviser, Axel Kilian, and reader Mario Gandelsonas between 2007 and 2013. The chapter on Cedric Price had an even earlier genesis in the Master's of Environmental Design program at the Yale School of Architecture led by Eeva-Liisa Pelkonen between 2005 and 2007, where Keller Easterling introduced me to the work of Price. It was the first of many intellectual introductions that she made. I'm also thankful for the valuable lessons that Claire Zimmerman and Peggy Deamer taught me there about naming your stakes and killing your darlings.

In the School of Architecture and beyond, my classmates had a big impact on me and include Anthony Acciavati, Pep Avilès, Alexis Cohen, Rohit De, Britt Eversole, Daniela Fabricius, Urtzi Grau, Gina Greene, Margo Handwerker, Alicia Imperiale, Lydia Kallipoliti, Joy Knoblauch, Evangelos Kotsioris, Anna-Maria Meister, Enrique Ramirez, Nick Risteen, Bryony Roberts, Sara Stevens, Mareike Stoll, Irene Sunwoo, Federica Vannucchi, Diana Kurkovsky West, and Grant Wythoff.

I spent time at a number of archives and institutions conducting the research that would become this book. During 2006, 2010, and 2013, I spent time at the Canadian Centre for Architecture, both in the Cedric Price Archive and teaching the "Toolkit on Digital" doctoral proseminar. I wish to thank the leadership and staff there: Phyllis Lambert, Mirko Zardini, Maristella Casciato, Giovanna Borasi, Albert Ferré, Lev Bratishenko, Mariana Siracusa, Renata Guttman, Colin MacWhirter, Natasha Leeman, Fabrizio Gallanti, Tim Abrahams, Howard Shubert, and Alexis Sornin. A special thank-you to Antoine Picon, with whom I taught and who has been a kind support to this project. Thank you also to MIT Special Collections and the Getty Research Institute.

A hearty thank-you to the MIT Press and to Doug Sery for his many years of conversation and support as *Architectural Intelligence* took shape, as well as to Gita Manaktala and Roger Conover. Marguerite Avery also supported this project from its germinal stages. Thank you to editorial assistant Noah Springer, copyeditor Erin Davis, and designer Erin Hasley; and to Chris Grimley of over, under for the cover design. And although this book would have been published, without Lisa Otto it would have had no images. Thanks to her and to Sarah Rafson for showing us the way. I wish to thank a number of other friends who have helped me with various aspects of the book: Judith Zissman, for telling me what to cut; Rob Wiesenberger, for helping with the puzzle pieces; Dan Klyn, for his feedback and encyclopedic knowledge of all things Richard Saul Wurman; Sands Fish, for hunting down images; Daniel Cardoso Llach, for generous attention and deep ideas; and Mimi Zeiger, for support both moral and architectural.

This book benefited from insightful interviews and conversations, across architecture, design, and the Web, with Dick Bowdler, John Frazer, Jesse James Garrett, Christopher Herot, Barbara Jakobson, Karen McGrane, Peter Merholz, Drue Miller, Tom Moran, Michael Naimark, Paul Pangaro, Nathan Shedroff, Gillian Crampton Smith, Phil Tabor, David Weinberger, Guy Weinzapfel, Terry Winograd, Richard Saul Wurman, and the members of the Face email list. I especially wish to thank Nicholas Negroponte, whom I interviewed twice, and who generously gave me access to his personal papers.

Much of what became this book was written in residence at the HUMLab at Umeå University in Sweden and in good friendship with the Umeå Institute of Design between 2010 and 2015. Friends in Sweden I want to thank include Elin Andersson, Emil Seth Åreng, Jim Barrett, Coppélie Cocq, Lorenzo Davoli, Carl-Erik Enqvist, Anna Foka, Mike Frangos, Stefan Gelfgren, Maria Göransdotter, Alan Greve, Stephanie Hendrick, Adam Henriksson, Karin Jangert, Anna Johansson, Finn Arne Jørgenson, Cecelia Lindhé, Mattis Lindmark, Fredrik Palm, Johan Redström, Jim Robertsson, Jon Svensson, Patrik Svensson, Johan von Boer, and Heather Wiltse. An especially big thank-you to Emma Ewadotter for making me feel at home in the tundra.

While I was a professor in the School of Journalism and Mass Communication at the University of Wisconsin–Madison from 2013 to 2015, my colleagues were a great support to both me and this project. They included Lisa Aarli, Dave Black, Janet Buechner, Rowan Calyx, Katy Culver, Greg Downey, Stacy Forster, Lucas Graves, Pat Hastings, Shawnika Hull, Young Mie Kim, Doug McLeod, Lindsey Palmer, Karyn Riddle, Sue Robinson, Hernando Rojas, Robert Schwoch, Hemant Shah, Dhavan Shah, Steve Vaughan, Mike Wagner, and Chris Wells. I will always miss James Baughman and our hallway conversations. Lew Friedland receives special mention for his mentorship and friendship that goes back to 1994 and the first website we built, and my deepest thanks for bringing me back to Madison. My friends in my renegade writing group read the first, tentative paragraphs of this manuscript: Emily Callaci, Kathryn Ciancia, Lucas Graves, Judd Kinzley, Nicole Nelson, and Stephen Young. Conversations on the porch with Mark Vareschi were also vital in shaping this book. Madison was a wonderful home, thanks to friends including Matthew Berland, Anjali Bhasin, Ralph Cross, Tullia Dymarz, Randy Goldsmith, Sarah Roberts, and Eliana Stein, and because of late-night conversations, again with Lucas Graves and Emily Callaci.

At Carnegie Mellon University, my students have helped me form and challenge the ideas in this book. They include Irene Alvarez, Ahmed Ansari, Jacquelyn Brioux, Anne Burdick, Deepa Butoliya, Francis Carter, Shruti Aditya Chowdhury, Victoria Costikyan, Saumya Kharbanda, Min Kim, Silvia Mata-Marin, Chirag Murthy, Aprameya Mysore, Kirk Newton, Dimeji Onafuwa, Lisa Otto, Olaitan Owamolo, Julia Petrich, Tracy Potter, Catherine Shen, Monique Smith, Alex Wright, Ming Xing, and Vikas Yadev. My School of Design colleagues have offered solid support. They include Eric Anderson, Mark Baskinger, Dan Boyarski, Charlee Brodsky, Wayne Chung, Melissa Cicozi, Jane Ditmore, Hannah Du Plessis, Bruce Hanington, Kristin Hughes, Meghan Kennedy, Gideon Kossoff, Austin Lee, Dan Lockton, Marc Rettig, Stacie Rohrbach, Darlene Scalese, Peter Scupelli, Kyuha Shim, Steve Stadelmeier, Andrew Twigg, Dylan Vitone, Matt Zywicka, and especially Terry Irwin, who granted me the time to complete this book. Across the CMU campus, I'm also grateful for a multifaceted group of colleagues that includes Mary-Lou Arscott, Daniel Cardoso Llach, Daragh Burns, Dana Cupkova, Anind Dey, Jodi Forlizzi, Stefan Gruber, Kai Gutschow, Eddy Man Kim, Steve Lee, Golan Levin, Adam Perer, Nida Rehman, Larry Shea, Francesca Torello, Christopher Warren, Scott Weingart, and John Zimmerman. You've all made Pittsburgh a welcome home, as have a group of folks who include Desi González, Jedd Hakimi, Jason Head, Val Head, Harriet Riley Lockton, Drue Miller, Becca Newbury, David Newbury, Sarah Rafson, and J. Eric Townsend.

I also wish to thank a cabal of coconspirators and purveyors of intellectual mischief that includes Eduardo Aguayo, Megan Sapnar Ankerson, Boris Anthony, Marit Appeldoorn, Jason Aronen, Jennifer Bove, Bryan Boyer, Benjamin Bratton, Jennifer Brook, Anne Burdick, Stuart Candy, Ben Cerveny, Elizabeth Churchill, Aaron Straup Cope, Matt Cottam, Cletus Dalglish-Schommer, Andy Davidson, Birke Dickhoff, Carl DiSalvo, Steve Doberstein, Nick and Heather Donohue, Jake Dunagan, Lia Fest, Adam Flynn, Laura Forlano, Anne Galloway, Jesse James Garrett, Marian Glebes, Sam Greenspan, John Harwood, Mocha Jean Herrup, Dan Hill, Joe Hobaica, Matt Jones, Jofish Kaye, Christian Svanes Kolding, Thomas Küber, Michael Kubo, Laura Kurgan, Mike Kuniavsky, Liz Lawley, Jesse LeCavalier, Ana Maria Léon, Jen Lowe, Joanne McNeill, Tom

Meyer, Stefano Mirti, Rudolf Müller, Ali Muney, Martin Nachbar, Chris Noessel, Erik Olofsson, Andrew Otwell, Erica Robles-Anderson, Frida Rosenberg, Brenda Sanderson, Caroline Sinders, Tristam Sparks, Nick Sweeney, Marcy Swenson, Craig Sylvester, Victor Szilagyi, Vicky Tiegelkamp, Anthony Townsend, Olga Touloumi, Phil van Allen, Greg Veen, Rodrigo Vera, Rowan Wilken, Janice Wong, and Alex Wright. I'd like to extend a special thank-you to Evangelos Kotsioris, Theodora Vardouli, and Fred Scharmen for collaborations on panels and articles related to these topics. A few special shout-outs: Enrique Ramirez expanded my field of vision, not just to architecture, but to airplanes, bass guitar, and beyond. He's had an enormous impact on how I see the world and on my path in life. Paul Dourish and I have traded ideas immaterial and material—he's a fellow traveler and a gateway to ideas and friendships of the first order. Not least, Paul introduced me to Janet Vertesi, my best woman and best friend, the person who always encourages me to be better. A particular thank-you to Pam Daghlian: when I wasn't sure how to get this book written, she reminded me that I knew how. Finally, my gratitude to the digital and real-life communities that feed me, including chix, the HC, the IxDA, the Eyeo Festival, my friends at Adaptive Path, and the numerous conferences and gatherings in which I've shared the ideas put forth here.

This book is supported by a grant from the Graham Foundation for Advanced Studies in the Fine Arts. Founded in 1956, the Graham Foundation for Advanced Studies in the Fine Arts fosters the development and exchange of diverse and challenging ideas about architecture and its role in the arts, culture, and society. Publication is also made possible in part by a grant from the Barr Ferree Foundation Publication Fund, Department of Art and Archaeology, Princeton University.

In closing, there's nothing without family. I'm so happy to have my brothers and their families: Andy, Carrie, Jack, and Maddie; Ben, Alexsis, and Sam; and my stepsister Darci and her daughter Fiona. I'm also grateful to the family I gained through marriage: Ruth and Randy; Isaiah, Jane, and August; Ben, Emily, Katherine, Sam, and Peter, and, in memory, Omar. I owe a debt of gratitude to my stepparents: to my stepmother, Carol, who shows me all the ways we continue to grow and learn; and to the memory of my stepfather, Chuck DuFresne, who shared my love of books and would've been happy to see this one. My parents have been everything to me: my dad, Mike, the first Steenson whose book I saw in print in grade school, and my mom, Mary, who I saw sworn in as a lawyer when I was little and as a judge when I was big—moments that made a huge impression on me. You've both been an enormous source of love and inspiration.

And most of all, I want to thank you, Simon King, for your love (and our perambulations with Emoji the dog). Here's to our adventures big and small, past and future. This book is for you.

1   Architects, Anti-Architects, and Architecting

What is the verb of "architecture"? That depends on who you ask.

A professional architect will tell you that architects *design*. Architects design buildings. They might have a hand in building them, but first and foremost, they design them. Yet the verb of digital structure for programmers and information architects designers is "architecting": designing a system, working holistically from parts to wholes, operating from above, setting in place foundations from below. From the perspective of digital designers and programmers, what architects do is analogous to what designers and programmers do in their most complicated and intricate work. The way designers and programmers use the term speaks to the idea of what an architect does, to the complexity of their work, and to the expertise that architects claim. In essence, they architect architectures.

Many architects criticize the uptake of architecture and architecting by non-architects. Becoming a licensed architect is a professional distinction achieved after several years of apprenticeship and a long set of challenging exams that takes months, if not years, to complete. Only after passing the registration exam can the designer of buildings call herself an architect. Once licensed and registered, architects can sign off on plans and drawings, legally assuming risk for projects.

It is illegal to call oneself an architect without the title, as Nathan Shedroff, founder of the early web design firm vivid studios, discovered in 1999 when he received a letter from the Board of Architectural Examiners. Shedroff (whom we'll meet again in chapter 4) wrote a column titled "The Architect" for a magazine about designing for the World Wide Web.

Dear Mr. Shedroff:

The Board has received information that you may be offering architectural services. Specifically, the Board received a copy [of] your article title "THE ARCHITECT" featured in New Media Magazine. In addition, your email address was identified as architect@newmedia.com.

Be advised that if you do not have a California license to practice architecture, you may be in violation of the Architects Practice Act, Business and Professions Code section 5536. This section states, in part, that it is a misdemeanor punishable by a fine and/or imprisonment for any person who is not a California licensed architect to put out any card, sign, or other device which might indicate to the public that he or she is an architect or is qualified to engage in the practice of architecture.[1]

Shedroff wasn't passing himself off as an architect in the traditional sense, but as amusing as the letter is, it underscores something important: that architecture is a high-stakes matter. It is a title and practice that architects defend, and a metaphor that the designers of systems reach for when they are working on complex problems and digital structures.

Architecture structures and scaffolds complex entities. It is no surprise that engineers, computer scientists, and digital designers reach out to architectural concepts when they want to express the complexity of their work. The notion of architecture provides a means for relating elements of a problem that are at different scales to one another. When non-architects adopt the term "architecture," when they use "architect" as a verb, they are seeking ways to bring complicated issues into relation with each other. They are looking to architecture as a metaphor for how humans interact with spaces. These notions of architecture and architecting are closer to each other than it might seem.

The purpose of this book is to explore that space between architecture and architecting. It centers on the work and practices of four architects: Christopher Alexander, Richard Saul Wurman, Cedric Price, and Nicholas Negroponte and the MIT Architecture Machine Group, starting in the 1960s and focusing on their work from the 1960s to the 1980s. In each case study, I look at the technological paradigms that each incorporated in their work, such as cybernetics, artificial intelligence, and the programs and interfaces that they used and developed. I then trace the influence of these architects on digital practices such as programming languages, information architecture, and other contemporary digital design practices from the late 1980s till the present day. I ask: In what ways were these practices architectural, and how did they push the boundaries of architecture? Similarly, how did their experiments with computing and technology push the bounds of the technological fields in which they were working? What did computational, cybernetic, and artificial intelligence researchers and engineers stand to gain by engaging with architects and architectural problems? How did architecture became useful territory for the imagination of new digital worlds?

At the same time the digital world was reaching toward architecture and architectural metaphors, the architects in this book weren't always sure whether what they were doing was still architecture. As Alexander, Wurman, Price, and Negroponte began to conceive of their work in terms of information processing and computational practices, they found themselves in a liminal space between the two fields, which caused them to question whether what they were doing was architectural at all, or something in opposition to it, or something new altogether. At times, they characterized themselves as anti-architecture and anti-architects. Robin Boyd wrote about the anti-architecture tendency in 1968, "It is fascinated by the population explosion and plugging-in and pop, by McLuhan, of course, and by systems and electronics; and it yearns for the day when it will be able to surrender itself completely to a computer." But some "realities" challenge anti-architecture: it is on paper; it "has not been built—yet."[2] Building anti-architecture would automatically cancel it, Boyd noted, by virtue of the fact that it would have become architecture.

Indeed, none of the projects in this book by any of the architects I write about directly resulted in constructed buildings. There are projects that were intended to be built but were not; there are design processes and tools, computer programs, and interfaces to use; there are digital environments to sit inside. What kind of architecture is it, when the fact of its construction isn't the point of it? And how did that perspective contribute to our metaphors for digital design and information architecture in its various forms today?

Meet the Architects

Christopher Alexander developed an operating system for order, first using computers and computation, then capturing the system in what he and his colleagues called pattern languages. His impact on programmers and digital designers is crucial: when programmers talk about patterns, or when digital designers talk about architecture, they are referring to Alexander. Yet architects remain ambivalent about his work, finding his methods overly moralistic and deterministic. Alexander incorporated aspects of cognitive psychology, heuristics, cybernetics, and early artificial intelligence in his work. Initially, in the early 1960s, he formatted architectural problems with set and graph theory, then used an IBM mainframe computer to run a program that analyzed those requirements. He employed different topological structures to visualize the architectural problems that accorded with the computational paradigms he had at hand, situating his rhetoric in favor of the operative visualization. As his structures grew in complexity, he abandoned computers for generative pattern languages that were more flexible and propagated the sense of order that so interested him. Best known for *Notes on the Synthesis of Form* and *A Pattern Language*, Alexander influenced programmers in the development of object-oriented programming languages, patterns in software, the wiki format that runs sites such as Wikipedia, and methodologies such as Extreme Programming. His approach to patterns is vitally important to human-centered designers, who look to pattern-based approaches to organize their work. So what of the disconnect between architects and system designers that Alexander seems to foment? What might architects learn from his influence on other fields? Anticipating the Internet of things and smart cities, Alexander told a 1996 audience of programmers, "You almost can't name a facet of the world which is not already, to some very strong degree, under the influence of the programs that are being written to manage and control those entities or those operations."[3] He asked to what extent programmers might be willing to take on "the responsibility for influencing, shaping, and changing the environment."[4] Should architects, designers, and developers of all kinds, all of whom operate in an increasingly digital world, do the same?

For Richard Saul Wurman, "information architecture" referred to the organization of information on the page, in a map, within a book, as a design language—and then, ultimately, to rolling these approaches outward to the city and the world at large. Accordingly, the term "information architecture" referred to clear structure and communication through graphics—applied fittingly and systematically at the urban scale, or in representations of information in books and atlases—a term he started to popularize in the mid-1970s. He began his career working in Louis Kahn's architectural practice and then led his own architectural practice in Philadelphia before shifting his focus. These days, Wurman is probably best known for founding the TED conferences, and has long understood events and conferences as a way to advance his ideas. He chaired the Aspen International Design Conference in 1972 under the theme "The Invisible City" and, in 1976, the AIA conference in Philadelphia under the title "Architectures of Information." The AIA conference brochure asked, "Wouldn't a city—any city—be more useful and more fun if everybody knew what to do in it, and with it? As architects, we know it takes more than good-looking buildings to make a city habitable and usable. It takes information: information about what spaces do as well as how they look; information that helps people articulate their needs and respond to change. That's what Architecture of Information is all about."[5] Wurman influenced a generation of software and web designers who took up the term "information architecture" and applied it to the structure and design of websites, software, and mobile applications. As the field of software design began to diversify, "information architecture" became the practice of structuring online experiences, particularly coinciding with the growth of the Web.

Cedric Price designed buildings that were determined by their flows of information. He incorporated cybernetic feedback loops in projects that challenged traditional relationships between architects, users, sites, and technology, in buildings and generative architectural projects that he proposed would learn from and respond to their users in surprising ways, such as the cybernetic Fun Palace (1963–1967, unbuilt) that he designed with radical theater director Joan Littlewood and cybernetician Gordon Pask; the Oxford Corner House proposal for a restaurant turned building-sized computer (1965–1966, unbuilt); and Generator, a networked, intelligent retreat center composed of a kit of responsive parts (1976–1979, unbuilt). Price playfully upended traditional architectural and system-design dynamics. He used cybernetics and information processing techniques to tease and challenge himself and the potential users of his buildings, supporting indeterminacy and the idea that a building never be locked down into one instance or one thing. And by designing buildings that worked like computers, multimedia environments, and distributed intelligence platforms, he made it possible to envision what it would be like to learn, play, and experience in a computerized world. Most of his work remained unbuilt, yet still exercised powerful provocations to fellow architects, students, and the British public, causing them to question what a building could be and how computation might change that notion. Although Price has exercised a less direct effect on programming and digital design than the other architects, designers, and technologists in this book, he is no less important.

Nicholas Negroponte, with his colleague Leon Groisser, founded MIT's Architecture Machine Group (AMG), a tinkerer's lab composed equally of architects and electrical engineers. Founded in 1967, it became the foundation for the MIT Media Lab, into which it was folded in 1985. Negroponte situated architectural research as a technical and scientific interest at MIT, collaborating with the Artificial Intelligence Lab (founded as the AI Project in 1959) and benefiting from Department of Defense and corporate funding. AMG initially designed programs for computer-aided design systems and interfaces on screen. Later, the scope of these projects grew in fidelity, as AMG's researchers designed room-sized, multiscreen simulations that surrounded the user, claiming that they were so realistic, the experience was "like being there." Negroponte ultimately claimed the term "media" for the MIT Media Lab—a deliberately loaded term for convergent systems that incorporated consumer electronics, graphics, publishing, learning, music, gestures, screens, and vocal commands. The research that AMG conducted contributed to practices that are still considered emergent, including artificial intelligence (AI), machine-learning, intelligent environments, virtual reality, remote sensing, and drone surveillance. Then as now, the MIT Media Lab is probably *the* lab that people think produces a vision of the digital future. Now in its third decade, it is more important than ever to critically examine how the lab arrived where it is today, where its vision might lead in the next thirty years, and the questions that its research might beg.

There are, of course, other architects and designers that this book could have followed but didn't: one such omission is Bill Mitchell at MIT, who was fundamental in framing the relationship between architecture and cyberspace. His long career, which bridged computing and architecture, began in the 1960s. He was dean of the School of Architecture and Planning until 2003 and led the Smart Cities research group at the MIT Media Lab. Mitchell was the author of many books, including *Computer-Aided Architectural Design* in 1977, and *City of Bits, e-topia*, and *Me++* in the 1990s and early 2000s. Another major case study could center on Carnegie Mellon University (where I am now a professor) and the work of Herbert Simon, Allen Newell, and architecture professor Ömer Akin, among others.

It is hard not to notice that the four major case studies in this book center on white men. In the earliest years of these practices, not many women were working with computation and architecture. But they weren't absent. In fact, M. Christine Boyer, professor of architecture at Princeton University (my dissertation adviser) received a master of engineering in computing and information science from the University of Pennsylvania and a master's and PhD from MIT in the Department of City Planning in the late 1960s, where her research involved mathematics, computation, and computational linguistics (she chose to do a PhD in city planning so that her work would not be funded by the military).[6] Many individuals that I write about in this book partnered and collaborated closely with women. Christopher Alexander worked closely with Sara Ishikawa, his coauthor of *A Pattern Language* and cofounder of the Center for Environmental Structure. Cedric Price and radical theater director Joan Littlewood were equal partners on their most famous project, the Fun Palace. Muriel Cooper was a vital force at MIT, first as design and media director of the MIT Press and later as cofounder of the Visible Language Workshop, where she pioneered the design of screen-based interfaces and immersive environments. Cooper was a close friend of Richard Saul Wurman, who included her work in his books, including a eulogy for her; she was also close to Nicholas Negroponte (whom she introduced to Wurman). David Reinfurt and Robert Wiesenberger's book, *Muriel Cooper* (MIT Press, 2017), begins to give her her due. In the late years of the MIT Architecture Machine Group and the founding of the Media Lab, women such as Peggy Weill and Judith Donath forged new territory for the lab. Contemporary digital design—and my view and experience of it for the twenty-four years I've worked in the field—would be nowhere without the contributions of Lucy Suchman, Jane Fulton-Suri, Elizabeth Churchill, Lisa Strausfeld, Gillian Crampton Smith, Shelley Evenson, Terry Irwin, Darcy Dinucci, and Joy Mountford, to name a few. Barry Katz's excellent book *Make It New: The History of Silicon Valley Design* addresses the contributions of some of these individuals to the world of digital design.

Architecture, by Definition(s)

The traditional definition of "architecture" is the practice of "building or constructing edifices of any kind for human use," according to the *Oxford English Dictionary*.[7] Architecture can refer to "the action or process of building" and the structures that result, both in abstract and concrete uses of the term. It also means the organization of the style, structure, and ornament of a building. But architecture is at least as much about the way a building is imagined, prefigured, and translated as it is about its construction. After all, most architects do not construct the building with their bare hands: their work is done on paper and in models long before a building stands. The word "model," too, is an architectural term: it initially referred to plans for building (the French *modèle* or Italian *modello* became the English "model" during the seventeenth century), derived from the Latin for *modulus*—an architectural term for "to measure." Models serve as the measure of an idea, the working through an image in one's mind, into a drawing, and into three dimensions. These conceptual notions of architecture are not a recent concept. The visionary architect Étienne-Louis Boullée wrote, in the late eighteenth century, "It is necessary to conceive (of architecture) in order to perform it. . . . It is this production of the mind, it is this creation that constitutes architecture that is of consequence to us: the definition of the art of production and bringing to perfection of any building."[8] To Boullée's mind, constructing a building was not what proved the architecture (that part was the "secondary art" of construction): it was the act of designing, the envisioning of detail, the specification that was the métier of the architect.

The architect and scholar Robin Evans wrote that architectural drawings were more like translations, both like and unlike the architectural object to which they relate. "To translate is to convey. It is to move something without altering it," he wrote in the opening lines of his 1986 essay, "Translations from Drawing to Building."[9] But that notion presupposes that even the most faithful translation is able to move something without changing it, because the feelings between languages don't move in a continuous fabric: "Things can get bent, broken, or lost on the way."[10] In a similar vein, architectural historian Beatriz Colomina wrote that architecture is "an interpretive, critical act."[11] She suggested that a building could be read and "interpreted" through a variety of theoretical methods, as one might do with a text ("theory, criticism, history, or manifesto,") or through representation ("drawing, writing, model making). "Interpretation is also integral to the act of projecting," she wrote.[12] All of this is to say that architectural design is a matter of prefiguring and processing, moving between image and language, interpreting and translating.

When engineers, programmers, and designers of different kinds describe the design and reproduction of complex systems, they call it architecture. Architecture means applying a structural approach to the design of complex systems, taking into consideration modular ways to program, and developing better interfaces for the user of a computer system. And while Evans and Colomina were not writing about computers, their notions of architecture as conception and translation are similar to computer architecture: "the conceptual structure and overall logical organization of a computer or computer-based system from the point of view of its use or design."[13] Engineers approach the design of software similar to the way an architect approaches the design of a building. This particular definition of architecture from the *Oxford English Dictionary* comes from the 1962 "Architectural Philosophy" that Frederick P. Brooks outlined in *Planning a Computer System*, a book about the world's first supercomputer, the IBM 7030, or Stretch. "Computer architecture, like other architecture," Brooks wrote, "is the art of determining the needs of the user of a structure and then designing to meet those needs as effectively as possible within economic and technological constraints."[14] The germ of Brooks's idea developed from John von Neumann's 1946 paper about the design of the EDVAC computer (one of the earliest digital computers) as the "organization of logical elements" of a computer and the instruction sets it follows. The architect of a system translated and transmuted these logical elements. The "conceptual structure" was a matter of not only schematics and wiring, but also interpretation and translation. Although the Stretch had the most intricate and complex circuitry of any computer of its time, its intricacies also led to its failures. It was never as fast as IBM claimed it could be (thirty times faster, not one hundred to two hundred times faster), and it took five years to realize, rendering it a commercial failure (it could be sold for $8 million, not $13 million, and with government agencies its only customers).

What lived on from the Stretch was its architecture. It formed the basis of the highly successful IBM 7090 and IBM S/360 computers, as well many non-IBM computers.[15] The architecture produced the seeds of its future propagation: the logics and the platforms that could be transferred onto a new system, and another system after that. Frederick Brooks, incidentally, was later influenced by Christopher Alexander, Herbert Simon, and the Design Methods movement, worked on design considerations for virtual reality, and authored a set of essays titled *The Design of Design* in 2010 that touches on many themes in this book.

Computers and the Changing Architectural Profession

While it may seem obvious, the connection of architecture to computing presumed something very basic: that an architect, planner, or designer could use a computer at all. Computers were rare, expensive, and slow. Only major educational institutions and big architectural and engineering firms, or ones that serviced military contracts, had digital computers (with few exceptions).[16] As early as the 1950s, architects at Skidmore Owings and Merrill (SOM) and Ellerbe & Associates used computers for risk calculations and cost estimates. The firm Arup used a computer to model the iconic sails of the roof of the Sydney Opera House, designed by Jørn Utzon. Computers cost as much as commercial airliners, and processing was expensive in terms of both time and capability.[17] Punching cards, debugging errors, and running programs all took hours, after which the programmer would still need to interpret the resulting data. Despite these barriers, computers were attractive to architects and designers, who found themselves interfacing with more systems, tackling more complicated design problems, and needing to conceptualize their work within a bigger systemic framework than ever before.[18]

In the 1960s, architects turned to computers because they recognized the growing complexity of architectural problems. Advances in information storage, transmission, and retrieval resulted in new possibilities—ranging from new institutions to new kinds of buildings and formal possibilities—that architects would need to both assimilate and accommodate, wrote British architect and architectural critic Royston Landau in 1968.[19] For architects, this meant changes in both the nature of their practice and what they designed. They needed to interface with more systems and handle problems of greater complexity. The architectural project, regardless of size, existed within a larger framework and needed to, as Landau writes, "be seen in its context as a component which has a relationship to other parts of its system."[20] Architects began to see that "information movement" had "a complementary effect on physical movement," which made the understanding of information networks a concern for "critical theoretical study."[21] Within this "information explosion and research revolution," architects themselves became nodes of an "information exchange network," in which an architect would develop "his own network of interests and special set of information antennae."[22] Not only would architects use informational mechanisms to structure their work, they would serve as communication nexuses that connected to other fields.

In the early to mid-1960s, architects including Christopher Alexander and Cedric Price used cybernetics to visualize the flows and feedbacks of the dynamics of design problems. In the late 1960s, architects like Nicholas Negroponte also turned to artificial intelligence, which offered the possibility of a system becoming more intelligent over time, by learning from its users and developing in tandem with them, with the idea that the system would evolve from how the computer was originally programmed, and from what both the architect and user might imagine on their own. New design processes emerged that had applications beyond architecture and into design, the social sciences, and beyond. Today, architects use computers in every aspect of their work, from computer-aided design (CAD) programs like AutoCAD that form the backbone of their work to algorithmic and parametric design tools that generate forms that couldn't exist without computation to visualizations of complex data. Not to mention, architects use computers as a matter of course for communication, publication, and the promotion of their work.

Augmenting the Architect

Just as architects turned to computers, engineers and programmers also turned to architecture. In the 1960s, computation, cybernetics, and AI researchers reached toward architecture. They did so through architectural use cases (such as with Douglas Engelbart's Augmented Human Intellect platform, as we will see below) or problems (Terry Winograd's SHRDLU language that manipulated piles of blocks, chapter 6), or through processes of abstraction and organization (Gordon Pask's second-order cybernetics, chapters 5 and 6, or Herbert Simon in *Sciences of the Artificial*), their manifestation of these routines in software (Ivan Sutherland's Sketchpad computer-aided design system, see below), or through direct application in the built environment (Mark Weiser's notion of ubiquitous computing, where the computer disappears into the environment, chapters 4 and 7). In architecture, these various engineers and researchers found not only a metaphor for building worlds, but also the justification for developing computational power that would make these worlds possible. Architecture offered the possibility of applying their work to tangible results that everyday people could understand.

The luminary engineer Douglas Engelbart, inventor of the computer mouse in 1963 and founder of the Augmented Research Center (ARC) at the Stanford Research Institute (SRI), used architectural scenarios and projects as a way to envision a future use case for rich computational experiences. Engelbart introduced the idea of an "augmented architect at work" in his proposal for the 1962 Augmented Human Intellect Study. Funded by the Air Force Office of Scientific Research, he proposed augmenting a human being, "increasing the capability of a man to approach a complex problem situation, to gain comprehension to suit his particular needs, and to derive solutions to problems."[23] Engelbart's system preceded Nicholas Negroponte and Leon Groisser's URBAN2 and URBAN5 urban design systems at MIT by six years (Negroponte referred to the proposal for the study in the bibliography of his 1970 book *The Architecture Machine*).

The setup that Engelbart imagined, from the beginning of his proposal, was not dissimilar from a contemporary architect's desk. Engelbart specified a good-sized screen, peripherals for designing and drawing, and a computer to process the work. "Let us consider an augmented architect at work," he wrote. "He sits at a working station that has a visual display screen some three feet on a side; this is his working surface, and is controlled by a computer (his 'clerk') with which he can communicate by means of a small keyboard and various other devices. He is designing a building. He has already dreamed up several basic layouts and structural forms, and is trying them out on the screen."[24] The relationship that the architect has with his computer is friendly—he "coaxed the clerk" to show him a perspective: "he has just coaxed the clerk to show him a perspective view of the steep hillside building site with the roadway above, symbolic representations of the various trees that are to remain on the lot, and the service tie points for the different utilities. . . . With a 'pointer,' he indicates two points of interest, moves his left hand rapidly over the keyboard, and the distance and elevation between the points indicated appear on the right-hand third of the screen."[25] Throughout the scenario, Engelbart's architect receives new computer data that he interacts with on the keyboard. "A structure is taking shape. He examines it, adjusts it, pauses long enough to ask for handbook or catalog information from the clerk at various points, and readjusts accordingly," Engelbart wrote. He enters data about aspects of the design and performs an analysis of how people will actually use the building, then saves the information so that it can be shared with architects and contractors. As the architect works with the computer, a proto-hyperlinked structure forms that "represents the maturing thought behind the actual design."[26]

To be clear, Engelbart's scenario was just that—a future vision of human–computer interaction. What is remarkable, however, is that it outlined the problems that intelligent computer-aided design systems would try to solve for the next fifty years. Architectural problems were multidimensional and programmatic, involving three-dimensional elements and real world attributes (such as traffic congestion in a building). Engelbart's research represented a new, developing notion of what a program was, in the definition of a computer program in the architectural sense of the term, which refers to defining the function of a particular space. Moreover, computer-aided design systems combined explicit information given by the user with implicit operations performed by the computer: design elements drawn by the user of a system would receive additional attributes from the system (such as Engelbart's stipulation that the "clerk" show how the doors swing, or the sun comes through a window). And ultimately, systems designed for architectural purposes would prove attractive and applicable to other uses. As Engelbart concluded, anything requiring the use of "symbolized concepts" would find his proposed system useful:

In such a future working relationship between human problem-solver and computer "clerk," the capability of the computer for executing mathematical processes would be used whenever it was needed. However, the computer has many other capabilities for manipulating and displaying information that can be of significant benefit to the human in nonmathematical processes of planning, organizing, studying, etc. Every person who does his thinking with symbolized concepts (whether in the form of the English language, pictographs, formal logic, or mathematics) should be able to benefit significantly.[27]

This last sentence deserves some emphasis. Architectural use cases could be applied to other contexts. Engelbart raised the possibility here, but this is something we will find throughout the histories elsewhere in this book. Finding novel applications of the digital and the spatial would change the way that people navigated learning, conversation, and information.

Beyond developing imperatives for computing power and peripherals, perhaps Engelbart chose to use an architect as representative in his earliest scenario about augmented human intelligence because it allowed him to show a vision of computing at scale. Most importantly, Engelbart understood something vital about the power of architecture: the fact that it is about building worlds.

The Architecture and the Computer Conference

With the computer, architects saw major changes coming to their discipline, not all of which were positive. It was clear that the traditional boundaries of architecture would shift, necessitating new skills and rendering others obsolete, as Royston Landau wrote.[28] With this "accelerating growth of information and knowledge" came "an increase in doubt."[29] That very feeling was in the minds of the attendees of the Architecture and the Computer conference in Boston in 1964. The question there was not *if* the computer would change architectural practice, but rather *how*. The six hundred conference attendees, a who's-who of architecture, planning, engineering, and computation research, traded visions and worries about how computers would change the field of architecture. The goal was to "alert the profession to an irresistible force which will radically alter the practice of architecture whether we plan for it or not," wrote conference organizer Sanford Greenfield in his preface to the proceedings.[30] Christopher Alexander was there, as was Marvin Minsky, the cofounder of MIT's AI Lab, and Steven Coons, the MIT mechanical engineering professor who, with Douglas Ross, led MIT's computer-aided design initiatives. Ivan Sutherland presented the Sketchpad computer-aided design system that he developed for his dissertation at MIT, and William Fetter, who popularized the term "computer graphics" and its development at Boeing, also presented. In fact, the Architecture and the Computer conference was important enough that Bauhaus founder Walter Gropius provided the conference's opening statement, read on his behalf. Gropius likened computing to an agent not unlike the forces of mechanization that Sigfried Giedion distinguished in *Mechanization Takes Command*. Although Gropius could not imagine architects having access to real-time computing, he imagined the creative possibilities that computers could afford. "It will certainly be up to us architects to make use of them intelligently as means of superior mechanical control which might provide us with ever-greater freedom for the creative process of design," he wrote.[31]

The conference's engineers and computation researchers most celebrated how computation would change architecture, perhaps not surprisingly. Marvin Minsky predicted that the computer's role could be "helpful on a very large scale," even in the most "conservative" estimate. Even the more "straightforward" possibilities he predicted included computer graphics systems that could sketch, render, or generate plans: by 1974, he envisioned that architecture offices would be able to use computer graphics, and to a large extent, he was right.[32] Minsky did not stop there—he projected forward to the mid-1990s.

For in no more than 30 years, computers may be as intelligent, or more intelligent, than people. The machine may be able to handle not only the planning but the complete mechanical assembly of things as well. Some computers now have scanners attached to them so they can see drawings; eventually computers will have hands, vision and the programs that will make them able to assemble buildings, make things at a very high rate of speed, economically. Contractors will have to face automation in construction just as the architects will have to face automation of design. Eventually, I believe computers will evolve formidable creative capacity.[33]

Minsky accurately captured both the concerns and the interests of architects and AI researchers in the 1960s, and many of his predictions did in fact come to fruition. Architects remained—and do still remain—concerned that computers might render them obsolete. Although other professionals (such as doctors, politicians, and policymakers) were facing the same concerns at the time, architecture had unique challenges. "It is perhaps unique to architecture that the resolution of these variables must express itself in a three dimensional form, and in the last analysis it is this form which is of principal importance," Greenfield wrote.[34] But could computers ever develop creative capacity? This was a question that captivated many of the architects and researchers in this book.

Computational Paradigms

In the 1960s, six areas of technological development were important for the architects that I write about in this book. The areas were not necessarily discrete, and overlapped with one another. I want to highlight them here: computer-aided design and computer graphics; symbiosis, problem solving, and cybernetics; and artificial intelligence.

Computer-Aided Design and Computer Graphics

The earliest computer-aided design programs incorporated the same basic functionality and operating models that contemporary CAD programs still maintain. Ivan Sutherland's Sketchpad, a two-dimensional computer-aided drawing system, was the subject of his PhD dissertation advised by Claude Shannon, Marvin Minsky, and Steven Coons.[35] Sketchpad attempted to model an understanding of the complexity of design processes. Computer-aided design programs like it, Coons said to the audience at the 1964 Architecture and the Computer conference in Boston, "will in a few years culminate in the kind of computer system and the kind of man-computer symbiosis we have in mind."[36] What Coons and Sutherland had in mind at the 1964 conference privileged the designer over a computer. Coons said, "The entire process is one of continuous communication between the designer and the machine, but one in which the designer is always in complete control. He is free to accept the implications of what he has done, as shown him by the computer, or to modify his original concept based on these implications."[37] Arguments such as this one served to assuage the fears of architects who did not want a computer taking over the role of the designer.

To use Sketchpad 2, a designer held a light pen and drew directly on the cathode ray tube screen, then performed operations on the lines that resulted. With a console of many dials, buttons, toggle switches, and knobs, the user correlated commands and operations to the drawn shapes. The designer could also create reusable archetypes: shapes, once drawn, could be employed whenever needed, and "icons" deployed that represented a set of replicable actions, such as commanding the computer to make a set of lines equal in length.[38] The next version of the system, Sketchpad 3, developed by Timothy Johnson (who later joined MIT's School of Architecture, where he taught computing), could render three-dimensional drawings. In just two to three years, the complexity that the program could handle improved substantially, as the cost of the system grew cheaper, the cost of processing dropped, and computers became smaller. Marvin Minsky noted the system's decreasing cost in 1964: Sketchpad ran on a machine worth $3 million but a similar system in the future (in 1970) would cost the same as a new car, a perspective he considered "conservative."[39]

Steven Coons exercised an enormous influence on entire ways of thinking about design and architecture from the earliest point of computer-aided design, an influence that stretched beyond just design. As Daniel Cardoso Llach points out in his book *Builders of the Vision: Software and the Imagination of Design*, computer-aided design was one of the first sites for research into what would become human-computer interaction. Beyond the technological advances from Coons's research, which include Sketchpad and the Coons patch (which calculated curves mathematically, later replaced by the more accurate Bézier curve), Coons developed new ways of formulating the role of machines in design. Rather than automating design, he turned the research agenda for CAD toward new modes of interaction and augmentation.[40] Coons's research also had ramifications for how architects would approach design on the computer: using it not merely as a drawing tool, but also as one for building. Cardoso Llach writes that the researchers "construed design representations as forms of *building*, which engendered a way of thinking about design as a structured process of information management, and enabled them to speculate about new forms of design work."[41] And as we will see in chapter 6, it was Coons's course that Nicholas Negroponte took as a college freshman, introducing him to the possibilities of design with the computer.

Computer graphics developed in close relationship to the aeronautics industry and within both mechanical and electrical engineering, supported by air force funding.[42] At Boeing, William Fetter and his superior, Verne Hudson, coined the term "computer graphics" in 1960.[43] It referred to the conversion of data to images, or as Fetter wrote in 1966, "a consciously managed and documented technology directed toward communicating information accurately and descriptively."[44] Boeing combined human factors research and computer graphics to simulate the pilot's movement within the cockpit.[45] Fetter, an art director, sought new ways to draw and to visualize complex relationships between the human body and the aircraft.[46] In 1962, he created a cockpit simulation in computer graphics for human factors purposes for Boeing and, in 1964, the "Boeing Man"—a computer graphical figure of a human being that articulated seven different movement systems.[47] It could be animated in order to visualize the range of motion of a pilot in a cockpit.[48] In the first half of the 1960s, Boeing used computer graphics for several purposes: acoustical engineering, engineering drawing, operations analysis, human factors, cockpit display systems, and aircraft carrier landings.[49]

Fetter understood computer graphics as an aspect of engineering communication, evidenced by the title of his book, *Computer Graphics in Communication*. He predicted—correctly—that computing and graphics would cause fields to converge: "Education to prepare for the effect of computers on engineering communication might take several approaches—each bridging a gap between engineering professions and communication and design professions. Bridging this gap will require educators to reduce the artificial barriers between different colleges within a university," Fetter wrote.[50] He suggested that engineers could take design courses, that communication students could take engineering courses, or that the professional world might shape the integration. Fetter continued:

Several professions exist that developed from the need to integrate significant technical requirements and human response. Architecture integrated structural technology and human response. Graphic design integrated printing technology and human response. In recent decades, industrial design integrated mass production and human response. As engineering and science develop,

Computer Graphics, by combining computing technology and human response, may emerge as one of the design professions.[51]

Fetter's suggestions presaged the approach of contemporary design programs and the later MIT Media Lab—and in the shorter term, the pedagogy of the Architecture Machine Group, as we will see in chapter 6.

Symbiosis, Problem Solving, and Cybernetics

Architects, including the ones discussed in this book, explored architecture as a problem-solving discipline and used heuristic processes to that end in their work. "Heuristics" means "serving to discover" and was popularized by George Pólya's 1945 book *How to Solve It*, a work that exercised a major influence not only on mathematics but also on fields such as cybernetics, cognitive psychology, artificial intelligence, and computer science.[52] Heuristic reasoning is provisional: it provides a framework for making plausible guesses, and these guesses derive from experience in how one solves problems— both one's own experience and the experience of observing others solving problems. In artificial intelligence and cognitive psychology both, researchers incorporated heuristics as they studied how people structured their own problem-solving. Research- ers modeled these functions in software and then applied the heuristics to other prob- lems. Architects also used these practices to conceive of architectural systems that could evolve and learn. Christopher Alexander used heuristics in the program at the center of *Notes on the Synthesis of Form* (as we will see in chapter 4), and Nicholas Negroponte used them in the vision of his URBAN5 computer-aided design system that would learn from its user through a question-and-answer dialogue (chapter 6).

Cybernetics provided a means for describing feedback and control within systems and organisms of all kinds, whether biological, computational, anthropological, or political. Coined as a term by Norbert Wiener in 1948, cybernetics (from the Greek for "steersman," *kybernetes*) revolved around the notion of feedback: a set of messages, exchanged without regard to their content, that control a system. A system undertakes an action, receives information about its performance, and corrects its course accord- ingly, not unlike the steersman of a ship.

What made cybernetics especially attractive was its applicability to organisms and entities of all kinds: animals, humans, governments, theaters and performances, art- works and buildings. It supported what Geof Bowker called a universal strategy. "In general, cyberneticians argued for the new age both conjuncturally (in terms of the current state of technology and warfare) and ideally (in terms of the grand unfolding of Ideas about humanity). The ability to shift between these two registers was a power- ful tool," Bowker wrote.[53] The facility with which cybernetics could make such moves made it all the more attractive to architects.

Two British cyberneticians played an especially influential role on architects and architecture. W. Ross Ashby influenced Christopher Alexander early in his career, in Alexander's work on *Notes on the Synthesis of Form,* as we will see in chapter 4. Ashby developed the Homeostat, an analog computer that was Ashby's "design for a brain."[54] It used electrical circuits to shock itself back into equilibrium as a mechanism to demonstrate how it adapted to change the way that a brain could. And Gordon Pask worked with Cedric Price and Joan Littlewood on the Fun Palace, a cybernetically responsive space that proposed to adapt to its users and modify them as they moved through and interacted with the building. Pask was also a long-term visitor at MIT's Architecture Machine Group on several occasions between 1968 and 1976, collaborating with the group on modeling techniques and design systems. Pask's 1969 article "The Architectural Relevance of Cybernetics" suggested that cybernetics could alter the interaction between the designer and the system with which the designer worked. Once architects understood themselves as systems architects, he suggested, they could cybernetically change their design practices. "Let us turn the design paradigm in upon itself; let us apply it to the interaction between the designer and the system he designs, rather than the interaction between the system and the people who inhabit it," he wrote.[55]

Cybernetics suggested how a building could be something more than a static entity, and the design process more than just the architect and the architectural team as they sketched and modeled. With cybernetics, architecture became a mechanism of information exchange and provided the groundwork for architecture as an interactive practice.

J. C. R. Licklider put in place one of the most enduring notions of intelligence and interactivity in "Man-Computer Symbiosis," published in 1960. He wrote, "Man-computer symbiosis is an expected development in cooperative interaction between men and electronic computers. It will involve very close coupling between the human and the electronic members of the partnership."[56] The goal of human-computer symbiosis was to make it possible for both entities to solve problems together, moving beyond computational preconfiguration and preformulation. Licklider underscored that such a way of working together would support new ways for humans and computers to "cooperate in making decisions and controlling complex situations without inflexible dependence on predetermined programs." Of Licklider's article, Paul Edwards wrote that it "rapidly achieved the kind of status as a unifying reference point in computer science (and especially AI) that *Plans and the Structure of Behavior* [by George Miller], published in the same year, would attain in psychology. It became the universally cited founding articulation of the movement to establish a time-sharing, interactive computing regime."[57] Even today, "symbiosis" is still a resonant aim for the goals of AI and human-computer interaction. We will see Licklider and symbiosis again throughout this book, particularly in chapter 6, in relation to Nicholas Negroponte and the MIT Architecture Machine Group.

Artificial Intelligence

When John McCarthy coined the term "artificial intelligence" in 1956, the concept of computers that could creatively solve problems was not new.[58] Histories of AI include automata and mechanics stretching back to the first century.[59] The field of artificial intelligence developed in the 1950s out of a systems theoretical, cybernetic interest in the function of the human brain as a model for machine logic. The 1956 Dartmouth Summer Research Project on Artificial Intelligence, as well as a set of papers between 1952 and 1961, outlined the key questions for what would become AI. Those defining the early discussion included Claude Shannon, John McCarthy, Marvin Minsky, and W. Ross Ashby. As for many cyberneticians or systems theorists, the interests of AI researchers expanded beyond computer science, including the fields of biology, neurology, mathematics, statistics, linguistics, management science, and psychology.[60]

Although AI research derived from cybernetics, it diverged from cybernetics' central interests into questions around systems that could learn or self-reproduce. The conceptual possibilities optimistically set forth by early AI researchers took decades longer to be realized. As Marvin Minsky wrote in 1961, "I believe . . . that we are on the threshold of an era that will be strongly influenced, and quite possibly dominated, by intelligent problem-solving machines. But our purpose is not to guess about what the future may bring; it is only to try to describe and explain what seem now to be our first steps toward the construction of 'artificial intelligence.'"[61]

Still, Minsky was more circumspect in just what intelligence meant in 1960, even though heuristics long continued to fill a central position in his conception of AI.[62] Intelligence and intelligent behavior was and is difficult to define. Sure, it was possible to use a set of practices such as heuristics or classification to make a computer act thoughtfully. "Is there something missing? I am confident that sooner or later we will be able to assemble programs of great problem-solving ability from complex combinations of heuristic devices," he wrote. But the techniques still didn't add up to the bigger questions. "In no one of these will we find the seat of intelligence. Should we ask what intelligence 'really is'?" Minsky asked.

My own view is that this is more of an esthetic question, or one of sense of dignity, than a technical matter! To me "intelligence" seems to denote little more than the complex of performances which we happen to respect, but do not understand. . . . But we should not let our inability to discern a locus of intelligence lead us to conclude that programmed computers therefore cannot think. For it may be so with man, as with machine, that, when we understand finally the structure and program, the feeling of mystery (and self-approbation) will weaken.[63]

Minsky refers to the problem of free will and self-knowledge, of modeling oneself and having a notion of oneself in order to reflect on one's being.[64] "Surely a machine has to *be* in order to perform," he writes. "But we cannot assign all the credit to its programmer if the operation of a system comes to reveal structures not recognizable or anticipated by the programmer."[65]

So was intelligence, as Minsky writes, a question of dignity, of the exponential increase in inductive power created by numerous processes? Or is it the notion of cleverness? Is intelligence a matter of a machine doing more than its designer planned, as Claude Shannon characterized W. Ross Ashby's Homeostat? Is it the quality that emerges when a system quickly processes decisions, learning from its prior states—adaptation, as Ashby called it? And what were architecture's stakes in asking this question?

In the chapters to come, we will see how architects, designers, and technologists modeled the impact of technology on how we live, and used technology to stretch the boundaries of architecture and architectural practice. We begin with Christopher Alexander, who has had quite possibly the biggest influence on programming and digital design of anyone in this book.

2 Christopher Alexander: Patterns, Order, and Software

Christopher Alexander, the architect, marveled that he was even speaking at a computer conference in the first place. In October 1996, he found himself giving the keynote lecture to "a whole football field" of software engineers and software designers at the ACM Conference on Object-Oriented Programs, Systems, Languages and Applications (OOPSLA for short) in San Jose, California.[1] "What is the connection between what I am doing in the field of architecture and what you are doing in computer science and trying to do in the new field of software design?" he wondered aloud.[2]

Alexander was, of course, no stranger to computers. He started working with them in the late 1950s and early 1960s, almost as early as it was possible for an architect to have access to one. By the time he stood on that stage in Silicon Valley, computation was no longer central to how he performed his work. But the software engineers who invited him to keynote the conference, surprisingly to him, found his writings about architecture very relevant. For them, Alexander articulated the logics, politics, and beauty of software architecture.

Alexander took the opportunity at OOPSLA to elevate the stakes of the work of software engineers. He told his audience, "I know you must realize the extent to which the world is gradually now being shaped more and more and more, indirectly, by the efforts of all of you who are sitting in this room—because it is you who control the function of computers and their programs."[3] The programs that software engineers were designing would have a profound effect on almost every aspect of the world, Alexander predicted. "It is the programs that control the shape of manufacturing, the shape of the transportation industries, construction management, diagnosis in medicine, printing and publishing. You almost can't name a facet of the world which is not already, to some very strong degree, under the influence of the programs that are being written to manage and control those entities or those operations," he said.[4] Software engineers wielded massive control and power through the programs they designed.

At that point, in 1996, it was clear just how much of this vision had come to pass, as the World Wide Web was exploding, and sophisticated, networked software had begun to reshape the corporate landscape. Alexander said that he figured the audience cared deeply about the "real physical world, and its shape and its design, its deep feeling, its impact on human life."[5] But Alexander's interest had less to do with expanding the control of programmers and more about the moral imperative of world builders like the software engineers and architects he was addressing. "Is there a chance you might take on the responsibility for influencing, shaping, and changing the environment?" he asked.[6] Alexander understood the stakes.

A Brief Biography

Christopher Alexander is one of the few architects that everybody seems to know. This popularity comes in part because he strived to clarify the logic of architecture in a way that made sense to non-architects, giving everyday people insight into how the rooms, buildings, streets, towns, and cities around them fit together. Since its publication in 1977, the yellow spine of *A Pattern Language* by Christopher Alexander, Sara Ishikawa, and Murray Silverstein is a frequent sight on the bookshelves of non-architects. It is the kind of present that parents give their college-age kids when they express interest in architecture. (Case in point: when I told my parents I wanted to go to graduate school for architecture, my stepfather gave me a copy of *A Pattern Language* for Christmas.) In fact, it is the number one bestseller for architectural criticism on Amazon.com.[7]

Alexander's theories also touch almost every element of our digital lives, whether you know it or not. If you've looked something up in Wikipedia; if you've learned to program in Java or C++, or used a program that was; if you've used a major website or played a video game—somewhere in there is an inspiration from Alexander that has influenced your actions. I speak from personal experience on this front: I first learned about Alexander on my first day of work as a producer at Netscape in April 1996, when Hugh Dubberly, then the creative director of the Netscape website, suggested we consider using patterns and pattern languages in our site redesign. That was six months before Alexander addressed the software engineers just a few miles up the road from OOPSLA in San Jose.

From his undergraduate studies onward, Christopher Alexander developed his systematic approach through a combined interest in mathematics, computation, and design. He was one of the first and very few architects in the early 1960s with the mathematical expertise to program and use a computer. Born Wolfgang Christian Johann Alexander in 1936 in Vienna and raised in England after his family fled the Nazis in 1938, Alexander completed two bachelor's degrees at Trinity College at the University of Cambridge: the first in mathematics, the second in architecture. Alexander's early years studying architecture at Cambridge coincided with the school's new focus on mathematics and computing, introduced by school head Leslie Martin, which formed the foundation of the architectural research programs that followed in the next decades. This logical approach influenced the work of Alexander and numerous architecture students who passed through it, including Peter Eisenman, Lionel March, and Philip Tabor.

Alexander moved to the United States and continued his architectural studies in the doctoral program at Harvard starting in 1958, during which time he engaged in a variety of collaborations outside of architecture, including with Harvard's Center for Cognitive Research, the Joint Center for Urban Studies of MIT and Harvard, and the MIT Civil Engineering Systems Laboratory. These collaborations introduced him to cognitive science, cybernetics, and artificial intelligence, all of which informed the design methods he developed. His dissertation committee reflected this interdisciplinary approach. Arthur Maass was a political scientist known for his quantitative modeling methods for water policy. Serge Chermayeff was an architect and industrial designer (with whom Alexander continued to collaborate after his degree, and with whom he wrote *Community and Privacy* in 1963). Jerome Bruner was a cognitive psychologist, who, with George Miller, founded the Center for Cognitive Studies. The center was funded by the National Science Foundation, the Ford Foundation, and the Department of Defense's Advanced Research Projects Agency and sought to bridge humans and "the devices man uses to amplify his cognitive control over the environment"—a theme and set of funders that I revisit in other chapters of this book.[8]

Alexander completed his PhD in architecture in 1962 and joined the University of California, Berkeley, architecture faculty in 1963. His dissertation was published mostly unchanged as *Notes on the Synthesis of Form* in 1964 and is still in print today. In 1967, Alexander founded the Center for Environmental Structure at Berkeley—where he remained until 1994—which developed patterns and pattern languages and published over twenty books and numerous other publications. Between 2003 and 2004, he published *The Nature of Order: An Essay on the Art of Building and the Nature of the Universe,* a four-volume theory of Alexandrian architecture. Alexander now lives in Arundel, England.

An Operating System for Architecture

Alexander's approach to architecture is important to people outside of the profession of architecture. It appeals to those who work with, analyze, and visualize complex sets of information, including software engineers and information architects. While traditional architects focus on the form and representation of a building by drawing and modeling it, Alexander instead sought to visualize the structure of the parts of a design problem and their relationships to each other. He believed that doing this adequately— mapping out the elements of a design problem and showing their interconnections to each other—created the form of the problem. Such structures were necessary because Alexander argued that the practice of architecture was too complex for designers to act on their own intuition—mapping the structure of the problem produced a better, more correct form than the one that sprang from the designer's imagination and intuition.

The scope of Alexander's interests is sweeping. He has studied this notion of parts to wholes in different ways: through set and graph theory, requirements and misfits, computation and heuristics, visualization and social network analysis. He retained and continued to incorporate some of these approaches while forcefully rejecting others when he better understood the problem he was trying to solve. For Alexander, it came to be that much more was at stake: questions of what he called "living structure"— morality, order, and objective goodness. In the books he wrote in the 1990s and early 2000s, especially the publication of his *Nature of Order* volumes, Alexander argued that it is possible to objectively define the properties of what makes something good, more "filled with life." Just as in his early work, when he believed he could design a system that could be objectively tested, his later work argued that it is possible to generate moral, meaningful spaces that can be empirically tested and proven as such.

Alexander, however, is often unpopular with architects. Although they concede Alexander's importance, they dislike his moralistic tone and disagree with him that there is an objective notion of goodness to be found in architecture. They don't like his blunt dismissal of design and are no fans of the buildings of Alexander's creation. More- over, the very works that make him popular with digital designers, programmers, and laypeople, such as *A Pattern Language* and *The Timeless Way of Building,* architects reject as oversimplifications of the complexities of design. Architects tend not to see architec- ture as a truth to be proven. But the digital developers and designers who follow Alex- ander's methods find the idea of this truth fundamental to their own view of their work.

In the pages that follow, I trace the influences that shaped Alexander's philosophies. I look at four key questions: What role did the computer play in his work? To what meth- ods did visualizing the structure of design problems lead Alexander, and what is the importance of these methods today? How did patterns provide a format and operating system for design that would prove potent for the digital age? And how did Alexander's ideas about language create new, generative architectures that could change the shape of the world? I then follow his influence in software design, architecture, and engineer- ing, and the paradoxical contention of Alexander among many of his fellow architects.

The Promises and Shortcomings of Computers

Even when the computer was brand new on the architectural scene, Christopher Alexander was already annoyed with how architects approached it. As architects grappled with how computers would change their practice for better or for worse at the Architecture and the Computer conference in 1964 (see chapter 1), their questions were already moot, as Alexander saw it. "In my opinion the question all these questioners ask, namely, 'How can the computer be applied to architectural design?' is misguided, dangerous, and foolish," he wrote in a strongly worded essay in the 1964 Architecture and the Computer proceedings.[9] It was like the proverbial person with a hammer who thinks everything looks like a nail: unless architects really conceptualized what the calculating power of a computer could do, they were likely to be wasting their time. "The effort to state a problem in such a way that a computer can be used to solve it, will distort your view of the problem. It will allow you to consider those aspects of the problem which can be encoded—and in many cases these are the most trivial and the least relevant aspects."[10]

But what if the computer could reconceive how architects thought about form? Not the frivolous form that sprang from the architect's ego, "an outpouring of personal secrets in plastic form," as he wrote, but rather form that was *in*formed—by a mapping of the structure of the requirements and relationships within a complex design problem?[11] That is where a computer could be a powerful aid. "The computer is a tool. It is a wonderful, almost miraculous invention," he wrote. "The more we understand about the complex nature of form and the complex nature of function, the more we shall have to seek the help of the computer, when we set out to create form."[12]

Alexander was speaking from personal experience that few architects had at that time. As a doctoral student in the early 1960s, Alexander gained access to the IBM 7090 computer in the MIT Computing Center through his collaboration with civil engineer Marvin Manheim and the MIT Civil Engineering Laboratory. This was no easy feat. Computers in the 1960s were scarce, and not many architects knew how to program them.[13] For Alexander, that was part of the attraction. He took the program that he and Manheim developed and applied it to his own doctoral dissertation research, published as the book *Notes on the Synthesis of Form*, in which he analyzed the relationship of design requirements for a village in India. By 1964, Alexander had already worked with a computer for several years to calculate and graph the relationships between requirements of a design problem. He struggled with the limitations of his programs and tools in representing the complexity he sought to find. While the computer could help him visualize the structure of the problem, visualizing design problems in a quickly graspable way was elusive. Alexander developed visual structures that corresponded to what his computer programs could calculate: trees, semilattices, and networks. Each visualization was more complex than the next, corresponding with what he could program on the computer, until he dispensed with the computer altogether.

Walking in the Footprints of the Gods

From *Notes on the Synthesis of Form* in 1964 to the four-volume *Nature of Order* series in 2001, Alexander continually pursued the essence of what generates order, the means to understand the elements and forces in a design problem, and their synthesis that produces understanding and meaning. Although he changed the names of the particulars and the method for how best to decompose a problem, rejecting his old methods for newer ones, he kept pursuing the notion of order throughout his work.

For Alexander, the purpose of design was to bring together all the parts of a design problem, break them apart along their natural joints to better understand them, and recombine them. He introduces this idea at the very beginning of *Notes on the Synthesis of Form*, in the epigraph, by using a passage from *Phaedrus* in which Socrates and Plato discuss how to make an argument. "First, the taking in of scattered particulars under one Idea, so that everyone understands what is being talked about. . . . Second, the separation of the Idea into parts, by dividing it at the joints, as nature directs, not breaking any limb in half as a bad carver might," said Socrates.[14] Later in that passage in *Phaedrus*, Plato states, "I am myself a great lover of these processes of division and generalization; they help me to speak and to think. And if I find any man who is able to see 'a One and Many' in nature, him I follow, and 'walk in his footsteps as if he were a god.' And those who have this art, I have hitherto been in the habit of calling dialecticians; but God knows whether the name is right or not."[15] For Alexander, the pursuit of order is nothing short of walking in the footprints of the gods.

Just as Plato and Socrates took apart an argument's "scattered particulars" along their joints in order to build it up to be stronger, Alexander broke down a problem into its constituent elements, examined how it comes apart, and built up a map of its relationships in putting the problem together again. By modeling the design problem as an information problem, it could be addressed rationally, in contrast to a designer acting according to internally held, unverifiable intuition in a "self-conscious" design process. "The opposition between these two aims, analysis and synthesis, has sometimes led people to maintain that in design intellect and art are incompatible, and that no analytical process can help a designer form unified well-organized design," he wrote.[16]

Alexander's theory of order derives from a number of disciplines, but in *Notes*, it mostly revolves around biological morphology, Gestalt psychology, and cybernetics.

Biological morphology, the study of the structure and relationship between structures of plants and animals, gave Alexander the vocabulary to examine the forces that make a form what it is in the world. Gestalt psychology, a branch of psychology that studies the relationship of the parts to the whole, provided a way to understand a design problem more holistically. Cybernetics gave him a means for modeling system stability in a set of informational inputs and outputs in feedback with one another. And he paired these notions with his computer program's ability to calculate many relationships between requirements of a design problem, and then he visualized the structure.

Form, Forces, and Fitness

There are three key components to the method in *Notes:* form, forces, and fitness. As Alexander wrote, form is the "part of the world over which we have control," and "context is that part of the world which puts demands on this form; anything in the world that makes demands of the form is context. Fitness is a relation of mutual acceptability between these two," he wrote.[17] Where a conventional architect creates form by drawing and making models in the shapes of buildings and rooms, Alexander equated form with the structure of the design problem. "The crucial quality of shape, no matter what kind, lies in its organization, and when we think of it this way we call it form," Alexander wrote in *Notes*.[18] He characterized form as a relationship between the "forces" of a design problem.

The idea of form as organization draws from D'Arcy Wentworth Thompson's 1917 book *On Growth and Form* that examined how biological form was determined by physical, chemical, or electrical forces—a "diagram of forces." Thompson wrote,

The form . . . and the changes of form which are apparent in its movements and in its growth, may in all cases alike be described as due to the action of force. . . . In an organism, great or small, it is not merely the nature of the motions of the living substance which we must interpret in terms of force (according to kinetics), but also the conformation of the organism itself, whose permanence or equilibrium is explained by the interaction or balance of forces, as described in statics.[19]

In Alexander's application, a designer acts on the boundary of form and context, a relationship complicated by the fact that, as Alexander wrote, "the form itself relies on its own internal organization and on the internal fitness between the pieces it is made of to control its fit as a whole to the context outside."[20] A designer can't change the context, but can create a form that adapts to the design problem. The designer then makes a reconciliation between "two intangibles: a form which we have not yet designed and a context which we cannot properly design," Alexander wrote.[21] It is important that the structure be able to adapt, that whatever the designer puts in place can change and evolve according to its context. For this reason, the problem the designer seeks to solve

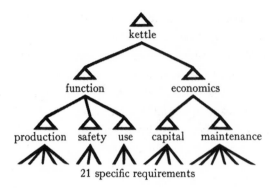

Figure 2.01

Alexander showed the relationship of requirements to each other in an object, using the example of the considerations that go into designing a kettle. By organizing the requirements in this fashion, a designer could break down the complexity of the design problem. *NOTES ON THE SYNTHESIS OF FORM* by Christopher Alexander, Cambridge, Mass.: Harvard University Press, Copyright © 1964 by the President and Fellows of Harvard College. Copyright © renewed 1992 by Christopher Alexander.

is structural, not representational. Good structure would be able to adapt to change, but typical architectural representation—drawings and models—were more like window dressing, not a structure that represented the essence of the design problem.

One of the most salient and influential points of Alexander's theory is the simple statement that good design is the absence of bad fit. Bad fit is "a single identifiable property of an ensemble, which is immediate in experience and describable."[22] It is the designer's job to make things fit, to fix the misfits. For example, think of a wobbly table. In order to stabilize it, you might try to fold a matchbook or nudge a shim under the table leg, using trial and error to fix the problem.

This is like what a designer does when addressing misfits at the boundary of form and context, an ability Alexander called "the designer's sense of organization."[23] When the designer outlines the set of requirements (misfits) that need to be addressed in a design problem, she is determining what the form needs to address. By analyzing and grouping the requirements, the designer can find the most appropriate physical solutions to fit the context. Alexander limited the scope of his investigations to misfits because it is easier to define what does not fit than what does—easier, he argued, than defining an open-ended list of requirements: although a designer could sit down and write up a list of requirements that a design problem needed to address—a field of attributes—how would the designer know when to stop?[24] In the simplest sense, this is what Alexander meant when he defined good design as the absence of bad fit.

Fitness is the psychological process of selecting the right tool for the job.[25] Alexander derived this concept of "fit" from Kurt Koffka's *Principles of Gestalt Psychology*. Koffka described how a child might choose between four possible sticks for pushing a ball between a set of bars: the skinny stick with a curved implement at one end is the obvious one for the job; the least suitable is a thick, pointed stick. "If . . . the child selects the proper stick this selection is due to intrinsic characters of the objects; the tool 'fits' the ball, and this fittingness acts as a principle of selection," he wrote.[26] "Since all problem solutions can be said to consist in finding the *fitting* part which will relieve the existing stress, a law of fittingness would be the most universal law to explain thinking, and with it the arousal of new processes."[27] A designer does the same thing when figuring out how to approach a design problem: correlating the shape and characteristics of the object and the context, then finding the right form and action that fixes the situation.

However, context and condition are not static—design problems of the slightest complexity can and will change. So how could a form adapt to the changes in its context? Alexander looked to cybernetics, and in particular, W. Ross Ashby's 1952 book *Design for a Brain* as a means to explore system equilibrium. Ashby sought to model how the human brain learned and adapted to differing circumstances. He built an analog computer, the Homeostat, which used cybernetic feedback loops to demonstrate how a system could continually stabilize itself. Constructed from magnets and electrical coils partly submerged in water, the Homeostat reacted to changes in its environment. Ashby wrote, "I propose the definition of that a *form of behaviour is* **adaptive** *if it maintains the essential variables within physiological limits*" (emphasis Ashby's).[28] The concept of adaptivity did not refer only to the human brain: it could refer to how an animal maintained its body temperature of other biological functions, as well as to higher level activities of humans interacting with their environment. This ability to bring a system back to equilibrium is called *ultrastability*.

Alexander took Ashby's homeostatic model and applied it to his design process. If a designer properly defined the requirements of the problem and the forces that connected them, then the resulting form and structure would be able to adapt to change, shocking itself back into equilibrium. Alexander devised his own hypothetical Homeostat to show how a system that followed his design process could reach equilibrium. It worked as follows: an array of one hundred lightbulbs turned on and off. If a lightbulb's direct neighbor turned on, there was a 50 percent chance that a light would turn off and a 50 percent chance that it would turn on again. When all of the lights were off for a second because they could not turn back on, the system was said to have reached equilibrium.[29]

Why did the designer need to go through this method? Alexander argued that the designer was designing for an increasingly complex world in which it was impossible to keep in one's mind all of the intermeshing systems with all of their details. "In spite of their superficial simplicity, even these problems have a background of needs and activities which is becoming too complex to grasp intuitively."[30] The complex systems of which he spoke sat within a growing ecosystem of other pressures, whether social, cultural, or informational.[31]

Furthermore, Alexander thought that most designers were intrinsically biased, likely to have the solution in mind before they began. Alexander believed that his method could fight these biases by making a model of the design problem and focusing the designer's attention on that, rather than the automatic image that he or she first intuits. "The designer as a form-maker is looking for integrity (in the sense of singleness); he wishes to form a unit, to synthesize, to bring elements together. A design program's origin, on the other hand, is analytical, and its effect is to fragment the problem," Alexander wrote.[32] By consciously working between analysis and synthesis, the designer would be able to create an adaptive system that could respond to change—creating a synthesis of form.

Visualizing Complexity

In the highway design projects that Alexander completed with Marvin Manheim and that influenced *Notes on the Synthesis of Form,* Alexander used a computer program to calculate *tree* structures. At that point in the early 1960s, he viewed all design problems as hierarchically organized, top-down structures with just two points of connection between each requirement because that was what his program could calculate. When his program could compute multiple points of connection between design requirements, then design problems became crisscrossed *semilattices,* able to support greater complexity. He then denounced trees as a dangerous way to structure a problem in his still-influential 1965 article, "A City Is Not a Tree." He also used the semilattice as an elementary method for social network analysis. Finally, in the late 1960s, he stopped using a computer to calculate relationships between design elements. He called the design problem a *network* and a language, with many possible connections and that no longer used (or could use) a computer because of its complexity. He explained the system and its accompanying philosophy in publications including *A Pattern Language* and *The Timeless Way of Building.*

Trees

Alexander began structuring design problems as trees in *Notes on the Synthesis of Form* and a set of projects and papers related to the design of highway exchanges. The program he used to generate the tree structures, he argued, demonstrated a certain amount of intelligence because of its consistency.

In their design of highway exchanges, Alexander and Marvin Manheim, then a civil engineering student at MIT, used computer programs called the Hierarchical Decomposition of Systems program, or HIDECS 2 and HIDECS 3. Written in FORTRAN, the HIDECS programs analyzed relationships between nodes for set theory problems. Alexander and Manheim made a list of 112 problems, including "Lanes too narrow," "Lanes too wide," and "Too much information for the driver to take in." Quickly comparing each requirement against another, they looked to see how each one addressed similar, neutral, or competing conditions, and then they immediately encoded the data in punch cards.[33] The computer ran an heuristic "hill-climbing" program to calculate the density of relationships in links. Hill-climbing is like hiking up a slope in the dark: taking a step, finding the next best foothold from there; the program chooses a variable, compares it to the other values in its array, selects the lowest (or the highest), moves onto the next variable, selects the lowest value in its array, and continues until no improvement or lower value can be made. The HIDECS 2 produced a symmetric, numerical matrix.[34] Alexander and Manheim used a graph to visually represent the relationship; both show the same relationships, on the left as a graph, and on the right as sets.[35] They then drew tree charts to represent the hierarchical tree suggested by the output matrices. Alexander argued that the only appropriate structure for a design problem was a tree because each requirement in HIDECS 2 could have only two points of connection, which led to a tree structure.

The HIDECS program was intelligent because of its consistent results, Alexander and Manheim claimed. "In view of the well-known difficulties associated with hill-climbing analyses . . . this [the near identical results] indicates a remarkable degree of stability. *We take it as evidence that the structure of the problem really does have the character described by the analysis, in some very deep sense,*" they wrote.[36] This intelligence was so powerful, Alexander stipulated, that HIDECS could be applied to "any collection of things whatever"—qualitative or quantitative, abstract or concrete, since it was the relationship between them that will matter, not their actual content.[37] Like Ashby's Homeostat, a "design for a brain," Alexander claimed his program was adaptive, ultrastable, and, indeed, intelligent.

But was it really? The hierarchy used to organize the elements of the design program provided order within Alexander and Manheim's program through control of

a.

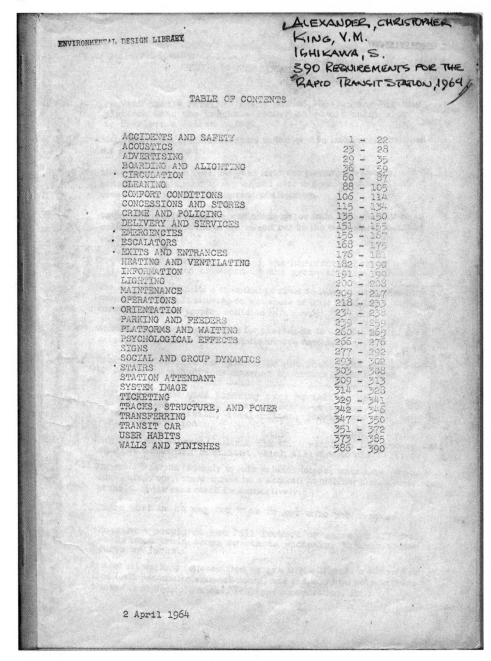

ALEXANDER, CHRISTOPHER
KING, V.M.
ISHIKAWA, S.
390 REQUIREMENTS FOR THE
RAPID TRANSIT STATION, 1964

TABLE OF CONTENTS

2 April 1964

Figure 2.02a and 2.02b

Alexander, with Sara Ishikawa and Van Maren King, applied the tree diagram and requirements grouping method to the design of the Bay Area Rapid Transit System (BART). Christopher Alexander, V. M. King, and Sara Ishikawa, "390 Requirements for the Rapid Transit Station" (Berkeley, CA: Center for Environmental Structure, 1964), 2. Courtesy of Christopher Alexander.

b.

ACCIDENTS AND SAFETY

HE 4491
542A4
cop DII
environ
design

(1) 1 9
Prevent people falling, being pushed, or jumping off the
platform onto the tracks - either to commit suicide or
to retrieve a fallen object.
40

(2) 36
Make it impossible for passengers to fall or step into the gap between
the platform and the train.
40

(3) 36
Make the change in level between train and platform so smooth, and
consistent from station to station and door to door, that there is no
danger of tripping during boarding or alighting.

(4) -27
To prevent people being dragged along by the train, no one must be in
contact with the outside of the transit car as the train starts to move
40   out of the station.

(5) -28
Prevent the accident in which the horizontal bar of a turnstile catches men or women in the groin as they push through.

(6) 34
The last minute rush for a train that is about to leave must not lead to
accidents, tripping, slipping on wet areas of floor skidding, stumbling,
bumping into other people, collision with moving ., etc.

(7) 34
Wherever it would be dangerous for passengers to run, the form of the
passage (or whatever else) must discourage running.

42 (8) -28
Make it impossible for people to get pushed and knocked down
by people in a hurry or crushed by crowds.behind them.

51 (9) 57
Passengers who ride standing must be able to keep
their balance without great effort even during
maximum acceleration, deceleration, jerking and
transverse motion

51 (10) 51
Anybody who stumbles in the car must within a few inches fall
against something resilient which will break his fall.

(11) 36 38
Anywhere a person is likely to lose balance (steps, transit car, ramp,
single step, etc.) there should be a handrail or grab bar placed just
at the point his arms reach for instinctively.

(12) 1
There must be no way for kids to get onto the tracks.

(13) 70
Make sure people do not fall forward or sideways off their
seats when train stops or starts suddenly, lurches around a
curve or jerks.

(14) 14
Protect all walking surfaces from water which will make a slippery surface (rain penetrating entrance doors, rain and mud from outside being
46   tracked in on people's shoes, seepage, condensation, etc.)

the elements and the process. Since HIDECS 2 was limited in what it could calculate, the "deep sense" of "character" was a product of the program's constraints. Only by adhering to strict hierarchies could Alexander's program overcome the shortcomings of hill-climbing analyses—and only through hierarchy did it display "intelligence." In the further development of Alexander's program and method, the hierarchy remained important for the system to maintain coherence. The intelligence resides in the hierarchy of the system, a concept that Alexander relied on for the next decades.

Alexander applied the program in *Notes* and his tree visualization method to a major project: the design of the Bay Area Regional Transit System (BART) in the San Francisco Bay Area in 1964. Donn Emmons, chief architectural consultant to the project, made Alexander the head of the research team. Along with his Center for Environmental Structure colleagues Sara Ishikawa and Van Maren King, Alexander and his team defined 390 requirements in thirty-three categories, ranging from "Accidents and Safety" to "Maintenance" to "Psychological Effects" that BART should address. Accidents and Safety, for example, included "Prevent the accident in which the horizontal bar of a turnstile catches men or women in the groin as they push through" and "Make sure people do not fall forward or sideways off their seats when train stops or starts suddenly, lurches around a curve or jerks."[38] The results, however, were met with derision by the engineers on the project.[39] According to a *Washington Post* article two years later, "The engineers called the report a 'joke book' and halted all research. They were not interested in anything, according to Alexander, but expediency and cost estimates."[40] Ironically, Alexander's program, which was developed in a civil engineering context, did not stand up to the biases of civil engineering culture. And Emmons, along with landscape architect Lawrence Halprin, resigned in 1966 because the engineers did not heed his recommendations regarding BART's impact on the communities it would affect.

Semilattices

Even before *Notes on the Synthesis of Form* was published in 1964, Alexander had already moved on to a new structure, the semilattice, thanks to the expanded capabilities of HIDECS 3. The new version of the program supported the visualization of more complex information structures because it calculated multiple links and variables that could overlap with one another and link to more than one node, unlike trees, in which relationships could not overlap.[41] Able to calculate more complicated relationships, Alexander could accommodate greater complexity in his models of urban structure. He wholly rejected the trees of just a year or two before, and celebrated the semilattice as the true way to format design problems.

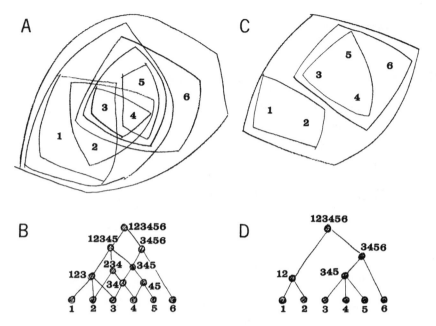

Figure 2.03

Alexander defined trees and semilattices as follows: Tree: "A collection of sets forms a tree if and only if, for any two sets that belong to the collection, either one is wholly contained in the other, or else they are wholly disjoint." Semilattice: "A collection of sets forms a semi-lattice if and only if, when two overlapping sets belong to the collection, then the set of elements common to both also belongs to the collection." Diagrams A and B show the relationship of overlapping sets that make a semilattice, whereas diagrams C and D show the independent sets that create a tree. "A City Is Not a Tree" favors semilattices and rejects trees. Christopher Alexander, "A City Is Not a Tree, Part 1," *Architectural Forum* 122, no. 4 (1965): 59. Courtesy of Christopher Alexander.

Alexander introduced his readers to the semilattice in his still popular two-part article, "A City Is Not a Tree," in 1965, a piece that continues to influence designers today for showing how elements of a city or complex city relate to one another. "The tree of my title is not a green tree with leaves. It is the name for a pattern of thought. The semilattice is the name for another, more complex, pattern of thought," he wrote.[42] A real city is a semilattice, he argued, whereas an artificial city is a tree. "You will have guessed from my title what I believe this ordering principle to be. I believe that a natural city has the organization of a semi-lattice; but that when we organize a city artificially, we organize it as a tree."[43] When one looks at the urban environment, one sees semilattices in the form of overlapping relationships between objects and social systems.

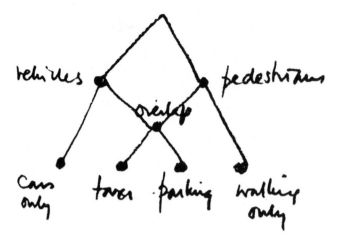

Figure 2.04
A semilattice diagram shows the relationships between the vehicles, pedestrians, and other objects
that make up a street corner in Berkeley. Christopher Alexander, "A City Is Not a Tree, Part 2,"
Architectural Forum 122, no. 5 (1965): 59. Courtesy of Christopher Alexander.

Alexander noted a street corner in Berkeley that has a number of different physical
elements that relate to it:

At the corner of Hearst and Euclid, there is a drug store, and outside the drug store a traffic light.
In the entrance to the drug store there is a newsrack where the day's papers are displayed. When
the light is red, people who are waiting to cross the street stand idly by the light; and since they
have nothing to do, they look at the papers displayed on the newsrack which they can see from
where they stand. Some of them just read the headlines, others actually buy a paper while they
wait.[44]

Objects and places corresponded to material and immaterial items in overlapping
sets, as he explains through his description of the objects that make up a street corner. For
instance, the newsrack, sidewalk, and stoplight created a set of fixed, material system
components. The immaterial, social aspects—the people crossing the street and the
news headlines—were the dynamic parts.[45] The crossovers referred to interdependent
systems: "The newsrack, the newspapers on it, the money going from people's pockets
to the dime slot, the people who stop at the light and read papers, the traffic light, the
electric impulses which make the lights change, and the sidewalk which the people
stand on form a system—they all work together," he wrote.[46] Mapping out these different relationships results in a semilattice. Alexander argued that his method is required
in order to visualize the semilattice. "You cannot bring the semi-lattice structure into a

visualizable form for a single mental act. In a single mental act you can only visualize a tree," he wrote.[47]

Yet every attempt Alexander made in "A City Is Not a Tree" to illustrate a semilattice in an architectural or urban-scale project failed, leaving him without a proof of concept for his model. Even luminary architectural projects such as Kenzo Tange's Tokyo plan, Paolo Soleri's design for Mesa City, and Le Corbusier's plan for Chandigarh all decomposed into trees. "You are no doubt wondering, by now, what a city looks like which is a semi-lattice, but not a tree. I must confess that I cannot yet show you plans or sketches," he wrote.[48]

The one exception was that of Karl Popper's notion of the open society, as characterized in 1945, which was a semilattice. If a closed society was like a "herd or tribe," in which people still lived in "concrete physical relationships" easily bounded by the physical senses, then the relations in an open society, by comparison, would be more dynamic, as Popper wrote.[49] Members of an open society might be more competitive than those in a closed society, whether food or social status was in contention. But the open society also offered choices to the people within it, giving rise to a "new individualism."[50] New relationships, too, would develop, and new forms of exchange and mutuality could arise. However, an open society could potentially become an "abstract society," Popper warned, in a passage that calls to mind the doomsayers of the Internet age: "We could conceive of a society in which men practically never meet face to face—in which all business is conducted by individuals in isolation who communicate by typed letters or by telegrams, and who go about in closed motor-cars. (Artificial insemination would allow even propagation without a personal element.)"[51]

Of course, people need both the close social relations that characterized Popper's notion of closed society and the benefits of individuation, cooperation, and exchange in an open society. Humans are biological beings, after all. And this is where Alexander's semilattice succeeded in a very important way: in the mapping of social relationships. "The reality of today's social structure is thick with overlap—the systems of friends and acquaintances form a semi-lattice, not a tree," Alexander wrote.[52] It marked Alexander's first forays into visualizing the structures of social networks.

As Alexander typically did when he developed a new approach, he rejected what came before—in this case, the tree. "It is this lack of structural complexity, characteristic of trees, which is crippling our conceptions of the city."[53] Reverting to the tree would produce the worst, most dire consequences:

But the city is not, cannot, and must not be a tree. The city is a receptacle for life. If the receptacle severs the overlap of the strands of life within it, because it is a tree, it will be like a bowl full of razor blades on edge, ready to cut up whatever is entrusted to it. In such a receptacle life will be cut to pieces. If we make cities which are trees, they will cut our life within to pieces.[54]

Alexander's semilattice is attractive to contemporary digital designers for the ways that it brings into alignment the individual, the architectural, the infrastructural, and the social. While humans have a primal relationship to trees and tree diagrams, it is also the first, often rudimentary organizational structure for visualization because it is easy to map.[55] But as the website or the company grows more complex, new representations of the structure become necessary and dynamic. The semilattice becomes a better way to map out a dynamic website, a service design ecosystem, the complex relationships between board members across multiple companies. Just as Alexander grappled with representing elements of a city with more abstract social relationships, around 2004 a number of interaction designers, such as Andrew Otwell, Dan Hill, and Tom Carden, applied "A City Is Not a Tree" to their own thinking about designing for networks at the scale of cities.[56] An interaction design studio at Carnegie Mellon's School of Design suggested that students spend a twenty-four-hour period observing an intersection in Pittsburgh in which they identified the different overlapping systems and components, with the goal of developing a more nuanced understanding of the design problem and where they might make their first design intervention. Might it be at the traffic light? The parking meter? The crosswalk? Or might it be broader, at the scale of transportation, or human-to-human interaction? Alexander's semilattice offers designers an approach for addressing design at different levels.

"A City Is Not a Tree" received its share of criticism. A decade after it appeared in *Architectural Forum,* Frank Harary and J. Rockey published "A City Is Not a Semilattice Either" in 1976. This critique of Alexander's method lauded the creativity of his approach but took issue with its mathematical inconsistencies. In particular, Harary and Rockey disagreed with his meshing of set and graph theory, arguing that doing so weakened both mathematic practices.[57] The critique is no surprise, given that Harary himself was a renowned graph theory scholar. Highway or road organization charts might follow such structures, Harary and Rockey wrote, "But this is not the case for a phenomenon so complicated as a 'living city,' which Alexander contends '*is and needs to be a semi-lattice*' (our italics)."[58] If anything, the semilattice is too simple, and more complex structures are necessary. They wrote, "The proper graphical representation of a city is a problem for which no easy answer can be found. Certain aspects may be represented by a tree or semilattice. A more complicated type of structure known as a 'social network' provides more promise as a realistic mathematical model when several different types of relations are involved."[59]

Harary and Rockey were right. Semilattices were too simple. But they were also right about social network analysis in ways they did not realize. Looking closely at

Alexander's work and the sources he cites, it is clear that he was attempting to perform social network analysis in an urban and architectural context, with visualization structures to match.[60]

Architecture and Social Network Analysis

Originally called sociometry, social network analysis uses a structural, graph theoretical approach to mapping relations between actors, focusing on the relations and not on the actors' attributes, just like Alexander's trees and semilattices.[61] Sociometry developed simultaneously out of several fields at once, including sociology, social psychology, and anthropology, starting in the 1930s and gaining traction in the 1950s and 1960s, with Harvard as an important locus during the years that Alexander attended. The most influential early work in social network visualization comes from social psychologist Jacob Moreno, who, in the early 1930s, developed node and line diagrams of human relationships called "sociograms." A Gestalt psychologist who immigrated to the United States in 1925, Moreno used information visualization to show the relationships of parts to wholes in a particular context, such as in a 1933 *New York Times* article about Moreno's sociograms that plotted the social relationships, friends, and foes among five hundred female students. Moreno explained, "With these charts . . . we will have the opportunity to grasp the myriad networks of human relations and at the same time view any part of or portion of the whole which we may desire to relate or distinguish"—a notion that feels familiar, considering the stated goals of Alexander's visualization strategies.[62] For Moreno, much like Alexander years later, revealing this "invisible structure" was the most potent part of his work. "If we ever get to the point of charting a whole city or a whole nation, . . . we would have an intricate maze of psychological reactions which would present a picture of a vast solar system of intangible structures, powerfully influencing conduct, as gravitation does bodies in space. Such an invisible structure underlies society and has its influence in determining the conduct of society as a whole," Moreno wrote.[63]

Alexander's 1966 project *The City as a Mechanism for Sustaining Human Contact* is his clearest attempt to apply social network visualization to the design of a city. In it, he presented a case in which he attempted to formally address how people become isolated from one another in cities, and how a pattern might bring them into closer contact. Urban form became a diagram for mapping out a social structure along the lines of Moreno's sociograms. The issue at hand is "autonomy-withdrawal syndrome," a term of Alexander's own invention that referred to a lack of social contact.[64] He defined the problem of human happiness in quantitative terms. "*An individual can only be healthy*

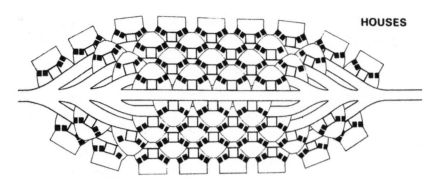

HOUSES

Figure 2.05
Although he struggled to find semilattices in existing cities, the structure that Alexander proposed in *The City as a Mechanism for Sustaining Human Contact* is a semilattice. He developed twelve pattern statements, requiring houses (the black squares) to be within one hundred yards of twenty-seven other houses, accessible on through streets, with communal rooms visible from the street and next to a garden. Tracing diagonal lines along the sides of the pads in the figure produces a semilattice diagram. Courtesy of Christopher Alexander.

and happy when his life contains three or four intimate contacts. A society can only be a healthy one, if each of its individual members has three or four intimate contacts at every stage of his existence."[65] The extreme negative case where an individual lacks contact could cause "extreme and well-defined social pathologies like schizophrenia and delinquency."[66] Alexander reasoned that adults are more or less beyond saving, but that if children had friends, then "autonomy-withdrawal syndrome" could be averted.

In order to prevent this syndrome, Alexander proposed spatial patterns that theoretically would put people in a neighborhood in contact with one another. He made twelve pattern statements calling for dwellings to be within one hundred yards of twenty-seven other houses, accessible on through streets, with communal rooms visible from the street and next to a garden.[67] The shape that accommodated the twelve geometric relations? A semilattice. Tracing diagonal lines along the sides of the pads in the housing development drawing in figure 2.05 approximates the sketches of semilattices that Alexander included in "A City Is Not a Tree" but that he could not offer in a working example. *The City as a Mechanism of Sustaining Human Contact* offered a visualization of a social network, applied to the geometric possibilities of urban design. The cure to "autonomy-withdrawal program" is living in a semilattice, physically manifested in the design for a neighborhood. His approach aligned with what other researchers attempted in the early days of sociometry and social network analysis. As Stanley Wasserman and Katherine Faust wrote in their history of social network analysis, "the experimentally designed communication structures employed by these researchers lent themselves naturally to graphical representations using points to depict actors and lines to depict channels of communications."[68] For *The City as a Mechanism,* human friendships and movement were those channels.

Admittedly, *The City as a Mechanism* seems to be backward-engineered from the spatial pattern of the semilattice to Alexander's declared mathematical requirements for happiness. But as an attempt at applying social network analysis to architectural and urban design, it is remarkable. Moreover, the problems that Alexander encountered in his own methods were the same kinds of problems that other social network analysts experienced as they attempted to visualize more complex relationships among their subjects of study.[69] "Perhaps a particular network method may appear to lack theoretical focus because it can be applied to such a wide range of substantive problems from many different contexts," Wasserman and Faust wrote, noting the difficulties that other social network researchers found in the 1960s. "In contrast, we argue that much network methodology arose as social scientists in a range of disciplines struggled to make sense of empirical data and grappled with theoretical issues."[70] Some of the inconsistencies in Alexander's methods can be explained by the fact that, like other practitioners of social network analysis, he was trying to do something that had not been done before in this manner and with this subject matter, and that he ran up against the limits of computational capabilities of the tools and the methods for visualizing the information. "The City Is Not a Tree" and *The City as a Mechanism for Sustaining Human Contact* meet those conceptions of practice.

Atoms, Relations, and Design Methods

The Atoms of Environmental Structure, written by Alexander and architect Barry Poyner, introduced the Relational Method that they developed in London, when collaborating on government architectural projects in 1965–1966. *Atoms* inspired a number of papers and practices in architecture and design. It particularly sparked argument in the burgeoning fields of environmental design and in the Design Methods movement, in the 1960s. *Atoms,* too, was controversial enough to garner reverberating criticism for more than a decade.

Rather than defining requirements or "needs" (a term used in the Design Methods Movement by John Christopher Jones and Bruce Archer), Alexander and Poyner opted for "tendencies," because, as they argued, people do not always know what their needs are. An architect or designer observed people as they pursued these tendencies, and would scientifically test the tendencies as hypotheses. *"A good environment is one in which no two tendencies conflict,"* Alexander and Poyner wrote.[71] Yet the conflicts might not be immediately evident. Rather than working on ameliorating bad fit, as in *Notes on the Synthesis of Form,* the designer's job was to resolve conflicts with a "relation"—"a geometrical arrangement that prevents a conflict"—what Alexander later called patterns.[72] The statement of the conflict is an if/then statement: if these conditions are to be found, then the following relations can prevent or fix the conflict. Alexander and Poyner believed that this system could be used to generate architectural form. "We believe . . . that it is possible to write a program which is both objectively correct, and which yields the actual physical geometry of buildings," they wrote.[73]

Atoms inspired a number of papers at the 1967 Portsmouth Symposium on Design Methods in Architecture. Poyner presented the paper there and Geoffrey Broadbent, the organizer of the symposium and an architect and Design Methods scholar, declared *Atoms* the likeliest candidate for Alexander's most significant work.[74] Alexander, however, did not attend and was already distancing himself from the Design Methods movement. He wholly rejected their uptake of his work. "I . . . want to state, publicly, that I reject the whole idea of design methods as a subject of study, since I think it is absurd to separate the study of designing from the practice of design," he wrote in a 1971 preface to *Notes on the Synthesis of Form.* "In fact, people who study design methods without also practicing design are almost always frustrated designers who have no sap in them, who have lost, or never had, the urge to shape things. Such a person will never be able to say anything sensible about 'how' to shape things either."[75]

Alexander's rejections of Design Methods did not stave off rejection by other architects. Lionel March attacked *Atoms* in his "deliberately contentious" 1976 essay, "The Logic of Design and the Question of Value," in his book *The Architecture of Form.* March, who also studied architecture at Cambridge, followed Alexander's path departing Cambridge, United Kingdom, for Cambridge, Massachusetts, to join the Joint Center for Urban Studies of MIT and Harvard after Alexander had left for Berkeley. He took issue with the scientific approach Alexander and Poyner claimed to follow, arguing that it was in fact not scientific, that it incorrectly used the models of logic it invoked, and that there was no such thing as the bias-free design to which Alexander and Poyner aspired. Note that these various critiques, as well as the critiques by Frank Harary and J. Rockey of "A City Is Not a Tree," were published nearly a decade after the original publication of *Atoms*—further evidence of the reverberations of his work.

Alexander's trees and semilattices demonstrate his concern with architecture as an information modeling and visualization process. In the 1960s, he tried again and again to structure architectural problems through computational formatting techniques, and his visualization methods changed accordingly, along with his terminology and arguments. With trees and semilattices, he found that the geometries he generated did not quite engender the sense of order he sought to systematize. The complexity he modeled would have required three-dimensional or dynamic mapping constructs to realize them, and certainly far more computing power than was readily available to him in the 1960s.[76] But there was one approach Alexander followed that he found to be the most promising part of his work in the early 1960s: the diagram—a quickly readable encapsulation of the design problem.

Diagrams

Although Alexander attempted to map complex design problems, he still hoped to communicate at a glance the nature of the design problem with a diagram. Diagrams in Alexander's method abstractly represent the forces in a subset of the requirements or, to put it in a graph theoretical sense, the edges between nodes. Unlike the direct relationships between requirements that trees or semilattices mapped, diagrams were intended to be interpretative, communicating the essence or feeling of the design problem. While trees and semilattices fell by the wayside for Alexander, diagrams became a foundational element of the patterns and pattern languages he later developed.

Initially, Alexander and Manheim developed the diagrams as a combination cognitive psychology and highway mapping exercise in a 1961 civil engineering class at MIT. For a region of I-91 between Northampton and Holyoke, they drew on a transparency over a composite photograph of the geographical area to "bring out its essential organisational features."[77] They developed twenty-six diagrams that illustrated the various forces indicated by the intersection of the requirements that the diagram addresses (figure 2.06a). For example, Alexander and Manheim used circles of different densities to represent the distance of emergency services along I-91, accompanying it with a textual description of the problem it approaches. Then, they rolled up the diagrams into a larger, master diagram that represented how the design problems related to one another (figure 2.06b).

Where diagrams did a good job communicating the design considerations for highway interchanges, their meanings were less clear in the "The Determination of Components for an Indian Village" in the appendix of *Notes on the Synthesis of Form*, which demonstrated Alexander's method applied to a redesign of a six-hundred-person rural village in India. In the example, Alexander grouped a list of 141 misfits into four categories: agricultural, transportation, religious, and cultural concerns, each of which could be addressed by some aspect of design for the village. The misfits included: "9. Members of one caste like to be together and separate from others, and will not eat or drink together"; "50. Protected storage of fodder"; "68. Easy access to drinking water"' and "95. Access to bus as near as possible."[78] He then drew a diagram for the subsets of requirements meant to evoke the context, but since the diagrams are not tied to an actual map or actual features, they were difficult to read. He wrote that "the program

a.

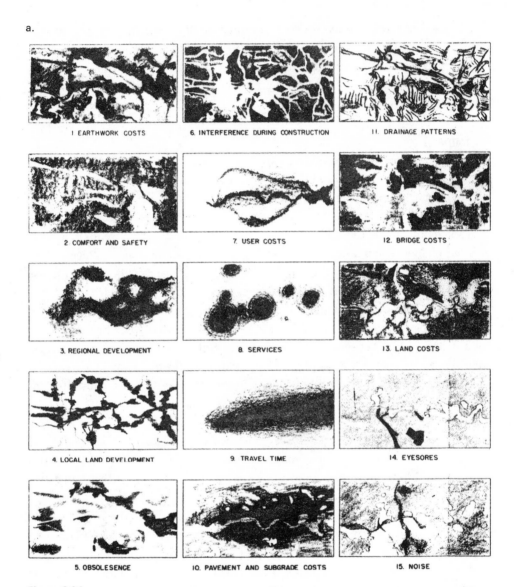

Figure 2.06a

Twenty-six diagrams show considerations in the locating of highway routes. They are more literal than the figurative diagrams of the Indian village that Alexander includes in *Notes on the Synthesis of Form*. Christopher Alexander and Marvin Manheim, *The Use of Diagrams in Highway Route Location: An Experiment* (Cambridge, MA: School of Engineering, MIT, 1962), 7. Courtesy of Christopher Alexander and MIT Press.

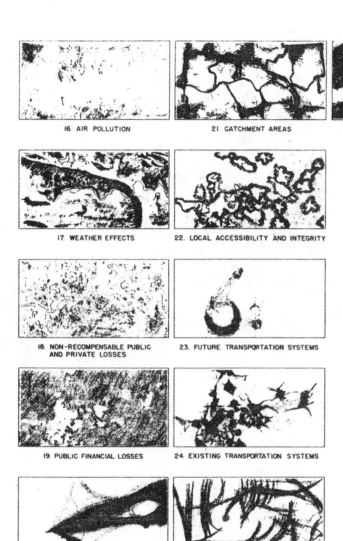

16. AIR POLLUTION

21. CATCHMENT AREAS

26. SELF-INDUCED CONGESTION

17. WEATHER EFFECTS

22. LOCAL ACCESSIBILITY AND INTEGRITY

18. NON-RECOMPENSABLE PUBLIC AND PRIVATE LOSSES

23. FUTURE TRANSPORTATION SYSTEMS

19. PUBLIC FINANCIAL LOSSES

24. EXISTING TRANSPORTATION SYSTEMS

20. MAJOR CURRENT TRAFFIC DESIRES

25. DUPLICATION OF FACILITIES

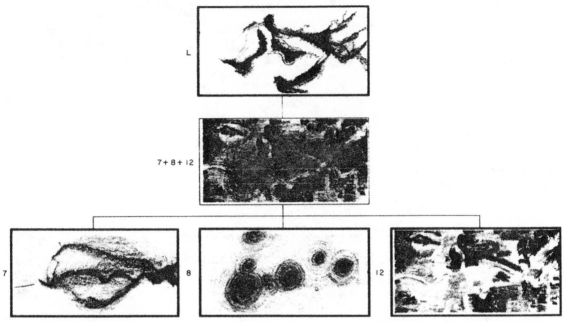

Figure 2.06b

The tree structure of diagrams for highway design, showing how the higher-level diagram encompasses aspects of the other diagrams. Christopher Alexander and Marvin Manheim, *The Use of Diagrams in Highway Route Location: An Experiment* (Cambridge, MA: School of Engineering, MIT, 1962), 12–13. Courtesy of Christopher Alexander and MIT Press.

will be used as a basis for the construction of diagrams from which we can develop a form," but never explained how the designer is to move from the diagram to the intervention in the village that would meet that diagram.[79] The diagram did not produce a literal model that could be translated, nor did it elucidate the relationships between the forces of a design problem. His further work in diagramming did not follow this form.

Instead of abandoning diagrams, Alexander wrote in the preface to the 1971 edition of *Notes* that they were the most important part of the puzzle he was trying to solve. He started referring to them as patterns. Patterns, he wrote, were a means to diagram "an abstract pattern of physical relationships which resolves a small system of interacting and conflicting forces" on a core level so that they represent just one set of these elements.[80] In their granularity, the patterns could be combined or studied together in myriad, if not infinite, ways. Patterns, he wrote, possessed "immense power."[81]

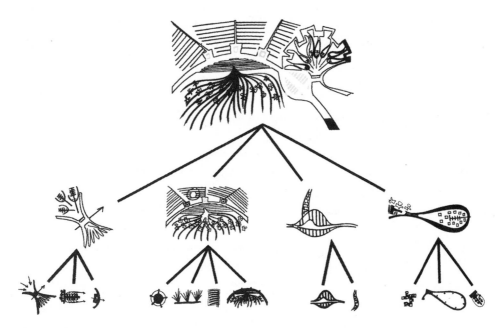

Figure 2.07
This composite diagram at the top of this tree rolls up all Alexander's subdiagrams that represent the dynamics of some functional aspect of the village in India that he used as a "worked example" in *Notes on the Synthesis of Form*. NOTES ON THE SYNTHESIS OF FORM by Christopher Alexander, Cambridge, MA: Harvard University Press, Copyright © 1964 by the President and Fellows of Harvard College. Copyright © renewed 1992 by Christopher Alexander.

Alexander jettisoned his visualization and structuring experiments with the computer and shifted his interest toward design patterns. Along with his colleagues at the Center for Environmental Structure, Alexander spent the next decade developing a network of patterns: a pattern language.

Networks and Pattern Languages

A Pattern Language is the body of work for which Alexander and his colleagues at the Center for Environmental Structure are best known, not only in architecture, but also in design, technology, and among the general public. The book was published along with *The Timeless Way of Building,* which outlines the theory and practice of pattern languages, and *The Oregon Experiment,* a worked example of patterns applied to the University of Oregon's campus.[82] The scope of the project is ambitious, to say the least. As Alexander and his coauthors wrote, it was "an entirely new attitude to architecture and planning" and the books were "intended to provide a complete working alternative to our present ideas about architecture, building and planning—an alternative which will, we hope, gradually replace current ideas and practices."[83] *A Pattern Language* inspired laypeople to think intuitively about designing their own spaces and find the patterns to help bring their ideas to fruition. And it also influenced programmers and digital designers in software and on the Web. It's safe to say that the contemporary digital landscape would look quite different, if not for *A Pattern Language*.

Design patterns were fostered by the Center for Environmental Structure (CES), founded by Alexander at the University of California, Berkeley in 1967. The CES served as a central control mechanism that gathered, researched, assessed, and shared patterns and pattern languages. Funded in part by the Kaufmann Foundation and the Bureau of Standards, it was structured as part research organization, part database, part alternative to an academic journal.[84] The CES would collect patterns from anyone who wanted to submit them, critique them, share them with subscribers, and research and apply the patterns to architectural and urban projects. The center even envisioned that the patterns might be able to be managed by a computer database by 1970, enabling the organization to put together just the right patterns for a subscriber's needs, like a custom academic journal without the lengthy publication process.[85] For a decade before the *A Pattern Language* was published, between 1967 and 1977, the CES detailed the grammar of the patterns. Alexander and his colleagues ultimately decided that a pattern should follow an explicit format that included a photograph that suggested the context, a paragraph that described it, a problem statement, a solution described instructionally, the confidence that the authors had in the pattern's universality, a set of diagrams, and the pattern's relationship to other patterns in the hierarchy of the language.[86]

Patterns are not new to architecture. Architects have long been interested in type and typology as a way to codify, categorize, and teach architectural style. In the early nineteenth century, architect Jean-Nicolas-Louis Durand classified the standard *éléments des édifices*—the elements of buildings that formed the basis of architecture in his book *Recueil et parallèle des édifices de tous genres, anciens et modernes (Collection and Parallel of Edifices of All Kinds, Ancient and Modern)*. He recorded the typology of architectural elements. As Antoine Picon writes, Durand's typology "is not a catalog of immediately applicable solutions but a system of classification that makes it possible to familiarize oneself with the various problems that may turn up in practice, but without any thought of covering them systematically."[87] A century later, Julien Guadet published his four-volume book *Éléments et Théorie de l'Architecture* in 1905 to teach students the practical elements of architecture that would allow them to design and construct logical and contextually appropriate buildings. By studying elements (e.g., walls, doors, rooms, porticos) and styles (e.g., religious, civic, military), the architecture student would learn to give form to concept—a sort of proto–pattern language. The difference between these typological approaches to architecture and *A Pattern Language* is that Alexander and CES's patterns described not only the elements, but also the problems that the patterns addressed and the relationships that they had to one other.

A pattern solves "a problem which occurs over and over again in our environment, and then describes the core of the solution to that problem, in such a way that you can use this solution a million times over, without ever doing it the same way twice,"[88] wrote Alexander, Sara Ishikawa, and Murray Silverstein and their other coauthors in *A Pattern Language.* Everybody has patterns in their mind for how to design or build something or solve a particular kind of problem, as Alexander explained in *The Timeless Way of Building*: "And all these rules of thumb—or patterns—are part of larger systems which are languages."[89] A pattern evokes, represents, and describes an image such that it can be acted on and built. The 253 patterns in *A Pattern Language* are organized in order of scale, from macro to micro. The book starts with global patterns for policy, institutions, infrastructure, and the definition of place, then moves to spatial relations for buildings and the spaces around them, then patterns for structuring and building a project. As Alexander wrote, "These patterns in our minds are, more or less, mental images of the pattern in the world: they are abstract representations of the very morphological rules which define the patterns in the world."[90]

The *language* of patterns is a format that organizes the parts, wholes, and relationships in a design problem. Built into the pattern language are both the means for sharing patterns and rule sets for generating new ones. This language is intended to be intuitive for its users, and the test of its success is how the patterns "feel." With pattern languages, Alexander had somewhat loosened his control over how people worked with his method. Patterns were intended to be intuitive and interpretative, and in *A Pattern Language*, Alexander and his colleagues advocated that a user include all patterns that seemed relevant, leave out those that didn't appeal, change them to suit taste, and include one's own ideas where appropriate in the scale. After all, the book's title is *A Pattern Language,* not **The** *Pattern Language.* Similarly, *The Timeless Way of Building* advocated following "the spirit of the pattern, not the letter."[91] Alexander wrote, "We tend to think of patterns as 'things,' and keep forgetting that they are complex, and potent fields. Each pattern is a field—not fixed, but a bundle of relationships, capable of being different each time that it occurs, yet deep enough to bestow life wherever it occurs."[92]

Put another way, pattern languages function like an operating system for design. They format information about the built environment, running the language along a decentralized, hierarchical network. The computer that governed Alexander's previous methods is no longer present, but the logic of computation still exists within pattern languages. By understanding the pattern language as an operating system, the translation to programmers and digital designers becomes even more apparent.

Operating the Pattern Language

Let's say someone wants to design a sunny living room for a house. She probably has an idea of what that room looks and feels like in her mind—the pattern in her mind—and she seeks out the patterns to help her articulate that idea. She would "make a language" (to use *A Pattern Language*'s terminology) by going through the list of patterns, finding a starting pattern that addresses the project's scope, then including both the smaller and larger patterns immediately before and after it, and looking at the suggested related patterns that provide context. This is her "base map." Pattern 159, "Light on Two Sides of Every Room," would serve as the base map.[93] It a vital pattern for the design of interior spaces—Alexander and his coauthors write that the pattern "determines the success or failure of a room."[94] In bold type, the problem statement reads, "When they have a choice, people will always gravitate to those rooms which have light on two sides, and leave the rooms which are lit only from one side unused and empty."[95] If rooms have light on both sides, people choose them over those that only have light on one side, they write. From that pattern, the reader could see its context for the pattern and other considerations she might like to take into account in designing her room. It is part of a group of ten patterns that represent the relationship of a room to the exterior of the building, including "Sunny Place," "Six-Foot Balcony," and "Connection to the Earth" that "prepare to knit the inside of the building to the outside, by treating the edge between the two as a place in its own right, and making human details there."[96]

"Light on Two Sides of Every Room" has a headline that, in this case, has two asterisks (two asterisks meant the authors were very certain about the pattern, "a deep and inescapable property of a well-formed environment," one asterisk means that the pattern was still tenuous and in development, and no asterisk means that they were quite uncertain but felt it important enough to include anyway[97]), a black-and-white photograph of the implemented pattern, and sketches diagramming its possible solutions. Below the headline is a black-and-white photograph of a room with sunbeams on the floor from two windows and an open set of French doors. An introductory paragraph notes that Pattern 159 shapes the edge of the room, and that it relates to patterns "107: Wings of Light," "106: Positive Outdoor Space," "109: Long Thin House," and "116: Cascade of Roofs"—the reader would refer to these for context but not include them in the list.[98] At the end of the statement, the authors provided a solution statement in bold type: "Locate each room so that it has outdoor space outside it on at least two sides, and then place windows in these outdoor walls so that natural light falls into every room from more than one direction."[99] A hand-sketched diagram followed that showed a room with light on two sides and a plan of five rooms configured so that all have light on two sides. Finally, the authors related this pattern to those that follow it, again, in colloquial language: "Don't let this pattern make your plans too wild—otherwise you will destroy the simplicity of Positive Outdoor Space (106) and you will have a terrible time roofing the building—Roof Layout (209)."[100] The reader would now have a number of considerations at hand that offered her possibilities and constraints that she could put to use as she designed her sunny living room.

The Language and System of Patterns

Alexander's concept of language is intended to be both an allegorical concept and a structuring mechanism. As an allegorical and emotional concept, language is "fundamental" to human nature, Alexander wrote.[101] All people have language; all people have patterns, and therefore all pattern combinations offer different semantic possibilities. The language is a universalizing concept, meant to explain "every single act of building" in the world.[102] Using the pattern language means engaging with a system of innate and intuitively derived feelings about space and place. It "gives each person who uses it the power to create an infinite variety of new and unique buildings, just as his ordinary language gives him the power to create an infinite variety of sentences," Alexander wrote in *The Timeless Way of Building*.[103] As a structuring mechanism, the language organizes the patterns, a notion that works in both a figurative and operational manner. It takes the place of the mathematical models and computer programs that Alexander used in his earlier career. The language represents the relations between parts, what he called a "finite system of rules which a person can use to generate an infinite variety of buildings" that hold together the elements within it.[104] Like a "genetic code" in a living being, the code of the language provides the means to produce and reproduce whatever humans might build.[105] It functions by coordinating and sequencing the network of connections in the pattern language.

Systems are holistic, composed of a set of interacting elements within them.[106] A system is different than the sum of its parts, to borrow from Kurt Koffka's famous statement in Gestalt psychology. Likewise, pattern languages are also holistic systems. They use a set of formats that compress spatial information, organized through hierarchies. It is similar to a computer's file system. When someone uses patterns in a design project, he is effectively running a program for design that generates space.

The standardized format of each pattern in *A Pattern Language* records the information of the problem it is intended to solve, relates it to other patterns, and makes it readily communicable. Its brevity and reduction to the essence of a design problem compresses its data. It is a notion that works in systems of other kinds. In a computer system, data compression increases storage capacity and efficiency by replacing redundant information with symbols and structure. Encoding the information reduces the size of the message, but the message must be decoded in order to reconstruct it. In patterns, a user reconstructs and recovers the relationships that are compressed by the patterns, forming their own specific spatial relationships in the process. The patterns use compression in both of these senses: as a format that encodes spatial information and as a mechanism that suggests interpretation on the part of its users.[107] Alexander wrote, "Each pattern is an operator which differentiates space: that is, it creates distinctions where no distinction was before. The operator is concrete and specific, insofar as it will always generate an instance of the pattern. But the operator is quite general, because it specifies the operation in such a way that its performance interacts with the surroundings."[108] The formatting and compression of the patterns make it possible to efficiently relate multiple patterns to each other. Reading two patterns against each other suggests connections between them that create more than the sum of their parts and that might suggest other meanings and uses than *A Pattern Language* provides. For example, in two patterns about water, "Bathing Room (144)" and "Still Water (71)," Alexander and his colleagues noted, "The compression illuminates each of the patterns, sheds light on its meaning; and also illuminates our lives, as we understand a little more about the connections of our inner needs."[109] The patterns do not need to explicitly state their potential uses—that is for the user of the language to decide. Together, they might refer to a bathroom in a house, a set of bathhouses, or a public swimming pool.

Not all of the guidelines Alexander and his coauthors offer about compression of patterns result in good design or an orderly solution, however. In language, a writer or speaker might compress a message not only for economy of words, but also for literary meaning, such as in a poem—a reader or fellow conversant then must recover what has been left out. But the authors also suggest cramming patterns into a project. "Every building, every room, every garden is better, when all the patterns which it needs are compressed as far as it is possible for them to be. The building will be cheaper; and the meanings in it will be denser," Alexander and his colleagues wrote.[110] They suggested that it would make for a rich building, in the way that a poem condenses multiple meanings in its lines. Yet they don't explain how more patterns make for a more economical building. More is rarely better in design, and one approach to making bad art or writing terrible poetry is to overload it with meaning.

Networks

The pattern language is a network with less hierarchy and more interconnection than Alexander's previous trees and semilattices. The introduction to *A Pattern Language* states, "Since the language is in truth a network, there is no one sequence which perfectly captures it."[111] But the network is not a sprawling one: it still relies on hierarchies in order for it to function properly. As in a computer's file system, the language helps the patterns to coalesce and make sense in relation to one another. Alexander wrote, "Each pattern sits at the center of a network of connections which connect it to certain other patterns that help to complete it. . . . And it is the network of these connections between patterns which creates the language. . . . In this network, the links between the patterns are almost as much a part of the language as the patterns themselves."[112]

To successfully deploy a pattern language, the user must do three things: follow the patterns in order, reach up to the patterns of greater scale just above, and reach down to the ones of smaller scale just below.[113] Each "sequence of these operators" further differentiates the image that the user has of what she is designing.[114] Like a file system, they are ordered in a "straight linear sequence [that] is essential to the way the language works."[115] As media theorist Cornelia Vismann wrote in her book *Files: Law and Media Technology*, lists contain "spatial logic," compressing the information required to perform transactions. The "in*forma*tion" passed among items in a list contains the logic of its format.[116] Applying Vismann's characterization to Alexander's work, the format and logic of the pattern language demands a scalar movement from large to small, universal to particular, general to more detailed, "always from the ones which create structures, to the ones which then embellish those structures, and then to those which embellish the embellishments," as Alexander and his colleagues wrote.[117]

What kind of network is the pattern language? We can compare it to the models in Paul Baran's famous 1964 diagram of networked communication systems and how they might fare in an attack. In Baran's model, a centralized network—which is ultimately what a tree is—is vulnerable to attack because destroying its center makes it impossible for any of the nodes to communicate with each other. If you take out the top node of a tree, the rest of the tree falls apart. A decentralized structure has a hierarchy of centers, each linked to its own galaxy of nodes, but destroying one of these networked nodes would cause its relatives to be lost. The least vulnerable and most secure structure is the distributed network, with multiple links to each node, all interconnected with one another. The distributed network offers a higher level of redundancy, so if one node were knocked out of service, communication could flow through the links and still be able to communicate effectively.[118] The pattern language network is more hierarchical than Baran's decentralized network, but not as robust as a distributed network. (Then

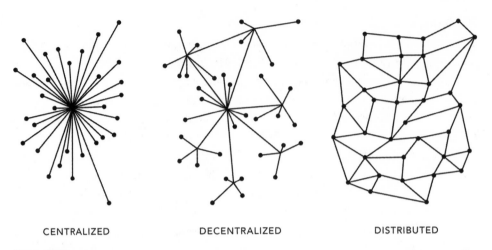

CENTRALIZED   DECENTRALIZED   DISTRIBUTED

Figure 2.08

Paul Baran characterized three kinds of networks similar to the ones depicted here: centralized, decentralized, and distributed. A centralized communications network was more vulnerable to attack, whereas communications could better reroute through a decentralized or distributed network. Pattern languages fall between decentralized and distributed networks. The distributed network topology was important for the architecture of the Internet.

again, it doesn't need to face coming under attack—as Baran's model of communications networks did.)

Skipping a pattern could break the relationships within the network, just as running a computer program and omitting a step could cause it to crash. Alexander and his coauthors underscored the fact that the success of a project depends on the user following the hierarchies, reaching up to the patterns of greater scale just above and to the ones of smaller scale just below in designing a project. Otherwise, it would fail, creating an "incoherent" image of what the user is designing. In the same manner that Alexander and Manheim argued that the HIDECS program was intelligent because it could produce consistent results that matched the structure of the analysis, Alexander argued that following the hierarchy demonstrates that the pattern language has "natural power to help us form coherent images."[119] While he claimed that the language is "not merely a network, but a network of networks, a structure of structures," in reality, the pattern network is still more like a semilattice that doesn't need a machine to compute it.[120] The pattern language represents what Alexander and his colleagues could master within a system of their own creation—this time a book, not a computer program.

These potential weaknesses of pattern languages were also their strength. As a network with limits, the system of the pattern language did not need to encompass every possibility for design, just a finite set. Moreover, as *A Pattern Language,* not ***The Pattern***

Language, it could address other subjects beyond that of architecture and the built environment. As a method for construing the elements of a design problem and their interrelationships, it could be used to represent more complex models of systems. And as a result, *A Pattern Language* and *The Timeless Way of Building* could apply to many different kinds of systems—particularly digital ones.

Generativity

There is one final, important element of Alexander's system: generativity. Generativity refers to the quality of multiplicity and holism, of a system that operates both as a set of rules and as a whole. A generating system is a kit of parts. *"Each pattern is a rule which describes what you have to do to generate the entity which it defines,"* Alexander wrote in *The Timeless Way of Building.*[121] He began exploring generativity long before *A Pattern Language* in an exhibition, the materials from which were published in 1968 for *Architectural Design* as "Systems Generating Systems." He introduced his notion of generative systems in four brief points:

There are two ideas hidden in the word system: the idea of a system as a whole and the idea of a generating system.

A system as a whole is not an object but a way of looking at an object. It focuses on some holistic property which can only be understood as a product of interaction among parts.

A generating system is not a view of a single thing. It is a kit of parts, with rules about the way these parts may be combined.

Almost every "system as a whole" is generated by a "generating system." If we wish to make things which function as "wholes" we shall have to invent generating systems to create them.[122]

Pattern languages have three characteristics that make them generative. First, they contain an inherent rule set that determines their logic. Alexander wrote, "It not only tells us the rules of arrangement, but shows us how to construct arrangements—as many as we want—which satisfy the rules."[123] In an interview with his biographer, Stephen Grabow, Alexander noted, "We give names to things but we don't give many names to relationships."[124] The pattern language was an attempt to address these relationships. "So it not only defines the sentences which make sense in a given situation; it also gives us the apparatus we need to create these sentences. It is, in other words, a generative system, which allows us to generate sentences that are appropriate to any given situation."[125] Following the operations in order, suggested by the system, creates a generative, coherent whole out of the parts the system is organizing.

Second, pattern languages and other generating systems produce effects greater and different than the sum of their parts. Alexander wrote in *The Timeless Way of Building,* "This quality in buildings and in towns cannot be made, but only generated, indirectly, by the ordinary actions of the people, just as a flower cannot be made, but only generated from the seed."[126] These systems may come to necessitate their own propagation, he suggests, when we use them. He wrote, "The patterns in the world merely exist. But the same patterns in our minds are dynamic. They have force. They are generative. They tell us what to do; they tell us how we shall, or may, generate them; and they tell us too, that under certain circumstances, we *must* create them."[127]

Third, in addition to their self-perpetuating properties, generating systems contain the mechanism for their own propagation. The pattern language, then, "like a seed, is the genetic system which gives our millions of small acts the power to form a whole."[128] A language can foster "a process of unfolding, like the evolution of an embryo, in which the whole precedes the parts, and actually gives birth to them, by splitting."[129] At the same time, the language grows through accretion. "Next, several acts of building, each one done to repair and magnify the product of the previous acts, will slowly generate a larger and more complex whole than any single act can generate," he wrote.[130] Alexander also saw it as a genetic allegory: in his description of "the timeless way of building," an unnamable quality that his systems are intended to elicit, he wrote, "*In this sense, then, we have found an example of the kind of code which does, at certain times play just the role in buildings and in towns that the genetic code plays in a living organism.*"[131]

Alexander was interested in the idea that a rule set—the syntax of a language—could generate a building "not as a mechanical technique (as might perhaps be naively understood in the automobile industry) but as a structural principle of natural creation as it is understood in modern science," wrote Stephen Grabow in his biography of Alexander.[132] "The idea that a set of known rules could actually generate a building is as disturbing as the idea that a human being is generated by a few genetic rules operating on chromosomes or that a poem is generated by a few grammatical rules operating on language. And yet that is precisely what Alexander is claiming," Grabow argued.[133]

Alexander referred to Noam Chomsky's generative grammar in an interview in his biography, stating that it was his intention to apply such a grammar to architecture.[134] The pattern language provides the syntax, wherein the patterns, when combined and executed by the user, reflect the language's semantics. Alexander channeled Chomsky's notion of deep and surface structures: while a pattern might have many potential instantiations on its surface, its sum of underlying possibilities are what make it generative. In essence, if a generative grammar can produce sentences regardless of the language, if genetic code can produce a bird, then a generative system can produce architecture. Alexander says, "*I'm making the statement that I can actually set up those rules so that if you follow a sequence of them in the order prescribed you will have a building.*"[135] The user of the language makes choices about what and how to use the language, based on context: it is the structure that makes this possible.[136] Again, genetics, languages, and architecture were inextricable in Alexander's view. Designing buildings or a town is "fundamentally a genetic process," he wrote.[137] Moreover, "patterns always come from languages"; these languages are analogous to the genetic code that shapes a living being.[138] Despite the fact that Alexander employed the notion of generative grammar, he argued that Chomsky's generative grammars were too basic, if not "primitive."[139] (Alexander was wrong on this count.) The "real stuff" that interested Alexander had to do with the architectural equivalent of the semantic networks: the interrelations of the words, their meanings, and their evocations with each other.

On one hand, generativity gives pattern languages a means to produce and reproduce themselves. The formatting and compression of the patterns and the sequencing provided by the language provide the framework for using the patterns as a program that creates form. But Alexander aimed further, toward semantics, allegory, and poetics, as well as the aspects of language that generate feelings, emotions, a sense of order—all of which extend beyond the structural, topological, and syntactic aspects of his program. These semantic conceptions equate the patterns with timeless cycles of life, with a program for the built environment, for the order of existence.

Ultimately, this is where Alexander wanted to land: a way to describe the generation and giving of life as a holistic system. Alexander attempted to describe what he called "life" and how it could be found in the world. In *The Nature of Order*, he wrote, "The quality I call life in these buildings exists as a quality. It is clearly not the same as the biological life we recognize in organisms. It is a larger idea, and a more general one. Indeed, what we intuitively feel as 'life' in these objects happens just as much in a purely abstract thing like a painting as it does in a functioning thing like a building, or in a biologically living system like a tree."[140] And these qualities are what digital designers and software engineers sought in Alexander's work—structure, harmony, and order.

Christopher Alexander's Digital Influence

"Christopher Alexander is a design person that other design people refer to a lot," wrote Stewart Brand in 1971 in *The Last Whole Earth Catalog*, presaging the influence that Alexander would have on designers and beyond.[141] As programmers and designers look to concepts from architecture to describe the complexity of the problems they seek to solve, they turn to Christopher Alexander's work. His approaches to architecture represent for them simplicity and simplification, adaptivity and adaptation over time, and a user-centered approach to design. Architecture stands for the primacy of structure for them, and Alexander's work offers a transformative framework for building systems.

Software developers and digital designers describe some of their most complex activities as architecture. But so pervasive is Alexander's influence in software and design that he is frequently the *only* architect that many programmers or designers name as an influence on their work. When I interviewed Kent Beck, he paused for a long time on the question of other architects. "Le Corbusier?" he asked. Alan Cooper named John Portman, who designed the Bonaventure Hotel in Los Angeles and the Embarcadero Center in San Francisco. As I noted at the beginning of the chapter, Alexander was "in the air" in the late 1980s and 1990s for the developers and designers of programming methods, software, and the early World Wide Web. Software engineers had taken up Alexander's work, applying pattern languages and the philosophies in *The Timeless Way of Building* to object-oriented languages and to software engineering. Designers, human-computer interaction researchers, and information architects theorized how patterns and languages contribute important methods to the emerging fields of user-centered design.

The rest of this chapter traces Alexander's influence on two different waves of software engineers and designers. First, I examine how pattern languages gave rise to software patterns, and how Alexander's work directly influenced the development of the wiki software format (that Wikipedia uses) and the Extreme Programming software development method. Then, I look at how the burgeoning practice of human-centered design modeled its practice in software and on the Web on tenets from Alexander. Finally, I loop back around to the singular influence of Alexander and the digital, and the distance architects keep from him, in order to find some productive ground in the tensions between the two.

Patterns in Software

Is it a coincidence that many programmers and digital designers spent their childhoods dreaming of architecture—only to design computer architectures instead? Software engineering luminary Kent Beck says that, growing up, he was fascinated by a book of house plans, one of which had a swimming pool running all the way through it. He obsessively sought out just the right graph paper to draw his own plans based on the ones in the book. Alan Cooper, a software engineer and interaction design pioneer, pondered the question of why programmers didn't become architects in the traditional sense. "The desire that makes these people want to be an architect is *not* satisfied by being an architect in most cases, but it is satisfied by being a software designer, an interaction designer, a software developer, a software engineer. This is where you get to do architecture: inside digital computers, and you don't get to do architecture out there in the built environment anymore," he said.[142] In Alexander, they discovered an architect who thought the way that they did about systems and computer programming.

Programmers found their way to Christopher Alexander's work in various ways. Some knew of *Notes on the Synthesis of Form* in the 1960s and 1970s.[143] Alan Cooper found it in his high school library in the late 1960s.[144] In the 1980s, a bootlegged, mimeographed copy of *A Pattern Language* purportedly passed hand-to-hand between programmers up and down the West Coast.[145] Beck first found *The Timeless Way of Building* when browsing the architecture shelves at the University of Oregon bookstore in 1979. Although he was fascinated with architecture, he says he didn't have the spatial acuity for the profession, but he still found himself in the aisle of the bookstore reading it bit by bit.[146] In the mid-1980s, he came across *Notes on the Synthesis of Form* and bought copies for himself and his group at Tektronix.[147] "I wanted a way to talk about programs," Beck wrote. For him and programmers like him, patterns offered an organizational structure for coding, providing a way to move between the larger framework of a program and the smaller pieces of code that he produced. "By the time I had been programming for a year at Tek Labs I was running into the limitations of my brain. I could write complicated programs but I couldn't keep them running when I tried to incorporate the excellent suggestions of my colleagues," he wrote.[148] Patterns provided a way to capture, distill, and communicate the best solutions in an abstract enough manner that other people could use them.

Beck and his colleague Ward Cunningham were the first programmers to apply Alexander and his colleagues' patterns to software.[149] In 1987, they were designing a system to test integrated circuits for semiconductors and grappling with how to program user interfaces in Smalltalk, an object-oriented language developed by computer scientist Alan Kay and his researchers at Xerox PARC in the 1970s and 1980s. Smalltalk was an interactive programming environment especially suitable for education and research. Kay had come up with the term "objects" in the late 1960s to describe repeatable modules of code.[150] Objects are similar to one another with minor variances, and so through "methods," they inherit code from a more general object or class.[151] Using objects makes it so the programmer does not need start from scratch each time, and instead relates modules to one another.

Cunningham and Beck wrote up their findings in "Using Pattern Languages for Object-Oriented Programs" for OOPSLA '87 (the ACM conference on Object-Oriented Programs, Systems, Languages and Applications, at which Alexander gave the keynote nine years later), outlining what they found inspirational about Alexander and how they applied five simple patterns to the design of their programs. "Computer users should write their own programs," they argued. "The idea sounds foolish when one considers the size and complexity of both buildings and programs, and the years of training for the design professions. Yet Alexander offers a convincing scenario. It revolves around a concept called a 'pattern language.'"[152] Pattern languages for software picked up steam, as a group of several engineers in the 1980s and 1990s including Cunningham, Beck, Richard Gabriel, and the "Gang of Four" (Erich Gamma, Richard Helm, Ralph Johnson, and John Vlissides) developed the practice in a set of meetings, conferences, and gatherings.[153] The "Gang of Four" promoted the use of "design patterns" that used the format and syntax of Alexander's patterns to capture and communicated object-oriented programming approaches. "Our solutions are expressed in terms of objects and interfaces, instead of walls and doors, but at the core of both kinds of patterns is a solution to a problem in context," they write.[154] These "micro-architectures" within the larger system architecture used pattern formats but, as they pointed out, did not form an entire language like Alexander's—either because object-oriented design was still new, "[o]r this may be simply because the problems encountered in software design are different from those found in architecture and are not amenable to solution by pattern languages."[155] Their early endeavors culminated in the best-selling book *Design Patterns: Elements of Reusable Object-Oriented Software* in 1994. There are now thousands of books and resources on using patterns in software, games, user experience, and interface design, among others.

Software and the "Quality without a Name"

Alexander began to engage directly with software engineers in the mid-1990s. Richard Gabriel, an engineer and poet, approached Alexander about writing the introduction to his 1996 book *Patterns of Software*. The "quality without a name" of Alexander's worldview was what Gabriel hoped to find in computer code. From the format of patterns to their compression in a poetic language, Gabriel sought to find applications that bridged architecture with software architecture. Alexander's introduction to *Patterns of Software* broached the question of whether higher standards through patterns could bring to bear the same spirituality in programming that he sought to locate in architecture. Alexander wondered about the possibility of "programs which make you gasp because of their beauty . . . and a growing knowledge, in the field of software engineering, of what this means."[156] Could code "breathe life?"[157] Or would that be too difficult because, regardless of the parallels that programmers tried to draw, computer code is more abstract than architecture?[158]

In his keynote at the OOPSLA '96 conference that opened this chapter, Alexander assessed the state of patterns in software at that point. He pointed out that patterns were not just a matter of capturing design decisions, but that the language and theory behind them had other functions. They had a "moral component," they were intended to be "generative," and they brought parts and wholes together, making "morphological coherence" in what they produced.[159] How would programmers know when a program was "good" in a moral sense, in that it supported the concept of life that so interested Alexander?[160] By this point in his career as he was writing the four-volume work *The Nature of Order*, Alexander argued that this moral goodness was something that could be explicitly defined and empirically tested in architecture. What was the analogous nature of order in software?

In an echo of ideas from "Systems Generating Systems" and *The Timeless Way of Building*, Alexander suggested computer code might carry forward the genetic and linguistic frameworks for producing patterns. "I am convinced that the equivalent of the genes that act in organisms will have to be—or at least can be—software packages, acting in society."[161] If programmers enacted it in this way, it could put decision-making in the hands of individuals, much the way that Kent Beck interpreted the possibilities of Alexander's work as a tool for social and political democratization of the design process. Alexander asked to what extent programmers might be willing to take on "the responsibility for influencing, shaping, and changing the environment."[162] If programmers and engineers were willing to take on patterns and their moral imperatives, then it was on them to build a better world. Not just a world imbued with computers, but also with a deep understanding of how computers contribute to the ecosystem in which they are located. "This is an extraordinary vision of the future, in which computers play a fundamental role in making the world—and above all the built structure of the world— alive, humane, ecologically profound, and with a deep living structure."[163]

Criticism of Design Patterns

Although design patterns are used so ubiquitously, many people have criticized their use, including the very people that inspired them. In fact, they sometimes could be viewed as a downright failure—whether in software or in the built environment. Alexander himself wondered how effective pattern languages could be in the sense that he designed them. He wrote in the introduction to Richard Gabriel's *Patterns of Software* book,

In architecture, the question, the question I have been asking is very simple: "Can we do better? Does all this talk help to make better buildings?" . . . Do the people who write these programs, using alexandrian patterns, or any other methods, do they do better work? Are the programs better? Do they get better results, more efficiently, more speedily, more profoundly? Do people actually feel more alive when using them? Is what is accomplished by these programs, and by the people who run these programs and by the people who are affected by them, better, more elevated, more insightful, better by ordinary spiritual standards?[164]

Alexander admitted in interviews with his biographer, Stephen Grabow (also referred to by Gabriel in *Patterns in Software*), that the patterns, when applied, often produced mediocre, geometrically uninteresting houses that did not produce the qualities of life he'd hoped they would have. Worse, the architects who used a pattern language might be glowingly enthusiastic about the process, only to have ended up designing "buildings that have this mechanical death-like morphology, even with the intention of producing buildings that are alive," Alexander said.[165] Before such a long view could be achieved, Alexander realized that it would require a broad engagement with the planning process: working with economics, zoning, mortgages, developers, and construction. It was a matter of "controlling the process," wrote Gabriel:

By controlling the process, you control the result, and if the control retains the old, broken process, the result will be the old, broken architecture.

This resonates with what we see in software development: The structure of the system follows the structure of the organization that put it together, and to some extent, its quality follows the nature of the process used to produce it.[166]

One of the biggest critiques of software patterns came from Alan Kay, who called patterns "the most disastrous thing about programming."[167] He didn't have a problem with Alexander's approach to patterns in architecture because Alexander "was looking at 2,000 years of ways that humans have made themselves comfortable. So there was actually something to it, because he was dealing with a genome that hasn't changed that much," Kay said about *A Pattern Language* and architecture. "But the bug in trying to do that in computing is the assumption that we know anything at all about programming. So extracting patterns from today's programming practices ennobles them in a way they don't deserve."[168]

Alexander might have agreed with Kay in one respect: he believed that there was no way to know "what a better program *is*" not within the limited history of software development.[169] But unlike Kay, he thought that it could be possible for programs to someday have the quality of life that he described in his later *Nature of Order* books—programs and computer environments, magically alive, that prove that they can "breathe life."[170] If this could be achieved, it would be the ultimate vaunting of software and software practices in an almost spiritual realm. But whether that could ever be achieved in computing was still the question.

Patterns and the Politics of Design

Traditionally, software engineers design the system architecture, hand off the decisions to be executed, and hope that costly changes do not need to be made—similar to how architects design buildings and hand off the drawings to engineers and contractors for construction. Yet when Ward Cunningham and Kent Beck first developed patterns in software, it was with the hope that users could begin to design their own environments.

Alexander's work not only provided a means to format programming problems, but also offered a philosophy of the social and political human truths of the design process. Beck said that Alexander's big vision resonated because of its "rearrangement of the political power in the design and building process."[171] This notion resonates with Alexander's realization that an architect needed to be involved not only in building but also in the planning process if she wanted to effect change in how design was done. Instead of handing down plans and pronouncements, the architect (whether of a house or a computer system) instead needed to consider the needs of the person who lives in the house or who uses the system.

Beck saw patterns as a way for the architect to put in place the conditions for a user to make decisions. Alexander's concept of "gradual stiffening" in Pattern 208 in *A Pattern Language*, influenced this idea: "The fundamental philosophy behind the use of pattern languages is that buildings should be uniquely adapted to individual needs and sites; and that the plans of buildings should be rather loose and fluid, in order to accommodate those subtleties."[172] Gradual stiffening meant that the parts of a design could be moved around before they set. They don't all need to be specified in advance on paper; instead, they can be tested in situ, shifted as needed, and firmed up when it is time. It was a radical concept, Beck explained, because it ran counter to the structure of programming in the world.[173] For contemporary platforms like Facebook, for example, there is no other way to design, Beck said. "In fact, you couldn't build it any other way. So I'd say that principle probably is the most important—Extreme Programming is the logical runout of taking gradual stiffening seriously."[174]

Beck developed Extreme Programming (XP), a set of practices and values in a new approach to programming, throughout the second half of the 1990s. XP breaks down programming tasks into smaller pieces that are planned incrementally and asks programmers to sit together and code together in pairs and continually test their code as they produce it. XP embodies values ("communication, feedback, simplicity, courage, and respect") that bind the community that uses them.[175] In *Extreme Programming Explained: Embrace Change*, Beck concluded the book with a chapter titled "The Timeless Way of Programming," tying XP back to Alexander. Beck saw in Alexander's work a fight against the "imbalance of power" in architecture that reminded him of the same disparities in software engineering, which is similar to Alexander's realization that the culture of design needed to change in order to support a different kind of design.[176] XP was an attempt to better align business concerns, users, and programmers with one another. Even though, as Beck wrote, Alexander failed in his attempt to reform architecture, programmers had a better shot. He concluded "The Timeless Way of Programming," the final chapter in *Extreme Programming Explained*, with a call for change: "We, in software, have the opportunity to create new social structures in which technical excellence is joined with business vision to create new products and services of unique value. This is our advantage."[177]

Extreme Programming was a foundational part of the Agile project management method. Rather than the waterfall method of project management, in which the customer delivers a set of requirements and a team develops the architecture, hands off the system architecture to the design team, and the design team passes its work to an implementation team to be coded, Agile works in shorter, collaborative sprints that can respond better to change. In 2001, the Agile Manifesto was developed by a group that included Beck and Cunningham. It includes four key points: "Individuals and interactions over processes and tools, working software over comprehensive documentation, customer collaboration over contract negotiation, and responding to change over following a plan."[178] Although there is criticism about Agile, the methods continue to be in use in companies big and small. They can also redistribute the power in a team, allowing for more team members to produce changes in the code and its management politics. Where Alexander's theories are concerned, they bring to light a changed politics of design.

The Wiki

The wiki, the website application format that runs Wikipedia, is also an Alexander-influenced concept. In 1994, Ward Cunningham started developing a database in Hypercard to track how ideas circulated within his company. Apple's Hypercard software used the idea of stacks of cards that a user could link to other cards in the database, enabled by a simple graphical user interface. Cunningham modified the system so that when he reached the end of a string of ideas, Hypercard automatically add a new card, with the effect of "push[ing] the edge out farther."[179] Hypercard was a single-user project, however, and Cunningham could run the program only off his desktop. When he attended the first Pattern Languages of Programs (PLoP) conference in 1994 at the University of Illinois, he was introduced to the World Wide Web and the Mosaic web browser that was developed at the university. His friends suggested building this database of "people, products and patterns" on the Web, and he called it WikiWikiWeb after the Hawaiian word for "quick."[180] In March 1995, he invited friends and colleagues to join, create, and collaboratively edit the web of pages at http://wiki.c2.com/.

What Cunningham found especially attractive was that the wiki matched the idea of a computer program emerging out of collaborative engagement. "We were very interested in how computer programs could form in an emergent way," he said in an interview with the Wikimedia Foundation. "We didn't have a master plan for the computer program. . . . [It was] unheard of at the time in computer programming, in a text system and a discussion board. . . . It was a demonstration of the very concept we were trying to explore for computer programming," he said. The WikiWikiWeb not only facilitated conversations about pattern languages, but also mirrored the philosophy behind them. It was more effective than using a regular email list. In order for this kind of conversation or programming to take hold, the community needs to trust each other and share openness. The code or the conversation could "grow from the center out."[181] People do not need to know each other, or even know that they might want to work together, but the wiki supports working toward a common goal.[182]

Cunningham has written extensively about the influence of pattern languages on the wiki and is quite clear about Alexander's influence on it. The wiki, he wrote in 2013, is an "elementary pattern language." Pattern languages and wikis both share the following characteristics:

Both are open-ended sets of information, consisting of unitary subsets (pages or patterns) connected by hyperlinks. . . .

Both are topical essays with a characteristic structure: overview (with links), definition, discussion, evidence, conclusion, further links. . . .

Both are structured to be easily creatable, shareable and editable by many people. . . .

Both are (in principle) evolutionary, falsifiable and refinable. . . .

Both aim to create useful ontological models of a portion of the world, as a more formalized subset of language. These are models of design specifically for pattern languages, and models of knowledge more generally for wikis.[183]

In essence, pattern languages and wikis are both worldviews. They are epistemological tools for capturing the rules around a set of information that governs a space, whether a space of knowledge (as in Wikipedia), the space of software, or the space of the built environment.

The wiki was never patented, although Cunningham briefly considered it in 1995.[184] This openness certainly helped enable its success. The biggest user of the wiki format, Wikipedia, was founded in 2001 and has over 5.4 million content pages, nearly 890 million edits, more than 10 edits per second and more than 30.9 million users as of May 2017.[185] Wikipedia is arguably the greatest demonstration of Christopher Alexander's philosophies.

Bringing Design to Software

At the same time as software engineers turned to patterns in programming languages, other designers and developers began to call for better design in software. As software grew in complexity and served a wider variety of needs, most programs weren't particularly well designed, a fact that became increasingly apparent as more and more consumers used and bought personal computers. Design often was a by-product of software engineering, something that concerned programmers and engineers only secondarily as they worked to meet business needs and technological constraints. In order to produce higher quality software, it was necessary to give thought to its design.

Just as software engineers had done with patterns, the burgeoning discipline of "software design" turned to Alexander's approaches for a way to situate their work. Alexander was the go-to architect whose work offered methods that worked for the designers of software, and his approaches became the operative term for what designers meant when they talked about architecture. Software designers saw their work as an analog to that of an architect: defining the structure of a livable environment.

Terry Winograd, the Stanford University computer science professor, was also looking to architecture and particularly Christopher Alexander's concepts on it as he articulated the emerging discipline of software design. In 1992, Winograd convened a group of designers, engineers, and business professionals, many of whom were affiliated with Interval Research in Pajaro Dunes, California, at a three-day conference, "Bringing Design to Software." As Barry Katz described it in *Make It New: The History of Silicon Valley Design,* the attendees "trained their artillery on yet another bastion of engineering that had rested comfortably on the pillars of functionality and profit."[186] Winograd had already begun to stake out a new way of thinking about design and architecture for human–computer interaction in 1990 when he gave the closing plenary at the SIGCHI conference on Human–Computer Interaction (CHI '90) that introduced a human-centered approach to design and proposed ways to educate these new professionals. As a result of that gathering, Winograd published an edited collection four years later, in 1996, *Bringing Design to Software,* that captured the emergence of design approaches in software. Things changed rapidly in the world of software as Winograd and his fellow authors worked on the book: they started it before most people had used the Internet, and published it in 1996, as the World Wide Web exploded and after the Netscape IPO had taken place.

The authors in *Bringing Design to Software* are a who's-who of digital design. Mitch Kapor, the designer of the Lotus 1-2-3 spreadsheet program, opened the book with a republication of his "Software Design Manifesto." The book also featured pieces by other important designers, including Gillian Crampton Smith, founder of the Computer-Related Design master's program at the Royal College of Art and the Interaction Design Institute Ivrea in Ivrea, Italy, with her husband Philip Tabor, an architect and educator who taught at the Bartlett and led the studio PhD program there; and John Rheinfrank and Shelley Evenson, design strategists who worked at Fitch, Doblin, and Scient, and were later professors at Carnegie Mellon.[187] The authors in Winograd's collection laid the groundwork for what would become a multifaceted set of approaches to the design of digital devices and experience that are still relevant today.

Those who engaged in "software design" had any number of job titles in the early 1990s. In fact, they still do today—they might be called interaction designers, user experience (UX) designers, or information architects—or all of the above. In the 1990s, the Association of Software Design defined software design as "the crossroads of all the computer disciplines: hardware and software engineering, programming, human factors research, ergonomics. It is the study of the intersection of human, machine, and the various interfaces—physical, sensory, psychological—that connect them."[188] More than a task performed by a specific person, software design was a way to develop a common language that could mediate between users, business, and programmers.

This shift toward design was very much needed, as Kapor argued in his 1990 "Software Design Manifesto": "Despite the enormous outward success of personal computers, the daily experience of using computers far too often is still fraught with difficulty, pain, and barriers for most people, which means that the revolution, measured by its original goals, has not as yet succeeded," he wrote.[189] For the developers of programs, typically engineers, design had not been the central focus, and understandably so: the way that software engineering worked, they had more pressing problems. "Perhaps the most important conceptual move to be taken is to recognize the critical role of design, as a counterpart to programming, in the creation of computer artifacts," Kapor wrote.[190] It was imperative for the designer to develop tools and models that could bridge the abstract and the conceptual, the underlying structure and the overarching experience.

Software design was conceived as a new form of architecture. Architecture—particularly through Alexander's theories and methods—became the means for articulating its aims. This took place on multiple scales: through a more general identification with the idea of the architect's role and, on a more specific level, using the lens of Alexander's work to better define that role. The methods that software designers used followed from Alexander's concepts of pattern, language, and order. Where architects set in place the plans for a building, designers set in place the plans for software. "In both architecture and software design it is necessary to provide the professional practitioner with a way to model the final result with far less effort than is required to build the final product," Kapor wrote. "In each case, specialized tools and techniques are used. In software design, unfortunately, design tools aren't sufficiently developed to be maximally useful."[191] Kapor suggested that a "theory of design for software" could apply the Vitruvian concerns as "Firmness: A program should not have any bugs that inhibit its function. Commodity: A program should be suitable for the purposes for which it was

intended. Delight: The experience of using the program should be a pleasurable one,"
he wrote.[192]

The designer as architect was distinct from the work of the engineer and provided
power beyond the stereotype of designer as window-dresser. "Architects, not construction engineers, are the professionals who have overall responsibility for creating buildings," Kapor wrote. "Architecture and engineering are, as disciplines, peers to each
other, but in the actual process of designing and implementing the building, the engineers take direction from the architects. The engineers play a vital and crucial role
in the process, but they take their essential direction from the design of the building
as established by the architect."[193] Similar to the distinction between architects and
engineers, software designers took into consideration an interrelated set of needs: the
functions the system needed to accomplish, the needs and the contexts of the users,
and the technical constraints and affordances. The movement between analysis and
synthesis, of bringing together the often competing concerns of software design, and
of working at a scale of complexity could only be described in architectural terms. It
isn't surprising that Alexander would also inspire software designers as he did object-
oriented programmers. Software design emerged at the same time and place as patterns
in software. Many of the people building the foundation of software design individually encountered Alexander's books as teenagers and college students.

Through Alexander's architectural theories, digital designers began to understand
the user as an inhabitant of a system of software.[194] This approach suggested that
instead of handing down plans and pronouncements, the designer of a system needed
to think of the user as someone dwelling within its space. In particular, designers took
up Alexander's concept of the "quality without a name," that Alexander introduces in
The Timeless Way of Building, one that refers to a "central quality which is the root crite-
rion of life and spirit in a man, a town, a building, or a wilderness."[195] As a user became
an inhabitant of a system, the question of software design became one that sought to
accommodate these notions of "life."

Software designers supported the notion of software being not just a conceptual
space, but one inhabited by a user, as Winograd wrote in an echo of Alexander in the
preface to *Bringing Design to Software:*

Software is not just a device with which the user interacts; it is also the generator of a space in
which the user lives. Software design is like architecture: When an architect designs a home or
an office building, a structure is being specified. More significantly, though, the patterns of life
for its inhabitants are being shaped. People are thought of as inhabitants rather than as users of
buildings. In this book, we approach software users as inhabitants, focusing on how they live in

the spaces that designers create. Our goal is to situate the work of the designer in the world of the user.[196]

Alexander envisioned architecture as a generative system wherein people develop structures appropriate to their needs. Winograd introduced the user as a way to make the considerations of the space of software alive to the programmers and designers of it. What would a designer need to know and understand about that user to make software that met his or her needs? What would that indicate about the space of software?

Alexander criticized software patterns programmers for focusing on patterns over the languages and hierarchies that held them together. For designers, however, language was fundamental to their work. John Rheinfrank and Shelley Evenson introduced design languages in their essay in *Bringing Design to Software*. They argued that design languages could be used for translating complex actions into simpler steps, such as with a complicated Xerox photocopier: someone working in an office might not know how to repair a photocopier, but they could follow a design language of forms and colors to master this unfamiliar task, making it possible to operate and unjam it. "Design languages are present everywhere in our constructed environment. Most design languages have evolved through unconscious design activities," they wrote.[197] Similar to how Alexander constituted language, Rheinfrank and Evenson defined design languages as a universal way to bring parts into a greater whole. "Just as natural (spoken or written) languages are the basis for how we generate and interpret phrases and sentences, so design languages are the basis for how we create and interact with things in the world," they wrote. "And, like spoken or written language, design languages are assimilated into our everyday activities, mediating our experiences with the world (often tacitly), and contributing to the perceived quality of our lives."[198] Through a focus on context in use, ever-evolving design languages benefit the user-as-inhabitant, providing a mode for understanding and for communication.

The architectural metaphor in software design is pervasive, but not without at least some critique. Winograd and Philip Tabor wrote a chapter called "Software Design and Architecture," in which they warned against uncritically embracing architecture. "We in the software profession may have much to learn from the ancient and rich tradition of architectural practice and architectural theory," they wrote. "At the same time, in drawing such a broad analogy, it is possible to fall into superficiality, finding attractive but misleading guidance."[199] For one thing, Winograd and Tabor reminded their readers that architecture is an analogy: architecture might be *like* some activities in software design but it wasn't *the same thing* as software design. They noted that a user didn't tend to see all of the minutiae and processes that add up to a building or a piece of software—"the whole is seen by the user as a unity," they wrote.[200] They asked what might be learned from the division of labor in architecture and the same in software design. Engineers determine the structure, architects address a program and determine its look, feel, and spatial experience, and builders construct the building. What about the legal liability that architects, engineers, and developers hold in traditional design and build: should software architects and designers have this same responsibility?

In his recent edited volume *Use Matters: An Alternative History of Architecture*," Kenny Cuppers writes, "Utility is central to what architects do in practice as they deal with clients, norms, and building regulations. . . . But utility also governs an unknowable universe of everyday experience that remains outside of the designer's direct control."[201] The everyday practice of architecture, he argues, is not an exercise of the primacy of form—it is a negotiation between drawing, computation, bureaucracy, and communication. "If a lot of architecture's meaning is made not on the drafting board but in the complex lifeworld of how it is inhabited, consumed, used, lived or neglected, that world is at once central and peculiarly under-explored."[202] Architectural practice could learn from the way that software designers, researchers, and programmers have taken up use and utility, and the ways that, for decades, their practices have postulated an inhabitant of the space of software. What might happen if architects discovered this new kind of user?

More recently, Alan Blackwell and Sally Fincher have suggested a reframing of Alexander's patterns for user *experience* (UX) as distinct from user interface. They argued that experience, not the facts of construction, were at the heart of Alexander's interests: software patterns are like an architect's specification of ornament on a building, not like the way that someone would feel in moving through the building. By capturing patterns that described the user experience, it might be possible to "design humane systems, rather than being distracted by the changing technical structures and ornaments that arrive with each generation of UI renderings," they wrote.[203] Such a vision of what patterns might offer gets closer to Alexander's vision of objectively, morally good software.

How Buildings Learn

In the same period that Terry Winograd and his collaborators put together *Bringing Design to Software*, Stewart Brand published another book about architecture that was influential for software and system designers, *How Buildings Learn: What Happens after They're Built*, in 1994. Although not an architect, Brand wanted to look at buildings as both objects and processes, "as a whole—not just whole in space, but whole in time."[204] Throughout the book, Brand refers to Christopher Alexander's work and conversations with him, as well as other architects in Alexander's circle, such as Sim van der Ryn, celebrating a dynamic approach in architecture to structure and evolution. The book, well received in architectural circles (including a favorable review in the *Journal of the Society of Architectural Historians*) was picked up by information architects and inter-action designers in the 1990s and early 2000s. Brand's book was attractive to digital designers and programmers because it focused on iteration and evolution—the kinds of concerns that early-generation Web designers shared as they developed user-centered design techniques and built websites that could accommodate change. For instance, Brand told the story of a campus planner who didn't put paths across the campus quad when it was first designed, instead waiting for the first snowfall to see where people put paths between the buildings: the right paths would emerge, and the planner would pave accordingly. "Some design is better if it's postponed," Brand wrote.[205] For digital designers, what is especially attractive about this story is the notion of bottom-up user actions determining the needs of a space—a question not only of how buildings learn, but of what designers could learn from their users.

Alexander's Unpopularity with Architects

Alexander is the architect who stands almost monolithically for architecture in software design and other digital design practices. He is often the only architect that many programmers and digital designers name as an influence for their work. Yet Alexander was and is extremely critical of architects, architectural design, and architectural prac-tice. Although he argues that architecture and geometry are of utmost importance to him, his aesthetics are conservative, and he repeats that he has no interest in how con-temporary architecture is taught or practiced today. This tendency distances him from many architects, who find him moralizing and reductive. This criticism of Alexander delights his technical followers, who like the practicality of his approach. Ironically, soft-ware design and patterns in software, which situated themselves as digital architectural practices, seems to be defined in the terms of an architect who stands counter to architec-ture, counter to much form and representation, and counter to contemporary practice.

Many architects believe in the intrinsic primacy and autonomy of architectural form, but they are less apt to believe in a *moral* system that makes it that way. Peter Eisenman, just four years younger than Alexander, has sought to define a system of order in architectural form-giving since his earliest studies. Alexander and Eisenman are not actually so far apart from each other, as historian Sean Keller and others have pointed out. Both architects attended Cambridge University at the same time, both use logic as a way to understand architecture, and both seek an underlying structure sepa-rate from the representation of the thing. Like Alexander, Eisenman was interested in a linguistic structure that defined the relations between objects. As Keller has pointed out, Eisenman and Alexander both play within a project of "architectural logic" that sought to define a rule-based system for generating architecture.[206] Eisenman seeks to define the "interior discursive formulation" of architecture, the "nature" of which architects have sought to describe since the fourteenth century.[207] He does so through the same interest in rational, logical, autonomous systems of design and "deep structure," a response to the problems caused by the increased socio-technical complexity of the world, writes Keller.[208] Eisenman tied the Platonic solids to architectural "intent, function, structure and technics."[209] Through an analysis of the work of Le Corbusier, Alvar Aalto, Frank Lloyd Wright, and Giuseppe Terragni, he defined a generative system that examined the internal "pressures" of formal interaction.

Yet their stances could not be more different. Eisenman claimed that he wrote his dissertation "The Formal Basis of Modern Architecture" because he so vehemently disagreed with Alexander's dissertation, published as *Notes on the Synthesis of Form*.[210] And a famous episode of the objectively moral versus objectively rational tendencies around Alexander within architecture took place in a debate in 1982, when Eisenman and Alexander debated at the Harvard Graduate School of Design about their approaches to design, about morality, rationality, and emotion in architecture. Moshe Safdie, architect and director of the Urban Design Program at Harvard's Graduate School of Design, introduced Alexander that evening, highlighting his challenges to conventionality and his humanistic approach: "I think Christopher Alexander throughout his professional life has always been at the cutting edge radically reexamining the conventional wisdom of the time. . . . And within all that diversity of activity, there has been one unity that has underlined it all and that is his basic humanism and his concern and affection for people," Safdie said.[211]

Eisenman criticized Alexander's pursuit of "feeling" in design, arguing instead in favor of rationality. Alexander argued that architecture must embody harmony and comfort, whereas Eisenman stood up for disharmony and dissonance. Eisenman brought up the too-thin columns in the arcade of Rafael Moneo's Town Hall in Logroño, Spain, an effect that was disturbing in photographs but that expressed an important discord in reality. Eisenman said of Moneo, "He was taking away from something that was too large, achieving an effect that expresses the separation and fragility that man feels today in relationship to the technological scale of life, to machines, and the car-dominated environment we live in."[212] Alexander responded in horror: "I find that incomprehensible. I find it very irresponsible. I find it nutty. I feel sorry for the man. I also feel incredibly angry because he's fucking up the world."[213] The audience broke into applause.

Of course, not all architects are formalists like Eisenman. Some of the difference in reception may be attributable to splits in architecture culture between the East and West Coasts. Architects such as Sim van der Ryn and Charles Moore valued Alexander's theories, and the University of California Berkeley School of Architecture was influenced by Alexander's methods. Not all of his students were pleased by it. Alexander's students at Berkeley who had to design houses using a set of fifteen patterns found it confining and reductive: "It made no sense to me, so I rebelled," said one of his former students.[214] One architect said, "I wouldn't feel educated if I didn't know about *A Pattern Language*, it's an important filter to analyze the world, but making an architecture student design patterns is like making us do color by number—it would drive you to a mad dérive with Guy Debord."[215] Others argue that his ideas work in the abstract but not in practice—an argument that Alexander himself has made continually over the years as he experimented with trees, semilattices, and pattern networks, only to discover that he didn't like the geometry and the architecture that resulted. Nonetheless, Alexander's moralizing and almost deistic approach to architectural truths make his work hard to stomach for many architects.

Recent trends in architecture show an interest in the architectural program, functionality, and the user, as architectural practices with that focus win major prizes. Consider the honors of Chilean architect Alejandro Aravena, winner of the 2016 Pritzer Prize in architecture and head of the studio Elemental, and of Assemble, the 2015 Turner Prize–winning British architectural collective whose members are the first non-artists to ever win the award.

Elemental designs and builds one half of a two-story house with government subsidies in what the studio calls "half a good house," and the residents of the house build out the other half over time according to their family requirements and as their finances allow. The studio first designed half-houses in Iquique, Chile, in 2002, when local residents threatened a hunger strike if the government built a high-rise for them—instead, Elemental designed houses with empty spaces that could be built out over time.[216] Elemental also designed the Villa Verde houses for a lumber company in Constitución, Chile, after a magnitude 8.8 earthquake in 2010 destroyed 80 percent of the buildings in the city.[217] These houses are split vertically down the middle: Elemental builds one half, the residents build the other. Aravena seemed to echo Alexander when he told an interviewer, "The beauty is that if there's any power in architecture, that's the power of synthesis. All those forces at play eventually can be synthesised in a design. We just have to understand that language and also do not forget that they way that we respond is to design. We do not have to become policy makers or economists. Our contribution to a problem is as designers."[218] Now, it should be noted that there is also criticism about the half houses. They are the most minimal housing standard for low-income residents. The client for the Constitución, Chile, project is a lumber company, who might have it in its best interest to produce the cheapest houses possible.[219] But the residents say they appreciate the homes, and that if there had been more money, they still would have preferred their houses; Elemental would have put the money into better public spaces.[220]

Assemble is an interdisciplinary collective of eighteen architects, artists, and designers who met while at university. Rather than parachuting in with an architectural intervention, they actively engage the people in the communities in which they work. The collective "champion[s] a working practice that is interdependent and collaborative, seeking to actively involve the public as both participant and collaborator in the on-going realization of the work," states Assemble's website.[221] They've designed the Yardhouse, a coworking space (now up for sale, as of December 2016, and called "one of London's most instagrammed spaces")[222]; the New Addington public square in Croydon, with a parade event and public space interventions; and the Granby Four Streets project in Liverpool, which worked with residents on home and garden renovations. All of these projects bring everyday people into the design process, enabling them to articulate how they want their communities to be in a latter-day echo of some of Alexander's tenets of design and the kinds of projects that Cedric Price pursued. *The Guardian* wrote, "They talk about research and listening hard to the needs of communities; they talk about the actual built fabric that might result from a project as not necessarily the most important aspect of their job, which is sometimes as much about setting up an organisation or scheme."[223] Assemble is less beholden to an agenda for form and representation. Yet the collective isn't anti-formal, either. They don't see their approach as standing in opposition to formalism, they told the *Los Angeles Times*.[224]

Firms like Elemental and Assemble have achieved critical accolades for their return to the kinds of participatory approaches that were popular through the 1960s and 1970s. Their practices show an engagement with people and their needs, whether as a means for building houses to combat poverty (such as Elemental's "half a house" idea) or for contributing to working-class, multicultural neighborhoods (such as Assemble's Granby Four Streets). There are echoes of Alexander in these approaches to design that also push the boundaries of contemporary architecture.

Conclusion

Christopher Alexander is a fundamental bridge between architecture and digital design practices. His work helps us understand how architects first grappled with digital complexity—concerns that endure today—and allows us to understand the influence of architecture on programming and practices such as interaction and experience design and information architecture.

Programmers and designers find Alexander more relevant than ever. His later four-volume work, *The Nature of Order*, inspires emerging design practices such as design for social innovation and transition design, practices that envision an ideal world that design processes can help to achieve. In a recent conversation about Alexander on Facebook, designer Marc Rettig said, "The more I dive into things like social complexity, the more I find myself referencing Alexander. . . . For me (not an architect), the stuff about stepwise decomposition of hierarchies of wholes, emphasizing *relationships* as you go is . . . well, it's relevant well outside of architecture, and it's gold."[225] Many design practitioners take up his call for design solutions that use his approaches to order and that appeal to something deeply resonant and meaningful.

On the other hand, many architects still reject Alexander's moralizing tone. But his work is more relevant than ever. We are in the midst of a new wave of architectural design and architecture pedagogy in which the computer plays an operative role and reshapes how we teach architects and how they conceive of their work. In some schools of architecture, instead of drawing, students learn "visualization"; in addition to construction, they adopt approaches to "fabrication"; they capture the information and decision-making around the architectural project in "building information models" (BIM).[226] Architecture and urban design studios become software companies, a move that Frank Gehry Studios made in 2002 by spinning out Gehry Technology, and that urban and regional planning firm Calthorpe Associates made recently by starting a new company, Calthorpe Analytics, that leverages their methods as modeling and planning software. Missing in these shifts, however, are the tool kits of user experience designers and interaction designers, who consider a user (or inhabitant) and the responsiveness of interfaces and environments. Equally missing is an understanding of how architects such as Alexander make human needs central. What might be learned from interaction design approaches to users—the ones that Alexander influenced—in addition to these visualization-minded approaches in architecture curricula?

Programmers and interaction and user experience designers exercise a steeply increasing influence on the built environment. Returning to Alexander's OOPSLA keynote, Alexander said that the programmers in his audience were powerful because they "control the function of computers and their programs. . . . You almost can't name a facet of the world which is not already, to some very strong degree, under the influence of the programs that are being written to manage and control those entities or those operations," he said.[227] Alexander made those statements in 1996, when there were just twenty million Americans on the Internet.[228] The influence is only compounded today. As buildings and cities are increasingly responsive, and our built environment imbued with artificial intelligence and governed by algorithms, it is vital for architects, designers, and programmers all to heed the warning implicit in Alexander's statement. As they design interfaces that control more and more of the world, there are potentially outsize consequences for the design and programming decisions they make.

3   Richard Saul Wurman: Information, Mapping, and Understanding

American Institute of Architects (AIA) Convention, Philadelphia

2016

The stage was dark except for two white leather chairs, spotlit for a conversation that promised to be a "kick in the pants."[1] Architect and Pritzker Award winner Rem Koolhaas sat stage right, his interviewer Mohsen Mostafavi, dean of the Harvard Graduate School of Design, sat to his left. The keynote title, "Delirious Philadelphia," referenced Koolhaas's 1978 book *Delirious New York,* while referring to the city in which the convention took place. In their provocative conversation, Koolhaas decried the ways that Silicon Valley and technology professionals had co-opted architectural vocabulary for their own purposes. "Architecture and the language of architecture—platform, blueprint, structure—became almost the preferred language for indicating a lot of phenomenon that we're facing from Silicon Valley," he said in conversation with Mostafavi.

Koolhaas might be complicit in that co-opting. He has spent much of his career taking on digital media as architectural material. For instance, in 2003, Koolhaas edited an issue of *Wired* magazine in which he introduced thirty spaces of a new order, reported on by a cadre of writers, critics, and researchers. "Where space was considered permanent, it now feels transitory—on its way to becoming. The words and ideas of architecture, once the official language of space, no longer seem capable of describing this proliferation of new conditions," he wrote. "But even as its utility is questioned in the real world, architectural language survives, its repertoire of concepts and metaphors resurrected to create clarity and definition in new, unfamiliar domains (think chat *rooms,* Web *sites,* and fire*walls*). Words that die in the real are reborn in the virtual," Koolhaas wrote in that issue of *Wired.*[2]

Back to 2016's "kick in the pants." Technology is fast, but architecture is slow, Koolhaas said to his AIA audience in 2016, seemingly forgetting his captivation with digital culture over the prior decades. "[Silicon Valley] took over our metaphors, and it made me think that regardless of our speed, which is too slow for Silicon Valley, we can perhaps think of the modern world maybe not always in the form of buildings but in the form of knowledge or organization and structure and society that we can offer and provide," he said.[3] In the conversation on the AIA stage, Koolhaas framed architecture in terms of its information architectures. But someone else had beat him to it, almost exactly forty years earlier, in the same city, at the same conference.

1976

In 1976, almost exactly forty years before Koolhaas's keynote, Richard Saul Wurman also gave the closing keynote in Philadelphia and at the national AIA convention that he chaired under the theme "An American City: The Architecture of Information." The convention brochure, its text laid out like a waving American flag, stated, "We are coming to know the importance of describing how physical space performs as well as how it looks. . . . Wouldn't a city—any city—be more useful and more fun if everybody knew what to do in it, and with it? As architects, we know it takes more than good-looking buildings to make a city habitable and usable. It takes information: information about what spaces do as well as how they look; information that helps people articulate their needs and respond to change. That's what Architecture of Information is all about."[4]

The sessions of the 1976 AIA convention would fit right into a conference today. There were talks on information design at the urban scale, public space and education, computing and media—as the convention brochure promised, "The Architecture of Information is a two-way process, and there are sessions on collecting and correlating information, as well as communicating it."[5] Buckminster Fuller gave a morning keynote (titled "Lucky to Have Bucky"). Jonas Salk, the virologist who developed the polio vaccine, delivered a talk titled "Visualization of Complex Ideas." Frank Gehry and Doreen Nelson introduced "The School Room: Analogue of the City" (their bios stated that Nelson was an designer of educational systems and Gehry "is noted for his design of corrugated paper furniture").[6] Several talks addressed computation and information, including that of William Fetter, a founding father of computer graphics, whose talk was titled "Computer Graphics and the Urban Perception," and Marley and Ronald Thomas taught attendees "How to Spec an 'Interface,' Detail an 'Input' and Supervise a 'Programming Process," and lectured on "The Architecture of Understanding." Other talks focused on the interface among cities, media, and communication, such as "Space Doctors: Understanding How People Use Public Spaces," by architect Don Clifford Miles (who helped to found the Project for Public Spaces); "Communicating the City" by Michael and Susan Southworth; and "Information about the Environment: Context and Meaning," by Jivan R. Tabibian. Ivan Chermayeff lectured about "Communication

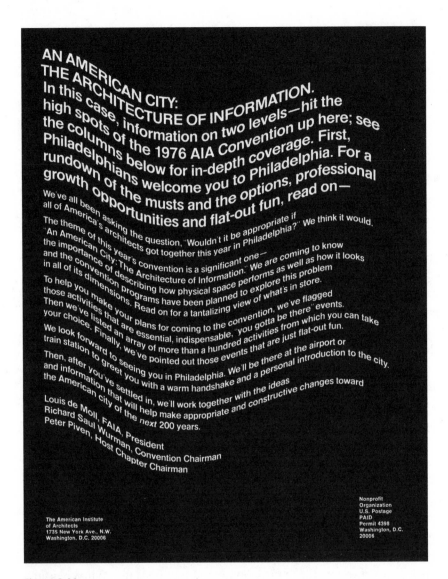

Figure 3.01

Richard Saul Wurman chaired the 1976 AIA convention under the theme "An American City: The Architecture of Information." It made information and its communication a concern of architecture, and made architecture an approach to organizing and navigating information. An American City: The Architecture of Information (Washington, DC: AIA, 1976). Image courtesy of The American Institute of Architects Archives, Washington, DC.

in Architectural Environments." It's not unlike a contemporary TED conference when you look at it, and that's no surprise: Wurman created TED.

For his closing keynote, "The Architecture of Information," Wurman told a fable. He gave the attendees an illustrated booklet, "What-If, Could-Be: An Historical Fable of the Future," illustrated by R. O. Blechman. What-If was a country celebrating its two-hundredth birthday, Could-Be was one of its oldest cities, and Wurman was the Commissioner of Curiosity and Imagination. The Commission—composed of citizens of all walks—issued edicts such as "Public Information Must Be Public,"[7] instituted a "Right to Copy"[8] instead of copyright, and built an Urban Observatory, where the citizens of Could-Be could easily find public information.[9] "After the *Urban Observatory* had overflowed City Hall and had its own building, a lot of the sophisticated techniques for information storage and retrieval that until then had been reserved for big corporations and universities, began to be used," Wurman said. "There were computers that could classify and update information; there were others that could generate maps, graphs and diagrams and display them on terminals or print them out."[10] Could-Be launched a good many initiatives for the city that made it transparent and accessible for its residents.

Yet the fable's conclusion wasn't a happy one. "You could say that in the desire to clarify and communicate, we'd created a proliferation of confusing and unintelligible information. *Everyone spoke of an information overload, but what there was in fact was a non-information overload.*"[11] We learned what the issue was, Wurman said: "performance, not products, . . . learning, not schools, . . . mobility, not highways. Communication, not signs and lighting, not light-poles. . . . The architecture of information, not information about architecture."[12] Unfortunately for those in the fable—and for those of us in the real world—the promises of Could-Be were not to be: the fable concludes with, "*In short in the desire to win, we had lost.*"[13]

So how could architects help? By understanding that architecture had to do with information, and that they could use their training as architects to organize it. They could approach design of information on a variety of scales, from maps and diagrams to large-scale graphics integrating with buildings and parts of the city to the built environment itself, neatly integrated with one another to promote better comprehensibility and understanding. "While the entirely self-revealing environment is as utopian an idea as the entirely self-revealing building or instructionless instrument panel," Wurman wrote in a 1975 article with Joel Katz titled "Beyond Graphics: The Architecture of Information," "as architects and designers we have a special opportunity and responsibility to make the environment more comprehensible and self-revealing, through more functional and self-revealing design."[14] Wurman and Katz did not see this as just adapting graphic design at the scale of the city—it was a matter of

Figure 3.02
The attendees of the 1976 AIA Convention received a booklet, an illustrated fable titled "What-If, Could-Be: An Historical Fable of the Future," illustrated by R. O. Blechman. Wurman was the Commissioner of Curiosity and Imagination of the country of What-If and the City of Could-Be. Wurman republished the contents of the fable in his 2009 book *Understanding Change and the Change in Understanding*. Image courtesy of Dan Klyn. Permission granted by Richard Saul Wurman.

"genuinely and sympathetically" integrating the information, unifying the experience of the city.[15] And, ultimately, these weren't new ideas, as Wurman saw it. In the conclusion of an *AIA Journal* article titled "An Interview with the Commissioner of Curiosity and Imagination of the City of Could Be" that previewed Wurman's AIA keynote talk, he included the lessons the commissioner had learned in the conclusion, two of which were, "Everything that has been enacted has been stated before, only nobody had heard it" and "Everything we have done has been visible before, only nobody has seen it."[16] The Commissioner of Curiosity and Imagination was and is correct to this day, as architects, designers, and programmers seek out middle ground to probe the interactions of information and architecture.

In this chapter, I examine the influence of the Commissioner of Curiosity and Imagination: Richard Saul Wurman. Wurman structured information to make things relative to one another, supporting new narrative interfaces and fostering a new view of convergence through conversation in his pursuit of what he calls "understanding." I examine how he mapped and structured information, both making it a concern of architects and translating architecture to the realm of communication. How does the architecture of information translate and mediate human understanding, and how did Wurman formulate that approach?

Understanding through Architecture

Richard Saul Wurman, born in 1935, popularized the concept of architectures of information, the profession of information architecture, and the title of information architect. Along with Christopher Alexander, he is *the* architect of influence on information architects and interaction designers. Wurman articulated the confusion of the early World Wide Web, offering the means to make it more navigable and, thus, more human. Throughout his career, Wurman has been interested in cities, communication, learning, mapping, information design, and conferences. Likewise, he was and is a prolific publisher, speaker, organizer, and instigator of ideas. He boils his career down to the singular pursuit of "understanding," to making information *inform*—finding the *form* in in*form*ation.

Wurman trained and worked as an architect—he completed both a bachelor and master of architecture at the University of Pennsylvania, worked for iconic architect Louis Kahn, then ran his own architecture practice till 1976. Bemoaning the ways that design fell short in making the world more meaningful, Wurman wrote, "That's why I've chosen to call myself an Information Architect. I don't mean a bricks and mortar architect. I mean architect as used in the words architect of foreign policy. I mean architect as in the creating of systemic, structural, and orderly principles to make something work—the thoughtful making of either artifact, or idea, or policy that informs because it is clear."[17] With this approach, he pushed the boundaries of how architects and designers configure their work, as Gary Wolf noted in a *Wired* magazine article in 2000 (a project that itself launched because of connections made at a TED conference).[18] "Richard Saul Wurman, trained as an architect of buildings, has become America's premier architect of information," state the first lines of the introduction in his 1989 book *Information Anxiety.*[19]

Wurman's work bridges design and architecture by claiming space through the structuring of information, whether in two or three dimensions, on the page or through social interaction. He developed methods to control information overload through mechanisms that categorize, serialize, spatialize, and typologize information. Moreover, he understood the dynamics of convergence, and promoted the sociality that learning and information sharing could provide. An interviewer wrote in 1976 that Wurman "keeps telling me that he's in communications and I keep telling him that he's in space."[20] Essentially, Wurman is in both places: for him, is there any difference between cities, publications, and information? He approaches them all in the same manner. He made the collecting and sharing of information not only an architectural endeavor, but also the right of the residents of a city. He developed (and continues to develop) information-sharing platforms that make the world more accessible. These platforms include the mapping methods he developed in his articles and atlases, the publications that assembled the work of numerous designers, and conferences such as the Aspen International Design Conference in 1972, the AIA Convention in 1976, and the TED conferences that he founded in 1984 and led until 2002. His work bridges space from the page to the person, with the fostering of understanding and learning at its center.

Of course, Wurman wouldn't necessarily see it this way. If you ask him, he will tell you that he is in the business of understanding. "I never thought that information would be important to architecture, I thought that understanding would be important to life," he told me in an interview.[21] The same axioms appear and reappear in his work. His words are so consistent that it is hard to figure out where to quote them first—1963, 1974, 2001, or 2013? There is also much to draw from: at least eighty-three books, the many conferences he produced, and more recently, websites and apps. His prolificness resists being cast in an interpretive light, as information architect Dan Klyn discovered in his research on Wurman and the application of his ideas to information architecture practices.[22] Wurman reminded him to keep it simple—to keep it dumb.

As a collector and promoter of ideas, Wurman crosses over other figures in this book. His edited volumes include maps that Christopher Alexander had a hand in designing, as well as some of Alexander's language on patterns. Wurman is a close friend of Nicholas Negroponte, who spoke at the first TED conference (and many since). Some of the themes that run through his work will also appear in other chapters of this book: convergence, generativity, and translation. In many different modes, this is what we will see Wurman do: translate architecture into a foundation for the digital world, translate printed information into a three-dimensional understanding, translate both of these modes into the social realm. Through Wurman's work, we better understand information and cities, interfaces and architecture.

In this chapter, I start with Wurman's 1996 book *Information Architects*. I jump back to 1963 to begin a discussion of his mapping-related publications and projects and the spatial and serializing strategies they use. Then, I look at his narrative interfaces: his information-organization techniques and what kinds of understanding they foster. Finally, I look at the convergent platforms he designed: the conferences and conversations his work sought to start. In conclusion, I revisit what is architectural about his approach and how it influenced digital design.

Information Architects

The world was drowning in so much information that everyone was choking on it. This chaos was the cause of so many problems in the world, from education to business to politics to health care. The world needed information architects.

Richard Saul Wurman's 1996 book *Information Architects* situated information architecture as a necessity in rectifying the deluge. "There is a tsunami of data that is crashing onto the beaches of the civilized world. This is a tidal wave of unrelated, growing data formed in bits and bytes, coming in an unorganized, uncontrolled, incoherent cacophony of foam," he wrote in the first lines of the introduction.[23] "And yet, through this field of black volcanic ash has come a group of people, small in number, deep in passion, called Information Architects, who have begun to ply their trade, make themselves visible, and develop a body of work on paper, in electronic interfaces, and in some extraordinary exhibitions. These people will be the wave of the future," Wurman wrote.[24] Information architecture was a noble calling. And the people that we will meet in the next chapter listened.

A richly saturated, 240-page coffee-table book, mostly black pages with white print, *Information Architects* presents the work of twenty designers and design practices. It shows numerous examples of information design, including the graphic design of publications, examples of wayfinding for public space, and software interfaces. At that time, the distinction between information design and information architecture did not yet exist—Wurman's book strove to be a polemic that introduced the distinction.

Information Architects celebrated work that crossed media boundaries, between new approaches to design for publications, software interfaces, mapping, sketching, and environmental design, work that could span, scope, and scale. What made the projects in the book architectural was the fact that they were in some way spatial. They organized space and human processes, something that all of the projects in *Information Architects* showcase in different ways.

The projects in *Information Architects* that spanned screen to page expanded the notion of what either could be on their own. Nathan Shedroff and vivid studios designed the CD-ROM *Voices of the 30s* as a curriculum, a "library in a box" that offered a thematic approach to the experience of living in the 1930s. It was designed to allow students to design their own paths through the material, a prescient approach for a pre-Web format. *Demystifying Multimedia,* a book and CD-ROM designed by vivid studios for Apple, feels like a software interface on a book page. It is a guide organized by the processes that one follows in designing multimedia projects (prototyping, production, testing, distribution). Working the way through the book is itself a multimedia process, even though it takes place on a book page.

Similarly, Maria Giudice and Lynne Stiles, principals of information design company YO, translated the processes of digital printing in the AGFA *Digital Color Pre-Press Guide,* a highly visual guide for designers.[25] Like the work of Shedroff and his team at vivid studios, Giudice and Stiles focused on the processes of completing a task, then organized the information and media that would best accomplish the task. For the Peachpit Press website, their first web project, they had to acknowledge that they did not have the same graphical richness as the AGFA book. "Designing for the Web, at least in these early days, means shrugging off attempts to control the 'graphic design' and focus on the interface: how the reader understands and accesses the content of the publisher's site and its network of pages," Giudice and Stiles wrote. "The most important aspects of a successful web site are organization and navigation—the design must support both."[26]

Other projects in *Information Architects* take the notion of information architecture forward into physical space, introducing how the exhibition design in museums organizes space and experience, such as in the work of Ralph Appelbaum, and the curation and information strategies of Donovan and Green and the Ronald Reagan Presidential Library. Erik Spiekermann, the founder of MetaDesign, demonstrated how a studio could produce systems ranging from the minute elements of a typeface all the way up to a strategy for reuniting a formerly walled city. *Information Architects* includes examples of both. The FF Meta typeface that Spiekermann and his colleagues at Sedley Place Design created was intended for the German Bundespost in 1987, but the post office didn't use it. Released commercially in 1991, the Meta typeface can be found out in the world at many scales, in books and magazines, bus-side advertisements, airport wayfinding systems, and transit maps. *Information Architects* also demonstrated how MetaDesign applied the logic of scale to a map and to a city at large. Spiekermann and his colleagues designed the post–Berlin Wall public transit map in 1992, a project that influenced how people found their way around Berlin. After the wall fell, Berlin began a lengthy process of consolidating the myriad transit systems of the two halves of the city, all of which were governed by different agencies. The goal was to design an adaptive map that could be updated by the BVG (Berlin Transit Authority). In so doing, the map helped to re-present and synthesize the city's reunification.

The information architects that Wurman introduced in the book were translators. They took human processes and interests, determined their informational requirements, and organized them accordingly. They understood that these processes unfold over time and space, and they designed interfaces that put them in order for their users. Thinking back to the definitions of architecture that I introduced at the beginning of this book, it is clear that these designers were thinking architecturally: conceiving and mapping, conveying and translating, measuring and modeling. Similarly, they were architecting as a verb: working from the minutiae to the major, fitting parts and wholes into something greater than the sum. Wurman claimed in the introduction of *Information Architects* that the practitioners of this burgeoning field would be the future. By these definitions, perhaps it's fair to say that they were.

Making Things Relative

A good map makes the relationships between different elements visible, promoting a greater sense of understanding in the process. As Richard Saul Wurman wrote in 1974 (and has repeated many times since), *"You can only understand something relative to something you understand.*[27] Wurman engaged with a variety of mapping projects throughout his career. Some were compendia: collections of maps and visualizations by his students and other designers, shown in relationship with one another. Published serially, they suggested relationships to one another that the viewer could then use to better understand their cities, the cities they've visited, cities of the past, cities of their dreams. The idea isn't new—architects since Jean-Nicolas-Louis Durand in the very early nineteenth century have shown elements of buildings in relationship to one another so that architects in training could learn architectural typology. But rather than highlighting the relationships between building types, Wurman used maps so that designers could better understand different kinds of data through the process of visualizing it, such as in the

Urban Atlas: 20 American Cities, or that could change the experience of navigating a city or a topic, as with the numerous *Access Guides* that Wurman's company produced for cities and various subjects.

For a designer, mapping and visualizing is a feedback loop—analyzing information, trying out different strategies of relating the elements to each other, looking at the results, returning to the data, and iterating again. The designer might learn that there's no there there, as she plots something that initially seems interesting in the data, or she may discover something more compelling in the process. For a map's user, engaging with the map underscores where he or she stands. It's the same thing with diagrams and visualizations that interpret complex sets of information. A good visualization makes connections apparent that wouldn't otherwise be readily visible. Beyond these considerations, something bigger is at stake in the process of mapping both in scale and in meaning. Clear, actionable information supports the denizens of a city. It activates them and gives them the opportunity to be better citizens. Obfuscating data and making it difficult to obtain, use, or map, by contrast, makes it more difficult for people to engage with the city.

In order to make his students aware of where they stood in relation to the world, Wurman introduced his first serial mapping project. In 1963, he assigned his second-year architecture students at North Carolina State University to develop models of the plans of fifty cities in North, Central, and South America, Europe, Asia, and North Africa, all at the same 1:7200 scale. The students built their maps on sixteen-inch Masonite squares, using green Plasticine, balsa wood, and paint.[28] Wurman published the maps in a book (*The City, Form and Intent*) that was republished in 1974 as *Cities: Comparisons of Form and Scale.* The fact that all cities were at the same scale and produced in the same color made it possible for the viewer to compare the size and distinctive features of the cities to one another. The book offered minimal information about each city: when it was founded, if it was burned, sacked, or conquered, its population over time, and sometimes a sketch, diagram, or line-drawn map to accompany the photos of the model. Beijing (at that time Peking) and Paris received a double page spread, with additional description preceding and succeeding the maps, where Tikal, Guatemala, received a column on a page. The maps abstracted many details that one might find in an atlas.

The reduced information in the book allowed Wurman to control the spatial relationships he wanted to highlight, privileging size above anything else. "Size is something on which you hang all your future visual images of a place," he said in an interview published in the 1974 edition. "We found that simply doing this one thing well—something apparently so simple yet which had never been done before—was a surprisingly heavy and satisfying job."[29] By serializing the maps, Wurman and his students isolated certain aspects of the cities above others. The choice demonstrated what his interviewer Joel Katz referred to as "the level of control you imposed on the problem in order to get such consistency in terms of both style, if you want to call it that, and quality."[30] Through the strategy of reduction of information and palette, and the serialization and repetition of form, Wurman and his students controlled the spatial rhetoric of the project: it didn't provide information about everything, just about one set of variables.

Whereas the *Cities: Comparisons of Form and Scale* reduced its inquiry to size and topographical relations, Joseph Passonneau and Wurman developed a new mapping convention in their *Urban Atlas: 20 American Cities,* a research project that began in 1962 and that involved a group of students at Washington University in St. Louis in 1965. Using a set of nested circles in different colors, the authors mapped the relationships of different kinds of demographic data onto the city. It still followed the same strategy of repetition of scale in order to foster relationships between the cities, but required the architects to determine what information about each city was most salient to map. While the maps looked like something that a computer might produce, they were not (they were painstakingly produced by hand by students who cut and pasted each dot onto the map), but the thinking that went into them followed a computational, cybernetic approach.

Through the experimental, visual language they developed, Passonneau and Wurman sought to better understand the relationship between information and its visualization. In an article about the project, Wurman and architect Scott Killinger wrote that the atlas wanted to address such questions as "What kinds of information, normally used by the designer, would find best expression in visual form?"; "What are the ground rules for visual display such that the graphic form can be produced easily and automatically be manipulated, aggregated, filtered, etc.?"; and "How do the graphic capabilities . . . feed back and influence the kinds of information that one wants to gather? What influence does this have on the form in which the information is gathered and the gathering technique?"[31]

The maps in the *Urban Atlas* were an architectural endeavor, in which the process of determining what data to map was the same as developing an architectural "program"—the determination of the functions and elements of a space.[32] "The programming and the forming of a design solution are best intertwined and are, together, a learning process by client and designer," Passonneau and Wurman wrote.[33] Ultimately, the map is the form of the program. "A program can be stated verbally, graphically, three-dimensionally, cinematographically, mathematically: that is to say, *the program*

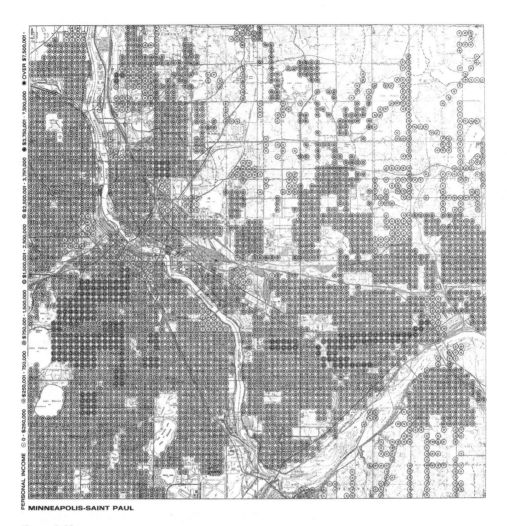

MINNEAPOLIS-SAINT PAUL

Figure 3.03

In their visualization of urban demographic data, Joseph Passonneau and Richard Saul Wurman produced *Urban Atlas: 20 American Cities*. The atlas was, among other things, a way to experiment on the feedback loop between the information that a designer might assemble and how it would be visualized. This map of Minneapolis/St. Paul shows personal income levels throughout the cities, the darker dots referring to higher income. Joseph R. Passonneau and Richard Saul Wurman, *Urban Atlas: 20 American Cities, a Communication Study Notating Selected Urban Data at a Scale of 1:48,000* (Cambridge, MA: MIT Press, 1968) with permission of Richard Saul Wurman and MIT Press.

itself has form."[34] This form presented relationships that would not have otherwise been visible. They wrote, "The form of the city, at all scales, is the crystallization of often invisible relationships. These may be the relationship of topography and transportation, the activities of a person or of an institution, they may be a history of psychic associations. *It is the work of the urban architect to capture in a geometric web, such varied and dynamic human and natural relationships.*"[35]

Between these two urban mapping projects, some important strategies emerged. First, Passonneau and Wurman made mapping an architectural concern. The process of designing multiple maps became the form and formulation of the designer's relationship with data. This perspective on mapping relates to what Wurman's mentor Louis Kahn wrote about the relationship of plan to form in *The Notebooks and Drawings of Louis Kahn*, a book that Wurman edited and designed with Eugene Feldman. "As notations in music reveal structure and composition for hearing, the plan is the score that reveals the structure and the composition of spaces in natural light," Kahn wrote in 1962, referring to the kind of drawing that shows the organization of spaces, typically in a top-down view.[36] There were productive limitations between plan and form, according to Kahn. "The plan expresses the limits of Form. Form, then, as a harmony of systems, is the generator of the chosen design. The plan is the revelation of the Form," Kahn wrote.[37] It was up to the designer or architect to determine how best to represent and control space, given the respective constraints of the model or the printed page—the plan, in this sense. What Wurman called form is the interface that provides the means for interpretation and experience for the viewer. As the architect or designer grapples with the constraints of the plan and the requirements of the data, the form emerges. The generator that Kahn refers to is the sense of understanding gained by the user of the maps. The form of the maps presented and revealed new relationships between the user of the map and the data that it put in context. They fostered a new understanding not only of the information, but the user's own situation within a city.

In 1971, Wurman collected sixty-four ways of seeing and interpreting cities in an issue of "Making the City Observable" that he guest-edited for *Design Quarterly*, published by the Walker Art Center. Whereas his North Carolina State and Washington University students produced map-models that controlled space and representation through their repetition and comparative typology, "Making the City Observable" had a different agenda. Page by page, Wurman built up examples of cities as themselves information and communication systems, as teaching and learning environments, and ultimately, posited a new way of not only seeing the world but being in it. "Making the City Observable" offered a much broader range of representations and visualizations

Figure 3.04
In the "Making the City Observable" volume that Wurman edited for *Design Quarterly*, he situated the cities as systems for information and communication and environments for teaching and learning. Richard Saul Wurman, "Making the City Observable," *Design Quarterly*, no. 80 (1971). Courtesy of the Walker Art Center.

of cities, including maps (the plan for New York, the Nolli Map, Sanborn Fire Insurance Maps, USGS maps), tours (Rettig's tours of Cambridge, Massachusetts; Nicholson's tours of London; a San Francisco tour for children); and graphics, diagrams, and visualizations (Christopher Alexander and Marvin Manheim's highway route locator project, William Fetter's Boeing Man, the Plan for New York, Lance Wyman's iconography for the Mexico City subway, Hertzburg's One Million). The last third of "Making the City Observable" mixes in some of Wurman's projects, including kits and curricula from the Group for Environmental Education (GEE!) that Wurman cofounded, and material from the City/2 exhibition, which told its visitors, "The city belongs to you."[38] He wrote in the introduction, foregrounding some of the ideas that followed:

Public information should be made public.

Information about our urban environment should be made understandable.

Architects, planners and designers should commit themselves to making their ideas immediately comprehensible.

Making the city observable implies allowing the city to become an environment for learning. The city can be made observable by developing a school curriculum about our man-made environment, by designing a clear subway map or by producing a ballot that people can understand and use intelligently.[39]

At the end of the issue of "Making the City Observable," Wurman proposed an "urban observatory," a city-based information center that worked like a predecessor to the Internet. In ways similar to Cedric Price's urban information center proposals (as we will see in chapter 5), Wurman's urban observatory was a "visual data center of the city and region" with multimedia content showing the history and future of the city.[40] "Visitors would be able to 'dial' any relationship among these aforementioned elements . . . and thereby understand the various relationships and correlations," Wurman wrote.[41] Throughout the city, in public buildings at the ground level, there would be a network of information nodes that allowed the city and its institutions to speak to its citizens. As an example of the longevity of pursuit for his ideas, in 2013, Wurman launched Urbanobservatory.org, in conjunction with Esri (the mapping technology company that produces geographic information software, or GIS) and RadicalMedia, a production company. Both a website and an installation at Wurman's WWW conference in 2012 and Esri International User Conference in 2013, the Urban Observatory allows its users and viewers to interact with data sets, compare maps, and, on the website, contribute their own.[42] "The Urban Observatory provides a framework for answering questions about cities through maps. Questions related to where people live, work, and play can be answered by comparative visual analysis."[43] The mission of the project rings familiar, and is consistent enough with Wurman's interests that he could have written the description in the 1960s, with a few updates to the words here and there.

The city, for Wurman, was a "message system," and its architectural patterns systematically communicated "subconscious messages" to the users of a city. "How does the city describe itself and make itself intelligible to the visitor and resident?" he asked.[44] More than just an issue of environmental graphics, the city's ability to communicate was a one-to-one relationship to its map. But in effect, the map was more than a guide to the city. It became a means of access. Wurman advanced this idea with his publication company, Access Press, that published the Access guides. The first guide, *LA Access*,

a.

b.

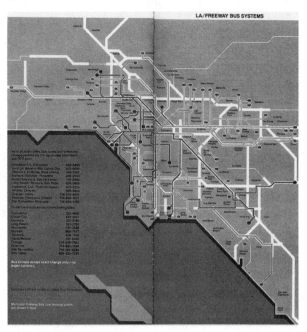

c.

Figure 3.05

LA Access was the first of many guides produced by Access Press, Wurman's publication company. He called it "Access" because the maps and guides were intended to offer a different kind of access to the city. This was the first edition of *LA Access* and was completely redesigned in future editions. It included an orientation to the public transportation system for Angelenos and would-be Angelenos, and a spread of iconic buildings in downtown Los Angeles, including the Bonaventure Hotel, designed by John Portman, and the Bradbury Building. Richard Saul Wurman, *LA/Access: The Official Los Angeles Guidebook* (Los Angeles: Access Press, 1980). Permission granted by Richard Saul Wurman.

was published in 1980 after Wurman moved to Los Angeles and found it hard to get acquainted with the city.[45]

The book opens with colorblocked maps of LA's regions, and abstracted, graphical maps of its freeways and public transportation. Each region of the city included maps, descriptions of highlights, distinctive line drawings of buildings, full-color drawings of theme parks, seating charts for theaters and event spaces like the Hollywood Bowl, and quotes from famous Angelenos. There were lists of two hundred important dates, tours that one could follow, and phone numbers to call. At roughly ten and a half by five inches, the guide fit nicely into the hand, making it easy to flip through the pages. The thirteenth edition of *LA Access* was published in 2008.

Wurman continued to apply his interest in access to many other guides, and not only just for cities. *Olympic Access*, in 1984, broke down the details of Olympic sports: in archery, for instance, with a mix of drawings and graphics of an archer holding a bow, the parts of a bow, the considerations of hitting a target. It also showed world records in each sport in relation to one another. The *Medical Access* guide from 1985 oriented readers to the human body and visits to the doctor and hospital, using Wurman and team's characteristic graphics and text. "I am concerned with public access to experience and to information, with giving people new ways to look at their environment, their lives," Wurman wrote in 1989.[46]

Narrative Interfaces

Wurman's books explore the space of information. They experiment with structure. We've seen this with his numerous books on mapping, whether his early projects in the 1960s or the more recent Access guides: they help their readers foster a new sense of space. This sense of space comes through the organization of information. Mapping is one approach to the spatialization of information—"A map is a pattern made understandable," Wurman wrote, and indeed, "every diagram is really a map of something," he wrote.[47] But there are other approaches, too, all of which change the potential for the forms that we might design. "The creative organization of information creates new information," Wurman wrote in the second issue of *Design Quarterly* that he edited, "Hats," in 1989. The issue wasn't about hats but about hat racks—ways to categorize information. He coined the acronym LATCH in 1996 to underscore the five information organization methods:

Location
Alphabet
Time
Category
Hierarchy

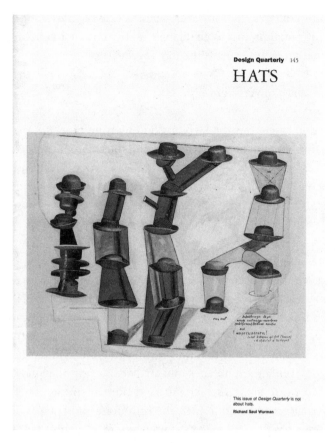

Figure 3.06
"Hats" had nothing to do with hats. Or rather, it had to do with hats in a metaphorical sense—ways to hang your hat as a metaphor for organizing information. Richard Saul Wurman, "Hats," *Design Quarterly*, no. 145 (1989). Courtesy of the Walker Art Center.

If someone were running a coat check, he could organize hats by location (where the hat was made, where the guest came from), alphabetically (beret, cowboy), chronologically (by guest arrival time), or categorically (by style), or hierarchically (by magnitude). Each suggests a different set of meanings. Consider how this might affect weightier matters. What might we learn in how we work through that data? Each categorization manifests a different understanding of the factors at play.

Moreover, the ways that we might choose to categorize the information becomes its own contribution. It formulates and generates tools to help us understand. Remember what Louis Kahn wrote: form, "a harmony of systems," generates design. So does the organization of information. Choosing a different structure or mode of organization changes the meaning and thus changes the form. The architecture of information changes the meaning of the information, just as changing the structure of a building would change its form. Information architecture is the form of rhetoric.

Communication, Convergence, and Conversation

Convergence is a dynamic that characterizes the blending and blurring of media and the channels that carry them. It used to be that information and the channel that carried it had a one-to-one relationship with each other. But with the growth of electronic media, this began to change. One channel, such as broadcast or print, could carry multiple kinds of media, and the service that a certain medium used to provide could now be carried by more than one channel. For example, the phone network used to carry only voice calls, but began increasingly to carry data and transmit information that a newspaper or television channel might have broadcast.

The changes that convergence introduced were and are radical. In his 1983 book *Technologies of Freedom*, Ithiel de Sola Pool (who coined the term *convergence*) described the "unprecedented flux" in everything surrounding human communication, expression, and knowledge production. "A panoply of electronic devices puts at everyone's hand capacities far beyond anything that the printing press could offer," he wrote. "Machines that think, that bring great libraries into anybody's study, that allow discourse among persons a half-world apart, are expanders of human culture. They allow people to do anything that could be done with the communications tools of the past, and many more things too."[48] The political ramifications of convergence interested de Sola Pool, who was the founder and chair of MIT's Political Science Department (and died in 1984, a year after *Technologies of Freedom*'s publication). Electronic communication opened up the possibility for more media representing more points of view to move to the fore, but also provoked new questions of governance and regulation.[49]

Both Richard Saul Wurman and Nicholas Negroponte harnessed these changes in the dynamics of communication. In particular, they understood that convergence offered new territory for reformulating the relationship of people to information and communication. Both men used the dynamics of convergence for their work in related ways: Wurman in his conferences, publications, and, later, his websites and apps, and Negroponte in the founding of the MIT Media Lab. I delve into Negroponte and convergence in chapter 6, but focus here on Wurman's adaptations of convergence.

Wurman collected and juxtaposed individuals and ideas, offering multiple levels of information, engagement, conversation, and experience, in both his conference and his publications. The goal for these vehicles was to change the way that readers and participants understood communication. For Wurman, cities and communication could not be separated from one another. Remember his idea of the city as a "message system" that conveyed messages from a sender to a receiver—conveyance came through the design of the city itself, which made it a concern for architects and designers.[50] Cities were also learning environments, or at least had the potential to be, if they could communicate more clearly. To put it differently, cities were the convergence of communication, learning, and experience—and Wurman wanted people to be challenged and changed by their experience with them.

In these next sections, I move between Wurman's conferences and publications, between 1972 and 1984, with an eye to today, as a means of tracing the ideas about convergence that each introduced. I begin with "The Invisible City," the 1972 International Design Conference in Aspen that Wurman chaired. Next, I move to Wurman's books *Information Anxiety* and *Information Anxiety 2*. I then return to the TED conference, which started in 1984. Finally, I revisit "The Architecture of Information," the AIA Convention that started off this chapter. How do we see information architecture after this expanded tour? Viewing Wurman's work in comparison with Rem Koolhaas's comments at the same convention forty years later, what can we learn from the memory of the city, from architecture's love/hate relationship with the Silicon Valley metaphor? The two are inextricable and inseparable, as we will see.

The Invisible City

Wurman produced conferences as a way of bringing together people, forces, and ideas, as multichannel experiences that combine text, graphics, conversation, and even moving around the city. In a 2012 video interview at the Cooper-Hewitt Museum, Wurman rattled off a long list of conferences he has produced that included the Aspen International Design conference, under the theme "The Invisible City," in 1972; the First Federal Design Assembly in 1973; the AIA Convention, under the theme "The American City: The Architecture of Information," in 1976; and the TED conferences that he chaired from 1984 to 2002. He continually plays with the format of the conferences and gatherings he is setting, bringing together unexpected figures in unusual conversations with one another.

In 1972, Wurman chaired the International Design Conference in Aspen under the title "Invisible City"—"invisible" for the ways the information and processes of a city are not visible to their residents and users, for a lack of awareness, availability, and access to a city's resources and information.[51] But if they were visible, cities could be places for new kinds of learning. The conference poster read:

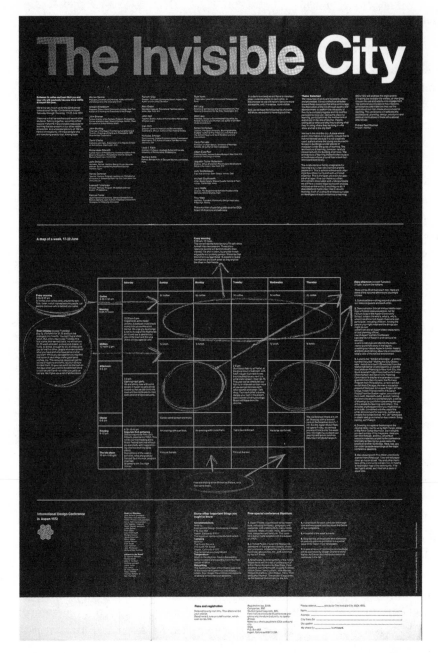

Figure 3.07
"In order to succeed we will have to make our ideas understandable to each other. In the process we too will have to become more accessible, and, in a sense, more visible," stated the poster for The Invisible City, the 1972 International Design Conference in Aspen, Colorado, that Wurman chaired. Image courtesy of International Design Conference at Aspen records, IDCA_0002_0018_001, University of Illinois at Chicago Library, Special Collections. Permission granted by Richard Saul Wurman.

The resources of a city are its people, places and processes. It is our collective attitudes toward these resources that either encourage the destruction of the city through apathy and abandonment or reaffirm the necessity of the city to civilized progress and life itself by participation and use. Use as the place for learning; participation as the involvement of everybody in the role of teacher. People telling about what and why they're doing what they're doing where they're doing it—the show and tell is the city itself.

We live in the invisible city. A place where public information is not public: a place that is not maintained because it is not creatively used: a place where the young are shunted to fenced-in buildings amidst islands of macadam under the guise of learning. The architecture of learning, however, rarely is concerned with the building of schools. The architecture of learning instead is the city as a schoolhouse whose ground floor is both bulletin board and library.

The most extensive facility imaginable for learning is our urban environment and the people in it. This is school without walls offering a boundless curriculum with unlimited expertise. This is the open university for people of all ages. If we can make our urban environment observable and understandable we will have created classrooms with endless windows on the world. Everything we do, if described and made clear, has to do with learning. Each of us should embrace our roles as developers of such invitations to learning.[52]

Wurman invited designers, architects, and educators to the Aspen International Design Conference to discuss new, alternative styles of education, such as classrooms without walls, or teaching that took place in the urban core, like using Montreal's Metro and vacant space in its stations for classrooms. As he would do in the future, Wurman mixed up the format, with more sessions that were talk-show style conversations—"more believable than a lecture," he said in an interview.[53] Speakers were called "Resource People" and included an equal number of educators or educational researchers as architects (there were urbanists, sociologists, and the head of the FCC). Louis Kahn spoke, as did Paolo Soleri (also the subject of a multimedia slide show). The conference screened films throughout about cities and education, including *The Idea of the City*, about the ugly development of urbanism, as well as Fritz Lang's 1927 masterpiece *Metropolis*, and *The Jungle,* the 1968 documentary by the Twelfth Street and Oxford teenage gang in Philadelphia.[54] Traditional designers such as Saul Bass and Ivan Chermayeff were relegated to the "Poster Group."

Changing the city required a shift from nouns to verbs, to the "performances" and "processes" of a city.[55] Rather than focusing on police cars, Wurman advocated framing the question in terms of safety, for example, which "might be a combination of *performances*—of people, and lighting, and of buildings" that would make for a different kind of experience within the city.[56] "It is difficult to talk about interest, about comfort, about communication, or safety, or lighting, or learning. It is easy to talk about light poles, schools, cars, roads, parks, cops, etc," he said in an interview about the 1972 IDCA. "And that's why I say the Invisible City is invisible because the performances are invisible."[57] The conference was a conversation about making a city's performance visible.

Convergence and Information Anxiety

Wurman characterized information overload as "information anxiety," a concern he sought to alleviate in his books *Information Anxiety* (1989) and *Information Anxiety 2* (2001). The specific nature of the anxiety in the first book came from the encroaching of the computer age on communication: more computers, more channels for communication, more information, less context, and therefore less meaning. "*Information anxiety* is produced by the ever-widening gap between what we understand and what we think we should understand," Wurman wrote in 1989. "*Information anxiety* is the black hole between data and knowledge. It happens when information doesn't tell us what we want or need to know."[58] In the introduction to the book, John Naisbitt, author of *Megatrends*, highlighted how much information anxiety had to do with convergence. Quoting from his own book, Naisbitt wrote, "The combined technologies of the telephone, computer, and television have merged into an integrated information and communication system that transmits data and permits instantaneous interactions

Information
Anxiety is produced
by the ever-widening gap between what we understand
and what we think we should
understand. It is the black hole
between data and knowledge,
and it happens when information doesn't tell us what we
want or need to know.
In this breakthrough book
Richard Saul Wurman ex-
plains why the information

explosion has backfired, leaving us inundated with facts but starved for understanding. John Naisbitt, the author of *Megatrends*, has written a provocative introduction to this essential map through the information jungle.

continued on back cover

Figure 3.08

The book *Information Anxiety* was intended as an antidote to information overload. Richard Saul Wurman, *Information Anxiety*, 1st ed. (New York: Doubleday, 1989). Permission granted by Richard Saul Wurman.

between persons and computers. . . . We have for the first time an economy based on a key resource that is not only renewable, but self-generating. Running out of it is not a problem, but drowning in it is."[59]

In *Information Anxiety*, Wurman threw a life preserver to readers who were drowning in information. The fifteen chapters of *Information Anxiety* were intended to be consumed quickly, and Wurman offered three approaches to reading the book. A reader could just take on the twenty-one-page table of contents for the quickest introduction to the book, a sort of syllabus for the topic of information anxiety. Or the reader could flip through the book to whatever interested him or her. It didn't need to be read in order. The marginalia, with quotes, drawings, and other items, as well as the illustrations, quotes, and diagrams throughout the text could attract a reader to whatever seemed most interesting and relevant.

The topics were the ones to which Wurman always returned. How to best find information, or structure it so someone else could find it? How could our interests be piqued

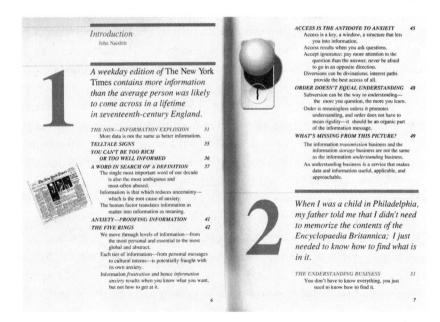

Figure 3.09
The table of contents in *Information Anxiety* was itself intended to alleviate information overload by making it possible to breeze through it and get a sense of the book's argument. Richard Saul Wurman, *Information Anxiety*, 1st ed. (New York: Doubleday, 1989). Permission granted by Richard Saul Wurman.

so we want to learn, and how would that learning take place? How was the news changing? How could we make decisions in an information glut? How would conversation change, and what might computers have to do with it? Again, it was a question of architecture and of form. A lack of architecture—of form—exacerbated information anxiety. "The word inform has been stripped out of the noun information, and the form or structure has disappeared from the verb to inform," Wurman wrote.[60] *Information Anxiety* was a social endeavor. It was like eavesdropping on a conversation, which it was intended to be. It was also situated socially: the inside cover of *Information Anxiety* is lined with fifteen praise quotes, including mentions from Alan Kay, John Sculley, Jay Chiat, Stewart Brand, Nicholas Negroponte, Senator Arlen Specter, and Craig Fields (who, at DARPA, funded much artificial intelligence and MIT Architecture Machine Group and Media Lab research). They read like a list of TED presenters, which, to an extent, they were.

The world looked quite different when Wurman published *Information Anxiety 2*, but still the scariest predictions from *Information Anxiety* remained unfounded. "Since *Information Anxiety* was published in 1989, the sky has not fallen," wrote Wurman in the first lines of the 2001 book. "We still use centuries-old languages to communicate, and we do not speak in the zeroes and ones of binary language. Humans have shaped computers more than they have shaped us."[61] If anything, the Internet opened people up to more human connection than ever before. More people had access to information that previously had been controlled and had shut people out. Still, information anxiety proliferated. More information meant more misinformation. How was a user to know what was what? Wurman's familiar axioms still applied. "Information is not enough." "Organization is as important as content." "It's not the what, but the how."[62] The sequel, *Information Anxiety 2* followed an even more social agenda (this time with twenty-seven praise quotes), with essays from other authors including Nathan Shedroff and Mark Hurst, CEO of Creative Good, a company devoted to customer experience. By the time Wurman had published *Information Anxiety 2*, there were many practicing information architects, many of whom were inspired by his work to make the web a more usable place. They took the organization of information to be a creative and generative exercise, one that suggested new strategies for experiencing the Web.

TED: Technology, Entertainment, Design

Everybody reading this book has probably watched a TED Talk. TED these days is a cultural phenomenon, a format, a meme—the very image of convergence. Wurman cofounded TED, short for Technology, Entertainment, and Design, in 1984. Harry Marks,

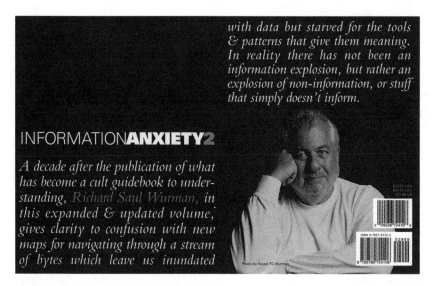

with data but starved for the tools & patterns that give them meaning. In reality there has not been an information explosion, but rather an explosion of non-information, or stuff that simply doesn't inform.

INFORMATION**ANXIETY**2

A decade after the publication of what has become a cult guidebook to understanding, Richard Saul Wurman, in this expanded & updated volume, gives clarity to confusion with new maps for navigating through a stream of bytes which leave us inundated

Figure 3.10

When Wurman published *Information Anxiety 2*, the Internet had brought a great deal more information to the world. "In reality there has not been an information explosion, but rather an explosion of non-information, or stuff that simply doesn't inform," stated the back cover of the book. Richard Saul Wurman, *Information Anxiety 2* (Indianapolis: Que, 2001), back cover. Permission granted by Richard Saul Wurman.

a retired television executive and computer graphics innovator, asked Wurman if he wanted to collaborate on a new conference concept. Wurman in turn approached Frank Stanton, former president of CBS (and a funder of Wurman's Access Press), and asked if he wanted to fund the project. They each committed $10,000, and TED was born.

At the first TED, three hundred attendees convened to experience a conversation that ushered in visions of the future. The speakers pushed the boundaries of technology, media, and society. Benoit Mandelbrot, the mathematician who popularized fractal geometry, talked about complexity and roughness and the patterns that fractals could find in them. Nicholas Negroponte made predictions about the future, many of which came true. TED was also an event that debuted consumer technology. The Macintosh computer had been announced in the iconic 1984 television ad and wasn't yet available, but Steve Jobs lent three of them to TED for demo purposes. (Marks owned three Apple Lisa computers, which may have been the impetus.)[63] There was a demo and giveaway of the compact disc by Sony president Mickey Schulhof, first introduced in 1982 but still largely unknown in 1984.[64] Conversation moved quickly because each talk was short, and if the speaker verged on talking for too long, Wurman would get up from his chair on the stage and walk over to him, encouraging a fast finish.

Yet the first TED was a financial failure. Although Wurman, Marks, and Stanton had agreed they would only go ahead with the conference if they had ample attendees for it to be a success, the room was only half full. Wurman nonetheless pushed the conference ahead, and the founders all lost about a third of their investment. In so doing, Wurman also lost Stanton's friendship, and Marks backed off from collaborating with him in the future.[65] It was six years before the next TED conference took place, but then the conference grew. Wurman ran the conference in Monterey, California, from 1990 until 2002, when Chris Anderson took over the conference as his successor.

TED ushered in a format for sharing a certain style of ideas—pithy, intelligent, inspirational. Today, it is run as a nonprofit "devoted to spreading ideas, usually in the form of short, powerful talks (18 minutes or less)."[66] In 2006, TED.com started sharing videos of its talks under a Creative Commons license. Today, the site now boasts over a billion page views, with talks translated into 112 languages by volunteers of the TED Translators project.[67] TED has franchises, from TEDx talks that take place in cities, communities, and on campuses, to the biennial TEDwomen conference, or the TEDyouth conference. The $1 million TED Prize supports work that will benefit the greater good, voted on by conference attendees. And the community fosters a class of TED Fellows.[68]

Criticism abounds that TED is elitist. The closest most people will get to TED is the TED.com website. The TED Global conference, now held in Vancouver, cost $8,500 to attend in 2017. Attendance is by invitation and application only, and it sells out a year in advance. The speakers throughout TED's history have been overwhelmingly male (only 27 percent of speakers were female as of 2012), white, Western and from the Global North.[69] Moreover, the celebrated format dumbs down the content, as critic Benjamin Bratton states. He refers to TED as "middlebrow megachurch infotainment . . . a combination of epiphany and personal testimony (an 'epiphimony' if you like)."[70] And many critics deride Wurman's ego. "At every TED, Wurman is teased mercilessly all weekend long," wrote Gary Wolf in "The Wurmanizer" in *Wired* in 2000. "Some of the gibes are about his weight or his egotism, but most are about his lust for patronage. Often, when Wurman turns his back, the conferees' good-natured facade disappears, and they marvel at what they see as his avarice and shamelessness."[71]

Criticism notwithstanding—or perhaps in full acknowledgment of it—TED is the poster child for Wurman's vision of convergence as a conversation: a conversation that is aspirational but at least partly accessible, and that changes what people know and how they see the world.

Conclusion

Let's return to the stage of the 2016 AIA Convention and the conversation between Rem Koolhaas and Mohsen Mostafavi that opened this chapter. Koolhaas has never given a TED talk, but his 2016 keynote conversation at the AIA Convention began to approximate one.[72] The images advertising the keynotes surely did—and in fact, MIT Media Lab professor Neri Oxman, who delivered her keynote talk the night before, is a TED speaker whose talk has garnered over 1.5 million views.[73]

In the conversation, Koolhaas took issue with what he saw as SiliconValley's co-opting of architectural metaphors. Recall again what he told Mostafavi: "They took over our metaphors, and it made me think that regardless of our speed, which is too slow for Silicon Valley, we can perhaps think of the modern world maybe not always in the form of buildings but in the form of knowledge or organization and structure and society that we can offer and provide."[74] Had he looked back in time to 1976, he would have found Richard Saul Wurman grappling with the same thing.

But there's something that Koolhaas was missing and that Wurman—and the other architects in this book—might remind him: that these metaphors in the digital actually come from architects and architectural practice, and architects developed knowledge structures and ways of organizing information to a burgeoning world of information and electronic media. Richard Saul Wurman was an early instigator in this regard, as we have seen with the publications and conferences he had devoted to a notion of understanding, but he wasn't the only one, as we've seen with Christopher Alexander and will see in the chapters to come.

Moreover, architecture has always been a tool of translation and mediation, to recall chapter 1. "What goes out is not always the same as what goes in," wrote Robin Evans of architecture's processes of translation from drawing to building, and we might say the same of architecture's movement from design to building to knowledge structures to information architecture.[75] Architecture doesn't look the same way at the other end, not when we are dealing with the verb of architecture. Koolhaas noted in his conversation with Mostafavi that the best architecture depends heavily on the contribution of engineers, at least half and half.

How might architects work with, and not against, Silicon Valley's appropriation of their metaphors? What would happen if they themselves appropriated the idea of architecting as a verb? If architects looked around at the architecting—at the systems that they literally, metaphorically, and physically design—they might open up vital new ways of interpreting the world, from physical to digital. And here, Koolhaas suggests important territory for architects of all kinds. "We're working in a world where so many different cultures are operating at the same time, each with their own value system. If you want to be relevant, you need to be open to an enormous multiplicity of values, interpretations, and readings. The old-fashioned Western 'this is' 'that is' is no longer tenable. We need to be intellectual and rigorous, but at the same time relativist."[76] As Richard Saul Wurman repeats, "You can only understand something relative to something you understand."[77] Perhaps the two keynotes aren't as far away as they might seem.

4 Information Architects

"What is the architecture part of information architecture?"[1] This is a question that Dan Klyn's University of Michigan students in the School of Information frequently asked him. Although Klyn was trained as a library and information scientist, he found himself turning to architecture to answer that question. "Most folks understand that if you want to build something remarkable, yet inhabitable and usable, the person that you call is an architect," Klyn said in a video, "Explaining Information Architecture." His starting point, when he teaches graduate students, is Richard Saul Wurman (he's become a biographer of Wurman) and Christopher Alexander. Klyn also introduces information architects and user experience designers to his love of architecture—guiding them on walking tours during conferences and encouraging them to build bridges of their own from their digital worlds outward, to the built environment and the history of architecture—and, above all, to his interest in Wurman and Alexander, for the foundations and inspiration they set in place for the practice of information architecture.

Information architects are designers who structure information and the experience of using software and the Web. Information architects (IAs for short) took on the mantle of architecture as a way to distinguish their practice from other forms of design. Adopting the title of architect spoke to the *idea* of what an architect does: developing blueprints and plans for design in spaces intended for human habitation. It also aligned these individuals with technical architects and separated them from graphic designers. When the practice of information architecture (IA) began to emerge in the mid-1990s, "design" connoted traditional graphic and communication design, marketing and advertising. Unlike formally trained graphic and communication designers, IAs tended not to be trained as designers. They came from any number of fields, including library science, anthropology, journalism, fine arts, human–computer interaction, and cognitive psychology, to name a few. The origins of the term "architecture of information" far predate Web-oriented information architecture. In fact, the term "architecture of information" was first coined in 1970 at Xerox and, as we saw in the last chapter, was popularized by Richard Saul Wurman starting in 1976, with some HCI researchers using the term as early as 1989–1990.

Most of the histories in this book focus on the work of a traditionally trained architect who reached out to computers and digital practice, but in this chapter I take a different approach, tracing the development of information architecture not through a main character but through a number of practices, conferences, and collaborations. We've already covered Wurman's influence, so here we begin with other elements in the history of information architecture: the early corporate concerns of managing information at IBM and Xerox in the 1960s and 1970s, then the 1990 ACM SIGCHI conference (Special Interest Group on Computer-Human Interaction, commonly referred to as "CHI"). We visit the book that many information architects name as a major influence, *Information Architecture for the World Wide Web* by Louis Rosenfeld and Peter Morville (first published in 1998, now in its fourth edition, and known as the "polar bear book" after the drawing of the animal on the cover); the professionalization, growth, and decline of information architecture and the umbrella of user experience and interaction design practices. Overall, this chapter turns around the same question that Dan Klyn's students ask him: What is architectural about information architecture? What was its initial disconnection from and, later, its connection to, an expanded notion of design? And what might architecture learn from the influences, interests, and practices of information architects?

Xerox, IBM, and the "Architecture of Information"

Long before the emergence of the Web, or even personal computers, major information technology companies such as Xerox and IBM saw their future in the corralling and managing of information. These imperatives have shaped the strategies of both companies over the last fifty years. Xerox set out its information management imperatives in a speech that announced the founding of Xerox PARC. Similarly, IBM understood the management of information as a corporate mandate to be achieved through consistency in design. It carried this notion forward with the design of breakthrough products like the IBM ThinkPad and the information architecture on IBM's Web properties, some of the first major websites in the early years of the World Wide Web.[2]

It wasn't Richard Saul Wurman or another architect but rather the president of Xerox, Peter McColough, who first coined the term "architecture of information" in 1970. He projected that the next decade of Xerox's growth would take place around the management of information. In an address to the New York Society of Security Analysts, he stated that the company's "basic purpose" was "to find the best means to bring greater order and discipline to information. . . . Thus our fundamental thrust, our common denominator, has evolved toward establishing leadership in what we call 'the architecture of information.'"[3] McColough suggested a structural, architectural approach that could be applied to the entire business and information landscape of Xerox. Xerox's interest in such an endeavor lay in what McColough called the company's "raw materials of advanced architecture of information technology. What we seek is to think of information itself as a natural and undeveloped environment which can be enclosed and made more habitable for the people who live and work within it."[4] To design and construct its next decade of information management design and technology, McColough said that Xerox would combine machines of all scales and sizes: "computers, copiers, duplicators, microfilm, communications devices, education techniques, display and transmission systems, graphic and optic capabilities," with "heavy research and global scope."[5] For Xerox, "architecture of information" meant developing products, services, and a research program to manage the onslaught of information overload. These statements served as the salvo for the foundation of Xerox PARC—the Palo Alto Research Center—to advance leadership in the new informational landscape.

IBM also long understood its strategic imperative as a structured, conceptual, and logical approach to information management. Its future was in the "business of controlling, organizing, and redistributing information in space," as John Harwood writes, and the company turned to design to accomplish it.[6] When IBM hired industrial designer Eliot Noyes as consultant director of design in 1956, the company wanted to both foster design excellence and use design to change its management structure to be more horizontal and less hierarchical. Noyes worked with a team of consulting design and architecture luminaries, including Charles Eames, Paul Rand, George Nelson, Marcel Breuer, Ludwig Mies van der Rohe, Paul Rudolph, and Eero Saarinen, who worked on every element of the IBM brand, from the design of computers and typewriters to the logotype and design language of all aspects of the company's communication to its showrooms and pavilions in world's fairs.[7] Noyes saw this as "environmental control," as he expressed in a 1966 interview: "If you get to the very heart of the matter, *what IBM really does is to help man extend his control over his environment*. . . . I think that's the meaning of the company."[8] To put it another way, Noyes understood the role of design as amassing and exacting power. The positioning of Noyes and the industrial design of IBM's computers reverberates today. Harwood argues that industrial design occupied a "liminal area of expertise" among the electrical engineers who design the technical architecture, the ergonomics and human factors engineers who fit the human body to the computer, and the architect who fits the machine to the room, integrating streams of data from all areas of expertise and fashioning "what Noyes and his colleagues at

IBM called the externals of the machine—its interface."[9] For IBM, the interface organized the myriad flows of information and bureaucracy, making it visible at the scale of a typewriter or a mainframe computer. The interface became the operative point of control.

"The Computer Reaches Out"

Although IBM and Xerox well understood that their futures lay in the management and control of information, and that design played a role in that endeavor, the interfaces to their machines were not particularly user-friendly. The concept of user-friendliness wasn't even coined till 1972, and it took till the early 1980s for it to become a common part of our vocabulary.[10] Engineers designed hardware interfaces and early text editors for their own purposes—to program and control computers. But once they began to solve hardware-level challenges, the computer began to "reach out," as Jonathan Grudin wrote in "The Computer Reaches Out," a paper on the history of user interfaces that he gave at the 1990 SIGCHI conference on Human–Computer Interaction (or CHI '90 for short).[11]

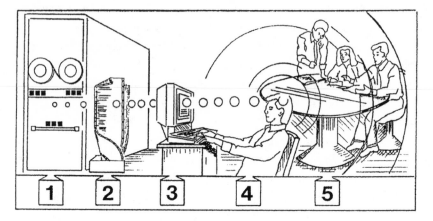

Figure 4.01
Jonathan Grudin's 1990 diagram is a sort of historical-conceptual timeline showing how, over the course of its development, the computer increasingly reaches out into the worlds and the minds of its users. Jonathan Grudin, "The Computer Reaches Out: The Historical Continuity of Interface Design," in *Proceedings of the SIGCHI Conference on Human Factors in Computing Systems*, CHI '90 (New York: ACM), 263.

Grudin's paper features a remarkable diagram: a sort of figurative timeline showing the "Five foci of interface development," each corresponding to and enabling a different level of interaction with the computer. The mainframe computer (1) and dot matrix printout (2) in the drawing (figure 4.01) corresponded to the interfaces that concerned programmers and engineers through the 1970s: "the interface at the hardware" and "the interface at the programming task."[12] Then, as research in ergonomics and cognitive modeling allowed for interface advances in computer terminals, engineers and computer scientists began to envision the terminal interface (3) as a way to engage users in a dialogue. The look and feel of software interfaces began to matter. The user in Grudin's diagram (4) has his hands on the terminal and looks through to all of the previous interfaces, all the way to the mainframe, all of which enable the interactions he has at hand. The computer acts on the user. "In a metaphoric sense, the computer is extending its grasp beyond the keyboard and the display surface on which fonts, color patterns, and menus are arranged—extending its knowledge into the mind of the user," Grudin wrote.[13] Ultimately, (5) is "the interface at the work setting" in which three people gather at a round table, conversing about the charts and papers before them. There is no computer, none that we can see. It isn't visible anymore. The computer has reached out through layer after layer of interface, until it weaves seamlessly into work, conversation, and the environment. It could be better called the social interface: work is merely the setting.

Grudin understood the profound implications of the computer reaching out. Like Eliot Noyes at IBM, like Peter McColough at Xerox, he understood that a computer's interaction with its users was a matter of controlling space. "In a sense, the computer is colonizing its environment—or, less threateningly, computers are progressively learning more about the world around them," he wrote.[14] The built environment could thus become both an input and an output for the computer. But the computer's reach did not stop there. Grudin likened its extension to the way a child reaches out to the world as she grows and learns—a limited metaphor, he acknowledged, for what a computer would want to do. "Whereas children master their own physical, perceptual, cognitive, and social functions, this paper presents the computer as gaining control over its own hardware and software functions, but then increasing its knowledge of our perceptual, cognitive, and social behavior."[15] The computer would gain agency. It would develop a disposition, in which it would seek to increase its tendrils into its our worlds by coming to understand us—a new take on the notion of human–computer symbiosis brewing since J. C. R. Licklider coined the term in 1960, and on the research by the MIT Architecture Machine Group (as we see in chapter 6).

This radical idea surpassed the way that some of Grudin's contemporaries were talking about computers and their interactions with users out in the world. At the time that Grudin wrote this paper for CHI '90, the notion of ubiquitous computing was being developed by Marc Weiser at Xerox PARC, in which the computer would disappear into the environment around us. "The most profound technologies are those that disappear," Weiser famously wrote in 1991. "They weave themselves into the fabric of everyday life until they are indistinguishable from it."[16] Quite the opposite of virtual reality, ubiquitous or "invisible computing is so strong that some of us use the term 'embodied virtuality' to refer to the process of drawing computers out of their electronic shells," Weiser wrote.[17] This is the inverse of the far more radical suggestion by Grudin: computers drawing *us* out of our shells, out into the world. It also underscores the architectural question of computing: the *architecting* that takes place when the computer reaches out, when the architect and designer reach for the computer and a new practice between the two emerges.

Architectural Education and HCI

At the same CHI '90 conference where Jonathan Grudin's paper, "The Computer Reaches Out," was presented, Terry Winograd gave a closing plenary talk, "What Can We Teach about Human-Computer Interaction?," in which he turned to the architecture studio as a model for training future software designers. Now an emeritus Stanford computer science professor and founder of the Human–Computer Interaction program, Winograd received a PhD from MIT, where he was a researcher in the AI Lab.

By 1990, Winograd had shifted his focus from AI to human–computer interaction (HCI). HCI was a booming field, and its practitioners needed to take into consideration the look and feel—the design—of software. But the pedagogical models from computer science fell short in educating tomorrow's HCI professionals. Winograd noted that computer science departments were not exactly known for looking outside their purview. By its nature, HCI was multidisciplinary: in order to develop good software, it was necessary to understand users and model their behavior, and then design interfaces that matched these models. Winograd quoted a letter from Mitch Kapor, the software entrepreneur who designed the Lotus 1-2-3 spreadsheet program: "As communities, [computer science graduate programs] lack the human-centered values central to a design oriented approach," Kapor wrote to Winograd.[18]

So how should HCI students be taught? Kapor, in the letter that Winograd read in his plenary, advocated following the model of architecture school, in which students learn structural fundamentals that they then apply to architecture problems in their design studios, where architectural critics shape the students work. "To design a building well, the student needs to understand the activities people intend to perform in it and the problems they are likely to encounter," Winograd said. "Knowing how to find out these things in a particular case is dependent on having a strong general understanding of how people are constituted and how they act, both individually and as part of a social organism."[19] Ultimately, to educate a designer in this burgeoning field, the educator acts more like a "coach" who introduces the student to new domains of knowledge and learning practices, situated in the real world with real-world users. This "guided learning" approach would be an experiment, Winograd admitted, but it would be necessary for HCI and computer science departments to shift their focus toward a new model of human-centered design.[20]

In the audience at CHI '90, Andrew Cohill heard Winograd's proposal. Inspired by the talk, Cohill proposed a new role in 1991: the information architect, the person who would guide a user-centered design process. At the time, Cohill was a PhD student in environmental design—a doctoral degree in architectural history and theory—who was studying how architects used computers and information systems. He contemplated how the tenets of design and architecture could be applied to the software engineering process. "In the future, we may see the high level design work now performed by a systems analyst performed by a member of a new discipline called information architecture; the practitioners of this discipline would be information architects," Cohill predicted.[21]

Just as architects and engineers played different roles for buildings, an "information architect" would focus on design across the software development process, distinct from the engineers who would work on the technical components. "The foundation of such a discipline would be training in design, and the primary role of the information architect would be to discover the deep structure of information environments, rather than on the shallow structure of data," Cohill wrote.[22] From this design background, the information architect would incorporate an understanding of organizational structures, human factors, and information systems. He offered six design principles for information architecture:

1. Design is a process; it is circular, repetitive, and unpredictable.
2. Design is intimate and idiosyncratic; it is a process that can be learned only through personal exploration and experience; it cannot be taught.
3. Design is an act of exploration; it is feedback-oriented, it requires a willingness to change, and it requires a sensitivity to the aesthetics of the final product.
4. Information architecture is concerned with information environments; these environments can be represented as self-contained, self-regulating structures composed of elements defined by interconnecting relationships.
5. The elements of an information structure are computers (hardware and software), people, and the physical and social environment in which people and computers communicate.

6. Information architects are designers. A fundamental grounding in design, combined with expertise in computer systems, organizational behavior, and ergonomics provide them with the knowledge to design information structures.[23]

Although Cohill was motivated by Winograd's proposal, he didn't think it went far enough. He didn't want information architecture to be an experiment or a short-term course, but rather an entire approach to design study and practice. The principles that Cohill outlined, several years before people would claim the title of information architect, are ones that information architects and other digital designers would agree with today. As the purview of information architects grew, they incorporated ethnographically oriented methods to learn about people and their potential needs, devised and structured digital information environments, and often led these digital design processes. As we will see later in this chapter, information architects in the early 2000s would find themselves talking about "Little IA" and "Big IA," the difference between classifying information for the Web and the ambitious and strategic vision of design led by information architects.

Information Architects and the Web

In the earliest days of the Web, resources were available about how to *build* a website but few about how to *design* one. Laura Lemay's very successful book *Teach Yourself Web Publishing with HTML in a Week*, which came out January 1, 1995, introduced the basics of Hypertext Markup Language (HTML), the Web formatting language, and the Netscape website offered a few pointers. But for the most part, people tended to learn Web design by *doing* Web design, by using the "view source" command on cool websites, looking at the HTML, and then trying the code out for themselves. These early Web tinkerers didn't necessarily think about an end user. Rather, they thought of themselves and their interests in playing with the Web's latest conventions and publishing whatever content they wanted. (I could include myself and my 1995 personal site, Girlwonder.com, in this category: a fine example of "just because you can doesn't mean you should," in terms of Web design.) The "cool" factor of websites stood in for a design sensibility. But as communications scholar Megan Sapnar Ankerson writes, what constituted cool could really be anything—"a hodgepodge so arbitrary, that it appears hard to draw out any defining characteristics of cool."[24] But design? For the most part, in the early days of the Web, it didn't exist.

Not surprisingly, the early Web was a messy place. It grew in an ad hoc manner because the tools and languages for building websites were not locked in a proprietary system. Before blogging systems took hold in the early 2000s, design conventions hadn't been locked down. This ease and openness was what made it evolve so quickly.

But it's also what made it inconsistent, if not chaotic. For this reason, information architects tasked themselves with providing structure, formatting, and sense to the Web. Information architect Christina Wodtke wrote about the chaos of the early days in a 2014 Medium post on the history of information architecture. "[The Web] wasn't very interactive. To be honest, it barely had any interface design either," she wrote.[25] What passed for interactivity had more to do with what a user did with browser buttons, such as bookmarking a page or filling out a Web form. "But what the Internet did have was information. Everybody put everything they had up on the Web, from help pages to marketing brochures. It was a mess, and someone had to make it all make sense. So while most software interaction designers declined to play with the very limited set of tinker toys the [I]nternet offered, others stepped up to fight the 'tidal wave of data.' And they become the first Information Architects."[26]

One of the first resources that promoted a structured approach to Web design and development was the "Web Architect" column authored by Lou Rosenfeld, Peter Morville, and Samantha Bailey on *Web Review* (itself one of the first weekly publications about Web design and development), which launched on August 17, 1995. In his introductory column, Louis Rosenfeld addressed the problems that the early Web presented. "What is Web site architecture?" he asked. "Well, Web users face a number of problems: awkward designs, confusing navigational aids, documents covered by walls of blue links, and on and on. In fact, at every level of a Web site's architecture, there are plenty of things that can and often do go wrong," he wrote. He wrote that Web architecture should take into consideration the site's audience, balance the site's design with its functionality, offer short-but-sweet pages, and extend to support future growth. "A 'good' architecture for a Web site succeeds at all levels of granularity," whether of the page elements, the page itself, or the overall structure, he wrote.[27] Ultimately, a Web architect would not hit the site visitor over the head with "your site's coolness factor"— he warned, "They'll get mighty sick of cuteness and splashiness after a while, and hey, let's face it: *A successful site should not concentrate on initially engaging the interest of new users. . . .* Don't sacrifice that functionality to aesthetics, because after the feeling of falling in love wears off, you'll be married to your Web site."[28]

Still, early IAs didn't trust design. It seemed at odds with the more serious, rigorous work of "architecture." Design was window dressing, the icing on the cake. "Architecture" meant solving problems. It meant being thoughtful. Rosenfeld, Morville, and Bailey advised budding Web architects to work at all levels of granularity to make good site blueprints (or site maps), employ appropriate metaphors in their design, and tune up their pages and site architectures. They did not suggest becoming designers—they instead advised their readers to think like architects.

The "Polar Bear" Book

As websites increased in complexity, library and information science approaches provided advanced ways to organize information. Library and information scientists were an important voice in the IA community, who defended the specificity of a scaffolding, structural process. Those were the fields that Louis Rosenfeld and Peter Morville came from, with master's degrees from the University of Michigan in Information and Library Science. Rosenfeld cofounded Argus Associates with UM professor Joe Janes and hired Morville, then a student, in 1994. Argus provided consultancy that focused specifically on information architecture, and its blue-chip clients included AT&T, Chrysler, and Dow Chemical. Was an academic degree from an I-school (an information science program) necessary? Rosenfeld and Morville were the first to say that IA didn't require this level of specialization. "You don't need a library degree to be a successful information architect. Despite the requirements listed in some job descriptions, it's hard to have had years of experience within this fledgling medium. More important . . . is common sense, plain and simple. The Web is too new for anyone to feel secure in claiming that there is a 'right way' to do things," they wrote.[29] But while the burgeoning discipline of information architecture was open to people from a variety of backgrounds, it did set out a right way, or at least a better way, to do things.

In the days pre-Google, it was hard to find information on the Web. Search engines existed, but they were not as effective as they are today, and without a usable information organization scheme, it was difficult to navigate a website. Information architects determined the appropriate organization schemes for a site, such as organizing information alphabetically, geographically, metaphorically, or by task; the navigation for the website, with keywords designed into the page; and the labeling schemas for the individual pages and their subsections. Information architects created site maps with information hierarchies showing how a user might move from one page of the site to another (these maps were originally called "blueprints.") "Sites that use well-planned information architectures are as magical as the phenomenon of routing users and packets respectively," Rosenfeld and Morville wrote."[30]

Information architects defined the architecture of a digital space or information environment. This notion is akin to what architects call the *program,* the function of an architectural space. Thinking about buildings as an analog encouraged early information architects to consider not just the design and the structure but also the inhabitant

Designing Large-Scale Web Sites

Information Architecture

for the World Wide Web

O'REILLY™   *Louis Rosenfeld & Peter Morville*

Figure 4.02

Louis Rosenfeld and Peter Morville published *Information Architecture for the World Wide Web* in 1998, more commonly referred to as "The Polar Bear Book" for the drawing of the animal on its cover. *Information Architecture for the World Wide Web*, 1st Edition by: Louis Rosenfeld and Peter Morville Copyright ©1998 O'Reilly Media, Inc. All rights reserved. Used with permission.

of a space. "What is it about buildings that stir us?"[31] ask Rosenfeld and Morville in their book, *Information Architecture for the World Wide Web,* first published in 1998 (referred to as the "polar bear book" because of the polar bear drawing on its cover and now in its fourth edition, published in 2016). Rosenfeld and Morville describe a set of buildings and environments in Ann Arbor—a smoky bar, a cozy café, or an office that used to be a garage. "Why so much talk about the impressions that physical structures make on us? Because they are familiar to us in ways that web sites are not. Like web sites, buildings have architectures that cause us to react. Buildings and their architectures therefore provide us with great opportunities to make analogies about web sites and their architectures."[32]

Rosenfeld and Morville talk about architecture differently than architects would. Architects, to recall the first chapter of this book, would refer to the design of buildings. They would be unlikely to say that buildings "have" architectures. It would be the apperception of the design that would cause a reaction. Rosenfeld and Morville appropriated certain metaphors of architecture in a different language than architects would use. In so doing, they gave early Web practitioners a way of looking at the world: seeing the scope of structure, the necessity of function and program, to use the architectural terms. Just as architects designed the program, the structure and engineering, and the overall experience of a building, an information architect determined the functionality, the structures and categories of the information the site provided, and the user experience—the way that someone would experience moving through the website. Thinking of the Web from an architectural perspective meant thinking of who might move through your website, in the same way that they might move through a built space: wouldn't you want it to be elegant, thoughtful, and attractive?

From Information Design to the Information Architect

Although early information architects were suspicious of design on the Web, just outside of their field was "information design," an established practice that had its own scholarly publication (the *Information Design Journal* from 1979 onward). Information designers focused on the presentation of information. As Robert Horn wrote in 1999, "The values that distinguish information design from other kinds of design are efficiency and effectiveness at accomplishing the communicative purpose."[33] Information design worked at multiple scales, with designers creating documents that were easy to find and understand, "interactions with equipment" (in the realm of human–computer interaction) and the navigation of "three-dimensional space . . . especially urban space, but also, given recent developments, virtual space."[34] This definition echoes Lou Rosenfeld's recommendation of considering the multiple scales of website granularity, from page element to page to website, in his first "Web Architect" column. The difference is that information design found a place in multiple kinds of design practice. It went by different names depending on where it was practiced: "information graphics" for a magazine, "wayfinding" for an architect, plain old "design" for graphic designers.[35] These fields shared an approach that started with cognitive science, working in an array of practices ranging from computer interfaces to data visualizations to urban space, by a number of different titles, and would eventually come to blend into the concerns of information architecture.

A number of pre-Web and emerging Web and software companies called their work information design before later differentiating their work as information architecture. For example, Karen McGrane, a user-experience designer who led the user-experience practice at the agency Razorfish from 1998 to 2006, was initially hired as an "information designer/writer." When she became the group manager, she took on the mantle of "information architect" and changed the name of the information design group to information architecture. "At the time, the term 'designer' was so strongly associated with graphic design—particularly in the agency world—that it made sense to latch onto the word architect," she says. Information design meant the design of charts and graphs, so it wasn't really the right term, particularly once Razorfish began to acquire data visualization companies that had that practice as their forte. "[Information architecture] connoted something more structural, less visual," she continues. "I think it also suggested the work of an architect in defining how a system or space should work and function, separate from what it should look like."[36]

Information architects and information designers were also different from visual designers, many of whom worked with Flash, a browser plug-in for vector-based animation and rich media on the Web. Flash files were very small, making it an attractive format for designers to deliver highly visual experiences on the Web. As Megan Sapnar Ankerson writes, "Flash appealed to a new vision of the web, one vastly different from the static, silent, textual form that imitated the aesthetics of print. . . . Its popularity rising with the dot-com bubble, Flash represented a transformative moment in web production discourse where presumptions concerning 'quality' web design (how the web should look, feel, sound, behave) were in flux."[37] There were vibrant communities around design, such as Kaliber 10000 (k10k), founded by Michael Schmidt, Toke Nygaard, and Per Jørgen Jørgensen in 1997, one of the first portals for Web designers, and the Dreamless.org forum founded by Joshua Davis that was in existence from 2000 to 2001. While I am not covering these design communities in this book, they are an important element—and sometimes element of opposition—in the more seemingly left-brained information architecture and usability testing approaches of the time. They demonstrated that the Web could push the boundaries of visual design in developing Web-native aesthetics.

Professionalizing Information Architecture

Information architects were particularly successful in organizing and professionalizing their practice by using blogs and email lists to support, educate, and provide resources for the community. The community developed its own conference, the IA Summit; an email list, SIGIA-L (which stood for Special Interest Group IA-List), in 2000;

a peer-reviewed journal, *Boxes and Arrows*, in 2002; and a non-profit institute, the Asilomar Institute of Information Architecture (which became the Information Architecture Institute in 2005).[38] Here, I want to home in on the IA Summit and *Boxes and Arrows*.

The first IA Summit took place in 2000—the first full-fledged conference devoted specifically to information architecture—and has taken place every year since. The organizers and sponsors reflected the two strains of interest in the field at that time, library science and Web consulting. Conference chairs Lou Rosenfeld, Gary Marchioni, and Victor Rosenberg came from library science backgrounds (Marchioni and Rosenberg were professors of library science at University of North Carolina–Chapel Hill and University of Michigan, respectively), and the Association of Information Science (ASIS) and dotcom Web consultancies Zefer, Sapient, and iXL sponsored the gathering. Speakers included Web and design luminaries including Clement Mok, Mark Hurst, Alison Head, and Jeff Veen. While many of the talks were introductory in nature, defining what information architecture was from the perspectives of the speakers, the IA Summit felt "edgy" and "experimental" as Rosenfeld said in 2001.[39] The summit galvanized not only the attendees but the broader IA community. By the time of the second IA Summit in February 2001, the SIGIA mailing list had exploded to more than 1,650 subscribers, and local IA groups had formed internationally. There were jobs for IAs, too, with at least a hundred online postings.[40] In short, it was a booming field, and information architects were keen on fostering its growth.

Another central endeavor gave the booming information architecture community a voice: *Boxes and Arrows,* a peer-reviewed, blog-based journal for information architects. The goal of *Boxes and Arrows* was to provide a critical position from which to explore the practice of information architecture. "Boxes and Arrows is the definitive source for the complex task of bringing architecture and design to the digital landscape," wrote *Boxes and Arrows* publisher Christina Wodtke in the site's first post. "There are various titles and professions associated with this undertaking—information architecture, information design, interaction design, interface design—but when we looked at the work that we were actually doing, we found a 'community of practice' with similarities in outlook and approach that far outweighed our differences."[41] *Boxes and Arrows* launched with eleven stories, including a comparison of three online bookstores, a discussion of the clash between design and the executive suite, and a review of Ray and Charles Eames's iconic film *Powers of Ten,* as well as pieces on participatory design, usability testing, government consulting, and the simplicity of Yahoo! Mail. Each week, *Boxes and Arrows* published several articles written by active participants in fields affiliated with information architecture.

Not everybody in the community agreed with calling the practice "architecture." Nathan Shedroff, author of *Experience Design* and the founder of vivid studios, one of the first Web design firms, was cynical about the titling. In the same launch issue of *Boxes and Arrows*, he criticized the self-named architects:

For a field that is barely even two years old, the exact same egomaniacal process is starting but, this time, with even less substance. I sat through a presentation last year of Experience Architecture which, as far as I could tell, had no new insights, processes, or techniques to offer other than what would already be covered (or uncovered) in Experience Design. The only reason for this title was to differentiate this one company's offering. . . . Can you imagine a group of Fashion Architects declaring their supremacy over Fashion Designers? Yes, that's what we've come to.[42]

It wasn't that Shedroff had a problem with information architecture: he wrote a column titled "The Architect" in *New Media* magazine (the title of which garnered him a cease-and-desist letter, as we saw in chapter 1) and counted Richard Saul Wurman as his mentor—he worked for him at his studio, The Understanding Business. Shedroff criticized the territoriality of claiming architecture. IA was too reductive in its framing, where design, or experience design, or interaction design, offered a broader framework.

Information architecture hit its peak around 2004. At its highest point, Wodtke and Morville had been interviewed by the *Wall Street Journal.* Using Google Trends to chart the relative interest in two search terms, "information architecture" and "user experience," shows a wide gulf between them in January 2004, with the lines hurtling toward each other over the next four years. By 2008, the lines intersect, and after 2009, interest in user experience overtakes that of information architecture, a gulf that continues to grow as information architecture drops considerably in interest.[43] This map of search interests corresponds to what was taking place in Web information architecture and user experience.

By 2009, seven years after Shedroff's critique, information architects started backing away from their title and began calling themselves designers. As we have seen, the practice of information architecture grew in opposition to design—the approaches and interests of information architects differed from those of designers in the late 1990s and early 2000s. Information architects had focused heavily on the professionalization of the practice and the claiming of the term "architect." Why did many of them begin to step away from that title?

There were strategic and structural reasons for the decline of IA and the rise of user-experience design (UX). First, there was the distinction between "big IA and little IA," a conversation that started in the community in 2003 after a blog post that Peter Morville wrote, a differentiation between the categorical work of the library science–oriented information architect (little IA), and the expanded purview of big IA, involving ethnographic research and design strategy. This distinction produced a split within the community as it began to separate out the different tasks in information architecture. In retrospect, the division could be viewed as a difference between the IA produced by library scientists and that of strategic designers, as Peter Merholz, Garry van Patter, and Dan Klyn have noted.[44]

Second, in the early days of the Web, interactivity took place largely by clicking links in the Web browser. Search engines were not as effective as they are now, and so structuring information was vital in order to make the Web usable and useful. In 2005, Tim O'Reilly coined the term "Web 2.0" to describe a new set of practices on the Web: interactivity on the page level, such as the slippy interactions with Google Maps and emergent social media with the photo-sharing Flickr. Jesse James Garrett and his colleagues at the user-experience studio Adaptive Path called this increasing functionality in the browser "AJAX," which stood for Asynchronous JavaScript+XML."[45] AJAX enabled the Web browser to render and produce more interaction without having to make a call to the server. Again, think about how quickly Google Maps responds to your clicking and dragging, or how the Google search engine makes suggestions for you as you type. These actions are provided by a JavaScript engine that the browser loads in an invisible frame that provides a much faster response than going back to the server for more information.

AJAX and its related technological approaches and Web 2.0 produced new approaches to design and new business paradigms. Social media exploded with Facebook, which launched on campuses in 2004 and, by 2007, was in heavy use by adults and teens alike. Twitter launched in 2006 and started becoming massively popular in 2007, with its terse character count and its extensibility across computers and mobile phones. And what about smartphones? Apple launched the iPhone in 2007 and Google the Android operating system in 2008, making the smart phone the site of interactivity.

Interaction Design
Interaction design is another umbrella term for design practices at the nexus of software design, human-computer interaction, information architecture, and interface design, among others (sometimes interchangeably, and sometimes fiercely defended). The question for interaction designers was not one of ontologies and facets of information, although they frequently engaged in the same kinds of user research (and what had been termed "big IA" in 2003). Interaction designers develop the function and the feeling of these human-machine-software interactions that move between multiple modes and apparatuses. Interaction designers specify, communicate, and prototype these actions.

Interaction design developed out of the edges of industrial design, the point at which the designer's purview needed to address the object, the interface, and the relationship between the two. It was coined as a term by Bill Moggridge, an industrial designer, and Bill Verplank, a mechanical engineer, in the 1980s. Moggridge designed the GRiD Compass, the first laptop, in 1980. When Moggridge turned it on for the first time, he found himself absorbed not by the form of the laptop but the software running within it. "All the work that I had done to make the object elegant to look at and to feel was forgotten, and I found myself immersed for hours at a time in the interactions that were dictated by the design of the software and electronic hardware. My frustrations and rewards were in this virtual space," Moggridge wrote.[46] Designing the interactive experience was at least as important as designing the device. He initially called this intersection of interface design and software "Soft-face." His collaborator Verplank suggested "interaction design."[47]

The practice of interaction design picked up steam in Europe, particularly at the Royal College of Art under the leadership of Gillian Crampton Smith. She founded the Computer Related Design MA program in 1990, adapting it from a CAD (computer-aided design) technology course into a new perspective on design. By 1998, Crampton Smith's program had a broader focus than that of Web-based information architects, with three areas of study: "interactive information worlds," "tangible computing," and "intelligent environments," the general areas that are taught in interaction design programs today.[48] Crampton Smith left the RCA to found a school, the Interaction Design Institute Ivrea in Ivrea, Italy. The two-year master's program educated students from more than twenty countries, from 2001 to 2006. Carnegie Mellon's School of Design launched its master's in interaction design in 1994, and has graduated students every year since. (Full disclosure: I am an associate professor in CMU's School of Design, and was an associate professor at the Interaction Design Institute Ivrea.)

Since interaction grew out of the design of tangible and physical objects, it was also well suited to architectural connections. Several faculty members at the Interaction Design Institute Ivrea were trained as architects (although in Italy, design degrees are conferred by schools of architecture, so this was not a surprise). For example, Stefano Mirti taught "Buildings as Interface" in 2003 at Interaction-Ivrea, a course that encouraged students to design for interactions at the urban scale and inspired master's thesis projects in the area. Architecture scholar and University of Michigan professor Malcolm McCullough saw the architectural possibilities and potencies in interaction design. "As ambient, social, and local provisions for everyday life, those realities have become part of architecture. Whereas previous paradigms of cyberspace threatened to dematerialize architecture, pervasive computing invites a defense of architecture. In sum, my essential claim is that interaction design must now serve our basic human need for getting into place," he wrote in his 2005 book *Digital Ground: Architecture, Pervasive Computing, and Environmental Knowing.*[49]

Titles in Flux

If you find the shifting titles and practice names confusing, you're not alone. It was a problem that needed to be fixed: IAs needed to unify under a different umbrella. "What is clear to me now is that there is no such thing as an information architect," Jesse James Garrett announced in the closing plenary of the tenth IA Summit in 2009. "Information architecture does not exist as a profession. As an area of interest and inquiry? Sure. As your favorite part of your job? Absolutely. But it's not a profession."[50] For as much as he and others grappled with calling themselves "designers" or working within "design," "experience design" had the extensibility to apply to many different kinds of design, "practiced independent of medium and across medium."[51] More could be gained by uniting forces and promoting what the umbrella of digital design practices shared—and that would be best done as user-experience designers. Garrett said he no longer had any interest in the distinction between the fields. The best decision would be to reach out and build bridges with the other people playing in the same field, rather than competing for limited attention. "There are no information architects. There are no interaction designers. There are only, and only ever have been, user experience designers," Garrett said.[52] (In 2016, he acknowledged that he was amending this position: he told the audience of his plenary talk at that year's IA Summit that he was more interested in a broader definition of experience and experience design, one that put humans and not users at the center.)[53]

The valence of these titles and practices will continue to change. Just as I list these titles here, new differentiations are taking place. A 2015 post on the Medium platform by Paul DeVay outlined the current stakes around the role of "product designer"—not someone trained in industrial design, but a designer with good visual design chops and some front-end coding capability, who works on a digital product and is managed by a product manager.[54] Seen broadly, someone with the same skills could be described by any of these terms. For people at the forefront of a new discipline, guarding titles is a matter of defining disciplinary territories. But one thing becomes apparent: the rejection of the title "designer" in favor of "architect" and then the consequent turn to designer.

The world of digital design today is clearly a much more sophisticated place than it was in the 1990s. It requires expertise that the early Web did not. In the Web's early years, using the View Source command revealed the code for the page and was the first point of education for would-be Web designers and architects. While it's still possible to do this, much more is hidden beneath the hood that is not readily apparent. On mobile apps, however, this isn't possible at all: it's a walled garden rather than an open and visible field. And to make things more complicated, our paradigms for digital media are not shaped by the information architecture of the Web, but rather by location and the personal data trails we generate. A different set of skills is necessary to code and build contemporary sites and apps—engineering skills.

This turn has consequences for the design labor force. As front-end Web development positions are increasingly filled by engineers and computer science graduates, workplace demographics begin to look more like those of computer science programs and less like those of design schools (which typically enroll more women than men): fewer women fill these roles at technology companies, and fewer still, coders of color (in 2016, 25 percent of the computing workforce is women, and fewer than 10 percent of those women are of color: 5 percent were Asian, 3 percent were African-American, and 1 percent were Latinx, according to the National Center for Women in Computing Technology).[55] To ensure a more diverse future in digital design, it will be necessary to pay attention to the architectures of race, gender, and class in education, hiring, and promotion practices. There is much work to be done.

Conclusion

Information architecture and its related practices emerged from the liminal space between multiple areas of expertise. Not quite fitting in with the concerns of graphic designers, practitioners of information architecture looked to fields outside their own to inform these practices: library science, human-computer interaction, and architecture. In so doing, they found metaphors and models on which they could build new practices for the new medium of the World Wide Web. The work of information architects reflected back on these fields. The field of library and information science related closely to the concerns of information architecture, developing research methods in tandem with the professional concerns of information architects. Likewise, information architecture intersected with the concerns of HCI research, such as in the use of ethnographic methods, as well as in the structuring of computer systems.

More importantly for our use here, information architects served as a point of translation of *architecture* to a digital world that would be radically changed by the Web. By using their version of architectural approaches, information architects made the early Web a habitable place at a time when few practicing architects saw its relevance. Information architects translate abstractions to the behind-the-scenes structures that enable digital experience. "Information architecture is the stuff that is never rendered in pixels and it's never rendered in code," says Dan Klyn, the information architect we started with at the beginning of this chapter. "Information architecture is about creating a marvelous set of abstractions that enable so many things."[56] The translation is the structuring and clarification that is necessary in the digital realm. This kind of honesty of organization of information is as vital as the honesty of material for an architect. For information architects, it is the verb of architecture.

5 Cedric Price: Responsive Architecture and Intelligent Buildings

"Technology is the answer, but what was the question?" asked British architect Cedric Price (1934–2003) in a lecture he gave by that title in London in January 1979—a question that is one of the best lenses for both understanding his work and framing its relevance. The iconoclastic architect argued that the point of architecture should not be to lock people down, but rather to open them up: "to ease up the choice, to free the opportunities of the individual user as to what they would do next," he told his audience.[1] How might architectural projects "generate new thoughts" in the minds of the people who interact with them?[2] How might architecture and technology work together, not for clarity and usability, but for some different purpose that the architect or technologist didn't predetermine? "I feel that the real definition of architecture is that which through a natural distortion of time, place, and interval creates beneficial social conditions that hitherto were considered impossible," Price said.[3] He concluded the lecture saying that "it's worth mentioning that with the advent of the microprocessor and the silicon chip more and more people are going to be in the situation where they themselves, have to decide what to do. Society, economic circumstances, will make no demands on their time, but they'll live just as long, unless they kill themselves through boredom."[4]

Price's projects, most of which weren't built, embodied the characteristics of technological and computational paradigms. The proposed Fun Palace collaboration (1963–1967) with radical theater director Joan Littlewood applied cybernetics at an architectural scale, in a building that would have learned from, responded to, and adapted with its users. The five-story multimedia Oxford Corner House (1965–1966, unbuilt), with movable floors, was an information environment with screens everywhere that were to project news and educational content. And the Generator project (1976–1979, unbuilt), a set of mobile twelve-foot cubes and walkways movable by crane, was designed to be recombined however its users wanted. Each element was to be fitted with a microcontroller and governed by a suite of computer programs. If its parts weren't moved around enough, Generator would get bored and redesign itself. These projects were decades ahead of their time and would still be radical if they were built today. Information architects and contemporary digital designers outside architecture probably are not familiar with his work. Yet his playfulness and his provocations make me wonder whether Price might be the secret patron saint of interaction designers and information architects.

Although Price's built projects weren't quite as revolutionary as the sketches and plans for some of his unbuilt work, they still were remarkable. The Snowdon Aviary at the London Zoo, designed with his friend and engineering collaborator Frank Newby, and Lord Snowdon, in 1961, features an aluminum tensegrity frame that pulls back large triangles, over which a mesh is stretched. As architect Will Alsop, who worked for Price in his early career, wrote, "It was designed for a community of birds and the idea was that once the community was established, it would be possible to remove the netting. The skin was a temporary feature: it only needed to be there long enough for the birds to begin to feel at home, and after that they would not leave anyway."[5] It is one of the few projects of Price that was built and is still standing. (The birds are still there, under the netting, too.)

And that was just it. For Price, it wasn't about the buildings themselves, it was about the interactions that they could shape, whether for the people (or birds) who used them or the architects who designed them. Compared with other architects interested in technology in the 1960s, Price's approach was different. It didn't have the graphic polish of that of his close friends at Archigram, who pushed graphic strategies and sci-fi representations of technology in projects like Walking City (a city-sized pod with legs that could walk from location to location), Plug-In City (a megastructure that would allow people in the city to plug their apartment into a different part of a huge frame), and the Cushicle and the Suitaloon, mobile, body-sized wearable environments that a person could expand when needed. Instead, Price pushed what was beneath the surface: designing provocative projects that worked through the ramifications of different technologies and the kinds of buildings, sites, and cities they produced.

Price saw enormous potential in using architecture and technology to reframe leisure and learning. Price designed buildings and architectural projects that facilitated open-ended, self-directed study. The buildings would provide a framework for learning, as would be expected, but with a twist: he designed them to learn from and respond to the people who used them. Price claimed that his Generator project was the world's first intelligent building, and perhaps it was—particularly because it actually showed how artificial intelligence could work in an architectural setting. As his friend and collaborator Royston Landau wrote, in Price's work, the purpose of technology was "to take part in the architectural debate, perhaps through contribution, disputation, or the ability to shock."[6] Price used technology as a provocation for change—change in the design process, change in how people interacted with buildings and cities, change in the status quo.

Cedric Price: A Brief Biography

Cedric John Price was born September 11, 1934, near the Staffordshire Potteries in west-central England to an upper-class mother, Doreen Emery, who came from a distinguished ceramics industry family, and a Welsh working-class father, Arthur Price. Cedric was homeschooled till age twelve because of World War II, and that educational experience helped cement his interest in unorthodox educational models. His father and uncles all worked in the field of design and were staunch leftists, qualities that shaped Cedric's own values.[7] His father Arthur went to night school to complete architectural training after his career with the Royal Marines ended. He started encouraging Cedric to design when he was eight and gave him his first book on architecture, *The Modern House in England*.[8]

Cedric completed a BA at St. John's College at Cambridge University from 1952 to 1955 and continued his studies at the Architectural Association from 1955 to 1957. He was mentored by Ernö Goldfinger, whom he assisted in the iconic exhibition, *This Is Tomorrow*, at the Institute of Contemporary Arts in 1956. Around that time, he became friends with Buckminster Fuller. Fuller's biographer said of their relationship, "I think one of the early clues that Cedric was different from other architects was that he saw something in Bucky that none of the others did. He saw beyond the images. As far as I'm concerned, Cedric is the only architect who really had any idea what Bucky was about."[9] Price founded his own practice in 1960, which he ran till he died in 2003. He taught at the Council of Industrial Design and the Architectural Association, and lectured frequently around the United Kingdom and the world.

Price was also a public figure and collaborated with many influential people over the years—a list that of course included architects, but also actors, directors, artists, and technologists. He was a dedicated member of the Labour Party, yet counted Conservative MPs as close friends.[10] Price's life partner, Eleanor Bron, is herself a well-known figure: a British film and stage actress who, in her early career, played the female lead in the Beatles movie *Help!* and whose name was the inspiration for the Beatles song "Eleanor Rigby."[11] Price's collaborators included the British theater director Joan Littlewood, and cybernetician Gordon Pask, with whom he worked on the Fun Palace and other projects, whose view on cybernetics shaped Price's interactive projects. (Pask also collaborated with Nicholas Negroponte and the MIT Architecture Machine Group.)

Cedric Price operated in the same territory as other key figures in this book, Christopher Alexander, Richard Saul Wurman, and Nicholas Negroponte. Alexander was especially interested in Price's approach to problem-solving and his cybernetic models to categorize and sort activities. Price shared the proposal for Potteries Thinkbelt with him when they met in April 1966.[12] Wurman and Price were both passionate about using architecture for new approaches to learning. They had met but didn't "know" one another, according to Wurman.[13] And although Gordon Pask worked with both Price and Negroponte, Price and Negroponte had never met.[14]

Price, however, owned a copy of Negroponte's 1995 book, *Being Digital*, now in the Canadian Centre for Architecture's collection. Price inscribed it: "GOOD—but dated."

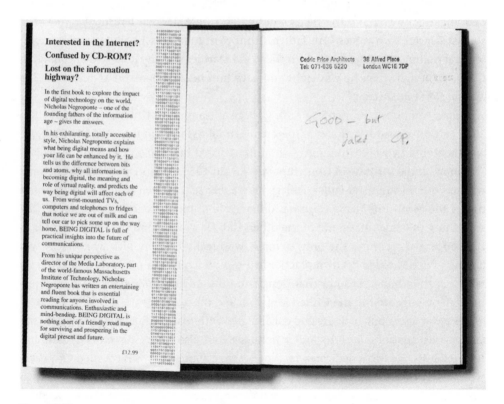

Figure 5.01
Cedric Price's copy of Nicholas Negroponte's 1995 book *Being Digital* reflects Price's opinion of Negroponte's work: "GOOD—but dated." Image courtesy of Collection Centre Canadien d'Architecture/Canadian Centre for Architecture, Montréal.

The Anti-Architect and the Anti-Building

An introduction to Cedric Price almost needs to start with the Fun Palace (1963–1967, unbuilt). The Fun Palace started as a collaboration with Price and the radical theater director Joan Littlewood, folding in many other coconspirators along the way.[15] It was an alternative theater, a leisure and learning center without a lesson plan, a cybernetic building that would respond to its visitors and modify them as they passed through it—all of those things. The Fun Palace was an anti-building, Price proclaimed, and he was CEDRIC PRICE, ANTI-ARCHITECT NO. 1," according to the letterhead that he doctored by hand for a 1964 memo about the Fun Palace.[16] If an architect was someone who created solid buildings that were constructed from long-lasting, traditional building supplies, then the anti-architect was someone who sought to understand and justify the social function and role for the architectural project, maybe not designing a building at all.

This concept of an "anti-building" is central to many of Price's projects: a framework can be reconfigured according to its users' whims and supports as many kinds of fun as possible (such as, in the Fun Palace, the ability to "exploit drinking, necking, looking, listening, shouting and resting") and that relies on the huge variety of activities to "determine the form for the site" (a form that would accommodate "water space, television and easy chairs, noise and cinema, darkness and toys, clowns and food").[17]

The Fun Palace, as in other Price projects, involved movable, modular components. Price and engineer Frank Newby strived to make as much of the Fun Palace as mobile as possible. Its components were integrated into a huge steel frame, nearly 780 feet by 360 feet, on a tartan grid that would enable the movement of portable stairways, pivoting escalators, and moving walkways.[18] Mobile gantry cranes (such as those for loading cars at a rail yard or ship's port) and cranes installed near the roof would place the ceiling, floor, and modules, and other pneumatic structures could be put in place where needed. Projection units would allow for different kinds of media spaces to be designed. Then as now, and as was the case with many of Price's projects, it's difficult to say exactly what it would have looked like. As his friend, architecture critic Reyner Banham wrote, "He may well not know [what it looks like], but that doesn't matter because it is not the point. Seven nights of the week, it will probably look like nothing on earth from the outside: the kit of service towers, lifting gantries, and building components exists solely to produce the kind of interior environments that are necessary and fitting to whatever is going on."[19]

Littlewood and Price invited cybernetician Gordon Pask, whom Price first met in the 1950s, to join the project in 1963. The introduction of cybernetics into the Fun Palace would allow the building as an organism to learn over time, anticipate the movements and desires of its visitors, and shift and change in response. Pask contributed "Proposals for a Cybernetic Theatre" that included "vehicles for a control system" that would offer new modes of audience participation.[20] From there, Pask convened the twenty-five-member Fun Palace Cybernetics Subcommittee that researched and proposed programmatic opportunities for the Fun Palace. The committee suggested using punch cards to manage resources and help avoid conflicts in the use of the space, and then learning from these patterns over time.[21] Roy Ascott, a member of the committee, even wanted to develop a "Jukebox Information System" that would accept queries from visitors and, over time, anticipate answers and develop informational pathways through the collected Jukebox responses. Later, this became the "Pillar of Information," an encyclopedia kiosk that could remember previous queries, developing its own model of the Fun Palace's visitors over time.[22]

For Pask, the Fun Palace was an opportunity to explore cybernetics at an architectural scale and to discover the social effects of such an endeavor. The committee produced a cybernetic diagram that showed how the "Input of Unmodified People" entering the Fun Palace would take part in the "Actual Network," with resulting "Output of Modified People."[23] Pask also proposed using the Fun Palace for a cybernetic study in the emotions that the space invoked, including a directive for the "determination of what is likely to induce happiness." He wrote, "In particular the issues of philosophy and theory and principle involved in determining what is likely to induce happiness and what role the organisation should play in relations to the leisure of an automated society."[24] This second notion is another example of the prescient thinking of Pask and Price. But is such thinking potentially dangerous? Consider the fact that in 2014, it came to light that the social networking platform Facebook was manipulating the amount of positive and negative content on personal news feeds in order to study the emotional impact on Facebook's users.[25] People were outraged. But in an increasingly automated world, this happens all the time. The Fun Palace modeled the possibility for it on an architectural scale decades earlier.

Price and Littlewood tried for years to get the Fun Palace built. They chased a series of potential sites and met with numerous politicians and citizen groups, only to see each possibility evaporate. By late 1966, it became clear that the Fun Palace would not succeed, but its final Mill Meads site remained empty for decades until the 2012 Olympics and is now the location of the London Aquatics Center, designed by Zaha Hadid—a rather different idea of leisure than Littlewood and Price had proposed.[26] Price did see too well what the Fun Palace inspired: the Centre Pompidou in Paris by Renzo Piano and Richard Rogers borrowed heavily from the Fun Palace design scheme, with the externalization of its structural trusses and the prominent escalators and walkways on the building's exterior. With its traditional program—a contemporary art museum—the Centre Pompidou aligned with Price's aesthetics more than his philosophy.

Price designed a smaller, less ambitious version of the Fun Palace, the Inter-Action Centre in Kentish Town, London, a local community center built in 1976. Its external trusses supported prefabricated modular components that plugged into the structure. Price never intended for any of his buildings to last forever, and he incorporated their planned obsolescence (he proudly touted his membership in Britain's National Institute of Demolition Contractors). Although some wanted to preserve the building for historic purposes, Price wouldn't support it. It was demolished in 1999. There were, however, tactical advantages to this demolitionist stance. When Price's projects were realized, such as the Inter-Action Centre, they came with problems. Mary Louise Lobsinger points out that the client contested the building's loose-fitting, off-the-shelf components, and the Inter-Action Centre's folio contains documentation of numerous complaints and legal threats.[27] Price's famous interest in planned obsolescence could also have to do with the fact that an architect in the United Kingdom can be held responsible for a building's faults in perpetuity—potentially even after the architect's death.[28]

Serious Fun and Games

Price's writings, drawings, notes, and projects are often wickedly funny, full of colorful metaphors. Architecture is eating, cooking, consuming, and digesting; it is a network, a computer, a brain; it is a game; it is play. While the work of the architect was structured—Price was very prompt, particular, and organized, as his friend Paul Finch wrote—the practice and process didn't need to be staid or fusty.[29]

Price took play seriously. This commitment to fun was not married to any single project, it was part of how he approached life, as numerous people recount in their stories about him. The first page of the book *Cedric Price Opera* is imprinted with his Hot Stuff Club President stamp (he, of course, was president; his brother and close friends and associates were the members). He started many clubs, and the Hot Stuff Club met for lunches that "were not to be believed," said Barbara Jakobson, a trustee of the Museum of Modern Art and collaborator with Price on the Generator project. Jakobson was one of two special overseas members and was given the title "Vole"; the vice-president always had to eat stuffed cabbage, she said.[30]

But this fun served a purpose: shifting perspectives, changing the playing field, revealing the dark underbelly. "Designing for delight and pleasure should very seldom be seen to happen, and must encompass—indeed nurture—doubt, danger, mystery and magic. . . . Distortion of time, space and substance is as necessary a design tool for pleasure as it is for religious architecture," Price told his audience in a 1989 lecture at the Architectural Association.[31] Warping the rules, processes, and materials could alter things enough to "generate pleasure," he said—as long as it wasn't taken too far. "Wonder is very tricky to design for, since it can usually be experienced only once," he said.[32]

One way to view Price's architectural practice is as an infinite game. Infinite games are played not to determine a winner or loser, but rather "for the purposes of continuing the play," as James Carse defined the term.[33] "Infinite players cannot say when their game began, nor do they care. They do not care for the reason that their game is not bounded by time. Indeed, the only purpose of the game is to prevent it from coming to an end, to keep everyone in play," Carse wrote.[34] Price introduced new rules to the architectural game, whether with the charts he made that poked fun at his clients or the responsive buildings that he proposed could not only be modified by their users, but could modify the users themselves, or even get bored of them. These rules extended architecture beyond the bounds of a building or a drawing's ordinary situation in time and space, changing their relationships with the people who designed and interacted with them.

The projects by Price that I introduce in this chapter are not just about representing information and computation in architecture. They also serve as a critique of social concerns and architectural practice, and engage in playful dynamics as a means for achieving subversive aims (albeit benevolently subversive ones). Moreover, these projects show Price's interest in architecture capable of educating and transforming its users by being changeable, not immutable. Although I touch briefly on some of Price's better-known projects, such as the Fun Palace and Potteries Thinkbelt, I concentrate on two projects that more explicitly represent networks and information systems: the Oxford Corner House Feasibility Study ("OCH," 1965–1966, unbuilt) and Generator (1976–1979, unbuilt). I contrast the centralized model of OCH with the distributed network of Generator. In these projects, it is apparent that Price "redesigned the figure of the architect," as Mark Wigley wrote.[35] In developing new programs, not only for the projects in front of him, Cedric Price broke apart traditional notions of architectural practice.[36]

Architectural Machines for Teaching and Conversing

It was not unlike a search engine designed as a building, if such technologies had existed in 1965. Cedric Price proposed an interactive, building-sized computer in the middle of London, an "information hive" and "teaching machine" in a once-famous restaurant run by J. Lyons & Co.[37] The Oxford Corner House (OCH) Feasibility Study (1965–1966,

Figure 5.02
Vellum sketches in pen over photographs of the Oxford Corner House. Left: the planetarium and upper floors. Center: the planetarium building out from the OCH on the left (recognizable from "HOUSE" on the facade). Right: the undoctored image. Image courtesy of Collection Centre Canadien d'Architecture/Canadian Centre for Architecture, Montréal.

unbuilt) was a proposal for an enormous information network, open twenty-four hours a day, with a capacity of seven thousand people. In Price's plans for OCH, news and images entered the building on chugging teleprinters, as closed-circuit TV cameras broadcast their output on hundreds of screens throughout the building. Hydraulic floors moved up and down on demand to create three-dimensional information spaces, and a powerful IBM System/360 computer in the basement, run by dozens of computer operators, stored and delivered individualized media and information to dial-up information carrels—a concept so experimental, it wouldn't even be fully invented for another five years. On the roof, OCH would have a planetarium that illuminated a starscape; in the basement, people could learn to drive on car-driving simulators. "The possibilities are limitless and will be constantly changing," Price wrote.[38]

The OCH project site was the Lyons Oxford Corner House restaurant on Tottenham Court Road at Oxford Street in London, built in 1928 and formerly a grand restaurant and dining complex. J. Lyons & Co., one of the largest catering and food companies in Europe, opened the five-location Corner House chain in 1909. Each of the chain's facilities offered opulent dining and sold J. Lyons's products and services (tea, hams, pastries, candies, and even hairdressing, theater booking, and food delivery to anywhere in

London) on the ground floor of the Corner Houses. The Corner House waitresses—called Nippies for their speed and nimbleness—achieved iconic status in pre–World War II London film and mass media. When Oxford Corner House originally opened, each of its four floors had restaurants with live orchestras, a total capacity of up to 2,200 customers at a time, and, for some of its years, operated around the clock—and it wasn't even the biggest or busiest Corner House restaurant.[39] By the 1960s, however, the British palate and tastes for leisure had changed, and the once grand Corner Houses had lost their luster.[40] Yet J. Lyons & Co. had much to gain in a successful renovation of the Oxford Corner House: the restaurant occupied a prime location in central London, its potential customer base was growing to the tune of fifteen thousand a year, and, moreover, the thirty-two-story Centre Point development, a concrete skyscraper designed by Richard Seifert, would only increase traffic to the area.[41]

Why Cedric Price for the project? After hearing about the Fun Palace, Patrick Salmon, the son of J. Lyons & Co. director Samuel Salmon, approached Price "to see whether such a scheme could be fitted into the Oxford Corner House." He wrote, "I think that there is an enormous potential in catering for the leisure activities of the populace and that we could well be letting a new social pattern if we went ahead with this scheme, as original as the Teashops were at the turn of the century."[42] The ten-month, £20,000 feasibility project took place from October 1965 to August 1966 and focused on research and concept development (it did not advance to a design or construction phase, and so there are no construction drawings for the project as there are for Generator, for example). The ideas that J. Lyons & Co.'s directors came up with on their own weren't a bad starting point: a center for gardening, skeet, cookery advice, a gin palace, a slightly racy Playboy Club, or even a computer-simulated sport center with pretend glider piloting.[43] Price, however, reframed the problem, as he tended to do. He suggested that OCH should aim

to establish a unique pleasure place providing constantly changing conditions and facilities for self-participatory leisure activities ranging from eating and drinking to self-pace learning and involvement with world news.

The people's nerve centre or City Brain must, through its design, provide the excitement, delight and satisfaction that a 20th century metropolis should offer—Piccadilly Circus and Hampstead Heath are not enough.[44]

The nerve center would amplify the density of one of central London's busiest corners in order to maximize civic connection and transformation through the delivery of information. As Price wrote in the OCH Feasibility Study Report, "The whole building is a vast teaching machine."[45]

Teaching Machines

Price's plans for OCH supported his view of education as a self-motivated, leisure-time activity enabled by communication technology. At the same time Price was completing the OCH study, he was also inventing and writing about novel ways that mobile architecture and communication technology could be used for education—with OCH as a "self-pace public skill and information hive" that was framed explicitly as a learning project, "unfettered by tradition, scholastic, economic, academic or other class strictures."[46]

OCH was influenced by a major project Price was working on during the same period. The Potteries Thinkbelt (PTb, as Price abbreviated it, 1964–1966, unbuilt) was a recombinable, modular university on rails, the plans for which Price shared and discussed with Christopher Alexander when they met. The Thinkbelt proposed a twenty thousand–student campus that would use portable, flexible building components that ran on rail infrastructure. The location for the Thinkbelt, the North Staffordshire Potteries, was the center of England's ceramic production for 250 years, producing well-known china and porcelain by Wedgwood, Minton, and many others.[47] (It was also just a few miles from where Price grew up.) After World War II, the area was economically depressed and polluted and lacked advanced technical education. Price hoped that PTb would bring a long-term reinvention of the region in the shape of research and knowledge, setting off a "catalytic effect."[48] By living with the students and being surrounded by learning initiatives, he wrote, "people will begin to demand an even bigger improvement in their socio-civic environment, and the entrepreneurial instinct will be awakened by the demand."[49]

PTb would combine mobile units along rail and transfer lines that had previously serviced the porcelain trade. Teaching would take place along the "Thinkbelt faculty areas," with modular structures for education of different kinds: seminars, self-study carrels, storage units for communication equipment, and "fold-out inflatable units" that supported lecture spaces for television or larger demonstrations. The modular housing units were to house both students and local residents awaiting housing, the "sprawl" (for families), the "crate" (a tower that the crates would plug into once moved by mobile crane), the hermetically sealed "battery" housing unit, and the one-to-two-person "capsule," which could be used as temporary housing. None of these housing ideas were new to architecture—the Metabolists in Japan, as well as Price's friends in Archigram, investigated and sometimes built such living spaces—but the combination of all of them along rail lines and for education was Price's own invention.

Unfortunately, the demand for PTb didn't arise. Price put forth his plans for the Thinkbelt at the same time as planning commenced for the Open University, which intended to deliver education over the airwaves on the radio and television. There was no real client for Price's project, and although he published its plans, those interested in new educational models supported Open University instead.[50]

Potteries Thinkbelt is important for how it architecturally reenvisioned education, information, and communication. The history of the rail network, after all, is one of piggybacking technologies: the telegraph wires followed the rail circuits in the mid-nineteenth century. In a sense, Price was also piggybacking technologies to his own ends. "The Potteries Thinkbelt proposed a new informational model of architecture, a landscape/network whose algorithmic and fluid, self-regulating behaviour mirrored the character of post-industrial information technologies. The mobile units were like information quanta, the switches and transfer stations like the logical gateways of a vast computer circuit," Stanley Mathews writes.[51]

A Centralized Information Machine

Where Potteries Thinkbelt was a plan for a distributed educational network across an entire region, OCH centralized these activities into a single body for the consumption of information. Price wrote that OCH would become

a centre for the ingestion, digestion and regurgitation of Information, on demand—Information for and available to, specific purpose, space-place and time.

Selection Feed-back
Display Retrieval
Distribution Evaluation
Storage Comparison

. . . In effect, the total and imaginative use of such techniques will introduce a new dimension to public enjoyment of metropolitan life, since it eliminates the need for movement and physical separation in order to achieve varied particular aims. In doing so it introduces new relationships between activities and individuals hitherto unimagined.[52]

The nervous and muscular system, too, extended outside the building, in keeping with the idea of "the people's nerve centre or City Brain" that Price proposed at the beginning of the project."[53] It integrated with the "physical communication network" of London, putting a lens on the experience of London as an urban hub and its relation to the world. Maximizing the traffic into OCH meant the possibility of maximizing the informational density, user activities, and circulatory action of people moving through the building. The urban fabric became part of the communication network that fed OCH, its nerves the lines of communication into and out of OCH, and the muscles the physical communication network—the traffic and transportation network over London, as numerous charts and maps for the project show.[54] Ideally, infrastructural range would bring more people into OCH: Price even investigated the possibility of an exor-bitantly expensive subterranean link between the OCH and the London Underground station at Tottenham Court Road.

Visitors to the Oxford Corner House would be surrounded by news and information on screens meeting the users from almost every vantage point. The further up into OCH one went, the more granular information would be available—that is, information on the lower level would serve larger audiences, smaller groups on the second and third floors, and individuals in study carrels on the upper floors. News monitors would dis-play "instantaneous news" on the first two floors, highlighting selected world, United Kingdom, and government news on a two- to four-hour cycle selected by OCH's edito-rial staff. Small group and individual "informational and audio-visual retrieval and dis-play" would reside on OCH's third and fourth floors, and carrels for individuals on the fourth, with editorial management and serving of content from computers, teleprinters, and a TV studio in the basement.[55] The OCH would offer news from all major British newspapers and television channels, as well as police, city, and government informa-tion, educational activities, conference facilities, exhibitions, and computer services via the public telephone network.[56]

The process of defining and mapping the information sources to the building was similar to conducting systems analysis in computing, only at the scale of a building. In this analysis, Price's office determined the sources for the content, associated them with activities and their locations in OCH, designed the network infrastructures, and developed the circulation flow and interface placements through sets of drawings. The modalities of the information (its type, frequency and amount) and requirements for transmission, storage, retrieval, and delivery determined the circulation patterns, screen placement, and modular, movable floors that made up the design of OCH.

Contributing to these activities was a study of communication dynamics in audi-ences large and small, in which Price's staff diagrammed interactions between people as an input into OCH's plan. Each type of exchange is accompanied by a sketch that shows the dynamics of communication and how participants would interact with one another. How might they pool, exchange or disseminate information, or "provide a sparkpoint for an open forum discussion?"[57] His office then used these communica-tion dynamics in the design of OCH's screens, through layer after layer of tissue paper drawings. The first floor supported big audiences with large screens, the second floor's screen density suggested that people might move through and look at whatever they walked past. Escalator flow studies outlined how people would circulate through the building without creating traffic jams or blockages. The upper floors of OCH rested on movable plates, powered by hydraulics that allowed them to be moved up and down to

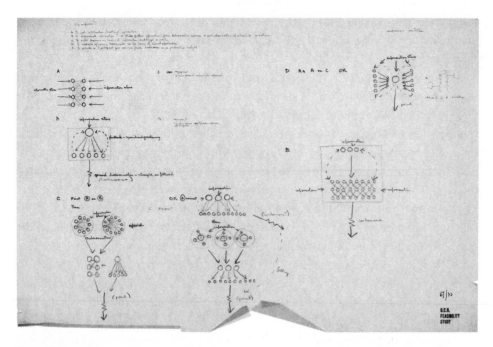

Figure 5.03
Price's office developed diagrams to explore models of information exchange and interpersonal dynamics, which in turn were used to determine the locations and density of screens throughout the Oxford Corner House. Image courtesy of Collection Centre Canadien d'Architecture/Canadian Centre for Architecture, Montréal.

create different information-screen-floor configurations within the space that accommodated different sizes of audiences. Combined plan/section drawings showed the focal reach of Eidophor screens through the building, a device that projected television images at the scale of a movie theater screen.[58]

In addition to viewing information at a distance on monitors or circulating through it by moving through the building, OCH's visitors would be able to retrieve and peruse it at close range, on their own initiative on smaller screens or in study carrels. The Oxford Corner House would contain as many as four hundred carrels that could deliver words, speech, still pictures, and moving pictures.[59] The carrels, designed by Sol Cornberg and used in the 1964–1965 World's Fair, had headphones, a microphone, speaker, and telephone handset that were used to receive and transmit speech; a monitor for receiving words and still and moving pictures; and a dial and keyboard for retrieving information from the computer and videofile system; two printers could give the user a printout of the session.[60] Cameras, too, would have provided the transmission for information called up on a computer, since at that time it was not possible to network computers to monitors throughout the building. Price wrote that the full media capabilities of OCH would support a new approach to teaching and learning. "[It] seems unnecessary . . . to use the conventional aids, such as teaching machines, language laboratories, etc., in each of the carrels. Language instructors, teachers, lecturers and conference speakers will have the information storage facilities of OCH to draw upon, and it would be possible in each case to relay both sound and pictures from the TV studio to any number of carrels," he wrote.[61]

Information Networks

To deliver the informational content, the OCH would have been filled with telephone and telegraph lines and closed-circuit TV lines snaking throughout the building—an enormous and complex undertaking. Much of the news transmission would take place from cameras mounted over teleprinters that broadcast their activity throughout the building. A camera mounted over each teleprinter would transmit news to up to 240 monitors throughout OCH, selected and switched by the editorial staff, changing on a five-minute cycle, or by visitor request. The proposed scale was massive: for news alone, twenty-one different newspapers—from thirteen news organizations—and four news agencies, each with their own teleprinters, would transmit words and images to the OCH's director of communications newsroom twenty-four hours a day via dedicated telegraph line, each printing onto its own teleprinter.[62] Similar network models were proposed for police information, Greater London, and United Kingdom government information and educational content. The full spectrum of information transmission and display comes together in a detailed drawing of all of OCH's networks: flows of words, still and moving pictures, thirty teleprinters with cameras, sixteen IBM display terminals and numerous other technologies making up its nervous system (Figure 5.04b). The staff to run the communications department would have been enormous. An organizational chart that Price included specified no fewer than 125 employees, not counting administrative or secretarial staff.

The Computer Brain of OCH

Turning the Oxford Corner House restaurant into a computerized learning and information hub was a more fitting concept than it might initially seem. It is clear that the capture and storage of news would have required a large computer system, and so Price's office sought a proposal from IBM for a computer to manage OCH's information stores. But before approaching IBM, they considered using a LEO (Lyons Electronic

a.

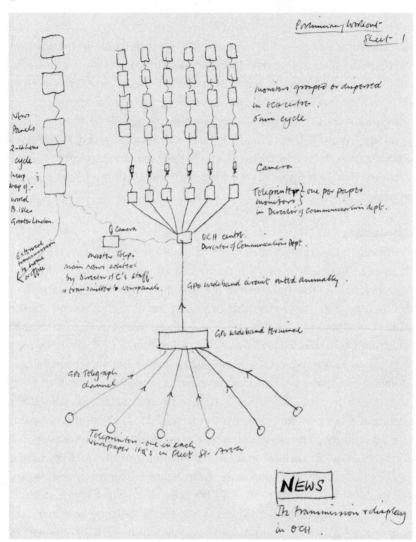

Figure 5.04a and 5.04b

Price's office produced detailed network diagrams showing how information would be transmitted into OCH from news organizations. From the bottom of the diagram: teleprinters would transmit via telegram into the OCH Director of Communications Office (small square, center) to teleprinters within OCH. Cameras trained on the teleprinters would then transmit their news throughout the building to monitors (squiggly lines and rectangles) and bigger screens (larger rectangles on left). The more detailed Communications Diagram shows the entire, gigantic information network for OCH, with thirty teleprinters, sixteen IBM displays, and the broadcast of words and images from outside into and throughout the building. Image courtesy of Collection Centre Canadien d'Architecture/Canadian Centre for Architecture, Montréal. The Communications Diagram Image courtesy of Collection Centre Canadien d'Architecture/Canadian Centre for Architecture, Montréal.

b.

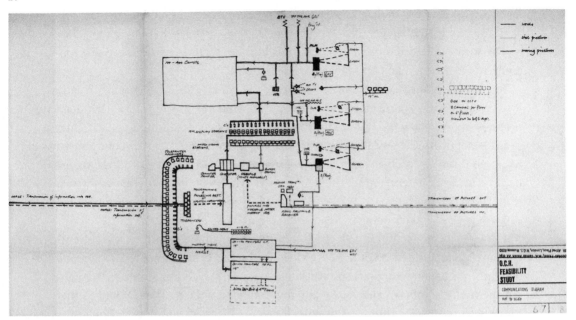

Office)—the world's first business computer, originally developed at J. Lyons & Co. The LEO computer started operation in 1951. It calculated inventory, payroll, and stock, and managed the bakery runs for J. Lyons & Co. LEO spun out as an independent company in 1954 and provided calculations for clients such as Ford Motor and the Ministry of Pensions. Even though it was no longer a part of J. Lyons & Co., the LEO remained a point of pride for the company.[63]

In 1966, when the OCH project started, few systems existed that would be robust enough to store, process, and transmit the amount of information OCH proposed. The first possibility Price's office considered was J. Lyons & Co.'s own LEO computer at their Cadby Hall headquarters, but not enough space remained on it, and so Price approached IBM. In his request for a proposal, he wrote, "Some of this information (and in time perhaps a very large amount of it) will have to be stored for future retrieval and display, and this, along with the question of how to control, code, and store a lot of incoming information, will form an important part of the feasibility study."[64] IBM proposed using an IBM System/360. The computer would take up a large part of the OCH's basement, both for all of its hardware consoles, drives, and terminals and for the dozens of humans that it would take to operate it.[65] It would have cost £844,000 if purchased outright, or £17,500 a month if rented, plus £50,000 for "special engineering facilities."[66] In pounds today, that would be equivalent to £14.77 million to purchase and £306,250 a month to rent. Those costs did not account for the labor, either: the IBM would have required twenty analysts to program it and at least that many to operate it. The sheer scale of information storage would have required two years of development, not to mention an enormous implementation budget.

In addition to the IBM System/360 computer, for storing still and moving images, Price's collaborator (and creator of British 3-D cinema) Raymond Spottiswoode proposed using a videofile system, in which pictures were stored in individual frames of a videotape—itself a radically new approach to image storage.[67] Spottiswoode himself had been inventing such a system that he proposed for OCH but learned that Ampex had one in development and specified it instead.[68] The videofile system alone—which would not be commercially available until 1969—was estimated to cost between £70,000 to £250,000 (or between £1.25 million and £4.38 million today).

Pause on the scope of this collaboration for just a second: the father of British 3-D cinema collaborating on a cutting-edge videofile system, to be delivered throughout a building by a gigantic computer installation, networked to information stores throughout the country, and experienced by moving through a building. The Oxford Corner House proposal was a multimedia machine.

A Conversational Machine

One aspect of Price's research for OCH was into the future of networks and information services. This research informed both the design of OCH and Price's thoughts on the potential for electronic learning systems. Two articles particularly informed the OCH project: "Computer Libraries" by Nigel Calder in *New Statesman* and "Towards an Information Utility" by John Laski in *New Scientist*.

"Computer Libraries" introduced the problems of interacting with information in an electronic system. Calder, the editor of the *New Scientist* (and who became one of England's best-known science writers) wrote that if we wanted to design systems that actually achieved human–computer symbiosis, "we have to give a lot of attention to the way we ourselves think. The problems become as much a matter of philosophy as of electronics."[69] The possibility of a library producing the exact, perfect search result could change the joy of reading and browsing. He wrote, "As users of books and libraries also know, there is a virtue in browsing. It is hard to imagine how a computer programme can provide the serendipity familiar to every book-lover."[70] Calder referred to MIT's experiment with such a system, Project MAC, a system that allowed multiple users to log in to a central computer from distant terminals (a project I detail in the next chapter). The question was, were people as ready for these advances as the technology was? "Behind it all is the problem I stated at the outset, and this can be paraphrased as understanding between men and machines," Calder wrote.[71]

If Price followed Calder's wisdom, then it's possible to imagine him devising OCH to permit people to both browse and pinpoint information they wanted to find. By circulating through the floors and moving between the screens, OCH's visitors would experience the serendipity of browsing. By sitting down at a carrel and dialing up information (suggested in another article he referenced: the National Computing Centre's "world index of computer information which could be made available for the price of a phone call," according to a 1966 article he included in this report from the *Times*) a visitor could find exactly what he or she sought.[72] Price also accounted for another consideration raised by Calder: the labor of cataloging and indexing information so that it could be found—which became the Information Storage project that Price's office pursued.[73]

The article "Towards an Information Utility," by John Laski, put forth a vision of the future that came to pass, in which computers, networks, and information would be widely available to everybody:

By 1996 computing power should be used by everyone as casually as energy is today. Access to computing power will be as widely distributed as electricity, and the wealth and well-being of the country will be dependent on the availability of adequate supplies. On the monopoly that will supply computing power for bulk transformation, storage and retrieval of information and for diffusion of information, will depend the quality of life for every member of the community. And the nation that first makes available computing power to its citizens as a public information Utility in this way will dominate the world economy just as the steam engine allowed Britain to dominate the world throughout Victoria's reign.[74]

Laski envisioned a "conversational machine" positioned between a user at a keyboard and an "immense national batch processor serving all regions."[75] From his perspective in 1966, the concept did not seem that far off—as early as the 1970s, if planning began soon. Laski's ideas sound similar to those of a young Nicholas Negroponte in his book *The Architecture Machine*. Laski predicted easy to use, personal interfaces for the Information Utility: "For output, there would be something as light, easy to read and pleasant to handle as a well-printed paperback. Perhaps I could be extravagant and get one with colour and discrimination as good as a coffee-table art book." There were many possibilities for Great Britain to succeed at building an information utility that could serve into the future—if only it weren't scuttled by British bureaucracy, Laski wrote.[76]

Was OCH perhaps the conversational machine that Laski envisioned? From its position at the center of a network and the social considerations it made, the idea seems

entirely plausible. OCH the conversational machine was a set of lenses that would capture and focus information for its users, on one end, connecting them to the country
at large—and, through the network, each other—on the other.

In the Oxford Corner House Feasibility Study, Price proposed an interactive, responsive building that aligned different instances of information and media. Different routes
would reveal different kinds of information, textual and graphical, moving and still,
to be experienced in shared and solo settings. The delivery of networked information
would be the spectacle, the experience coming together as the visitor moved through
the building. It is a physical and rudimentary analog, circa 1966, of what happens today
when we click on a link or type in an URL for a web page and its elements come together
across time and space to be constituted on the screen at that moment. It is similar to how
Katherine Hayles described the constitution of an electronic text. "Indeed, it does not
exist as an artifact at all. Rather, it comes into existence as a process that includes the
data files, the programs that call these files, and the hardware on which the programs
run, as well as the optical fibers, connections, switching algorithms, and other devices
necessary to route the text from one networked computer to another," she writes of
this set of electronic processes.[77] What kind of computer was OCH? As we have seen,
the OCH is a centralizing, localizing, urbanizing information machine. In the ways
that the OCH was proposed to store, transmit, and process information, it was a computer, to follow Friedrich Kittler's definition. In his book *Optical Media*, Kittler wrote,
"All technical media either store, transmit, or process signals and . . . the computer . . .
is the only medium that combines these three functions—storage, transmission, and
processing—fully automatically."[78] In OCH, Price designed the material experience,
in which a person moving through space would see information coming together at
a particular point in time. Except that OCH itself was a process, not a thing—a study,
not a constructed building. The sum of the work of OCH, to follow Hayles, "comes into
existence as a process," one that includes drawings, texts, articles, analyses, models,
and conversations.[79]

Price delivered the OCH Feasibility Study Report in September 1966. A 1967 news
clipping shared the actual fate of the Oxford Corner House:

The famous Lyons Corner House at the junction of Oxford Street and Tottenham Court Road is
to change hands.

The premises are being taken over from J. Lyons, the £70 million tea shop and catering concern, on a 99-years lease by Mecca.

Mecca, whose main interests are in dance halls, catering and bingo, will move in on June 1.
They have applied for planning permission to transform the Corner House into an entertainment
and catering centre.[80]

In an ironic twist, the purchase of the site by Mecca speaks in direct contradiction to Price's design brief from the year before, in which he wrote, "The necessary balancing of the programmed contents must avoid producing an entertainment 'Mecca'—rather it should create a 'launching pad' for further activities, interests and delight."[81] Like many of Price's projects, the prescience of his project became apparent decades after the fact. An obituary for John Pinkerton, the electrical engineer who co-led the team that designed the LEO, noted, "With his unfailing good humour, he would have enjoyed the thought of a LEO computer doing stock-control for a Lyons Corner House as the forerunner of a personal computer in a cybernet cafe."[82] Pinkerton probably did not know just how close he might have come.

Generator

Cedric Price's Generator (1976–1979, unbuilt) was an experiment in creating the conditions for shifting, changing personal interaction within responsive, reconfigurable architecture. A kit of parts, Generator consisted of 150 twelve-foot by twelve-foot mobile cubes, catwalks, screens, and boardwalks, all of which could be moved by mobile crane as desired by users. Generator was intended for small groups of visitors to Howard Gilman's White Oak Plantation on the coastal Georgia-Florida border. Since a retreat site composed of mobile, responsive components would likely prove to be an unfamiliar concept to its users, Price incorporated two social roles, "Polariser" and "Factor," to catalyze on-site interpersonal dynamics and logistical requirements. In addition, his collaboration with programmer/architects John and Julia Frazer stepped up this notion; they argued that Generator "should have a mind of its own."[83]

Price took responsiveness further with Generator than he did with the Fun Palace: it would become the first intelligent building, as Landau, Price, and Frazer have suggested.[84] "This scheme, the Generator, explores the notion of artificial intelligence, in which the environment itself becomes an intelligent artefact," Royston Landau wrote,[85] adding that it was "one of the first major investigations into an artificially intelligent architecture," and acknowledging the importance of Negroponte and the MIT Architecture Machine Group's work in this arena.[86] Landau even suggested "if the concept of artificial intelligence had not been created, then Cedric Price would have had to invent it."[87] More than an intelligent building, Generator was a vision for a networked site that could learn from and challenge its users. It is a different kind of configuration than we see in contemporary smart buildings, where "smart" typically refers to building operations and response to environmental, electrical, or security-related data. Generator was a model for distributed intelligence in built form.

Site, Menus, Cubes, Paths, and Barriers

The White Oak Plantation was a forest and wetland environment on the coastal border of Florida and Georgia, marked by slash pines, tall and slender with a fringe of needles on top. The Gilman family acquired the property in the 1930s, and in the 1970s, Howard Gilman sought ideas for the plantation that would support the arts, dance, and his other philanthropic pursuits. The napkin brief of the project read,

A building which will not contradict, but enhance, the feeling of being in the middle of nowhere; has to be accessible to the public as well as to private guests; has to create a feeling of seclusion conducive to creative impulses, yet . . . accommodate audiences; has to respect the wildness of the environment while accommodating a grand piano; has to respect the continuity of the history of the place while being innovative.[88]

The goal of Generator was to get its visitors to change it around, to get the mobile crane operator to move the cubes and walkways to suit a new activity. In order to model Generator's constant changeability, Price designed "menus": preconfigurations of Generator layouts of cube, screen, and path groupings that could be set up on the White Oak Plantation site. The menus got Price away from the requirement of determining a single instance of Generator; this way, he could provide many. These arrangements were the baseline narrative for the possibilities of Generator and its potential stories. The menu that awaited a user was one of many possible layouts.

To determine the menus, Price used two kinds of tools: questionnaires and a game. He asked Gilman to hand out a set of questionnaires for "remembering things you once wanted to do, never did, but now might have the chance to do with the help of GENERATOR," as the directions explained, and to hold onto the questionnaires afterward "to see if GENERATOR lives up to your aspirations.[89] On the "Activity Compatibility" questionnaire, for example, a user listed in a column all the activities that one might do with Generator and then compared each activity and marked whether it was compatible, neutral, or noncompatible. The responses ranged from serious to banal, including swimming, walking, bird watching, making love, sleeping, having a shit, and repairing a radio, to name a few responses.[90] His respondents then listed structural and architectural requirements that would support the desired activities, and then his office tallied the results into a master chart and presented to Gilman a list that excluded some of the more colorful suggestions but that indicated that Generator's users would want to read, enjoy music and dancing, go swimming, use a workshop, or even fell trees in the forest.

In translating these requirements to the initial menus, Price used the "Three Peg Game" to open the menus to chance, in which two players take turns trying to form a line of three pegs of the same color ("a mill"), vertically, horizontally, or diagonally; the game is won when the opponent can't make a move. Finally, the potential menus

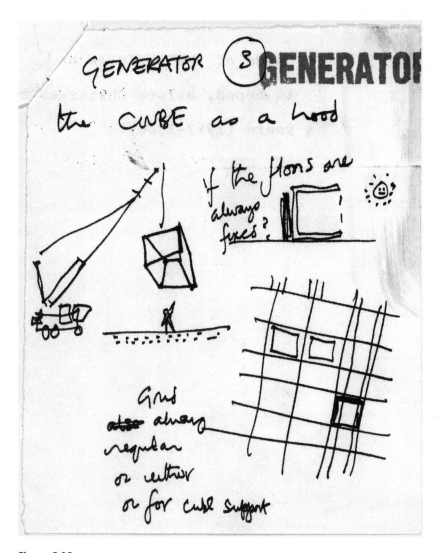

Figure 5.05

Price worked through some of Generator's elements, including the mobile crane, grid, floors, and cube supports in this sketch. "The CUBE as a hood," "if the floors are always fixed?" and possibilities for cube support. Image courtesy of Collection Centre Canadien d'Architecture/Canadian Centre for Architecture, Montréal.

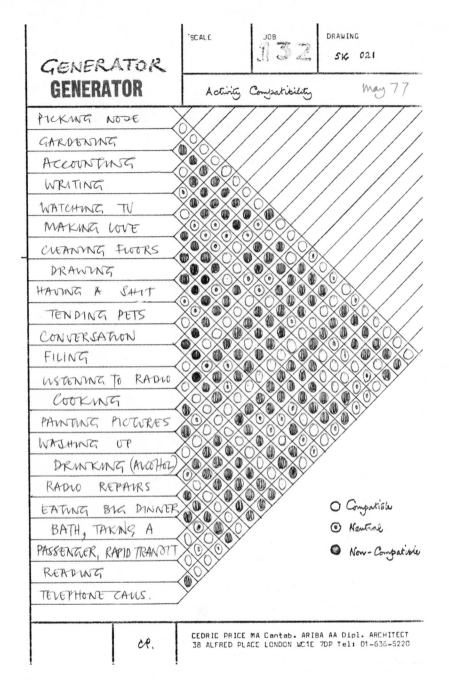

Figure 5.06

A completed Activity Compatibility questionnaire. The respondent was asked to think of all the activities he or she might like to do with Generator, then compare them against one another. The layouts of Generator's original menus were based in part on these compatibility questionnaires. Image courtesy of Collection Centre Canadien d'Architecture/Canadian Centre for Architecture, Montréal.

could be tried out with a set of blocks that looked like Legos: off-the-shelf plastic "Cubit" blocks and Plexiglas screens, laid out on a board that corresponded to the site and stored in cigar boxes when finished.

Ever fond of alimentary metaphors, Price said of the menus, in an interview with Hans Ulrich Obrist,

In defining architecture, you don't necessarily define the consumption of it. All the designs we did for Generator were written as menus, and then we would draw the menu, and because I like bacon and eggs for breakfast, it was all related to that bit of bacon and that bit of egg; they were all drawn, however cartoon-like, in the same order—not in the order the chef or cook would arrange them on your plate, but in the order in which the consumer would eat them. And that is related to the consumption or usefulness of architecture, not the dispenser of it.[91]

Price sketched Generator as a "limiting sausage," "extruding sausage," and "egg" to explain the menu concept. These menus recall his ideas of indeterminacy and conditioning: a cook can organize breakfast however he or she likes on a plate, but it is up to the person eating the food to arrange each bite. It was the same with architecture, in Price's view: how it is used a matter of personal choice and use.

While Price made hundreds of drawings for Generator, there is no single representation that captures it clearly. Looking at the sketches and menus of cubes, walkways, and their position on the landscape is like thumbing through a flip-book without the intermediate frames, each sketch a different, potential moment of Generator. The elements circumscribing the perspective are not stable, making it difficult to determine positioning: Is the viewer inside a cube peering out, or is the square a portal onto the landscape in front? Other playful drawings by Price's office show pneumatic cubes, eyeball cubes, and cubes of different materials, such as tile, while other drawings show the cubes being built up, constructed, or overgrown with weeds.

Given that there were 150 cubes and many drawings exploring their uses, it would seem that they were the most important aspect of the site. But Price's texts about Generator indicate that the boardwalks and catwalks that snaked around the site were equally, if not more, important than the cubes because they represented mobility and change. In "An Essay on Paths," Price described what a visitor to Generator would experience. "Tension is created by only certain groups of cubes being accessible by the b/ws [boardwalks]. Questions are begged.—Why does the path only link certain cubes? Are these cubes of lesser or greater significance? What else does the path do? What is it for if not a linking system?"[92] Generator's paths are like a flow of information, one in which the user is the informational packet, the message in transmission—an update of the ideas in the Oxford Corner House Feasibility Project ten years prior. Price continued, "Hence ambiguity is created by the well defined directive path being a facility for more than

a.

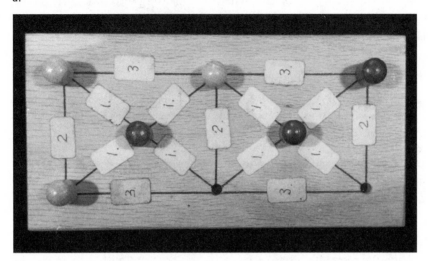

b.

Figure 5.07
Generator's design was also left open to chance: the Three-Peg Game was used in part to determine Generator's initial menus. Image courtesy of John Frazer.

simple communication. It can accommodate changes of pace. One may loiter, stop and sit or stand or one may indeed enter a cube. It is a USABLE path."[93] The path didn't make a directed flow of information; it represented possibilities and distribution, or different flows over time. A third set of components, screens and barriers, complicated the paths in Generator. They hung from rails and masts, cutting diagonals across the site. Price never committed to what they would be constructed from: perhaps canvas or panels woven from palm fronds on site. They supported Generator's ambiguity, encouraging the visitors to go different directions, to do different things, to change Generator to be more to their liking.

Price intended for users to question their own paths as they followed those of Generator, another example of challenging the roles of the architect and the user in Generator's consumption. One study for the menus told little stories around the intersections and angles of the paths that give indications of plot: "V.G. WALK AROUND TO ALL THE ANGLES," and "EXCELLENT. FULL OF EVENT+TAUT ACTION," read two statements in red permanent marker above the purple paths.

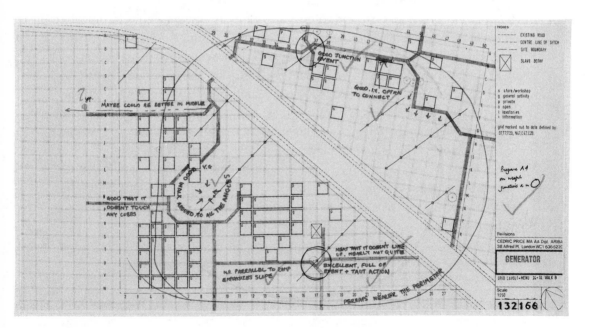

Figure 5.08
Grid layout, menu 24, with notations such as "V.G. Walk around to all the angles," and "Excellent. Full of event+taut action," in red permanent marker above Generator's purple paths. Image courtesy of Collection Centre Canadien d'Architecture/Canadian Centre for Architecture, Montréal.

The angles would have made for a more interesting wander around Generator; the intersections represented the possibilities for interpersonal connection or serendipity on the path. The paths, metaphorically speaking, asked questions that the users were to answer. If menus challenged the architect, then paths would challenge users in a friendly manner, causing them to question the ideas that they brought to Generator and spur them to see what else it could do.

The Social Generator

Generator was a social machine, designed to foster creative relationships. The project would not have come to be if not for Price developing relationships with arts patrons such as Howard Gilman, CEO of Gilman Paper Company; curator Pierre Apraxine; and collector Barbara Jakobson, who each not only funded the project but also played a role within it.[94] Price met Jakobson, a talented art collector and dealer who was a trustee at the Museum of Modern Art, in 1976.[95] Jakobson already had exhibited Price's drawings in the 1975 Architectural Studies and Projects show in the penthouse at MoMA, which she oversaw and Emilio Ambasz curated.[96] Price, Gilman, and Apraxine flew to the White Oak Plantation in 1976, and Gilman asked Price to "design a versatile building that could accommodate a somewhat contradictory program," Apraxine said. Before Price had an idea of what Generator would look like or be composed of, he and Jakobson collaborated on its program through letters, postcards, and in-person meetings in London and New York. It was no easy task, as Jakobson said. "His process was unbelievable—it was very hard," she said. "He would exhaust you into thinking, as he would say, 'Well maybe you don't need a new building; maybe you need a new wife. Maybe you need a walk in the park.'"[97] Or maybe you need a Generator.

How would people know how to engage Generator? From the beginning of its design, Price included two human roles to catalyze Generator's use, which he named "Polariser" and "Factor." Their job was to encourage interpersonal dynamics and manage logistical requirements. Price offered the following "zany definitions":

POLARISER—Modifies vibrations giving unity of direction and special meaning
FACTOR—One of the key components of any operation that contributes to a result
GENERATOR—A begetter[98]

Barbara Jakobson played the role of Polariser and collaborated with Price on Generator's program. Once it was in operation, Polariser's role would transition to encourage people to use Generator in novel ways. The role was imagined to be necessary until Generator gained enough momentum and had appropriately "conditioned" its users (this would take about a year, Price and Jakobson imagined).[99] In the meantime, Price assigned Polariser the following tasks:

To give unity of direction to the whole operation of the Generator while modifying the individual "vibrations" giving special meaning to the time and location of the causatory activities

To extend its delight and social usefulness beyond the site and before and after and on-site occasion

To be a world scout for creative appetites looking for an ideal meal setting

*Oxford Dictionary—Polarize—"Modify the vibrations so that the ray exhibits different properties on different sides, opposite sides being alike and those at right angles showing maximum difference, give polarity, give arbitrary direction, special meaning etc., to give unity of direction"[100]

Where Polariser's role was to translate social aims to Generator's operation, Factor was the operational force. The man behind that role was Wally Prince, the operations manager for the White Oak Plantation. His job was to coordinate and manage the site's activities, staffing, and maintenance, and to note the benefits of feedback through the system, as well as to operate the mobile crane to suit the menu.

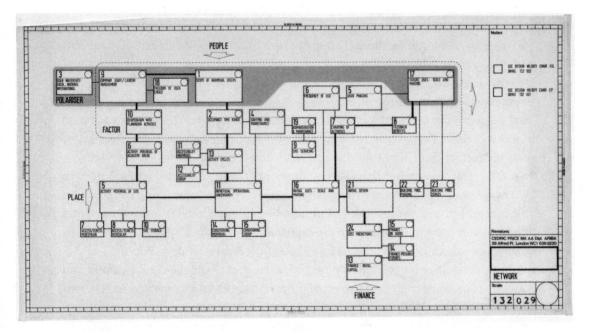

Figure 5.09

The Generator Network diagram highlights the social, operational, place-based, and financial inputs to Generator. It is based on a critical path diagram. "Polariser" corresponds to Barbara Jakobson's role as the social organizer; "Factor" refers to Wally Prince, the White Oak Plantation operations manager. Image courtesy of Collection Centre Canadien d'Architecture/Canadian Centre for Architecture, Montréal.

Generator's Network chart shows the roles of Polariser and Factor as a part of the informational dynamics that constituted the site: they resided on the critical path, represented as a flow of People that fed into Generator's relationship with the other task flows of Place and Finance. Factor's activities fell along the line that was bound to Place. In addition to the expected considerations, like pedestrian and vehicle access, the Network map also included a task called "Beneficial Operational Uncertainty"—which referred to enabling the appropriate amounts of indeterminacy, leaving some of Generator up to chance and change.

The Boredom Program

Could a bored building get you to change your mind? Two years into planning the Generator project, Price sought another means for supplying unexpected interactions between visitors, architect, and site. He contacted John and Julia Frazer, architects who wrote computer-aided design software, about developing programs for Generator.[101] Price concluded his letter to them with the line, "The whole intention of the project is to create an architecture sufficiently responsive to the making of a change of mind constructively pleasurable."[102] Although Price had considered using a computer and carrel system similar to OCH's in Generator's initial plans, noting "Personalised computer equipment:—games-individual or group tasks-forms-applications learning," the Frazers suggested taking the idea of an altered human–computer-architecture dynamic to another level.[103] They responded with a set of provocative proposals about Generator and interactivity, different than the traditional model of computer-aided design systems. The Frazers proposed that every component of Generator—each cube, screen, or walkway—would be outfitted with microprocessors. These sensors would connect with logic circuits in each structural element, and to a Commodore PET central computer that would run the programs and the peripherals. "If you kick a system, the very least that you would expect it to do is kick you back," the Frazers wrote to Price.[104]

To this end, they proposed four programs, three that would manage Generator and one—the Boredom Program—that would provoke its users into interacting with it. Programs 1 and 2 would manage the rules for Generator's layout and the use of its parts. As the "perpetual architect," Program 1 knew the structural implications for all of the components and could provide the "data to draw them."[105] Program 2 would keep an inventory of Generator's parts, calling attention to overuse and underuse of the components. Together, these programs provided instructions and schedules for Factor, the crane operator, so that he could move the cubes and other elements onsite. Generator's visitors would interact with Program 3, which addressed Price's initial request for a means to convince people to change their minds. The program "takes the form of an

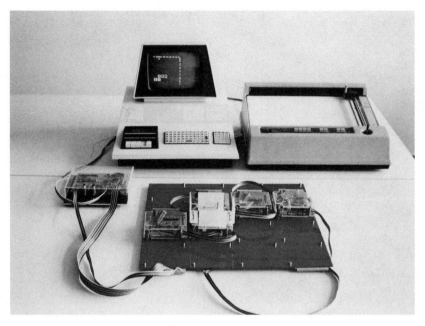

Figure 5.10
John and Julia Frazer's system that incorporated physical, screen-based, and plotting interfaces that modeled Generator's layouts: the screen of the Commodore PET computer represents the layout of the Plexiglas cubes. Image courtesy of Collection Centre Canadien d'Architecture/Canadian Centre for Architecture, Montréal.

interactive interrogation of changing requirements of the users of the site. They are invited to make proposals for improving or modifying the organization of the site," the Frazers wrote. It also was to serve as a "stimulus to the users to remind them that the site can and should be continually re-organized."[106] Program 3 would also couple with an "intelligent modelling kit" that the Frazers had designed, allowing users to prototype and visualize the outcomes of their design decisions. The tangible interface included a set of wired Plexiglas blocks on "intelligent beermats" that connected to both a computer and a plotter. The user would move the blocks; the computer would recognize the plans, display them on the monitor, and print out their menus.[107]

The Boredom Program, Program 4, was "the most powerful program on the suite," the Frazers wrote to Price.[108] When Generator's components were not reshuffled frequently enough, it would get tired of its users: "The program has been provided with a concept of boredom and in the event of the site not being re-organized or changed for some time the computer starts generating unsolicited plans and improvements," the

Figure 5.11
Detail of Generator's computer setup. Image courtesy of John Frazer.

Frazers wrote.[109] Generator's self-generated plans would then be handed off to Factor (Wally Prince), who would move Generator's parts in accordance with the new plan.

Generator's boredom routine is a direct nod to cybernetician Gordon Pask and his 1953 Musicolour machine. Musicolour was a cybernetic sculpture that accompanied a musical performer, turning and moving in response to the performance. The musician engaged in a feedback loop with Musicolour, and if the music became too repetitive, Musicolour would grow bored and stop responding.[110] The musician would then have to change what he or she was playing to reengage the machine. Yet Generator's model would have been the opposite: in order to spur the boredom routine, Generator's users would need to slow down to wait for the experience, to not interact with the site in the way that its architect and programmers intended. Boredom could not be a spectacle, as it was in Musicolour—boredom would have to be the character of the shift in agency.

The Boredom Program was the ultimate display of Generator's intelligence, measured by the changes it could encourage in its users. The Frazers wrote, "The computer program is not merely a passive computer aided design program nor is it just being used to assist with the organization of the site, but is being used to actively encourage continual change and adaptation to changing requirements. . . . In a sense the building can be described as being literally 'intelligent.'"[111]

But Generator having a mind of its own means the reverse: that the site makes demands on the user—that, separate from the architect's or user's intentions, the site and its components would have their own disposition. The Frazers wrote, "The intention of the architect in designing Generator is to facilitate the active and changing use of the site. The physical means of doing this is provided by the components and the site grid but it was felt that Generator should not be dependent entirely on the users for instigating the reorganization of the site but should have a mind of its own."[112] In Generator, it is neither the computer nor the user that offers the intelligence, it is a synthesis of the two, with the result something different and more unexpected than either could provide alone. This is the notion elucidated by J. C. R. Licklider in his 1960 article, "Man-Computer Symbiosis," which would become one of (if not the most) potent visions for human–computer interaction for the next two decades.[113]

In his influential 1969 article "The Architectural Relevance of Cybernetics," Gordon Pask argued that computers could change design paradigms by altering the relationship between the architect and the system.[114] "The glove fits, almost perfectly in the case when the designer uses a computer as his assistant. In other words, the relation 'controller/controlled entity' is reserved when these omnibus words are replaced either by 'designer/system being designed' or by 'systemic environment/inhabitants' or by 'urban plan/city,'" Pask wrote.[115] In this application of cybernetics to design, setting up some productive antagonism between designer and machine could help unsettle the traditional designer-determined hierarchy. "But notice the trick. . . . The designer does much the same job as his system, but he operates at a higher level in the organizational hierarchy," Pask continued. "Further, the design goal is nearly always underspecified and the 'controller' is no longer the authoritarian apparatus which this purely technical name brings to mind."[116]

Price and the Frazers were most interested in bringing to bear the unexpected results that arose from human–computer symbiosis—something that would surprise the architect as well as the visitor, to destabilize the traditional relationship that architects had to design and that ordinary people had to architecture. So while Price wanted to stir up the Generator visitor, perhaps he was stirring up his own relationship to indeterminacy—his own relationship to the stance of the architect, the visitor, the machine—and to architecture.

Returning to the Frazers and their programs, we see how notions of intelligence challenge traditional cycles of interaction. In a handwritten postscript in a letter to Price, John Frazer wrote, "You seemed to imply that we were only useful if we produced results that you did not expect. . . . I think this leads to some definition of computer aids in general. I am thinking about this but in the meantime at least one thing that you would expect from any half decent program is that it should produce *at least one plan which you did not expect.*"[117] By finding ways to change and adapt, and demanding that users change and adapt, Generator demonstrated its intelligence (and the Frazers, theirs).

But most important here is the nature of the instigation and provocation for change: it comes from boredom. The notion of intelligence that Price and the Frazers put forth is again different than Christopher Alexander's: Alexander designed systems that moved toward ultrastability and demonstrated intelligence by consistency, whereas Price's model of intelligence is a suite of programs that are cleverer than their users (and for that matter, their architect). An intelligent building for Price is one that challenges how its users think about it. Price's idea of intelligence is closer to Nicholas Negroponte's, where systems challenge their users, work in tandem with them, and become something more than either on its own.

Generator pushed the boundaries of both architecture and human–computer interaction in dynamics that are still provocative today. For instance, Madeline Gannon's Mimus is an industrial robot that was part of the exhibition *Fear and Love: Reactions to a Complex World*, at the Design Museum in London in 2017. Mimus's robotic arm swoops and swings around her enclosure, mimicking the people with whom she interacts—and gets bored with them if they don't respond enough to her. "An algorithm ranks everyone by interest level, and then Mimus goes to visit 'the most interesting' person. As long as that person works to stay 'the most interesting,' *Mimus* will stick with them. But once they get boring—like if they stand still for too long—*Mimus*' bored timer will start ticking," Gannon said.[118] Boredom makes the industrial robot seem like a creature, like a living thing—just as boredom is what brings a building to life and makes it intelligent.

"Re-Definition of ARCHITECTURE"

Generator demonstrated Price's theory of "life-conditioning," or architectural flexibility, to suit changing conditions. Conditioning took social considerations into account. In *The Square Book*, Price wrote that conditioning would rely on

recognition of the fact that as the availability network of invisible services increase in both intensity and content (credit cards and communication satellites) the residual activities requiring physical location, hardware, and access become more particular or "to taste." Thus the consciously planned and purposely built environment that exploits the potential of unevenness of environmental conditioning is likely to become one of the main contributions that architects and planners can make to society.[119]

Price's friend and collaborator, British architect Royston Landau called this a "philosophy of enabling"—one that showed Price's deeply held ethics about personal choice and flexibility: "*the effect an architecture may have on its occupants or observers.*"[120] Architecture could exercise a negative influence, but it could be "liberating, enhancing and supportive" as well.[121]

An undated sketch and handwritten text titled "An History of Wrong Footing—The Immediate Past," which seems to have followed Price's initial meeting with Gilman, frames the ideas that Generator sought to address:

The response of (architecture?) to the built environment is to the change in attitudes, requirements, aspirations and needs & demands of its users has usually been related to either the flexibility of "calculated slack" of the initial structure(s) & planned relationship of individual forms . . .

A further response to the capacity of the individual, group, institution & society to change its mind at intervals, frequencies & speeds unrelated to the normal time cycle of realization, utilization & obliteration of a building has been to engineer, physically, politically & economically

The socially delightful usefulness of responsive architecture has only recently gathered an establishment smart gloss and in so doing has cheapened the tight, nice original usage of the very word—responsive.[122]

If responsiveness had fallen short of the kinds of goals Price, Littlewood, and Pask pursued when they designed the Fun Palace, then Generator was an opportunity to achieve them, ten years later and with better technology. Price aimed higher still. Yes, he wanted to reclaim the concept of responsiveness for Generator. But on the reverse of an index card stapled to "An History of Wrong Footing," there is a list of seven items. The last of those items is: "Re-definition of ARCHITECTURE."[123]

Like many of Price's projects, Generator was never built. After nearly three years of design, the project was stymied by financial turmoil and a feud within the family-run Gilman Paper Company.[124] Moreover (and probably not surprisingly), the workforce did not support the project: the maintenance and labor requirements were too great. Howard Gilman was unable to clear that hurdle and had to abandon the project. White Oak Plantation did become a dance center, home to the White Oak Dance Project, founded by Mikhail Baryshnikov and Mark Morris in 1990, which operated until 2004. It then became a more conventional retreat center that supported Gilman's philanthropic interests. Sold in 2013, it is now the White Oak Conservation Foundation, a wildlife preserve for exotic animals and a more conventional conference center. Price and Gilman stayed friends throughout their lives (Gilman died in 1998), although it seems that Price likely felt wistful about the project's cancellation. In his files, Price made his own modification to an ad featuring Baryshnikov for the White Oak Dance project. Using Wite-Out, he painted the dancer some wings and roller skates.

Generator marked a point of emergence of important factors for responsive architecture: embedded, distributed, electronic intelligence; active computer-aided design tools; the correspondence of the model to the design tool; and questions of machine intelligence. John Frazer never gave up interest in the programs they designed for Generator—they served as exemplars of the vision for what he called "evolutionary architecture." Price never informed the Frazers that the project had been canceled—just that it was on hold. John Frazer approached Price about restarting the project in 1989, suggesting some fund-raising possibilities for doing so in 1995, and even brought it up again a year or two before Price's death in 2003.[125] Had they been able to build and implement their system, it would have been a remarkably prescient version of what today is known as a sensor network, one that demonstrates the architectural implications of distributed intelligence.

Price spoke about "computers and laziness" in 1989 in a lecture at the Architectural Association, stating that humans are best at making choices, computers are best at "taking infinite pains with a problem," he said. But he suggested that computers could also enable other dynamics. Referring to Generator, he said:

The development of computers that become "bored" through not being "exercised" enough could result in two fields of design activity which are both challenging and intensely useful. Firstly, the bored computer would produce its own possible solutions to a given set of circumstances, whether asked to or not. (This is in fact one of the programs John Frazer designed for our Generator installation in the USA.) Second, it is possible that the computer could establish a new language of what was hitherto considered incomparable. The lazy half-science of kinesthetics has always depended on just such comparisons. Designers and architects would be better employed in devising new languages of comparison for computers, than in using them to confirm the obvious.[126]

A new language for the incomparable: perhaps this is where Generator leaves us. Generator challenged the agency of the architect, of the user, of the building, of the site, of the computer. And if it did devise a new language of comparison, we might question what those comparisons would yield. How responsive might our architecture be to us? What might we ask in turn? What is the nature of this intelligence? Or would Generator simply get bored and take its leave?

Conclusion

Price combined technology with architecture to shake loose our expectations about what architecture could provide, to get people unstuck from the idea that architecture needed to be a steady and stable thing. He used technology and interactivity as a provocation for change within his projects and in his design process, with the ultimate, self-proclaimed interest of reframing architecture.

One of the tricky parts of much of Price's work is that it took place on paper and in process, and for the most part not as concrete interventions in the built environment. Price's drawings and charts, his collaborations and correspondence, influenced architects and other cultural, societal, and political figures, and presented concepts of a world that could be. Are these projects virtual architecture? Katherine Hayles offered a "strategic definition of 'virtuality.'" She wrote, "Virtuality is the cultural perception that material objects are interpenetrated by information patterns. The definition plays off the duality at the heart of the condition of virtuality—materiality on the one hand, information on the other."[127] At issue is the perception of these informational patterns taking priority over the materiality that carries them. "Especially for users who may not know the material process involved, the impression is created that pattern is predominant over presence. From here it is a small step to perceiving information as more mobile, more important, more essential than material forms. When this impression becomes part of your cultural mindset, you have entered the condition of virtuality."[128]

Ultimately, in Price's work, the purpose of technology is "to take part in the architectural debate, perhaps through contribution, disputation, or the ability to shock," as Royston Landau wrote.[129] By using technological systems and computational paradigms to render and represent information materially, Price played on the boundary between information, materiality, and possibility.

What if we step away from the Vitruvian architectural ideals of *firmitas, utilitas, venustas* (solidity, function, and beauty) and instead consider another set of architectural ideals: those that support designing for pleasure, surprise, and provocation?[130] To return to Price's lecture that opened this chapter, we act as though technology is the answer. And as technological architectures increasingly govern the built environment in which we live, we might want to ask ourselves: What *is* the question?

6 Nicholas Negroponte and the MIT Architecture Machine Group: Interfaces to Artificial Intelligence

In remarkable and sometimes unsettling ways, the MIT Architecture Machine Group experimented with the experience of artificial intelligence and how people would interact with it. The predecessor to the MIT Media Lab, the Architecture Machine Group was founded by Nicholas Negroponte and Leon Groisser and operated from 1967 to 1985, when it folded into the Media Lab. The Architecture Machine Group (AMG) integrated architecture with artificial intelligence, computer science, and electrical engineering. The group collaborated frequently with MIT's Artificial Intelligence Lab and experimented with its technologies, developing ideas from cognitive psychology, artificial intelligence, computer science, art, film, and human–computer interaction, among other disciplines.

The Architecture Machine Group lab was a tinkerer's haven for exploration of AI and architecture. But the group also took military applications and scaled them up to an architectural scale—to that of the built environment, to the world we live in. With the belief that sitting at a computer terminal was a lousy excuse for interactivity, the group developed conversational interfaces, and projects that showed how AI could affect the world around us—whether our interactions, our navigations of digital space in immersive media spaces, or how technology might be made portable enough. They conceived of simulations that would be so real, they could substitute for reality.

Since AMG received its funding from Department of Defense agencies such as DARPA and the Office of Naval Research, the group tailored many of its projects to the needs of these agencies. It was a strategic move on the group's part that allowed it to garner good funding and to work within the close relationships fostered by the DoD. The project Put That There used gestures and voice to manage ship fleets, and the Aspen Movie Map investigated the possibility of remote surveillance. And while these projects provided research opportunities to the group, their focus also underscores the fact that the purpose of many of the group's projects was battlefield command and control. Negroponte began to bridge the battlefield with entertainment as the group became the kernel of the MIT Media Lab, which was founded and funded primarily by corporate entities.

Negroponte developed a theory and practice of interaction among humans, computers, and the built environment, publishing books and articles about the idea of "architecture machines." What was an architecture machine? Was it a future vision of a digital environment? A simulation engine? A theory of robots or of software? A rallying cry for new research collaborations among architects, engineers, computer scientists, and artificial intelligence researchers? From Negroponte's perspective, it was all those things. The Architecture Machine Group forged new avenues of technical, computational teaching and research for architects. The group learned by tinkering, making, coding, and doing, pushing the boundaries of both architectural and engineering education.

In this chapter, my interest is in the relationships among artificial intelligence, engineering, and architecture that Negroponte and AMG forged. As we look forward to the next thirty years of digital media and architecture, *this* is the field on which we will all play, where AI and machine-learning intersect with our everyday world. Nicholas Negroponte was one of the people to see and to understand best where that nexus might lead. What are the implications of these demos and simulations when we scale them up? And, in an increasingly intelligent and responsive world, what might we learn from these important experiments?

"To the First Machine That Can Appreciate the Gesture"

In the out-of-the-way corner it first inhabited in Building 9 at MIT, the Architecture Machine Group experimented on interfaces and tools that bridged architecture, engineering, and artificial intelligence. Negroponte described the mission as follows: "The Architecture Machine has chronologically become a book, a minicomputer, a family of minicomputers, a small curriculum, a computer ethic, another book, and a catch-all for a variety of papers."[1]

With so wide a mission, one wonders what AMG did *not* aim to do. Indeed, Negroponte dedicated his first book, *The Architecture Machine*, "To the first machine that can appreciate the gesture."[2] Negroponte envisioned the "distant future" of architecture machines as something so pervasive that we would inhabit their worlds: "They won't help us design; instead, we will live in them."[3]

An *architecture machine* was Negroponte's term that referred to turning the design process into a dialogue that would alter the traditional human–machine dynamic.[4] In order to achieve this close relationship with the user, such a machine would have to incorporate artificial intelligence (AI) because, Negroponte wrote, "any design procedure, set of rules, or truism is tenuous, if not subversive, when used out of context or regardless of context."[5] Two of Negroponte's books, *The Architecture Machine* (1970) and *Soft Architecture Machines* (1975), and a number of articles expressed his theories and vision of these interconnections, distilled from the work of artificial intelligence researchers, cyberneticists, and other thinkers.[6]

The modus operandi of the Architecture Machine Group was one of tinkering and "bricolage," where the tools and technologies came from computing, engineering, and artificial intelligence.[7] The group performed demos of the work to its funders and visitors, a practice that continues today in the MIT Media Lab. AMG's shortcomings and successes, and perhaps most importantly, the group's interpretations of the results, were sometimes visionary and provocative and other times seemingly ignorant of the potential consequences of the group's vision. AMG experimented with systems that incorporated artificial intelligence, in projects that juxtaposed often grand ideas with limited and sometimes naive proofs-of-concept. As the lab grew in size and expertise, AMG experimented with immersive media rooms, storage and display media, speech and gestural interaction, and different kinds of audiovisual media and feedback. The goal of these projects—as AMG moved into the 1980s and the eventual founding of the MIT Media Lab—was the convergence of spatial and informational interfaces.

The lead protagonist, principal investigator, spokesperson, and director of the Architecture Machine Group was Nicholas Negroponte. Well-bred, well-spoken, and well-dressed, skilled at operating among technology, architecture, education, the corporate and private sector, and the military-industrial elite, by the time Negroponte founded the Media Lab, he presented himself as a sort of "hero" of what the hybrid digital world could achieve.[8] Born in 1942 into a wealthy Greek shipping family, Negroponte grew up in New York and Europe. He went to MIT, completing a bachelor of architecture in 1965 and a master of architecture a year later, in 1966. Doing so gave him the opportunity to work with computers, under the tutelage of Steven Coons, a mechanical engineering professor and computer-aided design pioneer whom Negroponte first met when he took a mechanical drawing class during his first year of undergraduate studies.[9] Five days after he completed his master's degree, Negroponte took over Coons's computer-aided design classes in the Department of Mechanical Engineering when Coons took a yearlong leave of absence.[10] When he returned, they taught together; Negroponte then transitioned to the Department of Architecture faculty in 1968, where he continued his teaching and his research as the cofounder of the Architecture Machine Group.[11]

Architects at MIT before the late 1960s did not pursue the kind of research that took place in the institute's more technical labs.[12] Around the time that AMG formed, MIT provided an imperative that its departments better align with what MIT president

Howard Johnson called a "science-based learning environment" as a "more effective laboratory for leadership," as the 1968 *MIT Report of the President* stated.[13] "We know that these are times when the most basic problems of our living arrangements can be solved only by the application of large technical systems; while, on the other hand, we feel a deep yearning for individual participation and expression and for the small-scale, person-sized contribution," Johnson wrote.[14] The School of Architecture and Planning began to alter its curriculum and pursued new research models. It was partly a move away from the traditional Beaux-Arts studio tradition of tutelage and critique, in which architects are trained as apprentices to a master architect. In the same 1968 report, Architecture and Planning dean Lawrence Anderson warned that this old model exercised "residual influence [that] remains as an incubus that dampens our enthusiasm for any panacea."[15] Anderson called for the department to look to other fields and collaborations, drawing attention to the "promise of new methodologies for problem solving, especially those supported by memory and retrieval systems and manipulative possibilities of the computer."[16] Architectural historian Felicity Scott writes that Anderson also sought to confront the "so-called 'urban crises'" characterized by the federal government and felt acutely in American cities.[17] To that end, the Urban Systems Laboratory was founded by the Department of City and Regional Planning at MIT in 1968. These were monumental shifts. Architecture, Scott writes, was no longer the grounds of solo expertise, but instead followed the formulation of other cybernetic, systems approaches from elsewhere on MIT's campus, from technical laboratories to social science research. As Scott writes, "While interdisciplinary architectural and urban research had of course taken place during the previous decades at MIT, as elsewhere, we can recognize at this moment a significant shift in the very conception of architecture."[18]

In founding the Architecture Machine Group, Negroponte and Groisser also built a framework for transdisciplinary research, an agenda of which Negroponte began to outline in 1966 in his master's thesis. He was influenced by collaborations between architecture and technology, and in his master's thesis cast the role of the architect as someone who "synthesized" different bodies of information.[19] "The research has compelled me to become more involved with the university and delve into other disciplines, some of them rarely associated with architecture," he wrote in the thesis preface. "In certain cases this sort of work has proved superficial and provides only a procedural retreading for the next act."[20] His thesis project, which blended architecture, engineering, and perception in a computer simulation of movement through an urban setting generated by a computer-aided design system, reflected the composition of his committee, which included members from both the Department of Architecture

(Gyorgy Kepes, Aaron Fleisher, Wren McMains, Imre Halasz, and Leon Groisser) and the Department of Mechanical Engineering (Steven Coons).[21]

The Architecture Machine Group began to formulate new venues and approaches for architectural research. Why couldn't architectural research look more like other research at MIT? Why couldn't it be more transdisciplinary? "As a profession we . . . have done little research," Negroponte wrote in his master's thesis. "All this work must take place within the academic world as we have no General Motors or NASA to sponsor philanthropic research. However, schools of architecture are still trade schools by nature and not compatible, at this moment, with the process of research."[22] Just six years later, this view of architectural research for which he advocated had come to fruition. Negroponte wrote in a 1971 proposal, "The sponsored research activities of the Department of Architecture have grown from a yearly cash flow of $256 in 1965 to $198,255 in 1970. Most of this growth results from emerging efforts in computer-related areas."[23] AMG's projects figured into that accounting and only grew throughout the 1970s—by 1980, its research budget had topped $1 million.[24] "This combining of modes, research and teaching, has led to an amplifying factor for results and a stimulation factor for potential hardware donors," wrote Negroponte.[25]

Teaching and Research

Teaching and research in the Architecture Machine Group lab complemented each other. The lab was the locus of classroom assignments in programming for the Department of Architecture and undergraduate and master's student research, usually in support of lab research projects.[26] It was "a way of thinking about thinking," as Nicholas Negroponte said in an interview.[27] In the architecture studio, students got their hands dirty with programming, using hands-on methods—an approach different than the abstract, symbolic way it was traditionally taught. Negroponte argued that traditional computing courses were inappropriate for teaching architects to program because, as individuals who worked with both the tangible and the representational, architecture students needed different teaching methods than the abstract, symbolic techniques taught in computer science.[28] "The student of architecture is an inherently tactile person," he wrote in *Soft Architecture Machines,* one who "is accustomed not only to working with his hands but also to physical and graphical manifestations; and he is accustomed to *playing* with these."[29] In the joint classroom-lab approach of teaching and research, students learned a way to think about thinking as they learned to program and tinker with input/output devices like tablets, light pens, cathode ray tubes (CRTs), and plotters.[30]

AMG lived and died by demonstrating its technologies. Learning by doing, building, and tinkering stood at the center of the group's mandate. Negroponte promoted the "demo or die" approach, as it became called at the Media Lab (current Media Lab director Joi Ito takes it further: it's now "deploy or die").[31] The "demo or die" ethos accompanies the futuristic picture that Negroponte painted in the group's proposals in its "orientation . . . [toward] the *discovery* phase of science-building."[32] AMG even coined the term "emergence exploration" for it: As one proposal explained, "Our approach, our stock in trade, has been the 'shakedown' of new ideas: building the prototype, interacting with it, demonstrating it, conferencing about it, enticing industry and making changes. Such is 'emergence exploration.'"[33] This "emergence exploration" of demo culture belonged to both working method and project deliverables because, as AMG argued, written text did not do the projects justice. In 1978, Negroponte and AMG principal researcher Richard Bolt championed their approach as an important aspect of the design of the Spatial Data Management System (SDMS). "The past two years of SDMS have enjoyed an omnipresent demonstration of the system itself," they write. "These live performances have allowed for critics and enthusiasts to have a hands-on experience with the interface, such as it stands."[34] Stewart Brand later criticized this tendency in his 1987 book *The Media Lab*, cautioning his readers to watch for "handwaving . . . what a speaker does animatedly with his hands as he moves past provable material into speculation, anticipating and overwhelming objection with manual dexterity—a deprecating 'you-know' featuring a well-turned back of the hand, or a two-handed symmetrical sculpting of something as imaginary as it is wonderful. Sometimes handwaving precedes creation, sometimes it substitutes for it."[35] Throughout AMG's history, the tension between demo-or-die and handwaving continued. "Wizard of Oz" techniques could simulate the effects of a technology or interface, but could gloss over the ramifications for the user of a system.

A Theory of Architecture Machines

Underlying the Architecture Machine Group's experiments and projects was Nicholas Negroponte's ideas about AI and interaction: a theory of architecture machines. Negroponte drew from cybernetics and artificial intelligence in his theory of architecture machines, articulated in his books *The Architecture Machine* and *Soft Architecture Machines,* and in articles and reports. He then used the Architecture Machine Group's projects as a way to manifest his theories in hardware, software, interfaces, and environments. In the simplest explanation, an architecture machine was Negroponte's vision of an intelligent environment that we would all eventually inhabit and that would eventually surround all of us.

An architecture machine would employ technological interfaces—screens, tablets, touch screens, video eyes, cameras, rooms—that felt comfortable and natural to use and that operated at a high degree of fidelity. Such an environment would respond intelligently and appropriately to its users in context. It would draw from a cognitive model of its users that could make inferences and learn and adapt over time.

Architecture machines were *symbiotic*. Almost any discussion of AI in the 1960s and early 1970s started with the concept of symbiosis from J. C. R. Licklider's influential 1960 article, "Man-Computer Symbiosis"; it was a natural point of departure for Negroponte, especially given that Licklider was a mentor to Negroponte.[36] Negroponte translated symbiosis as "the intimate association of two dissimilar species (man and machine), two dissimilar processes (design and computation), and two intelligent systems (the architect and the architecture machine)."[37] It suggested a dialectic in which dissimilar species, processes, and intelligent systems came together as "associates"— that is, allies or partners. "By virtue of ascribing intelligence to an artifact or the artificial, the partnership is not one of master and slave but rather of two associates that have a potential and a desire for self-improvement," Negroponte wrote.[38]

By distinguishing the partnership as different from a master/slave relationship, Negroponte was likely setting himself apart from his former teacher and colleague, Steven Coons, the MIT mechanical engineering and computer-aided design professor. Coons saw the human as the master, and the computer, the slave. In mutual engagement, they would work together by playing their carefully circumscribed roles, "where the computer and the man are mutually engaged in the learning creative process—the man as the general of ideas, and the computer as the appropriate slave," as Coons said at the Architecture and the Computer conference in 1964.[39]

Instead of being a slave, an architecture machine would serve as a bridge between the human and the computational, a personal computer that would learn through dialogue with its user. Not only would this theoretically result in a free-flowing conversation, but in a deeply personal relationship with the system. "The dialogue would be so intimate—even exclusive—that only mutual persuasion and compromise would bring about ideas, ideas unrealizable by either conversant alone," Negroponte projected. "No doubt, in such a symbiosis it would not be solely the human designer who would decide when the machine is relevant."[40] Such a machine would not only ingratiate itself to its human partner by modeling its behavioral and linguistic particularities, it would become something more than either the human or the machine alone, Negroponte believed.

Negroponte referred to Warren Brodey and Nilo Lindgren's characterization of dialogue in "Human Enhancement through Evolutionary Technology," the content and style of which Negroponte's writing imitated.[41] Brodey and Lindgren wrote, "Dialogue has to do with how people 'track' one another in learning novel views, in undoing structural obsolescence (in both skills and concepts); it is a kind of tracking that may exist not only between man and man but between man and machine as well."[42] Through a combination of analyzing and responding to sensory input, using "the new tools of artificial intelligence [that] make it possible to synthesize and model evolutionary processes in man," a dialogue would evolve—one that Brodey and Lindgren surmised would "draw its participants beyond the sum of their action or intent." "It evolves them," they wrote.[43]

By building a metamodel of themselves through dialogue, architecture machines would be *self-organizing learning machines*. This dialogue, this modeling process, was as important as what might emerge from it. "The architectural dialogue we are proposing is one in which the process of interacting is as important as the products of that interaction," Negroponte wrote. "The dialogue is not used to study or model the design process itself. . . . Instead, we are talking about a dialogue that shifts between states of goal-orientedness and states of playfulness (like [Warren] Brodey, [Avery] Johnson, and [Gordon] Pask) for the purpose of modelling the user," Negroponte wrote in *Computer Aids to Participatory Architecture*, the proposal for a 1971 NSF grant that supported some of the lab's early work.[44] The point was not for the system to model architecture, but rather to model the way the user understood architecture—a model of the model.

Negroponte underscored this point at the end of a passage in *The Architecture Machine* about how architecture machines would learn.[45] "The prime function of the machine is to learn about the user. It is to be noted that whatever knowledge the machine has of architecture will have been imbedded in it; *the machine will not "learn" about architecture*. The machine will indeed build a model of the user's new or modified habitat. But it is simultaneously building a model of the user and a model of the user's model of it."[46] He projected the ease in communication that a human would have with a close compatriot: "In the prelude to an architect-machine dialogue the solidarity of the alliance will rely on the ease of communication, the ability to ventilate one's concerns in a natural vernacular, and the presence of modes of communication responsive to the discipline at hand."[47] AMG applied these notions of dialogue, albeit with little success, to the URBAN2 and URBAN5 computer-aided design systems—Negroponte and Groisser's earliest projects (discussed below).

An architecture machine used *heuristics* to develop its models of human–computer interaction. Heuristics are rules of thumb and provisional techniques for problem-solving. In design, heuristics could be used for improving on design, developing the user model and interaction; on the programming level, they could be used to program deeper-level functions, routines, parameters, and procedures.[48] They were important as building blocks for artificial intelligence. Heuristics could start with layers of description, such as in the approach of MIT's AI Lab, in which mappings of real-world objects show the "relations" of "features" to each other, represented in the computer by interlinked networks of "ordinary language" strings.[49] Heuristic techniques would support architecture machines in "learning how to learn, and more important, the desire to learn," Negroponte wrote, in the hopes that machines would "mature" in a way similar to humans.[50] Problem-solving could improve on the model of the problem itself.

Another way to look at heuristics was "problem-worrying," a term coined by Stanford Anderson, professor of history, theory and criticism in the Department of Architecture at MIT. "Problem-worrying" demanded that the problem to be solved be as well determined as the methods used to solve it. It suggested "a dynamic involvement in the problem situation," involving "human purposes" and not just those of automation, Anderson said in in 1966 lecture.[51] Like the problems that AI researchers used heuristics to define, the entire scope of architectural problems could not be known at the outset of an architectural project: "The human purposes are altered by the very environment that was created to facilitate them," Anderson said. This continual assessment and reassessment, rendered in model and then some kind of form, whether in a representation, or technology, or interface, is how Negroponte proposed to approach design. He envisioned the design process of architecture machines as a continued heuristic modeling of models that learned from one another and that reflected the adaptation of human, machine, and environment. The source of connection between the elements would come through the interfaces to the architecture machine.

Architecture machines furthered the understanding of *human–computer interfaces*. "Interface," as the term was originally used in the 1880s, referred to "a surface lying between two portions of matter or space, and forming their common boundary."[52] It later came to refer to "a means or place of interaction between two systems, organizations . . . interaction, liaison, dialogue" and "(an) apparatus designed to connect two scientific instruments, devices, etc., so that they can be operated jointly."[53] Negroponte's model of interface picked up this last idea. For him, the interface was a feedback loop of an object to be sensed, a tool with which to sense it, and the mapping of its result for a new or different use. He called these elements the "event," "manifestation," and "representation," drawing from Nilo Lindgren's seamless model of interface, with the addition of another series of feedback loops that account for local behavior.[54] What counted as an "event" in the feedback loop involved sensory data, potentially "visual, auditory, olfactory, tactile, extrasensory, or a motor command."[55] The "manifestation" was hardware that could sense parameters such as "luminance, frequency, brain wavelength, angle of rotation," and that would turn this data into a "representation" that maps "the information into a receptacle that is compatible with the organism's processing characteristics."[56] The transference results in a multisensory, multimodal, and, eventually, necessarily multimedia approach to architectural problems.

Working with *audio, visual, and other sensory qualities* was thus an architectural endeavor because of the possibilities for creating interactive environments at the scale of rooms, buildings, and cities. "It seems natural that architecture machines would be superb clients for sophisticated sensors," Negroponte wrote. "Architecture itself demands a sensory involvement," one that he imagined the "machine partners" might need as well.[57] In *Soft Architecture Machines*, he expanded on this idea. "It is clear that computers need a wide variety of sensory channels and a host of effectors in order to witness and manipulate 'aspects' of the world, particularly those we use daily in our metaphors," he wrote. "However, to date, computers are by far the most sensory-deprived 'intellectual engines.' They are offered the richness and variety of telegraph-ese, with minor exceptions like computer graphics and a limited machine vision."[58] AMG, as a result, increasingly focused on the processing, storage, and transmission qualities of audiovisual technologies, working with videodisc storage and touch-sensitive screens, large light valve displays and handheld display devices, as well as with sound and speech recognition. The audiovisual qualities contributed to how a user perceived and conceived of space.

Negroponte argued the provocative point that architecture machine interfaces would need to be sensory in an almost human sense. "It is so obvious that our interfaces, that is, our bodies, are intimately related to learning and to how we learn, that one point of departure in artificial intelligence is to concentrate specifically on the interfaces," Negroponte wrote. This approach demanded the building of machines with a real world focus: embedded within the world, using sensing capabilities and engaging with the environment as human users and designers do. An architecture machine "should not only engage in dialogue with the world but also "must receive direct sensory information from the real world. It must see, hear, and read, and it must take walks in the garden."[59] This begs a question: How close did these machines need to be to the people who used them? "Does a machine have to possess a body like my own and be able to experience behaviors like my own in order to share in what we call intelligent behavior? While it may seem absurd, I believe the answer is yes," Negroponte wrote in one of his more poetic descriptions of architecture machines.[60]

Finally, architecture machines were designed to operate *on an environmental scale*—that of architecture and of cities—not stopping at the simple peripheral boundaries of the machine or user. The "soft" in the book title *Soft Architecture Machines* reflected what Negroponte envisaged would be not just an intelligent computer peripheral, but an intelligent environment. "I shall consider the physical environment as an evolving organism as opposed to a designed artifact,"[61] he wrote in the preface to *The Architecture Machine*. The organism that evolves *is* the built environment, *is* the architecture machine. Negroponte develops the idea from Warren Brodey's article "Soft Architecture: The Design of Intelligent Environments." Automation isn't intelligence, Brodey argued: it leads to "hard shell machines [that] multiply and control us."[62] Instead, Brodey imagined a "gentle control which stands in place of steel bones and stone muscles" that would potentially provide "creative flexibility" over the environment.[63] The problem is that "essentially stupid environments become more complicated, dials and toggles soon stand in massive array," Brodey wrote, portending the problems of interface development in command-and-control technologies. "All the skill of human engineering is required to avoid the mistakenly flipped switch that at supersonic speeds spells sure disaster."[64]

"The Closed World" and Funding for Architectural Research

The culture of funding sources shaped the Architecture Machine Group's priorities. Like other labs at MIT and other major technical institutions, the Architecture Machine Group received funding from educational grants, the National Science Foundation (NSF), corporations, the Department of Defense (especially the Advanced Research Projects Agency, ARPA—later DARPA), and the Office of Naval Research (ONR). DoD agencies tended to channel money to a brain trust that first formed during World War II—what historian and information scholar Paul Edwards refers to as the "closed world" in his book *The Closed World: Computers and The Politics of Discourse in Cold War America.*[65] As Edwards explains, this "closed world" consisted of a small network in a small field of individuals, with permeable boundaries between academia, the DoD, and industry. The directors of ARPA's Information Processing Techniques Office (IPTO) and similar organizations were recruited from this network.

AMG's patrons were some of the most important figures in defense funding, and their close relationship to Negroponte and the AMG was vital for the group's formation, funding, and future. Conversations with Negroponte are peppered with personal stories, of dinners and elevator conversations. His personal relationships with these individuals mattered a great deal to him, not only in terms of financial support but also for mentorship and the connections they brought to bear. Three of them, J. C. R. Licklider, Martin Denicoff, and Craig Fields were vital to AMG and, more generally, to technology development and transfer in AI, computer simulation, high-definition television, and the Internet. Marvin Minsky and Seymour Papert, of the MIT AI Lab, supported Negroponte as loyal friends and collaborators, in friendships that lasted until Minsky and Papert's deaths in 2016.

J. C. R. Licklider, who we have seen throughout this book, advanced a set of projects around time-shared computing and ARPANET by moving between institutions and placing sympathetic researchers in them. He circulated multiple times among institutions, moving among MIT, Bolt, Beranek & Newman (BBN), and ARPA/DARPA's Information Processing Techniques Office.[66] Licklider was a mentor to Negroponte and provided the initial funding for the HUNCH sketch recognition project, roughly $20,000–$30,000.[67] He put people in place in numerous institutions that helped realize his vision for time-shared computing, computer networking, and human–computer interaction. His articles, including "Man-Computer Symbiosis," were influential for many of the figures in this book.

Marvin Denicoff was director of the Information Systems Program at the Office of Naval Research from 1962 to 1983 and put in place the agenda and funding for artificial intelligence. By one account, he was "the 'grand old man' of all sponsors, . . . the patron of some of the most exciting AI research."[68] In the Information Systems Program, he supported "a multimillion-dollar per-year basic research grant program in such fields as artificial intelligence, robotics, computer graphics, man-machine systems, computer architecture, and software."[69] A civil servant who came from a liberal arts background—his graduate study included literature and linguistics—Denicoff also had a lifelong interest in playwriting and photography. His cultural interests were reflected in what he chose to fund, which made AMG an interesting candidate for support, and he even joined the MIT Media Lab upon his retirement, to work on projects in electronic theater. Marvin Minsky, in *Society of Mind*, acknowledged Denicoff's role in managing the MIT AI Lab's contracts, noting that Denicoff's "vision of the future had a substantial influence on the entire field."[70]

Craig Fields joined DARPA in 1974 and became the director of DARPA in 1990 (after which he was demoted in a political scuffle).[71] Unlike Licklider and Denicoff, who were a generation older than Negroponte, Negroponte and Fields were only four years apart in age. Fields was instrumental in funding AMG and early Media Lab projects, particularly around simulation environments and human factors projects. He had a reputation for aggressively supporting private high tech research.

To garner research support, Negroponte and his colleagues tailored the agenda of AMG for defense funding strategies, which in turn shaped the group's research. First, the group worked within limited, bounded environments called "microworlds." As the Vietnam War progressed and the defense funding landscape shifted in favor of applied and not basic research, AMG followed suit. The group turned to command-and-control applications. Finally, Negroponte and MIT president Jerome Wiesner began to raise corporate funding for what would become the MIT Media Lab under the aegis of media and consumer electronics. The group's work manifests the logics and agendas of these funding models in ways that are important (and maybe cautionary) for contemporary research in artificial intelligence and the built environment, particularly around how we model and prototype new worlds, and our expectations in how we deploy them.

Microworlds and Blocks Worlds

Like other artificial intelligence researchers in the late 1960s and early 1970s, the Architecture Machine Group worked within "microworlds," domains for artificial intelligence research that limited the number of variables in their models in order to focus certain problems such as computer vision and language dialogue. Such projects often involved the manipulation of stacks of blocks with natural language commands and peripherals, and accordingly were called "blocks worlds."[72] In artificial intelligence research, microworlds were closely bounded areas of inquiry that focused on specific AI problems while abstracting or ignoring others.[73] Although the projects did not always succeed as fully functioning programs and prototypes, they were provocative thought experiments and demos with sometimes troubling implications. AMG's early projects faced the same problems that AI researchers faced in their microworlds, in which the grand version of GOFAI ("Good Old-Fashioned Artificial Intelligence") did not succeed in producing what it promised.[74]

Microworlds were a useful construct precisely because they operated without regard to reality, contrary as it might seem, "partial, internally consistent but externally incomplete domains," as Paul Edwards described them in *The Closed World*.[75] The ability to isolate certain variables within a program and abstract aspects of a design problem "without irrelevant or unwanted complexity" was an attractive and powerful prospect: "Every microworld has a unique ontological and epistemological structure, simpler than those of the world it represents," Edwards wrote.[76] Focusing on a world known not to be real, or true, was all the more reason to perpetuate the development in this limited sphere. Marvin Minsky and Seymour Papert wrote, "One is absolutely dependent on having highly-developed models of many phenomena. Each model—or 'micro-world' as we shall call it—is very schematic; it talks about a fairyland in which things are so simplified that almost every statement about them would be literally false if asserted about the real world."[77]

Minsky and Papert celebrated the limitations of blocks worlds and justified their further funding. "We feel they [microworlds] are so important that we are assigning a large portion of our effort toward developing a collection of these micro-worlds and finding how to use the suggestive and predictive powers of the models without being overcome by their incompatibility with literal truth," they wrote.[78] Minsky and Papert argued that the separation of method from goal was not necessarily a negative thing—that the creation, evaluation and disposal of microworlds as a way to understand a problem was a valid method of problem-solving and heuristics.[79] "As long as one deals with 'toy' problems—puzzles, games, and other situations (some of which may be quite practical) in which little or no interaction with other aspects of reality are required, Artificial Intelligence techniques are generally quite advanced by human performance standards," Minsky and Papert wrote.[80] The problem was when its programs tried to model "things like space, and time, and people's desires, and economics, and design, etc. . . . Today's programs hardly approach the competence of a small child."[81]

The realm of space, time, desire, and design may have made for difficult problems to solve, but it was exactly the area that AMG explored in its projects. AMG followed the same strategy as Minsky and Papert, celebrating the shortcomings and failures of microworld research in order to justify the ongoing experimentation in their work. "Let us build machines that can learn, can grope, and can fumble," Negroponte wrote in the conclusion to *The Architecture Machine*, "machines equipped with at least those devices that humans employ to design."[82] The names of some of AMG's projects, such as HUNCH, SEEK, and GROPE embodied the philosophy of their design process. The very fact that these projects were imperfect justified further experimentation and development.

AMG projects used blocks worlds to constrain the scope of the design problems in such projects as URBAN5, the conversational urban design system; SEEK, a world of cubes reorganized by a robotic arm and inhabited by gerbils; and HUNCH, a system that recognized, interpreted, and rendered hand sketches on-screen. In keeping with the characterization that Edwards provides, the limitations and abstractions of AMG's microworlds had ontological and epistemological implications on the group's research. Although they provided a manageable framework for exploration, applying them to a larger scale, such as that of the built environment, became a thornier issue. After all, humans live between the interface and the infrastructure. So what happens to living creatures in the bounded territory of a blocks world? What happens to the user inside of a machine environment? What were AMG's researchers abstracting, what were they making concrete, and what did they brush aside in the process? And what was at stake in AMG's answers to those questions?

URBAN2 and URBAN5

The Architecture Machine Group's first architectural research projects were the URBAN2 and URBAN5 computer-aided design (CAD) systems.[83] It combined a simple graphical CAD program running on an IBM System/360 computer, in which the user manipulated ten-foot by ten-foot cubes with a light pen and engaged in a question-and-answer dialogue between user and computer.[84] A block, Negroponte wrote, "has few architectural impositions and many research conveniences,"—"research conveniences" referring to the advantages of blocks worlds.[85] Rather than acting like an intelligent designer, the system instead simulated an "urban design clerk" that could "monitor design procedures."[86]

In accordance with Negroponte's ideas about applying artificial intelligence to architecture, the goal of URBAN5 was to develop a model of its user through this conversation and, acting appropriately in context, ostensibly demonstrate its intelligence. The initial version of the system, URBAN2, was the class project for Groisser and Negroponte's 1967 course "Special Problems in Computer Aided Urban Design," sponsored by MIT and the IBM Scientific Research Center in Cambridge, taught as a computer workshop "by architects for architects."[87] Evidently, the special studies course and its approach proved "extremely popular," according to the 1968 MIT President's Report, and became a permanent part of the Department of Architecture curriculum. The next version of the system, URBAN5, became the first AMG lab research project.

The URBAN5 user drew and selected squares that represented blocks on a cathode ray tube (CRT) screen and assigned a "mode" to each block using a set of thirty-two buttons. As the user selected a block and a mode, the system would ask a preprogrammed question from a dictionary of approximately five hundred selections. For example, drawing two cubes next to each other joined them into a single volume, and the SURFACE mode gave the volume a quality, such as "solid."[88] Each cube had implicit and explicit qualities that URBAN5 automatically assigned to the blocks. If the user added a cube that cast shadows on another element, for instance, the system would update the natural light and visual privacy qualities, running the process in the background.[89] URBAN5 would ask contextually appropriate questions in language that an architect would understand, helping the user as she selected attributes and modes. The system would then look for "conflicts and incompatibilities" among the attributes, sounding "a nauseating bell" to alert the user, who then would fix the problem by typing in a response to a dialogue prompt or by selecting a new mode.[90] For example,

Figure 6.01

The URBAN5 user drew with a light pen and selected squares that represented ten-foot blocks, and then used the special keypad on the left to assign attributes and qualities to each block. *The Architecture Machine*, by Nicholas Negroponte, published by the MIT Press.

Architect All studios must have outdoor access.

URBAN5 I am sorry I do not understand.

Architect All studios must have access to the outdoors.

URBAN5 I am sorry I do not understand.

Architect A one-room residential unit must have outdoor access.

URBAN5 Now I understand. Furthermore, from now on, whenever you say "studios," I will assume you mean one-room residential units.[91]

After the discussion above, URBAN5 was supposed to learn the word "studios" and add it to its vocabulary of interactions with that user, and any time that user used the word "studios" or drew a one-room residential unit, the system used this new object. Negroponte and Groisser imagined that URBAN5 could eventually parse data from the user's interactions in order to create a more personalized interaction, or at least, "to gather personal manifestations and innuendos to be applied later in an attempt at congenial conversation with the designer," Negroponte wrote.[92] They thought that perhaps over time, this dialogue would be so particular to the user and URBAN5 that its original software could effectively die out, replaced by the user's unique interactions with the system.

But getting URBAN5 to respond intelligently was much more difficult than Groisser, Negroponte, and their students had realized. URBAN5's conversational style had more in common with the ELIZA psychotherapist computer program developed by Joseph Weizenbaum at MIT (1964–1966), which parodied the conversational patterns of a therapist in an initial psychiatrist interview.[93] The ELIZA program gave the illusion of meaningful conversation by following rules that recognize and decompose words and structures, and then transforming the sentence in response. An example dialogue with ELIZA ran as follows:

[User]   It's true. I am unhappy.

[ELIZA]   DO YOU THINK COMING HERE WILL HELP YOU NOT BE UNHAPPY

[User]   I need some help, that much seems certain.

[ELIZA]   WHAT WOULD IT MEAN TO YOU IF YOU GOT SOME HELP[94]

Although ELIZA acted cleverly, Weizenbaum never harbored illusions that it was actually intelligent. "A large part of whatever elegance may be credited to ELIZA lies in the fact that ELIZA maintains the illusion of understanding with so little machinery," wrote Weizenbaum. But over time, should ELIZA develop a bigger store of information or the ability to detect its users' sentiments and rationalizations, it would be said to have "belief structure" that could also potentially be simulated: effectively, a detectible epistemology.[95] Still, that seemed to be far off from where things stood in 1966. "It is useful to remember that the ELIZA program itself is merely a translating processor in the technical programming sense," Weizenbaum wrote.

At the same time that AMG was working on URBAN5 in the late 1960s, Terry Winograd was investigating a similar domain in his doctoral research at the MIT AI Laboratory: the use of natural language to manipulate spatial territories. He developed the SHRDLU system that investigated "complex language activity" in a blocks world.[96] (Despite the similarities, both Negroponte and Winograd say they weren't aware of each other at that time.)[97] The system presented a simulated robot with one arm and one eye, represented on a screen in "pretend" conversation with its human "FRIEND," responding to plain language commands about its blocks world and learning new vocabulary in context.[98] For example, a user might interact with the robot friend in this familiar manner:

PICK UP A BIG RED BLOCK.

—OK.

GRASP THE PYRAMID.

—I DON'T UNDERSTAND WHAT YOU MEAN BY 'THE PYRAMID.'

FIND A BLOCK WHICH IS TALLER THAN THE ONE YOU ARE HOLDING AND PUT IT INTO THE BOX.[99]

Winograd acknowledged SHRDLU's shortcomings in his dissertation. "First, at present it knows only about a tiny simplified subject. Second, most of what it knows has to be programmed, rather than told or taught. Finally, we can't talk to it at all! We have to type our side of the conversation and read the computer's."[100] Future research would need to address the structure and organization of information, and there was much more work to be done.

Dialogue was a sticky problem to perform well—difficult for Winograd, as his doctoral research, and almost impossible for Negroponte and Groisser. Winograd was circumspect about the scope of the challenges in his dissertation conclusion. "The challenge of programming a computer to use language is really the challenge of producing intelligence," he wrote. "Thought and language are so closely interwoven that the future of our research in natural language and computers will be neither a study of linguistic principles, nor a study of 'artificial' intelligence, but rather an inquiry into the nature of intelligence itself."[101] To design for artificial intelligence requires the designer or researcher to develop his or her own philosophy of intelligence. The problem came in the manifestation of these philosophies.

Negroponte stated that the failures of URBAN5 and the challenges of designing intelligent systems sparked him to write *The Architecture Machine*.[102] He admitted that the idea behind URBAN5 was "naively simple."[103] It seemed easy enough to design a system that monitored and clarified a user's commands. But Negroponte and Groisser underestimated the difficulty in handling the required abstractions of the system. "URBAN5 suggests true dialogue, suggests an evolutionary system, suggests an intelligent system—but, in itself, is none of these," Negroponte wrote.[104] He bemoaned the inability of a computer to absorb nonverbal and gestural cues that one would ordinarily pick up in conversation, writing (citing Weizenbaum, the ELIZA creator), "This all implies a congenial idiom, but it is still a narrow channel of communication that

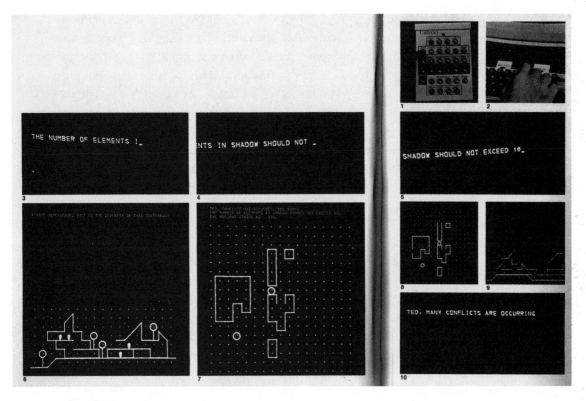

Figure 6.02
URBAN5 engaged its user in a question-and-answer dialogue about the design process. The ambitions of Nicholas Negroponte and Leon Groisser were greater than what URBAN5 would achieve—the "TED, MANY CONFLICTS ARE OCCURRING" statement seems to illustrate that fact. *The Architecture Machine*, by Nicholas Negroponte, published by the MIT Press.

ignores, as we have said, the language of gestures and the intonations available in face-to-face contact. The informal sensory and motor augmentation of understanding is verily 'unavailable to readers of telegrams—be they computers or humans.' But who designs environments by telegram?"[105] In subsequent publications about the project, Negroponte and Groisser backpedaled on URBAN5's original goals: a 1970 article is titled "URBAN5: A Machine That Discusses Urban Design." And even that title went too far: the system was too limited to simulate much of a discussion about urban design. Ultimately, Negroponte wrote, "Playing is learning, but URBAN5 has not been sufficiently sophisticated actually to frolic; instead it has inexhaustibly printed garbage."[106] If nothing else, he quipped, it was at least a friendly failure of a system.

URBAN5 suffered from the same problems that other blocks worlds did: inappropriate handling of abstraction and real-world constraints and too great a scope of the design problem at hand. Rodney Brooks, robotics professor and MIT AI Lab director from 1997 to 2007 criticized such blocks worlds approaches as "simple special purpose solutions to . . . more general problems,"[107] reflecting Negroponte's own critique of URBAN5 as "a barrage of special-purpose (little) architecture machines."[108] On one hand, as a menagerie of specialized programs, URBAN5 was not general enough to succeed at the problems of urban design. On the other hand, as an urban design program that attempted to build a natural language interface, it attempted too much. Despite IBM's funding and MIT's support, URBAN5 is perhaps best understood as an architectural blocks world, yielding the same cautions and lessons from other blocks world and microworld failings.

If microworlds had such shortcomings, then why did researchers use them? Terry Winograd said he chose to develop his SHRDLU system in a blocks world because it was the natural choice at that time, because many AI researchers conducted their projects in blocks worlds. In addition, the visual and conversational interface garnered attention for his project—even as commands for a simulated robot on a screen. "The fact that you could talk about something you could actually see was an important thing for getting people to pay attention to it," he said.[109] Microworlds made for good demos, and Winograd and Negroponte both knew that a project with a good demo was an attractive project to fund.

SEEK

It was a city designed to learn from its inhabitants. Constructed of cubes, it could be reconfigured at the whim of its residents.[110] A robotic arm would study the occupants' movements and then move the blocks in anticipation of their choices. The city's residents: gerbils; their locus: SEEK, displayed at the 1970 *Software* exhibition at the Jewish Museum in New York. SEEK used a mechanism "that senses the physical environment, affects that environment, and in turn attempts to handle local unexpected events within the environment."[111] A photograph on the exhibition catalog cover depicts a sea of mirrored blocks in a glass pen on a bed of wood chips, with two handsome gerbils in the foreground looking at the camera—the instigators of the aforementioned "unexpected events." A steel and Lucite electromagnetic hand, guided by a tangle of colored wires and a coiled cord, dominates the top half of the image. "Gerbils match wits with computer-built environment," states a caption. Inside the catalog, a double-page spread introducing the "Life in a Computerized Environment" section, opens to a rodent's-eye perspective showing the gerbil in its environment. The next pages present the five-foot by eight-foot pen of mirrored two-inch cubes, cables connected to a computer, three men in ties peering into the city, gerbils inhabiting it, and the robotic arm looming over the blocks.

SEEK's job was to manipulate and organize a blocks world to "show how a machine handled a mismatch between its model of the world and the real world."[112] It ran six programs: Generate, Degenerate, Fix It, Straighten, Find, and Error Detect, used to randomly lay out, reconfigure, align, and correct the blocks environment, using its arm and plastic attachments to stack, move, and vibrate the blocks into place.[113] The gerbils ("selected for their curiosity") introduced a dose of real-world chaos into the equation.[114] "The outcome was a constantly changing architecture that reflected the way the little animals used the place," Negroponte wrote.[115] But the system was not apprised of the presence of its rodent residents, he wrote. "Unbeknownst to SEEK, the little animals are

Figure 6.03
"Life in a computerized environment" from the perspective of the user (in this case, a gerbil) inhabiting it. From the SEEK project by the Architecture Machine Group, shown at the *Software* show at the Jewish Museum, 1970. Photograph: Shunk-Kender © J. Paul Getty Trust. Getty Research Institute, Los Angeles (2014.R.20).

Figure 6.04
The SEEK system involved a robotic mechanism that tried to stack and order blocks. When it was included at the *Software* show at the Jewish Museum in 1970, it also involved a community of gerbils that lived in its pen, making a mess of the blocks that SEEK tried to organize. *The Architecture Machine*, by Nicholas Negroponte, published by the MIT Press.

bumping into blocks, disrupting constructions, and toppling towers. The result is a substantial mismatch between the three-dimensional reality and the computer remembrances which reside in the memory of SEEK's computer. SEEK's role is to deal with these inconsistencies."[116] The actions of the gerbils were intended to highlight the shortcomings of the model in which they lived.

SEEK demonstrated both the potential and the problems of a responsive environment. On the one hand, it was intended to show "inklings of a responsive behavior inasmuch as the actions of the gerbils are not predictable and the reactions of *SEEK* purposefully correct or amplify gerbil-provoked dislocations."[117] But, on the other hand, its model fell short of these goals. "Even in its triviality and simplicity, SEEK metaphorically goes beyond the real-world situation, where machines cannot respond to the predictable nature of people (gerbils)," the catalog explained. "Today machines are poor at handling sudden changes in context in environment. The lack of adaptability is the problem SEEK confronts in diminutive."[118]

As Negroponte wrote at the beginning of *The Architecture Machine*, operating without regard to context may be dangerous, if not downright subversive: "Any design procedure, set of rules, or truism is tenuous, if not subversive, when used out of context or regardless of context."[119] SEEK demonstrated this very notion, advocating for the role of some manner of intelligence built into a responsive environment. "If computers are to be our friends they must understand our metaphors. If they are to be responsive to changing, unpredictable, context-dependent human needs, they will need an artificial intelligence that can cope with complex contingencies in a sophisticated manner (drawing upon these metaphors) much as SEEK deals with elementary uncertainties in a simple-minded fashion," he wrote.[120]

"Our bodies are hardware, our behavior software," as a pull quote from Ted Nelson states in the introductory essay to *Software*.[121] The situation couldn't be truer for the position of the gerbils: not only did they attack each other, SEEK tended to kill them.[122] To make matters worse, the *Software* show itself was deemed a critical failure for a number of reasons beyond SEEK: the show greatly exceeded its budget; the time-shared computer that supported many of the projects did not function ("due to problems, ironically enough, with the software"); the trustees of the museum censored the catalog; the Jewish Museum nearly went bankrupt; and after the Jewish Theological Seminary saved the museum, JTS demanded that it no longer show experimental art. The follow-up show at the Smithsonian was canceled.[123]

SEEK's technologies beyond the *Software* show belonged to other blocks world initiatives and collaborations in the MIT AI Lab, particularly in computer vision and the ability to parse conflicting sources of information (this time, without gerbils).[124] The AI Lab worked toward "building a practical real-world scene-analysis system": Marvin Minsky and Seymour Papert reported to ARPA that they were working on "visually-controlled automatic manipulation and physical world problem-solving."[125] The vision systems that Minsky and Papert researched also sought to make sense of everyday chaos: "automatic analysis of a desk top littered with books, pens, telephones etc., or the operation of an assembly-line under visual control so that the components do not have to be presented in precisely determined positions, or a vision system to guide a mobile automaton through unfamiliar terrain."[126] The Architecture Machine Group continued to work on these problems of spatial recognition and intelligence, frequently with the AI Lab's technologies, and the AI Lab mentored AMG students. Papert supervised architecture students Anthony Platt and Mark Drazen as SEEK incorporated the "Minsky-Papert eye," a video camera connected to a computer that "read" specific areas of a stack of blocks in order to draw them on a CRT terminal.[127] Negroponte wrote about these uses of SEEK, with no mention of the gerbils, in *The Architecture Machine*.[128]

Collaborating with Gordon Pask: Second-Order Cybernetics and Conversation Theory

The Architecture Machine Group collaborated with cybernetician Gordon Pask on two extended occasions: in 1973 on HUNCH, a program that attempted to recognize a user's hand sketch, as a part of a National Science Foundation grant for Computer Aids for Participatory Architecture and, in 1976, on Graphical Conversation Theory, a basic research proposal for almost $1.5 million in NSF funding. Pask was no stranger to artists and architects. He was keenly interested in cybernetic intersections with architecture and applied cybernetic principles to art and architecture throughout his career. He worked closely with Cedric Price and Joan Littlewood on the Fun Palace, and inspired ideas used in Generator (1976–1979). He was also a frequent and long-term visitor to the Architecture Machine Group and contributed the convoluted introductory chapter, "Aspects of Machine Intelligence" to *Soft Architecture Machines,* which involved a complicated proof of conversation theory with scribbled diagrams of feedback loops.[129] Pask's article, "The Architectural Relevance of Cybernetics" (see chapter 5) in which Pask suggested that computers could change the design paradigm by altering the relationship between the architect and the system, also influenced Negroponte and the researchers at the Architecture Machine Group.[130]

Pask pursued second-order cybernetics and, after the mid-1970s, "conversation theory," his advanced theories on second-order cybernetics.[131] Whereas first-order cybernetics produce a straightforward model of feedback in a system, second-order cybernetics takes into consideration the observer of the system and the observer's model of the system—a "cybernetics of cybernetics," as Heinz von Foerster put it.[132] Conversation theory, then, was a framework for describing how people gain knowledge through the use of natural language, object language, and metalanguages. Pask and the Architecture Machine Group applied second-order cybernetics to "1) model (in the machine) the user, his needs and desires; 2) refine the user's model of himself; 3) illustrate the implications to and expressions in physical form of both of these models," stated one report.[133] Pask and AMG applied conversation theory to computer graphics in an extension of a program called HUNCH, and eventually, to a bigger project called "Graphical Conversation Theory."

HUNCH

Following the concept that much architectural thinking happens as sketches on napkins and scraps of paper, HUNCH was a digital drawing system that attempted to recognize the sketches of its user, turning the stylus lines into data and using machine intelligence to translate and represent sketches. It also highlighted the difficulties in producing these representations and served as an example of the rhetorical handwaving in which the lab often engaged. HUNCH was the first student research project at AMG, pursued by James Taggart for his bachelor of architecture thesis in 1970 and his master of science thesis in electrical engineering in 1973. It was originally supported by AMG and the Ford Foundation, then received ongoing funding from the NSF,

MIT's Project MAC (under ARPA support), and a grant from the Graham Foundation for Advanced Study in the Fine Arts.[134]

Taggart and Negroponte chose sketching because it is the primary method within which architectural thinking manifests, "what architects do privately on the backs of envelopes, in the margins of telephone books or on the yards of yellow tracing stock used in the peace of a study or studio," wrote Negroponte.[135] In his master's thesis, Taggart breaks down how sketches function: they "act as a sort of physical memory" that operates in dialogue with the sketcher, allowing for sharing ideas that are hard to transmit in words and/or for recording such ideas for the person doing the sketching. The whole is greater than the sum of its parts, Taggart wrote: "The result of such a dialogue is that the information contained in the interaction is greater than the amount of information which could be contained in the sketch alone, or which the user could carry around in his head."[136] Drawing on (no pun intended) second-order cybernetics, the concept behind HUNCH was that it would develop a model of the user and how he or she drew, then develop "HUNCH's model of the designer's model of it," and then, finally, develop HUNCH's model of the user's model of its model of him in a slightly confusing construct, but central to Pask's cybernetics.[137] To use the system, a user drew with a stylus on a Sylvania data tablet and a series of programs and routines interpreted the pressure and speed of the stylus, then made inferences about lines intersection and latching, shape recognition, shading, and three-dimensional representation.[138] Negroponte quipped, "They range from recognizing a square, to recognizing a cube, to being a new brutalist."[139] HUNCH attempted to interpret the lines' meaning through the user's actions (the "model of the model"): retracing the lines in a sketch, for instance, would be interpreted to mean that the user intended to make a set of lines intersect, and what kind of architectural sketch it was—plan, section, axonometric, or orthographic.[140] These increasingly complex models were intended to produce the kinds of partnerships and symbiotic relationships that Negroponte and Groisser had unsuccessfully pursued with URBAN5.

Although HUNCH was developed for architectural sketches, AMG thought it could be used for a wider variety of purposes. "We believe that HUNCH will have general applicability as a front end to computer systems that require the graphical input of ideas which are not well formed" and for other situations in which a computer user might be "hampered by the means of input," Negroponte, Groisser and Taggart wrote.[141] Negroponte even imagined that the sketch system could eventually interface directly with a physical model, a sort of HUNCH meets SEEK. "In some sense it is a punchline to the demonstration program we employ to demonstrate the present workings of HUNCH; it is not an integral part of sketch recognition. However, consider the spectacle: you

sketch a perspective of an assemblage of housing units; behind you a machine is building them. You change your sketch; the physical model is changed."[142] A few years
later, Cedric Price's Generator included this function in the programs that John Frazer
designed for it.

However, there was a familiar gulf between AMG's—and more specifically,
Negroponte's—vision of HUNCH and what it could actually do: what the system actually produced was considerably more modest than its aims. The fidelity of the human
sketch versus the system's model of it proved very difficult to realize, and moreover,
HUNCH couldn't recognize curves, and so AMG left them out of the system and then
celebrated their exclusion.[143] "We have ignored curves for a long time. They are not
indigenous to architecture; we don't believe that sophisticated computer graphics techniques will lead to a proliferation of Gaudiesque architecture (in fact we might want
to discourage it). . . . Thus we are willing to recognize them, but in no sense try to 'fit'
them," Negroponte, Groisser, and Taggart wrote.[144]

Admitting failure on some aspects of sketch recognition again served as justification
for further experimentation. In a section of his master's thesis titled "LETDOWN," Taggart frankly assessed HUNCH: "It would be nice to be able to claim to have developed
the alert, provocative, interactive system mentioned in the earlier section. The system
which has been developed, HUNCH, falls short of this goal, however. Provocative it is,
although not in the manner described above," he admitted. "It is also moderately interactive. It does not, however, carry on anything which can be called a dialogue. . . . Yet
dialogue implies purpose and a developing context, and although HUNCH does know
a few tricks, once it has performed, all it can do is walk off stage."[145] What Taggart
considered a letdown, however, AMG supported. Negroponte wrote, "Sketch recognition has provided a medium of study with which to experiment on the embodiment
of fuzzy thinking, previously limited to linguistic approaches. . . . Otherwise, fuzzy
assertions and the vagaries we postulate to be inherent in searching through design
alternatives are relegated to caprice."[146] The undefined and imperfect correlated to the
problems of context, modeling, and fidelity and thus justified further research and
development.

The sketch-recognition input mechanisms in HUNCH remained an area of focus
for the Architecture Machine Group, a meshing of input mechanism and user modeling
that the group incorporated under the rubric of "idiosyncratic systems" that referred to
personalized computing paradigms. It also marked a difficult episode for the lab as it con-
tended with changes in the funding culture of defense-funded research that had emerged
in the early 1970s, and with other technical labs at American universities.

Changes in Funding Culture

The small successes and bigger failures of artificial intelligence research, along with changes in how universities could fund research, exercised a big influence on the Architecture Machine Group and other labs that relied on Department of Defense funding, and shaped the path that the AMG could take. Growing protest against the war in Vietnam forced MIT and other college campuses to reconsider military-related research. Until the Vietnam War, basic research—research that did not have a specific, determined end use—could be characterized as relevant to defense needs, even if it did not have an explicit defense component.[147] The Mansfield Amendment, introduced in 1969 by Senate majority leader Mike Mansfield and passed in 1970 at the height of the Vietnam War, sought to restrict military funding of academic research to only those projects "with a direct and apparent relationship to a specific military function or operation."[148] Restrictions tightened further in 1973, explicitly restricting DARPA funding to applied, tactical defense research. The National Science Foundation was intended to be the source of basic research funding, but its peer-review model operated differently than the "closed world" relationships of DoD sponsorship. Universities seeking funding were required to style their research proposals to appeal to specific military applications, or otherwise apply to the National Science Foundation—strategies that AMG followed with differing degrees of success.

The defense-funded "closed world" network ultimately enabled almost all development of computers and systems for artificial intelligence. This was by choice and by design: the funders felt like family.[149] Marvin Minsky later told Stewart Brand that ARPA trusted the AI Lab, "because they were us. For fifteen years the office down there was run by an ex-MIT person or equivalent. It was like having a patron."[150] Negroponte echoed the sentiment. "There was DoD funding, but it was through a real personality of someone [Marvin Denicoff of the Office of Naval Research] who was betting on us as people, not the ideas," he said in an interview.[151] The DoD supported AMG's work, particularly in the development of novel computer interfaces and simulation technologies for AI. It was an environment that Negroponte valued. "For me and my peers, getting Department of Defense money to do research was a great honor," he said in a 1995 interview. "There were no secrets. You were encouraged to publish. After all, it was military funding that developed the Internet, personal computers, multimedia, and artificial intelligence."[152] In short, the circular "closed world" played a major role in structuring not only the field of AI but also the Architecture Machine Group, granting a good amount of autonomy to the individuals who made funding decisions. As Negroponte told Stewart Brand in the book *The Media Lab*, "It [defense funding] was our bread and butter for a decade, and I wish it would become again."[153]

Vietnam itself only gets a brief mention in the Architecture Machine Group narrative. Negroponte said that he was more or less "oblivious," even though there was an increasing number of large protests in 1969 and 1970, some of which Negroponte said he'd attended.[154] What he regretted was the impact of protest on the research landscape at MIT. After the divestiture of Draper Lab, it changed the nature of all research, he said.[155] "I was the last of a generation that still emulated their parents. We thought it was cool to do things grown-ups did," Negroponte said.[156] It was not only his parents but also his brother that Negroponte looked up to: John Negroponte is a professor and career diplomat who was ambassador to Honduras, Mexico, the Philippines, and, more recently, Iraq, and whom Henry Kissinger included in the Paris peace talks intended to end the Vietnam War. John Negroponte later became deputy secretary of state and the first director of National Intelligence (appointed by George W. Bush).[157]

AI's First Failings

While the field of artificial intelligence had been successful in developing time-sharing platforms and networked computing, it did not succeed at answering the big questions it had posed in the 1950s and 1960s, when AI researchers claimed it would be able to model the human brain in software.[158] Alternate approaches such as expert systems were not much better (an approach that followed Allen Newell and Herbert Simon's heuristics, modeling knowledge on that of domain specialists, then applying these models to problem-solving).[159] As stated in the highly critical 1973 "Lighthill Report" from the United Kingdom, the fields of inquiry were too abstract to be practical, and progress on issues of natural language, machine translation, and speech recognition had fallen short of expectations.[160] As a result of this report, as well as fallout from the Mansfield Amendment, the big pools of funding that AI had enjoyed evaporated as research efforts turned to more specific and finite command-and-control applications.

One of the key problems was the very abstraction and reduction that both AMG and AI research had championed. Reduction was "a dangerous weapon," one of the issues that contributed to GOFAI's failures, as former MIT AI Lab director Rodney Brooks argued: "There is no clean division between perception (abstraction) and reasoning in the real world."[161] AI failed to solve the "hard problems" of perception and motor skills. Abstracting them reduced the possibilities of finding the proper solution in the future, he wrote.[162] The fact that the blocks world isolated certain problems while ignoring others reflected the shortcomings of microworlds in general, and even Marvin Minsky's celebration of the limitations could not sustain sponsorship enthusiasm. Brooks continued, "Eventually criticism surfaced that the blocks world was a 'toy world' and that within it there were simple special purpose solutions to what should be considered more general problems."[163] AI research operated under the slogan "Good representation is the key to AI." Thus the abstractions presented in microworlds were graspable, manipulable representations, but not extensible to what they themselves represented.

Thinking back to Minsky and Papert's characterization of microworlds as "a fairyland in which things are so simplified that almost every statement about them would be literally false if asserted about the real world," the problem with AMG's microworld models is that they *did* apply to the real world.[164] Negroponte did not intend for his ideas of dialogue and self-reflexive modeling to remain in the lab. The area of inquiry was still architectural, engaged with problems of designing for the built environment. And while Negroponte and AMG, like Alexander and, to a certain extent, Price, were more interested in the process than the end product, in AMG's case, the stakes and the impact were larger.

Graphical Conversation Theory and the National Science Foundation

The Architecture Machine Group banked on a grand proposal to the National Science Foundation: Graphical Conversation Theory, a proposal for a five-year, $1.42 million suite of projects on AI, interactive systems, computer graphics, and personalized computing.[165] In the Graphical Conversation Theory proposal, AMG likened the design process to that of "a conversation taking place between different perspectives which may exist within the mind of one or of several designers."[166] Graphical Conversation Theory expanded Nicholas Negroponte's theory of architecture machines, Gordon Pask's conversation theory, and AMG's multimedia research in sound, multimedia images, motion graphics, haptic feedback, and environments, providing a research plan to develop technologies to carry out this research under a large, well-funded umbrella.[167] The NSF rejected the proposal in a painful turning point for the Architecture Machine Group.

Producing the Graphical Conversation Theory proposal was an all-hands-on-deck moment in the lab. The six-hundred-page document, with a glossy, light-gray cover embossed with computer graphics, was created in six weeks by a team of nine researchers ("an experimental psychologist, a computer scientist of graphics upbringing, an operating systems expert, a hardware specialist, a cybernetician, an actor, an architect, a color theorist, and a technical voyeur," the proposal's introduction stated).[168] It opened with a long theoretical section that introduced conversation theory and evocatively titled projects like The Intelligent Pen, Drawing with Your Eyes, Seeing Through Your

Figure 6.05
The NSF proposal for Graphical Conversation Theory was a major production for the Architecture
Machine Group, in which the lab proposed uniting computer graphics, conversation theory, and
a number of research projects under one umbrella. It was not funded. Graphical Conversation
Theory proposal courtesy of Christopher Herot. Permission granted by Nicholas Negroponte.

Hands, and Painting Photographs. AMG proposed hardware prototypes that tied in
with concurrent AMG research into touch-sensitive and flat displays, color graphics,
memory, and the Scribblephone sketching system (HUNCH used over a phone line
with another user).[169] It also contained a two-hundred-page appendix of AMG papers,
reports, and book excerpts, as well as research already under way through corporate
support from companies such as IBM (the Media Room) and Department of Defense
support from DARPA (on the Spatial Data Management System) and the Office of Naval
Research (computer personalization).[170] AMG proudly touted the document in several

issues of the group's *Architecture Machinations* newsletter as the group produced it and delivered the proposal in November 1976.

But the NSF rejected the Graphical Conversation Theory proposal. There were four areas in which AMG apparently miscalculated: the project scope was bigger than what the NSF funded; its connection to artificial intelligence wasn't clear enough; the glossy design of the proposal wasn't met well within the NSF; and there was a misalignment between the peer-review culture at the NSF and the DARPA "closed world" that received and propagated defense research funding.[171] The bad news arrived "by an unsigned form letter bearing the wrong title (for the proposal)," wrote Negroponte, who angrily recounted the rejection in an August 1977 *Architecture Machinations* newsletter article, after retrieving the anonymized reviews through a Freedom of Information Act request.[172] "Interaction with NSF in our field is over!" wrote Negroponte of the debacle.[173] The NSF felt unfriendly and unpredictable to the lab, unlike the kickoff of AMG's 1973 proposal for the Computer Aids for Participatory Research program, which started with a panel visit from Gordon Pask, Ivan Sutherland, Herbert Simon, and Alan Kay, and unlike the collegial, "closed world" network of defense funding.[174] Negroponte's bitter feelings about the NSF continue to this day. "NSF is a beauty contest that you go through peer review and at the end of the conference you have no history, you start all over again," he said in an interview with the author. "ONR [the Office of Naval Research], you build up their confidence, they fund you because they trust you, they believe in you. So the DARPA funding, the DoD in general, was much better. I hated the NSF."[175]

The Graphical Conversation Theory rejection necessitated a shift in AMG's funding. One-quarter to one-third of AMG's funding had come from the NSF in 1976–1977, which required the group to shift its project priorities into different initiatives, with consequences for the group's research pursuits and funding relationships from that point forward. AMG had already begun to think of shunting their NSF research into DoD projects earlier that year. "*An important overview, again a feeling* is an emerging interest in computer graphics, inferred from both public and private sectors. In some sense we are seemingly coming out of an era of too many promises, too much cost, and too little application. We are also moving into an era where finally, after fifteen years, we can see basic and conceptual breakthroughs beyond SKETCHPAD."[176]

Perhaps the Architecture Machine Group knew that they were reaching far in their proposal. Negroponte certainly could sense the limitations. And so he and the AMG researchers regrouped. They continued to build and demo their work in their facilities, while following funding strategies of other groups like the MIT AI Lab, adapting their work for the research applications that the Department of Defense favored: command and control.

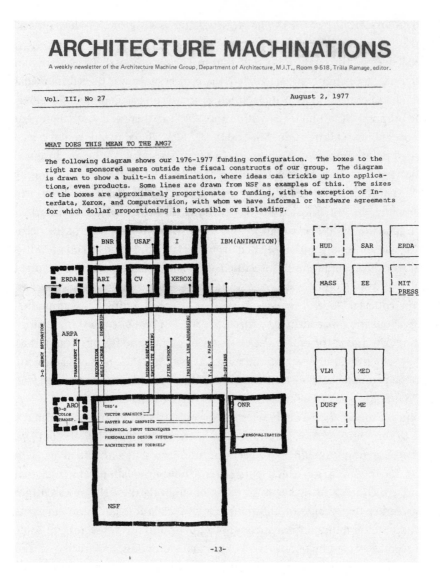

Figure 6.06
A diagram of the Architecture Machine Group funding configuration as it stood in 1976–1977, as
published in *Architecture Machinations,* the AMG newsletter for the lab and its friends. Nicholas
Negroponte, "NSF," *Architecture Machinations* 3, no. 27 (August 2, 1977): 10. Box 2, Folder 3, Institute Archives and Special Collections, MIT Libraries, Cambridge, Massachusetts.

Command and Control

In the wake of the Mansfield Amendment, Department of Defense agencies such as DARPA and the Office of Naval Research were required to prioritize projects with applied, tactical military applications and not basic research. In particular, they sponsored command-and-control projects. Command and control refers to a set of military activities concerned with handling a variable and quickly changing field of operation, including "the collection of data about the environment, planning for options, decision making, and dissemination of the decision" intended to lead to better strategic information and better command decisions.[177] Its history extends back to the Semi-Automatic Ground Environment system (SAGE, 1958–1983); its development is closely linked throughout the Cold War to J. C. R. Licklider's vision of symbiosis applied to combat, through "automation" (removing humans from "precision-critical machines" and replacing them with machine-based prediction) and "integration" (folding the person into the feedback loops operated by the machines, "by analyzing them as mechanisms of the same kinds of formalisms as the machines themselves," as Paul Edwards wrote).[178] Working on command and control proved attractive to university computing researchers who sought to develop better human–computer interaction; to the DoD, which wanted to better incorporate computers and computer interfaces into command and control; and to the Architecture Machine Group, who needed to carry on research after failing to win their NSF grant for the Graphical Conversation Theory proposal.[179]

In line with these changes in DoD funding priorities, Patrick Winston, director of the MIT AI Lab from 1972 to 1997, encouraged researchers to develop projects that met these new priorities.[180] "The mid 1970s were days in which you had to find a way of explaining the work in applications terms. It wasn't enough to study reasoning; you had to talk about how it might be applied to ship maintenance or something," said Winston in a 1989 interview. "I was seeking to find intersections between what the laboratory was doing and what DARPA was either interested in or could be persuaded to be interested in. So in some cases, it was a matter of pointing out the potential application of a piece of work."[181] Similar to the AI Lab, the Architecture Machine Group tailored its proposals to meet these criteria and garner these pools of funding. Even though projects shifted toward applied military research, DARPA still kept projects within a small network of trusted individuals, prioritizing its "closed world" of institutions and individuals. AMG developed a good relationship with Craig Fields, a rising star in the DARPA organization who championed electronics and commerce research (later taking a fall as a result) that extended to the founding of the MIT Media Lab.

The creativity of the demonstrations and the futuristic nature of AMG's projects likely contributed to the group's success in winning contracts that focused on graphical, auditory, and spatial interfaces under the aegis of command-and-control initiatives. AMG was like AI and robotics research groups that, as historian Stuart Umpleby wrote, "imagined a variety of futuristic electronic and robotic devices on battlefields. These science fiction-like descriptions proved to be quite popular in Washington, DC." The DoD received more funding for research from Congress, who "reasoned that the more automated the battlefield was, the fewer soldiers/voters would be killed or wounded."[182] AMG's information landscapes and simulations certainly fit the bill. The budgets for AMG's projects increased, leveraging relationships with electronics manufacturers, DARPA, and the Office of Naval Research. And in the process, AMG began to build a new vision of the future: of the architecture machines in which we might one day live, as Negroponte had suggested at the beginning of *The Architecture Machine*.

"Supreme Usability"

Usability typically refers to the ease of use of an interface, as well as ways that methods, tools, and processes improve interface design. When Nicholas Negroponte and Architecture Machine Group principal researcher Richard Bolt coined "supreme usability," they melded architecture, interfaces, and simulation technologies to engender a new kind of familiarity with computers. It presented new ways to navigate the digital, whether on the screen, in the battlefield, or in the living room. Supreme usability suggested a new level of human–computer interaction, "that is, that one can be oneself in the company of machines," Negroponte and Bolt wrote.[183] The integration, the oneness with machinery, would serve "'response compatibility' in its broadest sense."[184] In this regard, the human–computer-information environment would meld with place to best support action under "tactical conditions" in the Architecture Machine Group Media Room.[185] It was a step toward realizing Negroponte's theory of architecture machines.

Supreme usability was ergonomics on a grand scale, architecture that brought a human into alignment not only with physical affordances and information landscapes, but also with military logistics, entertainment, and the built environment. Projects from 1976 onward in the Architecture Machine Group, including the Spatial Data Management System (SDMS), the Aspen Movie Map, and Put That There, all swapped the model of a user working on a computational environment from the outside: they put the user into the computer, what Negroponte called "being in the interface."[186] "Mapping by Yourself," investigated mobile, digitally layered map devices—putting the user in the world with technology at his fingertips, and the "Data Space" proposal underscored the stakes for supreme usability, from the cockpit to the home. These late AMG projects all explored the conflation of human, the interface, and the built environment, in applications of Negroponte's theories of architecture machines both portable and all-surrounding.

The Media Room

The Media Room was the locus of many Architecture Machine Group projects that explored digital environments. It was a soundproofed space, eighteen feet by eleven feet by eleven and a half feet, with a six-foot-by-eight-foot screen built into the wall in front of the user, the other walls carpeted in dark pile fabric and sporting an octophonic sound system.[187] The center of the room featured the iconic Eames Lounge Chair outfitted with joypads (touch-sensitive joysticks), with two smaller touch screens in reach of the user, a ten-inch-square data tablet that the user could hold in the lap and operate with a stylus.[188]

In the Media Room, the user inhabited the terminal, rather than operating it from the outside. The computer is eerily absent. It had disappeared into the environment, or conversely, the room itself became the computer. AMG principal researcher Richard Bolt wrote that the Media Room was "a physical facility where the user's terminal is literally a room into which one steps, rather than a desktop CRT before which one is perched."[189] Stewart Brand described it in 1987 as a "personal computer with the person inside."[190]

One purpose of the Media Room was to foster research into a "sense of place" within data landscapes, by developing an "informational surround" that enveloped the user with multimedia content of different types, input and output interfaces, and that used spatial modeling for navigating information.[191] In Negroponte's early "fancies" (his word), his imaginations of the Media Room, he called it simply, "the Place" or "a computing place."[192] "Foremost, it will be totally quiet, isolated from the machine room, conceivably without even a door connecting directly to it (i.e., you will have to go out into the corridor and back into the machine room)," he wrote.[193]

The notion of information as place, in its simplest characterization, employed spatial metaphors for navigating information.[194] This "perceptual construct" offered visual and auditory cues that helped the user develop a spatial sense of the data landscape by using some qualities of "real space."[195] In the way that one remembers where a book resides in a full bookshelf or a specific note in a pile of papers on a desk, one would use the same mental process to navigate an information place. Negroponte referred to this the "Simonides effect," after the Greek poet famous for his memorization prowess—also known as a "memory palace." As Simonides set his poems and speeches to memory, he walked through a temple, situating each part of the speech in his mind to a location

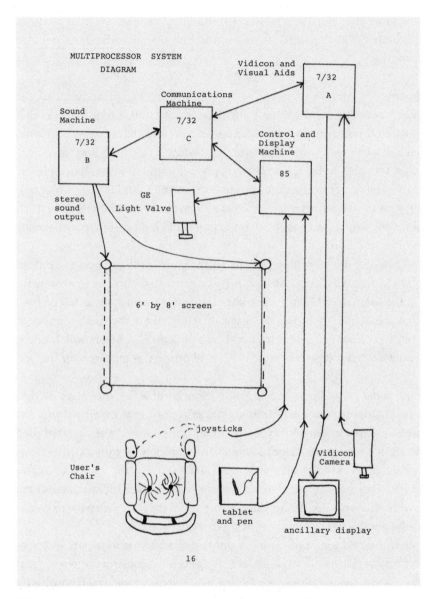

Figure 6.07
A schematic of the Media Room published in William Donelson's master's thesis, showing the chair with its joypads (joysticks), the cameras and displays, the tablet and pen, and the computers that would power the room out of view of the user. William Donelson, "Spatial Management of Data" (master's thesis, MIT, 1977), 16. Courtesy of MIT Institute Archives and Special Collections, MIT Libraries, Cambridge, Massachusetts.

or object—a column here, a garden there, an altar over there. When he later gave the speech, he imagined himself walking through the temple and correlated it to the oration. The landscape that Simonides walked through in his mind was akin to how a user would navigate an information place. One AMG proposal likened it to "the space that we perceive behind the surface of a mirror, or the virtual auditory space that we reconstruct when we hear a stereophonic recording," but could similarly be a "mental construct: for example the 221-B Baker Street of the detective, Sherlock Holmes, which space Conan Doyle addicts knew as well as they did their own living rooms."[196] It could potentially aid the memory, link abstract ideas, and help a user to process auditory and verbal information.[197] The geographer Yi-Fu Tuan characterized "place" as different than "space"; it has an "aura," an "identity."[198] As one gets to know a space, it becomes a place.[199] It is "an organized world of meaning," Tuan wrote.[200] Place calls attention to the familiar and the comfortable instead of the anonymous and systematized.

Spatial navigation in the Media Room's projects, along these lines, would render information and data familiar, organized, friendly, identifiable. "Work places" and information places would thus foster creativity and comfort where "work stations" dampened it, Negroponte and AMG's researchers postulated.[201] Negroponte wrote, "The 'place' or milieu that we envisage . . . is perhaps most directly conceived of as a compatible, comfortable place to be with computers. A state of mind, if you will. But states of mind have their objective correlative, and we have opted at the Architecture Machine Group to work toward realizing that correlate."[202] If an objective correlative, as the poet T. S. Eliot defined it, is about events that produce an emotion, then states of mind, as AMG saw them, were generated by what the group hoped would be a positive user experience of engaging information. The Media Room's spaces and interfaces would, to use Tuan's concept, organize meaning.

AMG's researchers also gave careful attention to the chair at the center of the Media Room, envisioning a sort of sci-fi dental chair before settling on the Eames Lounge Chair that the researchers doctored by inserting joypads (touchpad joysticks) for navigation. The chair was meant to elevate the experience of using the room, while underscoring the kind of calm, womblike place they intended the room to be. "It reflects convictions and positions about the nature and tone of human-computer interaction that we have attempted to actualize in the media room setting," Bolt wrote.[203] This attitude extended into other sensations in the user experience of the Media Room. "Just as the hands-on immediacy of touch-sensitive pads suggests a literal impatience with intangibles about data, so the decor as epitomized in the selection of the style of chair rebuts the premise that system users must live in severe, ascetic settings," Bolt wrote.[204] To put it another way, the chair repositioned the status of the user from someone

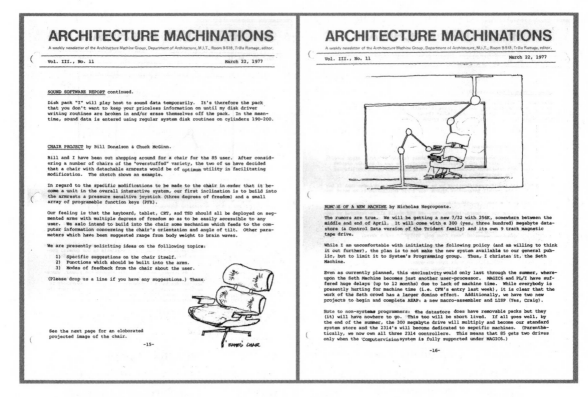

Figure 6.08
A sketch of the iconic Eames Lounge Chair (left) and a vision of how it might be connected to different apparatuses (right) in an article titled "Chair Project" in the *Architecture Machinations* newsletter. Bill Donelson and Chuck McGinn, "Chair Project," *Architecture Machinations* 3, no. 11 (March 22, 1977): 15. Box 2, Folder 2. Courtesy of Institute Archives and Special Collections, MIT Libraries, Cambridge, Massachusetts.

molded to a terminal to a person occupying a privileged position. Cognition scientist Alan Blackwell wrote in 2006 of it and other such technologies, "The users of these systems are made to resemble heroic explorers, adventurers, and wielders of technical power, rather than 'office professionals.'"[205] This choice probably did not hurt the demos that AMG gave of its systems.

The Aspen Movie Map

The Aspen Movie Map allowed users to "drive" down the streets of a hyperrealistic simulation of the town at hypothetical speeds of up to 160 miles per hour.[206] In the Media Room, the view of Aspen unfolded on the central wall-sized screen, with an aerial satellite map of the city on the left-hand touch display, and a street map view on the right-hand side—a mode called "helicoptering." (A later version coalesced into a single touch-screen interface.) The Aspen Movie Map was not (only) a reason for filming junkets to Aspen, but also a platform for exploring military simulation.[207] The project came in the wake of a successful recovery by the Israeli army of a hijacked plane in Entebbe, Uganda, in 1976: by simulating and rehearsing the rescue in the Negev Desert, the rescuers were better prepared, and most of the passengers and Israeli troops survived. Where Mossad and the Israeli army built a physical model of the airport in the desert, however, the Architecture Machine Group built a model of Aspen in digital images.[208]

The Movie Map promoted by Negroponte made "a 'new image of the city'; a brand of urban mapping," a reference to Kevin Lynch's book *The Image of the City*.[209] In that book, Lynch wrote, "The environment suggests distinctions and relations, and the observer—with great adaptability and in the light of his own purposes—selects, organizes and endows with meaning what he sees."[210] Aspen Movie Map is a digital tool that participates in this feedback loop, in which the user develops meaning by maneuvering the

Figure 6.09
The Aspen Movie Map, as viewed from within the Media Room. The user would sit in the chair and zoom through the streets of Aspen, with either maps or other images navigable on the ancillary screens. Courtesy of Architecture Machine Group and Nicholas Negroponte.

digital environment. Just as Yi-Fu Tuan defined place as the making meaning of space through familiarization and organization, the Aspen Movie Map would offer the making of meaning through simulation. The well-seated user, moving through virtual and distant spaces at his own speed, used maps and movies to build an image of a city or, rather, an image of a simulation.

To film the Aspen Movie Map, researchers including Andy Lippman, Michael Naimark, Peter Clay, Bob Mohl, and Walter Bender attached a film camera to a Jeep and photographed the street view and landmarks of Aspen, then converted the film to video. The images and maps were stored on videodisc—AMG had obtained one of twenty-five prototype MCA Discovision players (renamed LaserDisc in 1980) a year before it was available to consumers, which AMG used for audio-visual storage.[211] Each side of a videodisc stored fifty-four thousand frames of audiovisual content, and this greater storage capacity supported the faster and more dynamic transmission of information. The minicomputers served images, maps, and animations as the user "drove."

The notion of reality in a digital environment is determined by a user's perception of its experience. Here, the question became one of developing the appropriate perceptual cues for the environment. AMG researcher Scott Fisher argued in his master's thesis that achieving realistic environments was not just a matter of photoreality: "The proof of the 'ideal' picture is not being able to discern object from representation—to be convinced that one is looking at the real thing," he wrote. "But resemblance is only part of the effect. What is more important here is the process involved in 'unwrapping' the image. Evaluation of realism should also be based on how closely the presentation medium simulates dynamic perception in the real world."[212] The simulation that surpasses the real, creating images without reference is a Baudrillardian hyperreal. Of course, Ivan Sutherland in 1965 presented such a hyperreal interface in his "ultimate display," which would be "a room within which the computer can control the existence of matter. A chair displayed in such a room would be good enough to sit in. Handcuffs displayed in such a room would be confining, and a bullet displayed in such a room would be fatal. With appropriate programming such a display could literally be the Wonderland into which Alice walked."[213]

Aspen Movie Map researcher Bob Mohl wrote in his dissertation that "a novel form of spatial representation can be created which substitutes for the actual experience, . . . for pre-experiencing an unfamiliar locale that allows the acquisition of spatial knowledge to take place in a meaningful, natural, and accurate way."[214] This approach concentrated mapping, interface, and simulation into one flow, indistinguishable from one another—a combination of multiple perceptual modes. Mohl hedges the Movie

Map's limits: "Of course, it cannot measure up completely to the presence of being there. On the other hand, it provides some navigational aids which go beyond what is possible in the real environment."[215]

The key, however, is that AMG aimed to get there and believed that one day, it really would. A similar project that Negroponte wrote about in his 1995 book *Being Digital* showed how one might "helicopter" through a city made of information. DARPA program director Craig Fields in the Cybernetics Technology Office (who also funded the SDMS projects) "commissioned a computer-animated film of a fictional town, Dar El Marar. [216] The animated movie depicted a cockpit view from a helicopter flying around Dar El Marar, swooping into its streets, pulling back to see the whole townscape, visiting neighborhoods, and moving in close to see into buildings," Negroponte wrote in *Being Digital*.[217] The concept fused data interfaces with urban form, assuming that "you had built neighborhoods of information by storing data in particular buildings, like a squirrel storing nuts."[218] The purpose for swooping in and helicoptering into an Arabic-sounding, fictitious cityscape reinforces the combination of surveillance, information storage, and spatial memory, aligned again in the form of a city.

Spatial Data Management System (SDMS)

The Spatial Data Management System (SDMS) was a graphical user interface for moving through layers of information, an early version of a desktop interface, but projected on the wall. This four-million-pixel plane of information filled the six-foot-by-eight-foot screen in front of the user and contained smaller windows that represented graphical, textual, or moving images that the user could "find" and "peruse."[219] Four minicomputers worked in tandem to coordinate the navigation, control the system interaction, and serve the content that the user viewed from videodisc. As the user determined her own navigation path, the main minicomputer updated the images on the large and small screens. A "pixel window" that ran from a minicomputer scaled the images in real-time, while other minicomputers synchronized sound and managed the videodisc player.[220] The right-hand touch display presented an aerial view of "Dataland," the SDMS interface in its entirety, allowing the user to determine location within the data landscape.[221]

"Dataland" was a metaphor for location and a conceptual depth of increasing detail, its depth implied in terms of magnification and informational granularity.[222] An object that seemed fuzzy and low-resolution at a "distance" became clearer as one zoomed into it. Images, maps, and icons that represented entire systems of interaction populated the landscape: little photos "of animals, of people, even a miniature Landsat satellite photo of part of New England," wrote AMG principal researcher Richard Bolt.[223]

Figure 6.10
In using the Spatial Data Management System, the user would touch a "glyph" (an icon) on the touch screen and then zoom into the information for further navigation. The main object, such as a map, would display on the large screen before the user. Richard A. Bolt, *Spatial Data-Management* (Cambridge, MA: MIT, 1979), courtesy of MIT.

Zooming in to an image of a television set could start a TV program; zooming in to a photograph would open a set of photos that the user could move through. Bolt continued, "We see what appear to be book covers, television sets, a business letter, even a small image of an electronic hand-held calculator. Yet other items resemble emblems or 'glyphs,' not dissimilar from business logos"—what would now be called an "icon" on a computer desktop or smartphone.[224] In some futuristic handwaving, the book "glyph" might one day allow someone to "peruse" its text downloaded from "a computer-network-based 'book of the month' service" (a familiar concept today), not to mention that as a business logo, it suggested a whole set of commercial interactions familiar to contemporary web shoppers.[225]

The funded purpose of the SDMS, however, was managing tactical military tasks such as ship fleet management (as with Put That There).[226] The broader SDMS literature, especially Bolt's writings, do not hide the surveillant possibilities of the system, such as zooming in to map details. For example, the SDMS could provide a means to zoom from a map to a photograph of a specific street corner or attraction.[227] Such a function served as a means for investigating and becoming acquainted with foreign terrain.

Other movements into the information landscape fused one object category into another, with objects becoming the information that they provided: an image of a television set, complete with channel knobs and bunny-eared antennae, first becomes a TV screen and then the live action of a program. In *Spatial Data-Management*, as the user zooms into the image of a TV screen, we see an ostensibly Middle Eastern individual on the right side of the screen, wearing a kaffiyeh and holding an assault rifle. Closing in on that image launches video of the TV show *Columbo*, as Columbo walks up to the armed guard and shows his documents.[228] *Columbo* as a television show choice in the late 1970s might not be a surprise, but a scene with a man in traditionally Arab dress holding a gun, in a booklet for a DARPA project, indicates a specific use of navigating information: not watching TV but rather surveilling an enemy.

The metaphors in SDMS are familiar to us today, with Dataland one of many predecessors to the navigational metaphors that dominate contemporary human–computer interaction: the desktop.[229] Alan Kay's Dynabook portable computer and the Xerox Star used graphical user interfaces and desktop metaphors as early as 1972. Ted Nelson, who invented hypertext, described a multimedia-rich world of display interfaces in his 1975 credo, *Computer Lib/Dream Machines*: "The computer's capability for branching among events, controlling exterior devices, controlling outside events, and mediating in all other events, makes possible a new era of media. Until now, the mechanical properties of external objects determined what they were to us and how we used them. But henceforth this is arbitrary."[230] In the future, like the figure on the cover of *Computer Lib/Dream Machines*, we might fly through the air like Superman in Levi's, smoking a cigarette, tapping into a world of information on a touch screen.

The key challenges in Dataland arose from attempting to represent too many layers of information and from trying to compress information in multiple dimensions on a flat screen, a challenge other information designers and information architects have faced (see chapters 3 and 4). The SDMS organized the videodisc content into a hierarchical structure in order to make it navigable as nodes in a tree, with some images acting as "ports" that branched out into sublevels of images.[231] But as users navigated deeper into a hierarchy, they couldn't move laterally to another branch, nor could they figure out where they were in the tree so that they could navigate back to the top. As William Donelson wrote, "One recalls the Boston Common and its network of cow paths. Create a flat pasture, and the cows will take care of the rest. Break up the pasture into a multi-plane terrace system, and you must make provision for building as many bridges as there are two-way links to anticipate where any cow may care to wander."[232] This kind of approach is one that Edward Tufte criticized in his 1990 book *Envisioning Information*, in a chapter titled "Escaping Flatland." He wrote, "All communication between the readers of an image and the makers of an image must now take place on a two-dimensional surface. *Escaping this flatland is the essential task of envisioning information—for all the interesting worlds (physical, biological, imaginary, human) that we seek to understand are inevitably and happily multivariate in nature. Not flatlands."*[233] The problem is that "logical space" is not the same as actual space, and fusing the two types of space is the problem in developing schemes for information navigation. A bigger mess of photographs on a surface is still a mess.

Put That There

Further advances in the Media Room and SDMS platforms extended into gestural and sensorial realms. With "Put That There," AMG researchers Chris Schmandt and Eric Hulteen built a system that experimented with comprehending voice and gestural input; its ability to manage some level of abstraction gave it its name. The user, again sitting in the Eames chair, issued a voice command to create shapes and direct where they should go, with the ability to say "Put that there" or, "Move that over there." Coupled with two "space-sensing cubes"—one attached to the wrist, the other next to the chair that read the user's gestures—the system was able to address the commands in context. The first version of Put That There was demoed in 1980, and in 1983, Schmandt demonstrated the system's computer dialogue using a map of the Caribbean:

Schmandt   Pay attention. Create a red oil tanker.

System   Where?

Schmandt   There. (Points north of the Dominican Republic.) Put a blue cruise ship—

System   Where?

Schmandt   East of the Bahamas. Make a yellow sailboat.

System   Where?

Schmandt   North of that. (Points at Havana.) Create a green freighter.

System   Where?

Schmandt   East of the sailboat . . .

Schmandt   Put that there. (Points to the yellow sailboat and then points to the eastern edge of the screen)[234]

As the demo continues, Hulteen joins Schmandt, and they both issue commands and gestures to the system, showing how it parses the abstractions of "that" and "there" by interpreting the pointed location and the voice command in tandem. The obvious use, again, is military. A 1983 editorial in *The Tech*, the MIT student newspaper, noted that AMG projects were not about "creating very humanistic images," citing one "program whose purpose has aptly been described as 'put *this* bright red battleship *there*!' "[235] Another version, the "Put That There—Hack" demo plays with the artifice of it:

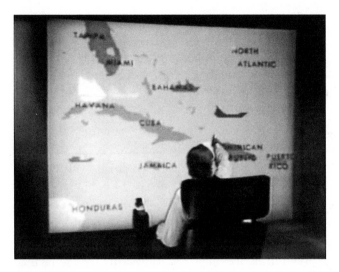

Figure 6.11
The user in Put that There used gestures and voice commands to move objects on a screen, such as ships. This version is from a 1983 video by the Architecture Machine Group. Permission granted by Nicholas Negroponte.

it concludes with the users getting up from the chairs and tearing apart the paper screen as the system babbles nonsense.[236]

The SDMS and Put That There are systems in a lineage of what Mark Poster called "the Western trend of duplicating the real by means of technology [that] provide the participant with a second-order reality in which to play with or practice upon the first order."[237] The information overlays designed by AMG for the command-and-control goals of automation and integration present a space that is at once detached and connected: detached in that the user is selectively isolated in the Media Room, connected in that he or she flows through these informational overlays. It provided, like later virtual reality systems, as Poster wrote, "prostheses for the real in order to better control it."[238] From the position of the Media Room, the input and output devices produce a doubling of reality that unsettles the real.[239] Aspen Movie Map project director Andy Lippman said of the project, "Its goal was to create so immersive and realistic a 'first visit' that newcomers would literally feel at home, or that they had been there before."[240] As long as someone sat in the Eames chair and navigated to wherever they wanted to go in Aspen, or issued whatever commands to Put That There, the displays of the large and small screens provided the only view out of the Media Room. The interface was the only way out.

Mapping by Yourself

Mapping by Yourself, a project pursued simultaneously with the Spatial Data Man-agement System (SDMS), was pitched as a "highly interactive, multimedia means for exploring models of geographical environments."[241] Where the Media Room created a surround in which to access information, Mapping by Yourself explored how to make maps and informational access portable. It proposed a new level of immersive experi-ence. "We are reminded of the prompt from Bell [Telephone ads]: '. . . it is the next best thing to being there,'" stated the Mapping by Yourself proposal. "This proposal is about being there."[242] A three-year, nearly $1 million project, Mapping by Yourself experimented with synchronized sound, digital layering, and haptic feedback.[243] From today's perspective, the Hand-Held Mapping Window looks like an iPad. AMG, col-laborating with Westinghouse, helped develop a six-inch-by-six-inch (projected to be twelve-inch-by-twelve-inch by 1980) thin-film transistor window that could be used for viewing and interacting with maps.[244]

Mapping by Yourself was unique among AMG's projects for its mobile and portable applications. "This kind of computer will get progressively smaller, lighter, less power consuming, and more portable. We envisage something larger than a pack of cigarettes yet smaller than a briefcase, substituting for all the paper maps in the field," stated the Mapping by Yourself proposal.[245] The direct military application for command and control here focuses less on automation and more on integration: in turning the task of map reading into more portable and actionable formats for military person-nel.[246] Developing a device that could fit into a briefcase, that could be carried onto the battlefield (or more comfortably navigated at one's desk than using the IBM Selec-tric typewriter in the background of the photograph here) was new ground for AMG. Mapping by Yourself ushered in questions around what it was that the researchers were designing and building; today, operating at the level of device, interface, content,

Figure 6.12
(a and b) The touch-sensitive, handheld window for Mapping by Yourself looks like a modern-day iPad. It was to be used for navigating maps while in the field. Architecture Machine Group, "Map-ping by Yourself" (Cambridge, MA: MIT). Courtesy of Nicholas Negroponte. (c) Guy Weinzapfel drew a number of stylistic studies for the Mapping by Yourself window, published in the *Architec-ture Machinations* newsletter: the Scandinavian, the Folded Sheet, the Military Chic, and the Star Wars models. (Note also that on page 7, Nicholas Negroponte announced that the weekly *Architec-ture Machinations* newsletter was about to go digital—in 1977.) Guy Weinzapfel, "MBY Hand-Held Display Designs," *Architecture Machinations* 4, no. 13 (June 5, 1978): 6–7. IASC-AMG Box 2, Folder 6. Courtesy of Institute Archives and Special Collections, MIT Libraries, Cambridge, Massachusetts.

a.

b.

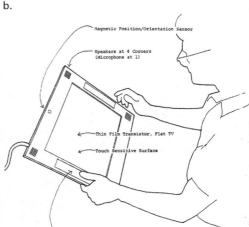

Magnetic Position/Orientation Sensor

Speakers at 4 Corners
(Microphone at 1)

Thin Film Transistor, Flat TV

Touch Sensitive Surface

Pressure Sensitive Grips

Conceptual Diagram of Equipment For Hand Held Mapping Window

c.

ARCHITECTURE MACHINATIONS

A weekly newsletter of the Architecture Machine Group, Department of Architecture, M.I.T., Room 9-518. Nobody, editor.

MBY HAND-HELD DISPLAY DESIGNS by Guy Weinzapfel

The thin film transistor (TFT) TV will arrive from Westinghouse
sometime in early August. Given this impending delivery and the
long lead time required to fabricate equipment to house it, I
have recently begun to design possible configurations for the
panel. The ultimate configuration will include at least the
following equipment:

    1) a 12" x 12" TPT display panel (from Westinghouse)
    2) a transparent touch sensitive surface to overlay it
       (from Elographics)
    3) a 3-D locating system (from Polhemus Navigation)
    4) pressure sensing gauges for each of the hand holds
    5) a gyroscopic force-feedback system
    6) four thin speakers

Four stylistic studies have been generated so far.

The SCANDINAVIAN Model:

This is the simplest of
the four. The hand grips
(and related pressure
sensing gauges) are iden-
tified by inlaid leather,
a la the SX-70. The four
speakers are located in
the four corners behind
simple perforation pat-
terns. All other features are innocuously disguised in the thin
panel. Unfortunately, this design leaves little room for the
force-feedback system.

The FOLDED SHEET Model:
This design stresses the
thinness of the TFT panel.
It also would be easiest
to fabricate. The hand-
holds need development
from their present form
in order to overcome the
hospital tray appearance.

The MILITARY CHIC Model:
Drawing on the recent
Japanese style, this ap-
proach provides the greatest leeway for extended
instrumentation (none of
the knobs shown in this
sketch have any real
function).

MBY HAND-HELD DISPLAY DESIGNS (continued)

The STAR WARS Model:
This at first startling
configuration offers the
advantage of spreading
the speakers, making the
panel truly three dimen-
sional and providing
space for the feedback
gyros at the greatest
possible moment arm.

One concept (at least) remains to be drawn. This would be an
ITALIANATE model noted by more anthropomorphically shaped hand
grips (perhaps like bow grips) and more contoured display bezel
and speaker enclosures.

In the next week, simple form mockups will be constructed to
evaluate size and shape effects and to test what kind of weight
limitations are to be used.

Your comments and/or thoughts on these concepts would be much
appreciated.

MACHINATIONS GOES ON-LINE by Nicholas Negroponte

Naomi Johnson has graduated. This concludes her editing of
Machinations, as well. Over the summer, we plan to come out
every two weeks or whenever there is sufficient material.
Additionally, we will go on-line, in part to make the editing
easier and in part to make it possible for people to append
their own news without the intermediary of a typist. Note
that its being on-line will allow for it to serve as "news"
without being printed. As such, we can expect less frequent
printings. Molly O'Donnell will be the editor through the
summer.

NSF PROPOSAL by Nicholas Negroponte

The following pages are taken from a small NSF Proposal
submitted jointly with the VLW to NSF's Office of Information
Science and Technology. (Note that it was on-line.)

Figure 6.13
The cover of the Mapping by Yourself proposal suggested augmented reality, an overlay of infor-
mation atop the world, a vision shown with a handheld postcard. Architecture Machine Group,
"Mapping by Yourself" (Cambridge, MA: MIT). Courtesy of Nicholas Negroponte.

and navigation is a concern that contemporary digital designers face. AMG seemed
to understand that it could change the nature of interactivity. "These machines are
themselves interfaces. They are hard and soft surfaces that mediate between a user and
a database. These surfaces are visual, auditory, or both. Also, these surfaces are reactive,
push back, and even interrupt the user. The underlying concept is that a very interactive
system offers insight and information though the interaction itself," AMG wrote.[247]
Mapping by Yourself made the logics of information, human, and spatial alignment
mobile, portable, and tactical.

Mapping by Yourself forecast another contemporary concept: augmented reality, in
which a portable screen provides an information overlay atop a real-world environment,
providing further narrative or visibility from what is already there. In the Mapping by
Yourself implementation, AMG suggested, "the photographs on the cover of this proposal and on the facing page illustrate our intentions for a light, hand-held mapping
'window' capable of presenting images of a modeled environment. Such images would

be 'played across' the surface of the display as the window is moved to new vantage points."[248] Mapping by Yourself's devices and windows were in fact realized and completed at the MIT Media Lab in 1992, as reported in "Advanced Concurrent Interfaces for High-Performance Multi-Media Distributed C3 Systems."[249]

Data Space

The culmination of the Architecture Machine Group's command-and-control projects was the proposal for Data Space, a vivid integration of the projects I've covered in this section that united simulation, command and control, and high-tech electronics from the home entertainment sphere, and that introduces the term "supreme usability."[250] It was a further development of the Spatial Data Management System (SDMS) project to run from 1978 to 1981 at $400,000 a year.[251] The very first sentences in the Data Space proposal highlight the monitoring and control systems of F-14 fighter jets, the sophistication of medical life support systems, and the fact that some fifty million US homes had color TV.[252] "The inherent paradox," Negroponte and Bolt wrote, "has been that we are proposing to develop human-computer interfaces, on the one hand as sophisticated in conception as a cockpit, on the other hand as operationally simple as a TV. From either perspective, the objective is the same: *supreme usability*."[253]

Data Space included advanced research into hand-eye-voice coordination. It incorporated gaze tracking that could make it possible for a user to travel and zoom through information spaces by merely looking at something on the large screen in the Media Room.[254] Combined with voice recognition, it would make for smoother commands. Three-dimensional sensing devices like wands or cubes could provide spatial orientation, allowing for a means to give directions by indicating, waving, or drawing in space. AMG would also further investigate touch-sensitive displays, long a subject of the group's research, and how they could scale to cover an entire wall. Finally, the position of the body would purportedly be able to be tracked through wearable technology, in a sort of wired "lab jacket" in which "the user is seen as a point in three-space, amidst data types (i.e. blocks)"; "directing on-coming targets"; "swimming through data in the sense of moving through Dataland by virtue of 'climbing around'" and "gestures of orchestration."[255] Some of these projects were eventually realized by the late 1980s and early 1990s in the MIT Media Lab.

Meanwhile, creating a viable simulation would require a conscientious relationship with DARPA in order to apply the systems to field conditions. Negroponte and Bolt wrote that they would "rely on close cooperation and interaction with DARPA to plan and implement realistic simulations or scenarios. . . . Again, to insure verisimilitude, we would look to DARPA for advice on how to bound the situation . . . and as to the nature of the simulation."[256] The "field exercise" of SDMS "in a data-base management task under 'tactical conditions' is an issue which warrants systematic exploration," they write. The high-fidelity special effects that AMG envisioned, along with measurable performance criteria, would combine to build appropriate field simulations. Yet this notion recalls the microworld approach of limiting the environment in order to better model criteria: How realistic could a limited simulation be? Further, in a simulation that substitutes for the real thing, there are no boundaries. Where does AMG stop and DARPA begin, and where does the simulation end? Returning to the concept of "supreme usability," not only was the notion intended to be a sort of great-scale ergonomics of well-being and informational integration, it set the stage for graphical and bombastic media environments.

The meshing of military sophistication with the ubiquity of consumer electronics would render both living room and battlefield easy and natural to navigate. "We look upon this objective as one which requires intimacy, redundancy, and parallelism of immersive modes and media of interaction. The image of a user perched in front of a monochromatic display with a keyboard, is obscured by the vision of a Toscaniniesque, self-made surround with the effervescence of *Star Wars*," Negroponte and Bolt wrote in the most colorful terms.[257] "We can anticipate that many military applications lend themselves handsomely. One need only consider, for example, ships: their size, range, crew, fighting power, and so on."[258] In this supremely usable landscape, the user could seamlessly access "computational facilities, graphical . . . facilities, live communications, real-time television."[259]

If "supreme usability" is "about being there," about generating a context in which human operator, interface, content, and the field condition are all brought together through a spatially navigated interface, the symbiotic relationship that Negroponte chased in his early projects becomes realized in a tactical human–computer-spatial relationship, in which the environment is also an actor in the feedback loop and circumscribed by an interface. As architectural historian John Harwood writes, the interface is the "hyphen between 'man' and 'machine' that articulates the system as a whole"; extending that relationship to AMG's later interfaces, the system as a whole incorporates the landscapes—both physical and informational—that it brings into alignment.[260] It is clear in AMG's projects that the interfaces they designed were not just intended to perform surface-level effects. We might recall that one definition for interface in the *Oxford English Dictionary* is that of a means of jointly operating two devices.[261] In this interpretation, an interface is operative and functional and not just a static boundary. Harwood wrote, "An interface is a complex apparatus that appears as a simple surface.

Although it seems to be unitary, it is always fragmentary and complex; although it seems to be two-dimensional, it is always at least three-dimensional and rendered in depth; although it seems to be solid and impermeable, it is always carefully perforated to allow strategically mediated interactions between man and machine."[262] "Supreme usability" makes the complex information-media environment seem simple, while masking the dynamics of perception and power both.

The only way out of these interfaces is through the simulation, which is to say through the nexus of the interface and the space that the user navigates: as long as the displays, whether wall-sized or handheld, show a map and a data territory, there are no boundaries. One of the five corollaries to interaction from AMG and Media Lab researcher Andy Lippman is that of the "impression of an infinite database."[263] The user has to have the idea that there are not just one or two possibilities, but rather many potential ways to navigate, myriad choices to make.

If that is the case, what are the bounds of the simulation? Benjamin Bratton writes, "Today *information is architecture by other means*, framing and contouring the relative motility of social intercourse. While the city remains a locus of this staging and dissimulation of security, it is supplanted by other network media that have assumed some of its traditional mandates."[264] When a user sits in the Eames chair and helicopters over a landscape of data, it is information as architecture that he or she navigates. For the designer, more potently, to build with information is to build an overlay on and in buildings and cities, with an impact on the people and environments it organizes. Moreover, the interfaces are "not just diagrams of virtual action to be taken, they are also mechanisms through which a user's motivation is first framed and then realized in the network and on the world. Modes of representation that were once cartographic and diagrammatic are now instrumental and mediational," Bratton writes.[265] Through mapping, simulation, and surround, the macroscale projects of AMG virtualize their subjects, to borrow a concept from Patrick Crogan. "Simulation will emerge as central to the virtualization of the citizen in the contemporary moment (with all its contradictions)," he writes.[266] The net result is that human agency becomes as logistical as the interfaces that organize it.[267]

Stewart Brand argued that Negroponte and the Architecture Machine Group had "moved beyond architecture" by the time that *Soft Architecture Machines* came out in 1975.[268] I disagree. The projects I have presented in this chapter show that, if anything, the opposite is very much the case. The Architecture Machine Group redefined and operationalized architecture as interfaces and digital environments. In *Soft Architecture Machines*, Negroponte wrote, "Ironically, the computer sciences, generally associated with elite and often oppressive authorities, can provide to everyone a quality of archi-tecture most closely approximated to in indigenous architecture (architecture without architects)," a blending of informatics, so-called primitive architecture, and control.[269] The Architecture Machine Group came close to achieving the notion of the architec-ture machine that Negroponte introduced in his first book, *The Architecture Machine*. He wrote, "I shall consider the physical environment as an evolving organism as opposed to a designed artifact. In particular, I shall consider an evolution aided by a specific class of machines. Warren McCulloch . . . calls them ethical robots; in the context of architecture I shall call them architecture machines."[270] The surrounding, mobile command-and-control interfaces by AMG treated the physical environment as an evolving mechanism with which to interact. McCulloch's ethical robots, as he imagined them in the 1950s, would be self-reproducing from elements they could pick up in the environment; moreover, they would learn, adapt, and be social, seeking contact with other machines. Ethical robots—and thus architecture machines—would have no limits to what they encompassed, reaching toward Negroponte's vision of architecture machines: "We will live in them."[271]

Media

The Architecture Machine Group started out by building microworlds that operated from the outside in and then designed command-and-control environments that simu-lated the world from the inside out. These paradigms culminated under the rubric of "media." This is where one chapter of the Architecture Machine Group story ends and another begins, when it was absorbed into the MIT Media Lab in 1985. A separate entity within MIT's School of Architecture and Planning, the Media Lab was and is still is the only lab at MIT to support its own degree-granting academic program and inde-pendent faculty.[272]

Why media? Negroponte said that "media" was ripe for claiming, especially because of its unpopularity: nobody else at MIT would try to own it. It was like consumer elec-tronics, in that "it has such a bad 'rep,' . . . which we are prepared to cleanse," he wrote in a 1982 memo.[273] Media was intended to connote home, learning, and creative inter-faces and not so much office automation, which was already the focus of much tech-nology research.[274] "By contrast, to my knowledge, nobody at MIT is addressing the home and, for that matter, no American university (to my knowledge) takes the world of consumer electronics seriously," Negroponte wrote.[275] When the Media Lab was dedi-cated in 1985, he used the name to concretize its stance. "In the late 1970's, when the concept of media technology was being developed at MIT, the very use of the word media was problematical because it connoted impersonal, one-way channels of mass communication, and even (at worst) the least common denominators of intellectual quality," he wrote. "Today the Media Laboratory challenges these assumptions."[276]

"Media" referred to the increasing overlap of three industries: the broadcast and motion picture industry; the print and publishing industry; and the computer industry, famously illustrated by a Venn diagram of Negroponte's "teething rings."[277] Negroponte claimed that by the year 2000, the rings would converge and sit atop each other, rather like bracelets.[278] The different convergences were ultimately represented in the interests of the Media Lab, where "media" meant the combination of entertainment, education, publishing, and computing—as well as the spaces, environments, and worlds that the Architecture Machine Group had built.

Negroponte's use of the term "media" recalls that of "convergence," coined by MIT political science professor and department chair Ithiel de Sola Pool (whom we met briefly in chapter 3).[279] A technological condition in which computing devices become more compatible, convergence referred to the alignment and unification of content, media, delivery, and governance. In his 1983 book *Technologies of Freedom*, de Sola Pool wrote:

A process called the "convergence of modes" is blurring the lines between media, even between point-to-point communications, such as the post, telephone, and telegraph, and mass communications, such as the press, radio and television. A single physical means—be it wires, cables, or airwaves—may carry services that in the past were provided in separate ways. Conversely, a service that was provided in the past by any one medium—be it broadcasting, the press, or telephony—can now be provided in several different physical ways. So the one-to-one relationship that used to exist between a medium and its use is eroding.[280]

Convergence is not a destination but rather a process that works in what de Sola Pool called "dynamic tension with change."[281] This dynamic shifts the relationships between media organizations, telephone carriers, regulatory bodies, and consumer audiences, as he wrote in *Technologies of Freedom*, which we continue to see today in different ways.[282] "Driven by cross-ownership," de Sola Pool wrote, these relationships reflect the fact that infrastructure, media, and content no longer unite with one another but "blur the boundaries" between the press, government regulation, and delivery.[283]

The Media Lab

The Media Lab was the result of a seven-year fund-raising effort by Negroponte and MIT president emeritus Jerome Wiesner, who raised $40 million as well as an additional nearly $4 million in operating expenses, primarily from major corporate sponsors in the United States and Japan. These corporate sponsors granted the Media Lab their pre-competitive research budget for shared access to the lab (pre-competitive research is a bridge between basic research at a university and competitive research conducted in a corporate lab). Negroponte and Wiesner visited more than a hundred companies, ultimately receiving sponsorship from forty companies in a number of sectors, including automotive, broadcast, film, newspaper and information, toys, media technology, photography, and computing technology.[284] Japanese technology and telecommunication provided 18 percent of AMG's early funding.[285] These sponsors, along with another 10 percent from DARPA and a smattering from the NSF, provided the foundation for the Media Lab, an amount that grew $6 million in its second year, and by 1990, $10 million.[286]

The Media Lab launched in 1985 with eleven research labs, with four encompassing the former Architecture Machine Group (Electronic Publishing, Movies of the Future, Speech, and Human–Machine Interface), and three (Speech, Spatial Imaging, Human–Machine Interface) funded by DARPA.[287] The core interests of AMG—spatiality, speech, gesture, eye tracking, videodiscs, media storage, and "interface as a place"—pull through these initial groups, in particular those run by Bolt, Schmandt, and Lippman. Beyond AMG's researchers, a number of the people heading groups had close relationships with Negroponte and AMG, such as Muriel Cooper and, as previously established, Minsky and Papert. In these ways, the Media Room and the concept of information as a navigable space that AMG researched and developed became a part of the concept of convergent media that the MIT Media Lab promoted.[288]

A $45 million building designed by I. M. Pei, the Wiesner Building, or E15, became the first home of the Media Lab. Its planning commenced in 1978, while AMG was still in full swing; its construction began in 1982, and the building was dedicated in December 1984 in honor of Jerome and Laya Wiesner. "It is the smallest, but most challenging and most interesting building I worked on at MIT," Pei said of this, his fourth building at MIT, but, "I wouldn't want to repeat it [the experience] too many times."[289] The 114,000-square-foot rectilinear building, tiled on the exterior with aluminum, comprised lobbies, theaters, video-production space, computer studios, and some 44,500 square feet of "variable loft space."[290] It is not one of Pei's more notable commissions, and although he termed it "interesting," Pei himself described it not as a "statement" but rather as a " 'space-making object.' "[291]

In tune with that assessment, Negroponte's conception of the Wiesner Building as a "medium" for a "space-making object" is fitting. He wrote a 1980 memo titled "The Building as a Medium" that explored "electronic presence built in" for the Arts and Media Technology Building.[292] Negroponte incorporates into the memo the same interests that AMG pursued in its later years—information as place and informational surround—postulating how they might be designed for and fit into the building in what he called "pure speculation about the future of computing and communications, insofar as how it might affect our building and how we might prewire for it," he wrote.

Such an approach might not make for the most daring architecture, but would highlight the fidelity of the building's interfaces. "It is unlikely that our fantasies (shared or not) of what the future holds will have a dramatic architectural impact," Negroponte wrote. "Nevertheless, it would be foolhardy to suggest that a large part of the building is for Media Technology, research and teaching, if the building itself does not include some built-in innovations."[293] Some of these ideas have the familiar, extravagant tone: an Experimental Media Theater—"the 'pulse' of the building"—might feature "Aristophanes' *Peace* produced with Trageous riding a rocketted dung-beatle [sic] and monster(s) belching napalm" (one is reminded of the "Toscaniniesque surround" in the Data Space proposal.)[294] "Equally important might be its use as an informational surround for an audience of one, . . . a kind of mental orgasmatron."[295]

Beyond the colorful ideas Negroponte proposed, the information spaces would support and be shared by the building's residents. The plans also envisioned "a large number of computing devices that can be built into the building. The building should have an electro-mechanical presence sufficient for us to talk to walls and have them talk back—for robots to serve us coffee, and for doors to know when they are open or closed."[296] The interior of the building reflected changing notions of where computing could take place: centralizing computing storage meant that terminals could be distributed throughout the building (although there was still a centralized Terminal Garden when the building opened, a space that brought together students twenty-four hours a day).[297] Negroponte advocated "putting terminals in lounge-like situations, in nooks and crannies, throughout the building [to] cast a cubicle privacy, library-like, which could be very attractive for work and play, and would draw upon the sophistication of our networking to emulate face-to-face contact when assistance of one kind or another is required."[298] The building was itself an architectural register of the "teething rings" Venn diagram, wired for convergence.

Negroponte wrote that "a computer room may have almost no computers in it, but instead store vast amounts of information, armies of disc drives, being a repository for everything from wire services to atlases."[299] The nerve fibers of the building would be "literally hundreds of miles of twisted pairs, coax, and fiber optic cables. While these do not have to be laid in advance, large and easy to access chaseways will be required, considerably more extensive and flexible than an ordinary building," he wrote.[300] "Over the next 25 years the distinctions among data, voice, and picture will disappear in the sense of each being a devoted link or network (if the FCC doesn't stymie advances)."[301] Similar to Cedric Price's proposals for Oxford Corner House and the

Fun Palace, throughout the Wiesner Building one would find public electronic information displays. Architect Pei proposed a "sign board"—an "array" of fifty to one hundred television monitors in a configuration that could be as large as twelve feet by sixteen feet. Each could be individually tuned to a broadcast, serve as a pixel in a big image, or be sequenced to show moving video, such as a figure that moves across all of them (so long as they weren't broken or turned off, a problem with information displays, Negroponte noted).[302] On a smaller scale, Negroponte envisioned "information fountains"—kiosks that might use voice recognition and building and office information—though he noted that privacy would be a concern.[303]

Despite the future tense of Negroponte's plans, he stated that he did not want to overdetermine the building's digitality. "We should be very careful not to build-in today's visions of tomorrow, making the building like the Enterprise, only to find it rather banal ten years hence (let alone rather inconvenient in the meantime). It is easy to speculate and to imagine a science fiction environment which knows all about us, moonboot-wearing people who are transported by computers at our feet, through neon passages, etcetera etcetera," he wrote.[304] "Instead, I suggest we conceive some modest examples and where possible prewire for a future when the building itself might be the infrastructure for experiments and research that have to do with a physical environment that computes."[305] The Wiesner Building was intended to be an interface and informational surround at a bigger scale than the Media Room or any single AMG experiment. Its purpose was not only education and research but also performance and display, the labs themselves the stage for the "demo or die" culture born in AMG and transported to the Media Lab.[306]

Media, in the manner that Negroponte, the Architecture Machine Group, and eventually the Media Lab defined it, is the culmination of different methods, interfaces, spaces, and technologies. As media converge, however, it is not just the vertical markets of broadcast, publishing, and computing that are brought into alignment. Timothy Lenoir and Henry Lowood refer to the emergence of the military-entertainment complex, and they, along with Jordan Crandall, Patrick Crogan, and others underscore the way that video game entertainment feeds back into the military simulations that spawned them in the first place.[307] Eyal Weizman points out that in the process of "civilianization," technologies move from the military sphere into the civilian sphere, becoming technologies everyday people use but that bring along their attendant power structures.[308] De Sola Pool wrote that, despite the dynamics of convergence, "there will always also be a return to the universal system because of the extraordinary convenience of universality."[309] If this is the case, then what is the universality to which media returns?

Conclusion

Nicholas Negroponte and the Architecture Machine Group worked at the crossroads of AI and the interfaces of the physical environment. The group sought to extend interaction to the human body and the space that the body occupied. Core to AMG's approach was a stretching of the boundaries of architecture, artificial intelligence, engineering, and art. The group believed that AI belonged in the hands of architects, filmmakers, and artists, not just engineers and computer scientists. And when all of the above worked together, synergistic and productive work emerged, as AI was modeled and manifested by people who built worlds, a notion that reflected back on AI and computer science research. AMG explored possibilities for personal computing, graphical user interfaces, and handheld devices; it put in place foundations for virtual reality in work that was later carried on in the Atari Research Lab and the Media Lab; it built simulation environments for both videogames and the battlefield. The funding of the group affected the flavor of its work, and when the group lost its bid for National Science Foundation funding, it hastened its uptake of Department of Defense funding—not a difficult choice for Nicholas Negroponte to make because he (as well as groups like the MIT AI Lab) preferred the culture of defense funding, with its close network of long relationships.

The experiments and projects that the Architecture Machine Group carried out explored how theories of artificial intelligence could function at the scale of the body, the room, or the city. These explorations also taught the group's researchers about how to take apart a system of intelligence in order to understand it, and to reconstruct it at a different scale and with different qualities of interaction. The approach echoes cognitive psychologist Ulric Neisser's description of understanding computers as a way of understanding the workings of a brain:

First, let us consider the familiar parallel between man and computer. Although it is an inadequate analogy in many ways, it may suffice for this purpose. The task of a psychologist trying to understand human cognition is analogous to that of a man trying to discover how a computer has been programmed. . . . He will not care much whether this particular computer stores information in magnetic cores or in thin films; he wants to understand the program, not the "hardware."[310]

In programming a computer, one comes to understand the analogy of the program as the key to comprehending the function of the brain as an information processing organ. "Although a program is nothing but a flow of symbols, it has reality enough to control the operation of very tangible machinery that executes very physical operations," he continued. "A man who seeks to discover the program of a computer is surely not doing anything self-contradictory!"[311] The same goes for the designers and engineers who try to build an intelligent environment. The researchers at AMG took this further, trying to understand the experience, not just the utilization, of responsive spaces. In the work of the Architecture Machine Group, we find scenarios for how that might play out when scaled up to the real world. Negroponte and AMG understood the stakes of this research for the future better than most. The group's projects and research are extraordinarily important, even when they seem to be producing silly, insignificant experiments. There are lessons to learn in the questions and the framing of the Architecture Machine Group.

Negroponte went further than Le Corbusier's characterization of a house as a "machine for living in"—his notion of an architecture machine would respond to its users, surrounding and enveloping them. Negroponte said about designing for architecture machines, "The fantasies of an intelligent and responsive physical environment are too easily limited by the gap between the technology of making things and the science of understanding them," he wrote in 1975. "I strongly believe that it is very important to play with these ideas scientifically and explore applications of machine intelligence that totter between being unimaginably oppressive and unbelievably exciting."[312] This space—between oppressive and exciting—is a tidy encapsulation of where we stand, inside of the architecture machine.

7 Architecting Intelligence

On stage at the World Economic Forum in Davos, Switzerland, in 2015, at a panel called "The Future of the Digital Economy," the world's most powerful technology executives painted a sunny picture of the technological future. Satya Nadella (CEO of Microsoft), Vittorio Colao (CEO of Vodafone), Sheryl Sandberg (COO of Facebook), and Eric Schmidt (former Google CEO and executive chairman of Alphabet, Google's parent company) shared their visions for the future, in which enough broadband could solve almost all human challenges, whether of poverty or the building of democracies.

But what made news headlines was something that Eric Schmidt said in answer to an audience member who asked about the future of the Internet. "I will answer very simply that the Internet will disappear," Schmidt said. He continued,

There will be so many IP addresses . . . so many devices, sensors, things that you are wearing, things that you are interacting with that you won't even sense it. It will be part of your presence all the time. Imagine you walk into a room, and the room is dynamic. And you—with your permission and all of that, you are interacting with the things going on in the room, a highly personalized, highly interactive, and very, very interesting world emerges because of the disappearance of the Internet.[1]

This isn't a new idea, of course—it's ubiquitous computing, a concept that Mark Weiser introduced in 1991. "The most profound technologies are those that disappear," Weiser wrote. "They weave themselves into the fabric of everyday life until they are indistinguishable from it."[2] That's the world that Schmidt describes: a world of sensors and intelligence that becomes the material of our daily lives. It becomes our architecture. But one thing is striking in Schmidt's statement: the handwaving of "your permission and all of that." Schmidt, and by extension, Google and its parent company, Alphabet, stand ready to simply shrug away the permission you may or may not have given to any number of companies. How do you opt in? How do you opt out? What happens if this new dynamic world fails?

I started this book with the word *architecting*, a deliberately uncomfortable term. Architecting is what designers and programmers call the design of complex systems. They use "architect" as a verb, something that conventional architects do not do. They architect when they build a structure and relate detail to it. And when they want to talk about the role of humans in those systems, they call it architecture. This book is also about conventionally trained architects who take unconventional approaches to architecture in their design of complex systems. Whether they would say it or not, under this definition, they architect. Architecting permits an exploration of the mechanisms behind and within design, and expands the boundaries of practice. It provides the means to model the implications of computation, generativity, and intelligence.

Throughout the book, I've traced the development of different technological paradigms, such as cybernetics and artificial intelligence, that architects explored at the scale of buildings and the built environment. How do architecting and architecture work when AI is a part of the world around us, when algorithms determine so many aspects of our daily digital lives—our search results, the job postings we see, the movies we might watch, the people we might date? Those who design artificially intelligent systems don't make nouns—objects, buildings, things—they make verbs. They architect machine learning algorithms—the steps that a program will follow to complete a task. They put in place a set of starting conditions, after which the programs program themselves. You'll notice I've used the words design and architect here, and that's what machine-learning experts do. They're building statistical models that evolve and learn. They're developing generative frameworks. They are architecting. But where are the architects and designers who design these algorithms into the built environment?

As we have seen, digital and physical architectures are increasingly inseparable from one another. Rob Kitchin and Martin Dodge refer to this condition as "code/space," when the spaces of software and the spaces that we live in every day become one and the same: the code and the spatiality coconstitute themselves.[3] An airport gate or a supermarket is a code/space because they will cease to function the way they are intended to if the programs running them fail: the airport turns into a tumultuous waiting room space, the supermarket becomes a dumb warehouse until the cash register systems run again, Kitchin and Dodge write.[4] But the scale of code/space can be much more expansive than a particular room or building. When Delta Airlines and British Airways experienced system-wide computer crashes in 2016 and 2017, respectively, thousands of flights were grounded for days: the airspace was a code/space that couldn't function without software. My Pittsburgh neighborhood itself is also a sort of code/space. I live a mile from Uber's Advanced Technology Group, the headquarters for Uber's autonomous vehicle division. I can't go a day without passing one of the self-driving cars, and I always note that while there is a driver, the hands are never on the wheel. The cars have a failsafe, a takeover mechanism from the human, but they still rely on the code to do their work.

Architects make models. What could we learn from the Architecture Machine Group and AI Lab in their early years at MIT, when researchers built microworlds? How do they scale up? The stakes change as we scale from an interface, from movie recommendations to moving vehicles. What happens at the scale of a building or a city? From the perspective of machine learning, it's worth asking what code is brought to bear and how it might affect and change the space that it cocreates. Do the code and the space hang in balance with one another? One way to ask this question is by considering the ramifications of the self-driving vehicle: What happens if a passenger is killed because of the car's error, as happened with a Tesla Model S in Autopilot mode in May 2016?[5] Or if the car had to "decide" between killing its own passenger or others on the street?[6] As rhetoric about AI, smart cities, and the Internet of Things ramp up, policymakers, technologists, and venture capitalists loosely toss around technological ideas that have a massive impact on the world in which we live.

But we're smarter than that. This is something that Antoine Picon, one of the best chroniclers of the *longue durée* of engineering, architecture, and the smart city points out. Rather than the usual tropes of technological utopianism or technology's damning effects, we could understand that we've already prefigured a post-rational, cyborg world of artificial life. In this sense, "the entire city could be considered intelligent in a new way, founded on the interaction and composition of the perceptions and deliberations of multiple entities, human, non-human, and often a mix of the two."[7] Or are we? In "A Cyborg Manifesto," Donna Haraway writes, "A cyborg is a cybernetic organism, a hybrid of machine and organism, a creature of social reality as well as a creature of fiction."[8] The cyborg is, she reminds us, "an ironic political myth faithful to feminism, socialism, and materialism."[9] Cyborgs are hybrids, but hybrids are not neutral. And we should remember that our algorithms are not neutral, either. A machine-learning algorithm learns from a corpus that it reflects and repeats. Data are not neutral. They reflect biases of their creation and creators. How might algorithms further perpetuate gender or race biases in harmful ways?[10] Eli Pariser warns his readers of "filter bubbles," which is what happens when a search engine gives a user information based on her profile and its interpretation of her preferences, and begins to exclude other kinds of information that falls outside of the user profile. Not only might a user not see a broader range of political information, but might also see a lesser range of job opportunities, for example.[11] What about questions of implicit bias or racial profiling? What biases are baked into the system? How might they be fought? And what are the ramifications for the marriage of these technologies at the urban scale?

There is a vital need for architects and for architecting, for both conventionally trained architects and people who design complex systems, to take on artificial intelligence as material for design.[12] Designers and architects build and bring things to bear at a scale with which people can interact with them, walk through them, inhabit them. What might their tools and materials look like? What might they need to know? The case studies in this book have introduced some approaches over the last fifty years, but what will come now? There are new courses for artists, musicians, and now designers and architects to learn machine learning.[13] In March 2017, I co-organized a three-day conference as part of the AAAI Spring Symposium Series titled "The User Experience of Machine Learning" with Elizabeth Churchill and Mike Kuniavsky.[14] Among the key conclusions of the symposium was that designers and those who are concerned with user experience could exercise an impact on AI in several ways, particularly around the issues of automation, agency, and control, on one hand, and bias, trust, and power on the other. Designers can make interactions more transparent and can contribute to the ethical development of the systems with which they interact.

Moreover, architects and designers might find some ways forward by looking back at the examples in this book: wrangling data and finding ways to analyze and represent it, or developing patterns and systems, like Christopher Alexander did, or supporting the experience of navigating or experiencing a city, as Richard Saul Wurman did. Architects could design totally new formats for buildings and spaces in collaboration with AI experts, to follow the Cedric Price example. Or they might take the elements of machine learning to push the field for designers and architects, working in tandem with engineers, as Nicholas Negroponte and the MIT Architecture Machine Group did, into new modes of research.

As Malcolm McCullough wrote in 2004, "Digital networks are no longer separate from architecture." Now it is time to update his statement for a built environment that increasingly needs to work with artificial intelligence. "We would be wiser to accept them as a design challenge, to emphasize their more wholesome prospects (which are less likely to develop by default), and to connect them with what we value about the built world."[15] The nouns and the verbs of architecture are changing. We have both an opportunity and an imperative: understanding the digital past and engaging these new tools and technologies in projecting an architectural future.

Notes

Chapter 1

1. Letter from Chantal Suarez, Board of Architectural Examiners, to Nathan Shedroff, June 10, 1999.

2. Robin Boyd, "Antiarchitecture," *Architectural Forum* 129 (1968): 85.

3. Christopher Alexander, "The Origins of Pattern Theory: The Future of the Theory, and the Generation of a Living World," *IEEE Software* 16, no. 5 (October 1999): 80, doi:10.1109/52.795104.

4. Ibid., 81.

5. Richard Saul Wurman, "An American City: The Architecture of Information," convention brochure (Washington, DC: AIA, 1976), 1, 4.

6. M. Christine Boyer, personal communication with Molly Wright Steenson, August 5, 2016.

7. "architecture, n." OED Online. December 2016. Oxford University Press. http://www.oed.com/view/Entry/10408?rskey=cArsyD&result=1&isAdvanced=false.
   Parts of this section have been previously published in *New Geographies* by the Harvard Graduate School of Design, and in *interactions,* published by the ACM. Molly Wright Steenson, "Architecture Machines and the Internet of Things; or, The Costs of Convergence," *New Geographies* 7 (2015); and Molly Wright Steenson, "Microworld and Mesoscale," *interactions* (July–August 2015), 58–60.

8. Étienne Louis Boullée, "Architecture, Essai sur l'Art," in *Boullée and Visionary Architecture: Including Boullée's Architecture, Essay on Art* (London; New York: Academy Editions; Harmony Books, 1976), 119. Translation mine. He continues: "The art of building is thus but a secondary art that, in our opinion, would be suitably belong to the scientific components of architecture." The original: *"Il faut concevoir pour effectuer. . . . C'est cette production de l'esprit, c'est cette création, qui constitue l'architecture, que nous pouvons en conséquence, définir l'art de produire et de porter à la perfection tout édifice quelconque. L'art de bâtir n'est donc qu'un art secondaire, qu'il nous paroît convenable de nommer la parti scientifique de l'architecture."*

9. In Robin Evans, *Translations from Drawing to Building and Other Essays* (London: Architectural Association, 1997), 154.

10. Ibid.

11. Beatriz Colomina, "On Architecture, Production and Reproduction," in *Architectureproduction*, ed. Beatriz Colomina, series Revisions: Papers on Architectural Theory and Criticism (New York: Princeton Architectural Press, 1988), 7.

12. Ibid.

13. *OED Online*, s.v. "architecture," accessed July 2017, http://www.oed.com/view/Entry/10408?rskey=cArsyD&result=1&isAdvanced=false.

14. Werner Buchholz, ed., "Architectural Philosophy," in *Planning a Computer System* (New York: McGraw-Hill, 1962), 5.

15. Brooks went on to coin the term "the mythical man month" (nine women can't give birth to a baby in one month). By the 1980s, his research included virtual reality for architectural purposes. He may have understood the architectural translation of function to space at that time better than we might ever have imagined.

16. Boston Architectural Center, *Architecture and the Computer* (Boston: Boston Architectural Center, 1964), 33.

17. According to Fernando Corbat of MIT. See Jennifer Hagendorf, "M.I.T. Laboratory for Computer Science," *CRN*, November 10, 1999.

18. Royston Landau, *New Directions in British Architecture* (New York: G. Braziller, 1968), 115.

19. Ibid., 107. Landau was director of graduate studies at the Architectural Association from 1974 to 1993. Throughout the 1960s, he taught at MIT and the Rhode Island School of Design; from 1969 to 1974, he taught at the University of Pennsylvania. He applied heuristics to architectural problem-solving in a paper titled "Toward a Structure for Architectural Ideas" that he developed at MIT; organized the Decision-Making Symposium at the Architectural Association; and attended and spoke at the seminal Architecture and the Computer conference at the Boston Architectural Center, all in 1964. He sometimes worked with Price and contributed an essay to Price's *Square Book* in 1984. See also Francis Duffy, "Royston Landau: Power behind an International Architecture School" (obituary), *The Guardian,* November 20, 2001, http://www.guardian.co.uk/news/2001/nov/20/guardianobituaries.highereducation.

20. Landau, *New Directions in British Architecture*, 115.

21. Ibid., 100.

22. Ibid., 43 and 14.

23. Douglas Engelbart, "Augmented Human Intellect Study" (Air Force Office of Scientific Research, 1962), http://sloan.stanford.edu/mousesite/EngelbartPapers/B5_F18_ConceptFrameworkPt1.html.

24. Ibid.

25. Ibid.

26. Ibid.

27. Ibid.

28. Landau, *New Directions in British Architecture*, 12.

29. Ibid.

30. Boston Architectural Center, *Architecture and the Computer* (Boston: Boston Architectural Center, 1964), 8.

31. Ibid., 67.

32. Ibid., 45. By 1974, computers that could make graphics and could produce plans and sections existed. It took longer for the architect to be able to step outside and view the design, but even as early as 1967, architects produced animated fly-throughs that showed what it would be like to maneuver through a project.

33. Ibid.

34. Ibid.

35. Steven A. Coons, "Computer-Aided Design," *Design Quarterly* 66/67 (1966): 8. Sketchpad was developed on a TX-2 computer in MIT's Lincoln Laboratory (before Project MAC, the time-shared computing project started). MIT's Lincoln Laboratory, founded in 1951 and directed by F. Wheeler Loomis, supported applied military research including air defense control. The lab worked in conjunction with other labs at MIT, including the Digital Computer Laboratory run by Jay Forrester. See Karl Wildes and Nilo Lindgren, *A Century of Electrical Engineering and Computer Science at MIT, 1882–1982* (Cambridge, MA: MIT Press, 1985), 295.

36. Boston Architectural Center, *Architecture and the Computer*, 26.

37. Ibid., 48.

38. Coons wrote in detail about the functions of the original Sketchpad program: "Sketchpad was purely graphical and purely geometrical. One could draw with the light pen on the screen—straight lines, circles and other surfaces. It could not solve any problems that had to do with abstraction, other than the abstractions of geometry itself. The operator could impose constraining relationships such as: 'Make these two lines parallel to the computer.' That, of course, is a geometrical abstraction and the computer program could follow such an instruction. But the designer could not say to the early Sketchpad: 'This line represents a piece of structure with a certain thickness and with certain cross-sectional characteristics, made of a certain material and obeys certain physical laws.'

Sketchpad had toggle switches that commanded the computer to satisfy such constraining relationships as the operator imposed. There were four knobs beneath the screen of a cathode ray tube which were used for four kinds of motion applied to the drawing on the screen: a rotation, a horizontal translation, a vertical translation and a change in magnitude. The precision of the graphic information presented on the screen is one part in ten million which means one thousandth of an inch in eight hundred feet! This made it possible to enlarge, look at a small region, change it and then push it all away from the viewer (by reducing its size) so that the entire structure could be visualized. Sketchpad could attach one line to the end of another separated line by means of toggle switch instruction, even if the light pen would not attach the lines precisely on the screen. The computer interpreted the instruction in such a way that the two lines were attached with mathematical precision at the end point, so that they were truly concurrent." Steven A. Coons, "Computer-Aided Design," 8.

39. Boston Architectural Center, *Architecture and the Computer*, 45.

40. I am grateful to Daniel Cardoso Llach for his the insights here about Steven Coons. This discussion of interaction and augmentation is a central theme in his book *Builders of the Vision*.

41. Daniel Cardoso Llach, *Builders of the Vision: Software and the Imagination of Design* (London: Routledge, 2015), 67.

42. Boston Architectural Center, *Architecture and the Computer*, 26.

43. William Fetter, "Computer Graphics," *Design Quarterly* 66/67 (1966): 15.

44. Ibid.

45. Boston Architectural Center, *Architecture and the Computer*, 33.

46. Fetter, "Computer Graphics," 15.

47. Ibid., 19–20.

48. Ibid.

49. Engineering drawing translated measurements and engineering data into the necessary projections (orthographic, oblique, isometric, dimetric, trimetic, central perspective) while additional shading, motion, or color rendered the drawing legible. Operations analysis could be used to model a flight path in a mountainous region and the visibility of an aircraft from a radar station, with additional hand drawing and erasing to make the computer graphics more legible. Experiments with cockpit display systems served as hybrid motion picture and computer graphic prototypes: such representations cost much less than building a demonstration system. And by generating computer graphics at intervals of one second each per animation cell, Boeing could simulate aircraft carrier landings that took into account the pitch and roll of the aircraft and its angle as it descended toward the carrier. Ibid., 17–22.

50. William A. Fetter, *Computer Graphics in Communication* (New York: McGraw-Hill, 1965), 104.

51. Ibid.

52. George Pólya, *How to Solve It: A New Aspect of Mathematical Method* (Princeton, NJ: Princeton University Press, 1945), 113. Allen Newell studied with Pólya at Stanford as well. Marvin Minsky, Herbert Simon, and Allen Newell all cited the importance of Pólya to heuristics and AI. See also

Marc H. J. Romanycia and Francis Jeffry Pelletier, "What Is a Heuristic?" *Computational Intelligence* 1 (1985): 48.

53. Geof Bowker, "How to Be Universal: Some Cybernetic Strategies, 1943–70," *Social Studies of Science* 23 (1993): 113.

54. W. Ross Ashby, *Design for a Brain: The Origin of Adaptive Behavior* (New York: Wiley, 1960), 16.

55. Gordon Pask, "The Architectural Relevance of Cybernetics," *Architectural Design* 39, no. 7 (1969): 496.

56. J. C. R. Licklider, "Man-Computer Symbiosis," *IRE Transactions on Human Factors in Electronics* HFE-1(1960): 4.

57. Paul N. Edwards, *The Closed World: Computers and the Politics of Discourse in Cold War America* (Cambridge, MA: MIT Press, 1996), 266.

58. Other participants at the conference felt it should be called "automata studies." In fact, Shannon and McCarthy edited a volume titled *Automata Studies* in the Annals of Mathematics Studies (Princeton University Press, 1956). It included articles by the editors and John von Neumann, W. Ross Ashby, and Marvin Minsky, among others.

59. Pamela McCorduck, *Machines Who Think: A Personal Inquiry into the History and Prospects of Artificial Intelligence*, 2nd ed. (Natick, MA: AK Peters, 2004), 113.

60. Ibid.

61. Marvin Minsky, "Steps toward Artificial Intelligence," *Proceedings of the I.R.E.* 49, no. 1 (1961): 8.

62. Minsky noted that heuristics, when successful, needed to be applicable to different kinds of problems, even if they sometimes failed. Ibid.

63. Ibid., 36.

64. Ibid.

65. Ibid.

Chapter 2

1. Christopher Alexander, "The Origins of Pattern Theory: The Future of the Theory, and the Generation of a Living World," *IEEE Software* 16, no. 5 (October 1999): 72, doi:10.1109/52.795104.

2. Ibid.

3. Ibid., 80.

4. Ibid.

5. Ibid., 81.

6. Ibid., 80.

7. As of 2003, it was still selling ten thousand copies annually. Emily Eakin, "Architecture's Irascible Reformer," *New York Times,* July 12, 2003, http://www.nytimes.com/2003/07/12/books /architecture-s-irascible-reformer.html.

8. George Miller and Jerome Bruner, "Application for Grant, Harvard Center for Cognitive Studies: General Description," April 8, 1960, 1, Box 1, Papers of Jerome Bruner, National Science Foundation, 1959–1961 (HUG 4242.9), Harvard University Archives. In Alise Upitis, "Nature Normative: The Design Methods Movement, 1944–1967" (PhD diss., MIT, 2008), 72.

9. Christopher Alexander, "A Much Asked Question about Computers and Design," in *Architecture and the Computer* (Boston: Boston Architectural Center, 1964), 52.

10. Ibid.

11. Ibid., 54.

12. Ibid.

13. Design questions about design and the role of computation and, eventually, the computer were of interest to engineers as early as the 1940s. See Daniel Cardoso Llach, *Builders of the Vision: Software and the Imagination of Design* (London: Routledge, 2015).

14. Christopher Alexander, *Notes on the Synthesis of Form* (Cambridge, MA: Harvard University Press, 1971), iv.

15. Plato, *Phaedrus,* 265d, quoted in Alexander, *Notes on the Synthesis of Form,* iv.

16. Ibid., 116. In contrast, the "unselfconscious" model presents a one-to-one relationship between the context and the form: there is an "actual world" problem that the unselfconscious (read: primitive) designer solves by designing a form. In his view, the unselfconscious culture does not have design or architecture in the big sense: instead, there are just simply instinctual ways of building that the culture knows how to do. "Since the division of labor is very limited, specialization of any sort is rare, there are no architects, and each man builds his own house," he wrote. In this idea, Alexander celebrates this "primitive" notion of design, as he calls it. The formulation is problematic for many obvious reasons. Alexander, *Notes on the Synthesis of Form,* 38.

17. Ibid., 18–19.

18. Ibid., 134.

19. D'Arcy Wentworth Thompson, *On Growth and Form* (Cambridge: Cambridge University Press, 1917), 16.

20. Alexander, *Notes on the Synthesis of Form,* 18.

21. Ibid., 26.

22. Ibid., 23.

23. Ibid., 18.

24. The limitation is one that W. Ross Ashby, author of *Design for a Brain,* also uses in delimiting the number of variables in a problem, since any "real 'machine' has an "infinity of variables"—"a system is . . . defined as *any set of variables* that he selects from those available on the real 'machine.'" W. Ross Ashby, *Design for a Brain: The Origin of Adaptive Behavior* (New York: Wiley, 1960), 16.

25. Kurt Koffka does acknowledge limitations in his model of fitness that challenge Alexander's later choices in the organization of Alexander's model. Wrote Koffka, "Since 'fittingness' . . . is a relation between at least two things, it is not only the problem which must be organized in a special way so as to make something fit it, there must also be objects which can fit the problem so organized. Since these objects need not be perceptually present, this imposes a certain condition on traces if they are to fit into the problem. They also must be organized, and organized in special ways. And often the form of the problem will influence the organization of the objects: i.e., an object will become the kind that fits, because it is exposed to the stress of the problem. Kurt Koffka, *Principles of Gestalt Psychology,* International Library of Psychology, Philosophy and Scientific Method (New York: Harcourt, Brace, 1935), 642.

26. Ibid., 638.

27. Ibid.

28. Ashby, *Design for a Brain,* 58. Emphasis Ashby's.

29. Alexander, *Notes on the Synthesis of Form,* 39.

30. Ibid., 3.

31. Ibid., 4.

32. Ibid., 116.

33. Christopher Alexander and Marvin L. Manheim, *The Design of Highway Interchanges: An Example of a General Method for Analyzing Engineering Design Problems* (Cambridge: Department of Civil Engineering, Massachusetts Institute of Technology, 1962), 25.

34. Alexander and Manheim, *The Design of Highway Interchanges,* 25.

35. In *Notes on the Synthesis of Form,* Alexander uses M to represent the nodes and L to represent the links. If the links between two elements are in conflict, then the link carries a negative sign; if the links are concurrent, they have a positive sign; if the relationship is more or less important, it can be weighted accordingly. Alexander, *Notes on the Synthesis of Form,* 80. The tree decomposition he shows breaks down the requirements into subsets; what interests Alexander is pulling apart the links and branches into their natural points of division. "Each subset of the set M which appears in the tree will then define a subproblem of the problem M. Each subproblem will have its own integrity, and be independent of the other subproblems, so that it can be solved independently." Alexander and Manheim, *The Design of Highway Interchanges,* 83.

36. Ibid., 85. Emphasis Alexander and Manheim's.

37. Alexander, *Notes on the Synthesis of Form*, 79.

38. Christopher Alexander, V. M. King, and Sara Ishikawa, "390 Requirements for the Rapid Transit Station" (Berkeley, CA: Center for Environmental Structure, 1964), 2.

39. Allan Temko, "Obituary—Donn Emmons," *San Francisco Chronicle*, September 3, 1997, http://www.sfgate.com/news/article/OBITUARY-Donn-Emmons-2829136.php.

40. "Washington Commuter, If He's Lucky, May Profit from Bay Area Blunders," *Washington Post*, August 7, 1966.

41. Alexander defined trees and semilattices as follows: Tree: "A collection of sets forms a tree if and only if, for any two sets that belong to the collection, either one is wholly contained in the other, or else they are wholly disjoint." Semilattice: "A collection of sets forms a semi-lattice if and only if, when two overlapping sets belong to the collection, then the set of elements common to both also belongs to the collection. He hyphenates "semi-lattice," but contemporary use of the term does not. Accordingly, I will use the unhyphenated form. Christopher Alexander, "A City Is Not a Tree, Part 1," *Architectural Forum* 122, no. 4 (1965): 59.

42. Ibid., 58.

43. Ibid.

44. Ibid.

45. Ibid., 58–59.

46. Ibid., 58.

47. Christopher Alexander, "A City Is Not a Tree, Part 2," *Architectural Forum* 122, no. 5 (1965): 60.

48. Ibid.

49. Karl Popper, *The Open Society and Its Enemies* (London: Routledge, 2012), 166.

50. Ibid., 167.

51. Ibid., 166.

52. Alexander, "A City Is Not a Tree, Part 1," 62.

53. Ibid., 60.

54. Alexander, "A City Is Not a Tree, Part 2," 61.

55. Harary and Rockey write, "The title of Alexander's article places his topic squarely within graph theory, yet he introduces another branch of mathematics, namely set theory, to support his argument. Furthermore he tries to induce a mathematical theory of the city from a certain number of particular and limited examples. . . . Alexander defines trees in terms of sets and hence bypasses graph theory and the usefulness it brings to bear on structural models. Unfortunately,

his use of the logically equivalent set theoretical formulation of trees, and later of semilattices, avoids the natural and intuitively simple and meaningful formulation of these intrinsically structural configurations in terms of graph theory. Further, and more important for empirical applications, the theorems of graph theory are thereby overlooked." Frank Harary and J. Rockey, "A City Is Not a Semilattice Either," *Environment and Planning A* 8 (1976): 377.

56. Ibid., 379.

57. Ibid., 383.

58. Although British anthropologists used social network analysis in the 1950s and 1960s to study urban relationships, they did not address issues of form, architecture, or design in their work, which reinforces the uniqueness of Alexander's application of such practices to architecture.

59. Manuel Lima provides an eight-hundred-year history of tree diagrams in *The Book of Trees: Visualizing Branches of Knowledge*. See Manuel Lima, *The Book of Trees: Visualizing Branches of Knowledge* (Princeton, NJ: Princeton Architectural Press, 2014).

60. See Andrew Otwell, "Structure and Situated Software," March 30, 2004, https://web.archive .org/web/20050213061449/http://www.heyotwell.com/heyblog/archives/000305.html; Dan Hill, "Trees, Lattices, Suburbs, and Software," April 6, 2004, http://www.cityofsound.com/blog/2004/04 /trees_lattices_.html; and Tom Carden, "Architects, Social Networks and Hypertext," September 28, 2004, http://www.tom-carden.co.uk/2004/09/28/architects-social-networks-and-hypertext.

61. Stanley Wasserman and Katherine Faust, *Social Network Analysis: Methods and Applications*, Structural Analysis in the Social Sciences (Cambridge: Cambridge University Press, 1994), 4.

62. "Emotions Mapped by New Geography: Charts Seek to Portray the Psychological Currents of Human Relationships," *New York Times*, April 3, 1933.

63. Ibid.

64. Christopher Alexander, *The City as a Mechanism for Sustaining Human Contact* (Berkeley: Center for Planning and Development Research, University of California, 1966), 12.

65. Ibid., 11. Italics Alexander's. (He uses italics frequently as a stylistic convention; italics shown in his quotes are original unless otherwise noted.)

66. Ibid., 12.

67. Ibid., 34–35.

68. Wasserman and Faust, *Social Network Analysis*, 13.

69. "Whether the model employed seeks to understand individual action in the context of structured relationships, or studies structures directly, network analysis operationalizes structures in terms of networks of linkages among units. Regularities or patterns in interactions give rise to structures." Ibid.

70. Ibid.

71. Christopher Alexander and Barry Poyner, *The Atoms of Environmental Structure* (Berkeley, CA: Center for Planning and Development Research, University of California Institute of Urban & Regional Development, 1966), 9.

72. Ibid., 11. I am referring here to the Center for Planning and Development Research working paper publication of *Atoms,* as published by Alexander and Poyner in July 1966. The document underwent several revisions, included different examples, and was presented republished in different locations and formats.

73. Ibid., 1.

74. *Design Methods in Architecture,* Architectural Association Paper Number 4 (London: Lund Humphries, 1969), 7, 9. In Upitis, "Nature Normative," 178.

75. Alexander, *Notes on the Synthesis of Form,* "Preface," 2.

76. While sociograms made relationships more readily visible, their layout was effectively "arbitrary": Wasserman and Faust write that "different investigators using the same data could produce as many different sociograms (in appearance) as there were investigators." Wasserman and Faust, *Social Network Analysis,* 78. In response, sociomatrices—a matrix formulation of data for social network analysis—grew in popularity throughout the 1940s. By the 1950s and 1960s, researchers began using computers to calculate their data, reinforcing the importance of sociomatrices over the more visual sociograms. Ibid., 79.

77. Christopher Alexander and Marvin L. Manheim, *The Use of Diagrams in Highway Route Location: An Experiment* (Cambridge: School of Engineering, Massachusetts Institute of Technology, 1962), 89.

78. Alexander, *Notes on the Synthesis of Form,* 137–139. A 1957 article on urban morphology and India in the *Journal of the American Institute of Planners* could have inspired the Indian village example. Pradyumna Prasad Karan describes Indian urban patterning of streets and buildings through an examination of their form on maps. Alexander does not cite this article, but there are a number of articles and works that he does not cite. See Pradyumna Prasad Karan, "The Pattern of Indian Towns: A Study in Urban Morphology," *Journal of the American Institute of Planners* 23 (1957): 70–75.

79. Alexander, *Notes on the Synthesis of Form,* 95.

80. Ibid.

81. Alexander, *Notes on the Synthesis of Form,* "Preface." In this preface, Alexander completely rejects the Design Methods movement and its uptake of his process.

82. Although numbered as volumes, the three books were published out of order. *The Timeless Way of Building,* volume 1, was published in 1979. *A Pattern Language,* volume 2, was published in 1977. *The Oregon Experiment,* volume 3, was published in 1975.

83. Christopher Alexander, Sara Ishikawa, and Murray Silverstein, *A Pattern Language: Towns, Buildings, Construction* (New York: Oxford University Press, 1977), title page.

84. Christopher Alexander, Sara Ishikawa, and Murray Silverstein, *Pattern Manual (Draft)* (Berkeley: Center for Environmental Structure, University of California, 1967), 1.

85. Ibid., 5.

86. Frank Duffy and John Torrey published "A Progress Report on the Pattern Language" in the *Emerging Methods in Environmental Design and Planning* volume that came out of the Design Methods Group First International Conference in Cambridge in 1968. Both Duffy and Torrey had worked on the early notion of the pattern language as graduate students at UC Berkeley, where Torrey was a member of CES. Their article supports the typological use of patterns but criticizes the communication and control processes of the CES. "It is not true that the problem of communicating patterns to users and critics has been solved. All attempts so far have floundered on the rock of precision, being either too general or too limited." Francis Duffy and John Torrey, "A Progress Report on the Pattern Language" (paper, Emerging Methods in Environmental Design and Planning Conference, Cambridge, MA, June 1968), 268.

87. Antoine Picon, "From 'Poetry of Art' to Method: The Theory of Jean-Nicolas-Louis Durand," in *Jean-Nicolas-Louis Durand: Précis of the Lectures on Architecture: With Graphic Portion of the Lectures on Architecture* (Los Angeles: Getty Publications, 2000), 45.

88. Alexander, Ishikawa, and Silverstein, *A Pattern Language*, x.

89. Christopher Alexander, *The Timeless Way of Building* (New York: Oxford University Press, 1979), 202.

90. Ibid., 181.

91. Ibid., 265.

92. Ibid., 263.

93. Alexander, Ishikawa, and Silverstein, *A Pattern Language*, xix.

94. Ibid., 747.

95. Ibid.

96. Ibid., xxix.

97. Ibid., xiv.

98. Ibid., 747.

99. Ibid., 750.

100. Ibid., 750–751.

101. Alexander, *The Timeless Way of Building*, 208.

102. Ibid., 192.

103. Ibid., xi.

104. Ibid., 204.

105. Ibid., 192.

106. Christopher Alexander, "Systems Generating Systems," *Architectural Design* 38 (1968): 606.

107. Samuel Levin wrote a deeper exegesis of the function of compression in poetry that proved useful for this understanding. See Samuel Levin, "The Analysis of Compression in Poetry," *Foundations of Language* 7 (1971).

108. Alexander, *The Timeless Way of Building*, 373.

109. Alexander, Ishikawa, and Silverstein, *A Pattern Language*, xlii–xliii.

110. Ibid., xliv.

111. Ibid., xviii.

112. Ibid., 313–315.

113. Alexander argues, albeit without providing examples of the experiments, "We have been able to show, experimentally, that the more a sequence of patterns meets these three conditions, the more coherent a person's image is. . . . On the other hand, the more a sequence of patterns violates the three conditions, the more incoherent the person's image becomes. . . . And this is why a pattern language has the natural power to help us form coherent images." Ibid., 380.

114. Ibid., 373.

115. Ibid., xii.

116. Cornelia Vismann, *Files: Law and Media Technology*, Meridian (Stanford, CA: Stanford University Press, 2008), 7.

117. Alexander, Ishikawa, and Silverstein, *A Pattern Language,* xviii.

118. Paul Baran, *On Distributed Communications Networks: I. Introduction to Distributed Communications Networks* (Santa Monica, CA: The RAND Corporation, 1964), 16.

119. Alexander, *The Timeless Way of Building*, 380.

120. Ibid., 341.

121. Ibid., 182.

122. Alexander, "Systems Generating Systems," 606.

123. Alexander, *The Timeless Way of Building*, 186.

124. Stephen Grabow, *Christopher Alexander: The Search for a New Paradigm in Architecture* (Boston: Oriel Press, 1983), 46.

125. Alexander, *The Timeless Way of Building*, 186.

126. Ibid., xi.

127. Ibid., 182.

128. Ibid., xiii.

129. Ibid.

130. Ibid., xiv.

131. Ibid., 192.

132. Grabow, *Christopher Alexander*, 9.

133. Ibid.

134. Ibid., 47–48.

135. Ibid., 48.

136. Ibid., 49.

137. Alexander, *The Timeless Way of Building*, 240.

138. Ibid., 199.

139. Grabow, *Christopher Alexander*, 50.

140. Christopher Alexander, *The Nature of Order: An Essay on the Art of Building and the Nature of the Universe* (Berkeley, CA: Center for Environmental Structure, 2002), 45.

141. Portola Institute, *The Last Whole Earth Catalog; Access to Tools* (Menlo Park, CA: Portola Institute, 1971), 15.

142. Alan Cooper, Skype interview by Molly Wright Steenson, April 23, 2015.

143. Edward Yourdon, "Historical Footnote on Design Patterns" (comment), April 20, 2009, http://codetojoy.blogspot.com/2009/04/historical-footnote-on-design-patterns.html?showComment=1240261080000#c5317107911198912272.

144. Alan Cooper, Skype interview by Molly Wright Steenson, April 23, 2015.

145. Kent Beck, Skype interview by Molly Wright Steenson, April 10, 2015. See also Grabow, *Christopher Alexander*, 127.

146. Beck, Skype interview by Molly Wright Steenson.

147. Kent Beck's Facebook page, "Patterns Enhance Craft Sidebar: My Personal Crisis," February 6, 2015, https://www.facebook.com/notes/kent-beck/patterns-enhance-craft-sidebar-my-personal-crisis/908356345863897.

148. Ibid.

149. Beck and Cunningham were the first to "actually do something" with patterns, said Beck. Kent Beck, Skype interview by Molly Wright Steenson, April 10, 2015. See Reid Smith, "Panel on Design Methodology," OOPSLA '87 Addendum to the Proceedings, October 1987; and Kent

Beck and Ward Cunningham, "Using Pattern Languages for Object-Oriented Programs," 1987, http://c2.com/doc/oopsla87.html.

150. Stefan Ram, email communication with Alan Kay, July 23, 2003, http://www.purl.org/stefan _ram/pub/doc_kay_oop_en.

151. Richard P. Gabriel, *Patterns of Software: Tales from the Software Community* (New York: Oxford University Press, 1996), 4.

152. Christopher Alexander, "Foreword," in *Patterns of Software: Tales from the Software Community*, by Richard P. Gabriel (New York: Oxford University Press, 1996), v–xi.

153. Jim Coplien created a catalog of "idioms," an early notion of patterns for the C++ language that were used at AT&T; Marc Sewell brought them to IBM; and Erich Gamma, a programmer in Switzerland, applied object-oriented patterns in his doctoral dissertation.

154. Erich Gamma et al., *Design Patterns: Elements of Reusable Object-Oriented Software* (New York: Addison-Wesley, 1994), 12–13.

155. Erich Gamma et al., "Design Patterns: Abstraction and Reuse of Object-Oriented Design," in *ECOOP' 93—Object-Oriented Programming*, ed. Oscar M. Nierstrasz, Lecture Notes in Computer Science 707 (Heidelberg: Springer Berlin Heidelberg, 1993), 417.

156. Christopher Alexander, "Foreword," in Gabriel, *Patterns of Software*, viii.

157. Ibid., ix.

158. Ibid., viii.

159. Alexander, "The Origins of Pattern Theory," 74.

160. Ibid., 77.

161. Ibid., 79–80.

162. Ibid., 81.

163. Ibid., 82.

164. Alexander, "Foreword," in Gabriel, *Patterns of Software*, vi–vii.

165. Grabow, *Christopher Alexander*, 128.

166. Gabriel, *Patterns of Software*, 59.

167. Drew Binstock, "Interview with Alan Kay," *Dr. Dobb's*, July 10, 2012, 4, http://www.drdobbs .com/architecture-and-design/interview-with-alan-kay/240003442. Thank you to Annette Vee for the insight.

168. Ibid.

169. Alexander, "Foreword," in Gabriel, *Patterns of Software*, vii.

170. Ibid., viii.

171. Beck, Skype interview by Molly Wright Steenson.

172. Alexander, Ishikawa, Silverstein, *A Pattern Language*, 963.

173. Beck, Skype interview by Molly Wright Steenson.

174. Ibid.

175. Kent Beck, *Extreme Programming Explained: Embrace Change* (Reading, MA: Addison-Wesley, 2000), 2.

176. Ibid., 154.

177. Ibid.

178. "Manifesto for Agile Software Development," http://agilemanifesto.org/.

179. "Ward Cunningham, Inventor of the Wiki," YouTube video, 17:12, posted by the Wikimedia Foundation, May 23, 2014, https://www.youtube.com/watch?v=XqxwwuUdsp4.

180. Ibid.

181. Ibid.

182. Interview with Ward Cunningham by Jim Fleming, *To the Best of Our Knowledge*, http://www.ttbook.org/book/transcript/transcript-ward-cunningham-wiki-way.

183. Ward Cunningham and Michael W. Mehaffy, "Wiki as Pattern Language," in *Proceedings of the 20th Conference on Pattern Languages of Programs*, PLoP '13 (The Hillside Group, 2013), 6–7.

184. Sean Michael Kerner, "Ward Cunningham, Wiki Creator," December 8, 2006, http://www.internetnews.com/dev-news/article.php/3648131.

185. "Wikipedia: Statistics," Wikipedia, https://en.wikipedia.org/wiki/Wikipedia:Statistics.

186. Barry M. Katz, *Make It New: A History of Silicon Valley Design* (Cambridge, MA: MIT Press, 2015), 158. Katz's history of design in Silicon Valley is an excellent resource.

187. In the interest of disclosure, I know these individuals well. Gillian Crampton Smith was the director of the Interaction Design Institute Ivrea in Ivrea, Italy, and Philip Tabor was a visiting professor; I was a faculty member from 2003 to 2004. I previously worked with John Rheinfrank and Shelley Evenson at Scient from 1999 to 2001.

188. Terry Winograd, *Bringing Design to Software* (New York: ACM Press, 1996), xv.

189. Mitch Kapor, "A Software Design Manifesto," in Winograd, *Bringing Design to Software* (New York: ACM Press, 1996), 3.

190. Ibid.

191. Ibid., 6.

192. Ibid., 5.

193. Ibid., 4.

194. Portions of this section on architecture and inhabiting the space of software were presented in a paper at the Design Research Conference 2016 in Brighton, England. See Molly Wright Steenson, "The Idea of Architecture, The User As Inhabitant: Design through a Christopher Alexander Lens," *Proceedings of DRS 2016, Design Research Society 50th Anniversary Conference*, Brighton, UK, June 27–30, 2016, http://www.drs2016.org/127/.

195. Alexander, *The Timeless Way of Building*, ix.

196. Winograd, *Bringing Design to Software*, xvii.

197. John Rheinfrank and Shelley Evenson, "Design Languages," in Winograd, *Bringing Design to Software*, 65.

198. Ibid.

199. Terry Winograd and Philip Tabor, "Profile 1. Software Design and Architecture," in Winograd, *Bringing Design to Software*, 10.

200. Ibid., 11.

201. Kenny Cuppers, *Use Matters: An Alternative History of Architecture* (London: Routledge, 2013), 1.

202. Ibid.

203. Alan F. Blackwell and Sally Fincher, "PUX: Patterns of User Experience," *Interactions* 17, no. 2 (March 2010): 31, doi:10.1145/1699775.1699782.

204. Stewart Brand, *How Buildings Learn: What Happens after They're Built* (New York: Viking, 1994), 2.

205. Ibid., 187.

206. Sean Keller, "Systems Aesthetics: Architectural Theory at the University of Cambridge, 1960–75" (PhD diss., Harvard University, 2005), 97.

207. Peter Eisenman, *Eisenman Inside Out: Selected Writings, 1963–1988* (New Haven, CT: Yale University Press, 2004), ix.

208. Keller, "Systems Aesthetics," 89.

209. Peter Eisenman, "The Formal Basis of Modern Architecture" (Zurich: L. Müller, 2006), 6.

210. "Discord over Harmony in Architecture: The Eisenman/Alexander Debate," *Harvard Graduate School of Design News* 2 (1983): 16.

211. Moshe Safdie, unpublished introduction to Christopher Alexander and Peter Eisenman debate, 1982. Thank you to Dan Klyn for sharing the text of Safdie's introduction.

212. "Discord over Harmony in Architecture," 16.

213. Ibid.

214. Molly Wright Steenson's Facebook Page, January 8, 2015, https://www.facebook.com/maximolly/posts/10100721200649914.

215. Molly Wright Steenson's Facebook Page, July 23, 2016, https://www.facebook.com/maximolly/posts/10101251669101884

216. Sam Greenspan, "Half a House," *99% Invisible*, October 11, 2016, http://99percentinvisible.org/episode/half-a-house.

217. Ibid.

218. Anna Winston, "Architects 'Are Never Taught the Right Thing' Says 2016 Pritzker Laureate Alejandro Aravena," *Dezeen*, January 13, 2016, http://www.dezeen.com/2016/01/13/alejandro-aravena-interview-pritzker-prize-laureate-2016-social-incremental-housing-chilean-architect. Thank you to Daniel Cardoso Llach and to Sam Greenspan for insights about Aravena and Elemental.

219. Personal communication between Sam Greenspan and Molly Wright Steenson, November 7, 2016.

220. Ibid.

221. Assemble Studio, "Info," http://assemblestudio.co.uk/?page_id=48.

222. Betty Wood, "Turner Prize-Winners Assemble List Their Yardhouse Studio for £150,000," *The Spaces*, December 14, 2016, http://thespaces.com/2016/12/14/assemble-yardhouse/.

223. Charlotte Higgins, "Turner Prize Winners Assemble: 'Art? We're More Interested in Plumbing,'" *The Guardian*, December 8, 2015, https://www.theguardian.com/artanddesign/2015/dec/08/assemble-turner-prize-architects-are-we-artists.

224. Christopher Hawthorne, "Assemble Might Have a Turner Prize, but the London Collective Continues to Defy Categorization," *Los Angeles Times*, April 28, 2016, http://www.latimes.com/entertainment/arts/la-ca-cm-assemble-architecture-20160501-column.html.

225. Marc Rettig comment on Molly Wright Steenson's Facebook Page, January 8, 2015, https://www.facebook.com/maximolly/posts/10100721200649914.

226. Students at Yale School of Architecture currently take a required sequence of up to four courses titled Visualization I-IV that takes on these topics. Columbia University's Graduate School of Architecture, Preservation and Planning no longer teaches a course on representation, but rather the history of visualization starting in the nineteenth century. "Yale School of Architecture M.Arch. I," http://architecture.yale.edu/school/academic-programs/march-I.

227. Alexander, "The Origins of Pattern Theory," 80.

228. Pew Research Center, "News Attracts Most Online Users," December 16, 1996, http://www.people-press.org/1996/12/16/online-use.

Chapter 3

1. "2016 AIA National Convention Keynote Speakers Finalized," AIA, February 18, 2016, https://www.aia.org/press-releases/4326-2016-aia-national-convention-keynote-speakers.

2. Rem Koolhaas, "The New World: 30 Spaces for the 21st Century," *Wired,* June 2003, http://www.wired.com/2003/06/newworld.

3. Diana Budds, "Rem Koolhaas: 'Architecture Has a Serious Problem Today,'" *Fast Company Co.Design,* http://www.fastcodesign.com/3060135/innovation-by-design/rem-koolhaas-architecture-has-a-serious-problem-today.

4. Richard Saul Wurman, "An American City: The Architecture of Information," convention brochure (Washington, DC: AIA, 1976), 1, 4–5.

5. Ibid., 4.

6. Ibid.

7. Richard Saul Wurman, *33: Understanding Change and the Change in Understanding,* 1st ed. (Norcross, GA: Greenway Communications, 2009), 20.

8. Ibid., 21.

9. Ibid., 20–21, 26.

10. Ibid., 26.

11. Ibid., 58. Emphasis Wurman's.

12. Ibid., 59.

13. Ibid. Emphasis Wurman's.

14. Richard Saul Wurman and Joel Katz, "Beyond Graphics: The Architecture of Information," *AIA Journal* 64, no. 10 (1975): 45.

15. Ibid.

16. "An Interview with the Commissioner of Curiosity and Imagination of the City That Could Be," *AIA Journal* 65, no. 4 (1976): 63.

17. Richard Saul Wurman, *Information Architects,* ed. Peter Bradford (Zurich: Graphis Press, 1996), 16.

18. Gary Wolf, "The Wurmanizer," *Wired,* February 1, 2000, http://www.wired.com/2000/02/wurman/.

19. Richard Saul Wurman, *Information Anxiety,* 1st ed. (New York: Doubleday, 1989), 27.

20. My, "Lifeboat #5: Richard Saul Wurman," *Journal of Information Architecture* 3, no. 2 (Fall 2011): 9, http://journalofia.org/volume3/issue2/02-my/. Originally published as My, *What Do We Use for Lifeboats When the Ship Goes Down?* (New York: Harper & Row, 1976). Dan Klyn confirmed

with Richard Saul Wurman that "My," the interviewer, is really Morton Yanow. Dan Klyn, personal communication with Molly Wright Steenson, July 20, 2016.

21. Richard Saul Wurman, Skype interview with Molly Wright Steenson, November 3, 2014.

22. Dan Klyn, "Make Things Be Good: Five Essential Lessons from the Life and Work of Richard Saul Wurman, UX Week 2013," http://2014.uxweek.com/videos/ux-week-2013-dan-klyn-make -things-be-good-five-essential-lessons-from-the-life-and-work-of-richard-saul-wurman.

23. Wurman, *Information Architects*, 15.

24. Ibid., 18.

25. Maria Giudice was a designer for Access Press and art director at The Understanding Business, Richard Saul Wurman's studio. She was a partner at YO until 1997, when she founded Hot Studio. She sold Hot Studio to Facebook in 2013. Maria Giudice, LinkedIn, https://www.linkedin .com/in/mariagiudice.

26. Wurman, *Information Architects,* 81.

27. Richard Saul Wurman, *Cities—Comparisons of Form and Scale: Models of 50 Significant Towns and Cities to the Scale of 1:43,200 or 1"=3,600'* (Philadelphia: Joshua Press, 1974), 60. Italics Wurman's.

28. Dan Klyn writes about the process that Richard Saul Wurman asked his students to follow in Dan Klyn, "A Comparison in Pursuit of 'The Masterworks of Information Architecture,'" *ASIS&T Journal*, June/July 2016, https://www.asist.org/publications/bulletin/junejuly-2016/a-comparison -in-pursuit-of-the-masterworks-of-information-architecture.

29. Wurman, *Cities—Comparisons of Form and Scale*, 60.

30. Ibid., 62.

31. Richard Saul Wurman and Scott W. Killinger, "Visual Information Systems," *Architecture Canada* 44, no. 3 (March 1967): 37.

32. Joseph R. Passonneau and Richard Saul Wurman, *Urban Atlas: 20 American Cities, a Communication Study Notating Selected Urban Data at a Scale of 1:48,000.* (St. Louis, MO: Western Print and Lithographing, 1966), 2.

33. Ibid.

34. Ibid. Italics Wurman's.

35. Ibid., 1. Italics Wurman's.

36. Louis I. Kahn et al., *The Notebooks and Drawings of Louis I. Kahn* (Philadelphia: Falcon Press, 1962), 2.

37. Ibid.

38. Richard Saul Wurman, "Making the City Observable," *Design Quarterly*, no. 80 (1971): 91.

39. Ibid., 6.

40. Ibid., 76.

41. Ibid.

42. "Urban Observatory Turns Spotlight on Understanding at 2013 Esri International User Conference," Esri, July 9, 2013, http://www.esri.com/esri-news/releases/13-3qtr/urban-observatory-spotlight-2013-esri-international-user-conference; and "Urban Observatory," http://www.urbanobservatory.org/.

43. "Getting Your City Involved," Urban Observatory, http://www.urbanobservatory.org/pdfs/G65568_Urban-Observatory-How_to_get_involved_Flier_9-14-2.pdf.

44. Wurman, "Making the City Observable," 90.

45. Nadia Amoroso, *The Exposed City: Mapping the Urban Invisibles* (London: Routledge, 2010), 66 cf. 44.

46. Wurman, *Information Anxiety*, 47.

47. Richard Saul Wurman, *Hats* (Cambridge, MA: MIT Press for the Walker Art Center, Minneapolis, 1989), 14, 16.

48. Ithiel de Sola Pool, *Technologies of Freedom* (Cambridge, MA: Belknap Press of Harvard University Press, 1983), 231.

49. Ibid., 2. For example, should an electronic article enjoy the same First Amendment protections as one published in print? In 1980, the question was still up for grabs—the chairman of the American Federal Communications Commission (FCC), had recently suggested that might not be the case, and a Senate bill that explicitly extended First Amendment protections to electronic media was introduced, under the assumption that they might not otherwise be entitled to them, de Sola Pool noted.

50. Wurman, "Making the City Observable," 88.

51. Wurman says that although Italo Calvino's book shares the same name, it was a coincidence that they both used the title. Wurman claims, "I had it first!" Richard Saul Wurman, Skype interview with Molly Wright Steenson, November 3, 2014. Perry Berkeley and Richard Saul Wurman, "The Invisible City," *Architectural Forum* 136, no. 5 (May 1972): 41.

52. *The Invisible City*, International Design Conference in Aspen, Colorado (IDCA: 1971). International Design Conference at Aspen records, IDCA_0002_0018_001, University of Illinois at Chicago Library, Special Collections.

53. Ibid., 64.

54. "Program, IDCA1972, The Invisible City," undated, International Design Conference in Aspen, 1950–1988, Box 22, Reyner Banham Papers, 910009, Box 22, Folder 3, p. 3, Getty Special Collections, Los Angeles, CA.

55. Wurman uses the word "processes" in the poster (figure 3.07) and "performance" in Berkeley and Wurman, "The Invisible City," 42.

56. Ibid., 41.

57. Ibid., 42.

58. Wurman, *Information Anxiety*, 34. Italics Wurman's.

59. Ibid., 27.

60. Ibid., 38.

61. Richard Saul Wurman, *Information Anxiety 2* (Indianapolis: Que, 2001), 1.

62. Ibid., 10–11.

63. Dan Klyn, personal communication with Molly Wright Steenson, July 16, 2016.

64. Mickey Schulhof and TED Blog Video, "Sony Demos the CD at TED," YouTube video, 2:21, October 1, 2012, https://www.youtube.com/watch?v=WABAlJHPdnw.

65. Wolf, "The Wurmanizer."

66. "Our Organization," TED.com, http://www.ted.com/about/our-organization.

67. "TED Translators," TED.com, https://www.ted.com/about/programs-initiatives/ted-translators.

68. "TED Fellows Program," TED.com, http://www.ted.com/about/programs-initiatives/ted-fellows -program.

69. Cassidy R. Sugimoto et al., "Scientists Popularizing Science: Characteristics and Impact of TED Talk Presenters," *PLOS One* 8, no. 4 (April 30, 2013): e62403, doi:10.1371/journal.pone.0062403.

70. Benjamin Bratton, "We Need to Talk about TED," *The Guardian,* December 30, 2013, https:// www.theguardian.com/commentisfree/2013/dec/30/we-need-to-talk-about-ted.

71. Wolf, "The Wurmanizer."

72. The US director of Koolhaas's Office of Metropolitan Architecture (OMA), Joshua Prince-Ramus, gave one in 2006, when he introduced the Seattle Public Library to the TED audience.

73. Neri Oxman, "Design at the Intersection of Technology and Biology," TED.com, March 2015, https://www.ted.com/talks/neri_oxman_design_at_the_intersection_of_technology_and _biology.

74. Diana Budds, "Rem Koolhaas: 'Architecture Has a Serious Problem Today,'" *Fast Company Co.Design*, May 22, 2016, http://www.fastcodesign.com/3060135/innovation-by-design/rem-kool haas-architecture-has-a-serious-problem-today.

75. Robin Evans, *Translations from Drawing to Building and Other Essays* (London: Architectural Association, 1997), 154.

76. Budds, "Rem Koolhaas."

77. Wurman, *Cities—Comparisons of Form and Scale*, 80.

Chapter 4

1. Dan Klyn, "Explaining Information Architecture," *The Understanding Group*, July 20, 2016, http://understandinggroup.com/information-architecture/explaining-information-(architecture/.

2. Alex Wright, Skype interview by Molly Wright Steenson, May 24, 2016.

3. Douglas K. Smith and Robert C. Alexander, *Fumbling the Future: How Xerox Invented, Then Ignored, the First Personal Computer* (New York: W. Morrow, 1998), 50; C. Peter McColough, "Searching for an Architecture of Information," presented at the New York Society of Security Analysts, New York, March 3, 1970. McColough's use of the term first came to my attention in Louis Murray Weitzman, "The Architecture of Information: Interpretation and Presentation of Information in Dynamic Environments" (PhD diss., MIT, 1995), 12.

4. Smith and Alexander, *Fumbling the Future*, 50.

5. Ibid.

6. John Harwood, *The Interface: IBM and the Transformation of Corporate Design, 1945–1976* (Minneapolis: University of Minnesota Press, 2011), 5.

7. Ibid., 4.

8. Scott Kelly, "Curator of Corporate Character . . . Eliot Noyes and Associates," *Industrial Design* 13 (June 1966): 43. Emphasis John Harwood's; Harwood, *The Interface*, 5.

9. Harwood, *The Interface*, 61.

10. *User-friendliness* was first coined as a term till 1972, and found its way into popular discourse (a newspaper is user-friendly, for instance) in the early 1980s. "user-friendly, adj." OED Online. December 2016. Oxford University Press. http://www.oed.com/view/Entry/276172.

11. Human–computer interaction was exploding as a topic of interest. CHI '90 had 2,300 participants, up 39 percent from the year before. Jakob Nielsen, "CHI '90 Trip Report," June 1, 1990, https://www.nngroup.com/articles/trip-report-chi-90/.

12. Jonathan Grudin, "The Computer Reaches Out: The Historical Continuity of Interface Design," in *Proceedings of the SIGCHI Conference on Human Factors in Computing Systems*, CHI '90 (New York: ACM), 261–268, esp. 263.

13. Ibid., 264.

14. Ibid., 263.

15. Ibid., 267.

16. Mark Weiser, "The Computer for the 21st Century," *Scientific American* 265 (1991): 94.

17. Ibid., 94–98.

18. Mitch Kapor letter, quoted in Terry Winograd, "What Can We Teach about Human-Computer Interaction? (Plenary Address)," in *Proceedings of the SIGCHI Conference on Human Factors in Computing Systems*, CHI '90 (New York: ACM, 1990), 445.

19. Ibid.

20. Winograd, "What Can We Teach about Human-Computer Interaction?" 449.

21. Andrew Cohill, "Information Architecture and the Design Process," in *Taking Software Design Seriously: Practical Techniques for Human–Computer Interaction Design*, ed. John Karat (Boston: Academic Press, 1991), 99.

22. Ibid.

23. Ibid., 101.

24. Megan Sapnar Ankerson, "How Coolness Defined the World Wide Web of the 1990s," *Atlantic*, July 15, 2014, http://www.theatlantic.com/technology/archive/2014/07/how-coolness-defined -the-world-wide-web-of-the-1990s/374443/.

25. Christina Wodtke, "Towards a New Information Architecture," February 15, 2014, https:// medium.com/goodux-badux/towards-a-new-information-architecture-f38b5cc904c0.

26. Ibid.

27. Louis Rosenfeld, "Design—Structure and Effectiveness," *Web Review* (Archive.org), November 27, 1996, https://web.archive.org/web/19961127163741/http://webreview.com/95/08/17 /design/arch/aug17/index.html.

28. Ibid.

29. Louis Rosenfeld and Peter Morville, *Information Architecture for the World Wide Web*, 1st ed. (Sebastopol, CA: O'Reilly, 1998), xiv. Dan Klyn also points out Joe Janes's role. Janes is currently a professor at the University of Washington. Dan Klyn, personal communication with Molly Wright Steenson, July 20, 2016. See Michael Beasley, "Interview with Lou Rosenfeld, Part One," http://michael-beasley.net/interview-with-lou-rosenfeld-part-one.

30. Rosenfeld and Morville, *Information Architecture*, 8.

31. Ibid., 1.

32. Ibid., 1–2.

33. Robert E. Horn, "Information Design: The Emergence of a New Profession," in *Information Design*, ed. Robert Jacobson (Cambridge, MA: MIT Press, 1999), 16.

34. Ibid., 15–16.

35. Ibid., 17.

36. Karen McGrane, email with Molly Wright Steenson, May 19, 2016.

37. Megan Sapnar Ankerson, "Writing Web Histories with an Eye on the Analog Past," *New Media & Society* 14, no. 3 (May 1, 2012): 393, doi:10.1177/1461444811414834.

38. The Asilomar Institute for Information Architecture understood its mandate in similar architectural terms: it was founded to "advance the design of shared information environments" by supporting "research, education, advocacy and community service" and "build[ing] bridges to related disciplines and organizations." Asilomar Institute for Information Architecture Annual Report, 2002–2003," http://www.iainstitute.org/sites/default/files/annual-reports/iai _annual_report_2003.pdf.

39. "ASIS&T Summit: Practicing Information Architecture," February 3, 2001, http://www.asis .org/Conferences/SUMMITFINAL/welcom&warmup_files/v3_document.htm.

40. Ibid.

41. Christina Wodtke, "Welcome to Boxes and Arrows," March 11, 2002, http://boxesandarrows .com/welcome-to-boxes-and-arrows.

42. Nathan Shedroff, "The Making of a Discipline: The Making of a Title," March 11, 2002, http://boxesandarrows.com/the-making-of-a-discipline-the-making-of-a-title.

43. Google Trends, information architecture and user experience, https://trends.google.com/trends /explore?date=all&q=information%20architecture,user%20experience.

44. GK van Patter, "IA's Unidentical Twins: An Information Architecture Transformation Story," *NextD Journal*, April 4, 2007, https://issuu.com/nextd/docs/unidentical_twins; and Dan Klyn, personal communication with Molly Wright Steenson, July 20, 2016.

45. Jesse James Garrett, "Ajax: A New Approach to Web Applications," Adaptive Path, February 18, 2005, http://adaptivepath.org/ideas/ajax-new-approach-web-applications/; and Jesse James Garrett, personal communication with Molly Wright Steenson, May 25, 2016.

46. Bill Moggridge, *Designing Interactions* (Cambridge, MA: MIT Press, 2007), 13.

47. Ibid.

48. "Interaction Design, Gillian Crampton Smith, Royal College of Art, London," Seminar on People, Computers, and Design, Stanford University Program in Human–Computer Interaction, September 26, 1998, http://hci.stanford.edu/courses/cs547/abstracts/98-99/980925-crampton -smith.html.

49. Malcolm McCullough, *Digital Ground: Architecture, Pervasive Computing, and Environmental Knowing* (Cambridge, MA: MIT Press, 2004), xiv.

50. Jesse James Garrett, "IA Summit 09—Plenary," *Boxes and Arrows*, April 5, 2009, http://boxes andarrows.com/ia-summit-09-plenary/.

51. Ibid.

52. Ibid.

53. Jesse James Garrett, "The Seven Sisters," May 11, 2016, https://medium.com/@jjg/the-seven -sisters-9c2a7c49c0d0.

54. Paul DeVay, "What Is Digital Product Design?" June 2, 2015, https://medium.com/@node source/what-is-digital-product-design-93caad4e4035#.tisof9snr.

55. National Center for Women in Computing Technology, https://www.ncwit.org.

56. Patrick Quattlebaum, "A Conversation with Dan Klyn: Richard Saul Wurman & IA for UXers," Adaptive Path, http://adaptivepath.org/ideas/a-conversation-with-dan-klyn-richard-saul-wurman -and-ia-for-uxers/.

Chapter 5

1. Cedric Price, *Technology Is the Answer, but What Was the Question?* (London: Pidgeon Audio Visual, 1979).

2. Ibid.

3. Ibid.

4. Ibid.

5. Will Alsop, "Flight of Fancy," *The Guardian,* June 17, 2005, https://www.theguardian.com /artanddesign/2005/jun/18/architecture.

6. Royston Landau, "A Philosophy of Enabling," in *The Square Book*, ed. Cedric Price (London: Architectural Association, 1984), 11.

7. Biographical details here come largely from Stanley Mathews's book. Stanley Mathews, *From Agit-Prop to Free Space: The Architecture of Cedric Price* (London: Black Dog, 2007), 19. Mathews was the first to write a dissertation about Cedric Price, one that he based on not only archival research but also on interviews with Price and his circle before Price's death in 2003. Both Mathews's dissertation and his book were vital resources for my research, especially when I began researching Price in 2005.

8. Ibid.

9. James Meller, interview with Stanley Mathews, January 28, 1999, in Matthews, *From Agit-Prop to Free Space*, 34.

10. The Cedric Price Memory Bank project, at http://cedricprice.com, shows the intersections among people, places, and ideas that crisscrossed Price's life.

11. Alisha Jackson, "The Beatles' 'Eleanor Rigby' Was Almost Called 'Daisy Hawkins,'" *WZLX CBS Local*, April 28, 2015, http://wzlx.cbslocal.com/2015/04/28/the-beatles-eleanor-rigby-was -almost-called-daisy-hawkins/.

12. Cedric Price and Christopher Alexander, meeting notes, April 28, 1966. Fun Palace document folio DR1995:0188:526, Cedric Price Archive, cited in Stanley Mathews, "An Architecture for the

New Britain: The Social Vision of Cedric Price's Fun Palace and Potteries Thinkbelt" (PhD diss., Columbia University, 2003), 343.

13. Richard Saul Wurman, personal communication with Molly Wright Steenson, November 25, 2016.

14. Nicholas Negroponte, personal communication with Molly Wright Steenson, September 30, 2013.

15. Eventually, "the project was so collaborative that it is difficult to say exactly who designed what, its very authorship was as fluid and indeterminate as the design itself," wrote Stanley Mathews. Mathews, *From Agit-Prop to Free Space*, 76.

16. Mark Wigley and Howard Shubert, "Il Fun Palace di Cedric Price=Cedric Price's Fun Palace," *Domus*, no. 866 (2004): 19; and Stanley Mathews, "Cedric Price as Anti-Architect," in *Architecture and Authorship*, ed. Tim Anstey, Katja Grillner, and Rolf Gullstrèom-Hughes (London: Black Dog, 2007), 142.

17. Wigley and Shubert, "Il Fun Palace di Cedric Price," 19.

18. Mathews, *From Agit-Prop to Free Space*, 78.

19. Reyner Banham, "People's Palaces," *New Statesman,* August 7, 1964, in Cedric Price, *The Square Book* (London: Architectural Association, 1984), 59.

20. Gordon Pask, "Proposals for a Cybernetic Theatre," in Mathews, *From Agit-Prop to Free Space*, appendix B, 274.

21. Ibid., 118.

22. Ibid., 119.

23. Gordon Pask Diagram of the cybernetic control system of Fun Palace, from a document related to a meeting of the Cybernetics Subcommittee, January 27, 1965, Cedric Price Archive, Montréal. In Mathews, "An Architecture for the New Britain," 120.

24. Fun Palace Cybernetics Report, 1964, Cedric Price Archives. Cited in Mathews, *From Agit-Prop to Free Space*, 119.

25. Vindu Goel, "Facebook Tinkers with Users' Emotions in News Feed Experiment, Stirring Outcry," *New York Times,* June 29, 2014, http://www.nytimes.com/2014/06/30/technology/facebook-tinkers -with-users-emotions-in-news-feed-experiment-stirring-outcry.html.

26. Mathews, "An Architecture for the New Britain," 169.

27. Mary Louise Lobsigner, "Programming Program: Cedric Price's Inter-Action Center," *werk, bauen+wohnen* 94, no. 12 (2007): 38–45.

28. Insights from an informal conversation with Howard Shubert in July 2010. Architects in the United Kingdom must carry professional indemnity insurance and run-off insurance for their

practices. "Professional Indemnity Insurance," Architects Registration Board, accessed October 7, 2012, http://www.arb.org.uk/architect-information/professional-indemnity-insurance/.

29. Paul Finch, "Breakfast with Cedric," *Volume* (42), January 13, 2015, http://volumeproject.org /breakfast-with-cedric/.

30. Barbara Jakobson, interview with Molly Wright Steenson, New York, November 29, 2006.

31. Cedric Price, "Cedric Price Talks at the AA," *AA Files* 19 (1990): 32.

32. Ibid.

33. James P. Carse, *Finite and Infinite Games* (New York: Free Press, 1986), 3.

34. Ibid., 6–7.

35. Wigley and Shubert, "Il Fun Palace di Cedric Price," 22.

36. Ibid.

37. The OCH Feasibility Study represents the work of a network of architects and media experts that Price orchestrated. Keith Harrison represented the office and drew the intensive network diagrams that outlined the structure of information to its served interfaces, with additional assistance from Peter Eley. Raymond Spottiswoode, a British producer and director who invented and patented 3-D movie technology in Great Britain, developed the screens and image-serving technologies. Sol Cornberg, a designer and inventor who worked on the earliest TV studios, designed the carrels. He believed that electronic brains from which people could retrieve information from home, car, or office should replace universities and invented a number of viewing devices (including a bowling ball viewing apparatus); Geoffrey Hellman, "Educational Alcove," *New Yorker*, September 7, 1963, 29; and Sol Cornberg, "Creativity and Instructional Technology," *Architectural Design* 38, no. 5 (1968), 214–217.

38. "Extent of Ex-Site Static Communication Possible," undated, Box 3, OCH Feasibility Study Folio, DR1995:0224:324:003, Cedric Price Archives, Montréal: Canadian Centre for Architecture (hereafter, CPA).

39. "An Electronic History of J. Lyons & Co. and Some of Its 700 Subsidiaries," http://www.kzwp .com/lyons/index.htm.

40. "Where Have All the Nippies Gone?," undated article clipping, Box 1, OCH Feasibility Study Folio, DR1995:0224:324:001, CPA.

41. In a 1961 memo, five years before Price's engagement began, a J. Lyons & Co. memo noted that visits to OCH were decreasing as the number of employees in the area was increasing, to the tune of fifteen thousand per year. Stated the memo, "If we wish to share in the increased prosperity which will undoubtedly come to the district then we must first learn what are the eating habits of people already in the area, and devise ways of catering for them either better or cheaper than do our competitors." "Memo: Developments in the Oxford Corner House Area," July 14, 1961, Box 1, OCH Feasibility Study Folio, DR1995:0224:324:001, CPA.

Price also included in the Feasibility Study an article by Reyner Banham on Centre Point. Reyner Banham, "An Added Modern Pleasantness," *New Society*, April 28, 1966, 19–20, Box 1, OCH Feasibility Study Folio, DR1995:0224:324:001, CPA. See also Stephen Bayley, "At Last, Things Are Looking Up at the End of Oxford Street," *The Guardian*, September 30, 2006, http://www.guardian .co.uk/artanddesign/2006/oct/01/architecture.

42. Memo to Geoffrey Salmon from Patrick Salmon (cc: Anthony and Michael Salmon, "Regarding 'Fun Palace' or 'A Trap for Leisure,'" September 20, 1965, Box 2, OCH Feasibility Study Folio, DR1995:0224:324:002, CPA.

43. The J. Lyons brainstorming included more quotidian activities: gardening, skeet, anything trendy in the United States, cookery advice, a gin palace, a Playboy Club, and the more imaginative computer-simulated sport center with simulated glider piloting. "Brainstorming re: OCH" memo to Patrick Salmon from Mr. Riem, August 25, 1965, Box 1, OCH Feasibility Study Folio, DR1995:0224:324:001, CPA.

44. "Memo, OCH Feasibility Study," September 23, 1965, Box 1, OCH Feasibility Study Folio, DR1995:0224:324:001.

45. "OCH Feasibility Study Report, 'Carrels,'" Section 6, Box 3, OCH Feasibility Study Folio, DR1995:0224:324:003, CPA.

46. Cedric Price, "Self-Pace Public Skill and Information Hive," *Architectural Design* 38, no. 5 (1968): 237.

47. Mathews, *From Agit-Prop to Free Space*, 203.

48. Cedric Price, "Potteries Thinkbelt," *New Society*, no. 192 (June 1966): 15.

49. Ibid., 17.

50. Mathews, *From Agit-Prop to Free Space*, 231.

51. Ibid., 238.

52. Cedric Price, OCH handwritten notes, "Internal Communication & Exchange potential—Static Communications," undated, Box 2, OCH Feasibility Study Folio, DR1995:0224:324:002, CPA.

53. "Memo, OCH Feasibility Study," September 23, 1965, Box 1, OCH Feasibility Study Folio, DR1995:0224:324:001, CPA.

54. Ibid. The first elements that Price's office researched were the physical infrastructures of the city as they intersected the OCH site. For example, the User Watershed studies analyzed traffic into central London—pedestrian, private car, and public transportation—in order to determine the "intent, appetite and free-time capacity of the potential users." This included mapping and statistics of all boroughs of London and its surrounding regions, with statistics of trips made across London for work and pleasure at present and projected to 1981. Cedric Price, notes on User Watershed, undated, Box 2, OCH Feasibility Study Folio, DR1995:0224:324:002, CPA. An article titled "London '81: Booming! Bulging!" from July 1966 highlighted potential concerns for OCH: Price

wrote "day-time importance" next to a passage on commuting. "Check cross river access routes," he wrote in the margin, and he underlined passages and question-marked passages on the decline of bus passengers and increase in private car use, particularly cross-town London Central, and a projected doubling in the increase of private car traffic for shopping and social excursions. Judy Hillman, "London '81: Booming! Bulging!," *Evening Standard*, July 12, 1965, 12, Box 1, OCH Feasibility Study Folio, DR1995:0224:324:001, CPA.

55. "Preliminary Draft of Distribution of Services (Crib Sheet)," May 6, 1966, Box 1, OCH Feasibility Study Folio, DR1995:0224:324:001, CPA.

56. Originally outlined in a memo between Keith Harrison for Price and Sol Cornberg, December 8, 1965, Box 1, OCH Feasibility Study Folio, DR1995:0224:324:001, CPA.

57. Undated colored-pencil drawing, drawings folio, OCH Feasibility Study Folio, 67/32, DR1995:0224:324:041–056, CPA.

58. Still and moving images (television and film) would be transmitted to OCH. News agencies would send images via fax machine over a regular telephone line; a Communications Department staff member at the OCH would "control all incoming pictures, and be able to switch any of them through to the large public viewing screens by placing the picture under a vidicon camera linked to one of the Eidophors"—which projected to one of three movie theater–sized screens. Each Eidophor cost £20,000; three were recommended, for a total of £60,000, and three film projectors would have cost £16,000. "OCH Feasibility Study Report," Sections 3–5, Box 3, OCH Feasibility Study Folio, DR1995:0224:324:003, CPA.

59. Keith Harrison, Memo: "Office: ref IBM meeting," June 21, 1966, Box 2, OCH Feasibility Study Folio, DR1995:0224:324:002, CPA.

60. Cornberg, "Creativity and Instructional Technology," 214.

61. "OCH Feasibility Study Report, 'Carrels,'" Section 6, Box 3, OCH Feasibility Study Folio, DR1995:0224:324:003, CPA.

62. Keith Harrison and Cedric Price, Memo to Sol Cornberg, December 8, 1965, Box 1, OCH Feasibility Study Folio, DR1995:0224:324:001; and "Communications Report," Section 2, undated, Box 3, OCH Feasibility Study Folio, DR1995:0224:324:001, CPA.

63. LEO's genesis lay in the 1947 visit to the United States of two J. Lyons directors who were sent to see the ENIAC, the first general-purpose computer, after which J. Lyons & Co. invested £20,000 in a computer at the University of Cambridge, the EDSAC. It was a success, and so production began on the LEO, led by John Pinkerton and David Caminer, with a twenty-person team. Princess Elizabeth saw a demonstration of LEO's first calculations in 1951 and LEO spun out as an independent company in 1953 and provided calculations for clients such as Ford Motor and the Ministry of Pensions. It merged with English Electric Ltd. in 1963, which bought out Lyons, merged with Marconi, and eventually joined with International Computers and Tabulators. *Times* (London), January 22, 1998; and S. H. Lavington, *Early British Computers: The Story of Vintage Computers and the People Who Built Them* (Bedford, MA: Digital Press, 1980), 72.

64. Letter from Price to K. T. Woodward, IBM, May 6, 1966, Box 1, OCH Feasibility Studio Folio, DR1995:0224:324:001, CPA.

65. The system consisted of a processor, disk storage unit, backup, two printers, and sixteen four-by-nine-inch cathode ray tube monitors to display information.

66. OCH Feasibility Study Report, "Communications," Section 3, Box 3, OCH Feasibility Study Folio, DR1995:0224:324:003, CPA.

67. He wrote further that it could have stored up to 350,000 images on a fourteen-inch reel and served fifty to one hundred people at a time. There was only one in existence at the time of the Feasibility Study, but this did not seem to pose a problem for Spottiswoode, who expected that other installations were being developed—the Ampex Videofile was publicly introduced in 1969. OCH Feasibility Study Report, "Communications," Section 3, Box 3, OCH Feasibility Study Folio, DR1995:0224:324:003, CPA.

68. Raymond Spottiswoode, letter to Cedric Price, July 21, 1966, Box 1, OCH Feasibility Study Folio, DR1995:0224:324:001, CPA. Finalized in "Storing and Retrieving Still Pictures," OCH Feasibility Study Report, "Communications," Section 3, Box 3, OCH Feasibility Study Folio, DR1995:0224:324:003, CPA.

69. Nigel Calder, "Computer Libraries," *New Statesman* 72 (1966). In OCH Feasibility Study Folio, Text Box 2, DR1995:0224:343:002, CPA. "Symbiosis" likely refers to the work of J. C. R. Licklider, author of "Man-Computer Symbiosis," *IRE Transactions on Human Factors in Electronics* HFE-1 (1960): 4–11.

70. Nigel Calder, "Computer Libraries," *New Statesman*, October 7, 1966. In OCH Feasibility Study Folio, Text Box 2, DR1995:0224:343:002, CPA.

71. Nigel Calder, "Computer Libraries," *New Statesman* 72 (1996).

72. "World File for Computers," *Times* (London), August 26, 1966. In OCH Feasibility Study Folio, Text Box 2, DR1995:0224:343:002, CPA. The first computer at the National Computing Centre would be a LEO—the LEO KDF 9. The company had been purchased by English Electric and then later Marconi, so the computer was an English Electric Leo Marconi KDF 9.

73. Price's office developed the Information Storage project, an electronic information scheme for the office, between 1967 and 1968. The self-funded project investigated storage banks and computers to catalog the information in the office, and also researched the possibility of developing information systems for outside clients. The project is interesting for what it reveals of how Price situated his practice inside a much bigger world. The scope of the project's taxonomy seemingly classifies the entire universe. Dick Bowdler, Price's part-time employee who ran his own communications technology consultancy, drew from the information schemes for Oxford Corner House and the British Midlands Institute Headquarters in his proposal for the Information Storage project. An electronic information system for Price's office could potentially perform four different tasks: "information retrieval," "solution of equations," "critical path analysis," and, possibly, computer-aided design. Price ultimately pursued only the information retrieval

function, because a machine that could handle all three would be prohibitively expensive. The cost would be somewhere in the range of £20,000 to £50,000 and would need to be managed by a computer bureau, where the connection costs would be £6 per minute. See Memo from Dick Bowdler, January 30, 1968, Box 1, Information Storage, DR1995:0232:001, CPA; and Box 1, Information Storage, DR1995:0232:001, CPA.

74. John G. Laski, "Towards an Information Utility," *New Scientist*, September 29, 1966:726. In OCH Feasibility Study Folio, Text Box 2, DR1995:0224:343:002, CPA.

75. Ibid., 727.

76. Ibid., 726.

77. N. Katherine Hayles, *My Mother Was a Computer: Digital Subjects and Literary Texts* (Chicago: University of Chicago Press, 2005), 93.

78. Friedrich A. Kittler, *Optical Media: Berlin Lectures 1999* (Cambridge, UK: Polity, 2010), 26.

79. Hayles, *My Mother Was a Computer*, 93.

80. "Mecca Takeover Corner House," *Evening Standard*, January 12, 1967, Box 1, OCH Feasibility Study Folio, DR1995:0224:324:001, CPA.

81. "From the design brief, letter to Raymond Spottiswoode," June 16, 1966, Box 1, OCH Feasibility Study Folio, DR1995:0224:324:001, CPA.

82. "Obituary of J. M. M. Pinkerton," *Times* (London), January 22, 1998.

83. John Frazer, Letter to Cedric Price, January 11, 1979. Generator document folio DR1995:0280:65 5/5, CPA.

84. This was a point that particularly interested John Frazer. Price went back and forth on it in his notes. John Frazer, letter to Cedric Price, January 11, 1979. Generator document folio DR1995:0280:65, 5/5, CPA.

85. Royston Landau, "An Architecture of Enabling—The Work of Cedric Price," *AA Files* 8 (Spring 1985): 7.

86. Ibid., cf. 4.

87. Ibid.

88. Paola Antonelli, "Interview with Pierre Apraxine," in *The Changing of the Avant-Garde: Visionary Architectural Drawings from the Howard Gilman Collection*, ed. Terence Riley (New York: Museum of Modern Art, 2002), 150.

89. Price, "Activity Charting Directions," November 28, 1977, Generator document folio, DR1995:0280:108–133, CPA.

90. Price, "Activities Chart," undated, Generator document folio, DR1995:0280:415–436, CPA.

91. Cedric Price et al., *Re-CP* (Basel: Birkhäuser, 2003), 58.

92. Essays on Paths, volume 1. Generator document folio DR1995:0280:459–480, CPA.

93. Ibid.

94. Gilman's art patronage is perhaps his greatest legacy and includes the highly regarded Howard Gilman Photography Collection, now at the Metropolitan Museum of Art, and the Howard Gilman Visionary Architectural Drawing Collection at the Museum of Modern Art. Pierre Apraxine curated both collections. Gilman supported Rudolf Nureyev and sponsored Mikhail Baryshnikov when he defected to the West. The White Oak Plantation would become the site of the White Oak Dance Project, founded by Baryshnikov and Mark Morris, in 1990.

95. Barbara Jakobson, interview with Molly Wright Steenson, New York, November 29, 2006. Art Net was a gallery curated by Peter Cook of Archigram.

96. "Architectural Studies and Projects," Museum of Modern Art press release, March 13, 1975. Jakobson had been appointed the head of the Junior Council at MoMA in 1970. In 1975, she came up with the idea for the show and encouraged the architects to sell their drawings. The show included works on paper by a number of architects, including John Hejduk, Peter Eisenman, Ettore Sottsass, Superstudio, Raimund Abraham, and Price; many of the drawings were sold during the show, for between $200 and $2,000, a boon to architects in a time of austerity.

97. Barbara Jakobson, interview with Molly Wright Steenson.

98. Cedric Price, "Further Respectably Zany Definitions," Memo to Gilman Paper Company, September 5, 1977. Generator document folio DR1995:0280:65, 1/5, CPA.

99. Barbara Jakobson, "Polariser Notes from February 1978," to Cedric Price, February 24, 1978. Generator document folio DR1995:0280:65, 1/5, CPA.

100. Cedric Price, "Polariser* Potential (Draft)," to Barbara Jakobson, August 4, 1977. Generator document folio DR1995:0280:65, 1/5, CPA.

101. John Frazer studied at the AA from 1963 to 1969, returning in 1989 to direct Diploma Unit 11, the AA's computer-related architecture module, where Julia Frazer became head of computing—a position she still holds today. In the late 1970s and early 1980s, the Frazers were engaged in teaching and researching at Ulster Polytechnic's Art and Design Center, Julia as a tutor and John as director of design research.

102. Cedric Price, "Letter to John Frazer," December 20, 1978, Box 4, Generator document folio, DR1995:0280:65, 4/5, CPA.

103. Price, "Notes for File," July 8, 1977, Box 1, Generator document folio, DR1995:0280:65, 1/5, CPA.

104. John Frazer, "Letter to Cedric Price," January 11, 1979, Box 5, Generator document folio, DR1995:0280:65 5/5, CPA.

105. Cedric Price, "Description of Computer Programs," undated, Box 1, Generator document folio, DR1995:0280:65, 1/5, CPA.

106. Ibid.

107. Ibid.

108. Ibid.

109. Ibid.

110. Gordon Pask, "A Comment, a Case History and a Plan," in *Cybernetics, Art, and Ideas*, ed. Jasia Reichardt (Greenwich, CT: New York Graphic Society, 1971), 77.

111. Ibid.

112. Price, "Description of Computer Programs," undated, Box 1, Generator document folio, DR1995:0280:65, 1/5, CPA.

113. Nigel Calder referred to the concept in his article, "Computer Libraries" that in turn inspired Price's OCH project (as well as Nicholas Negroponte, as we will see in the next chapter).

114. Pask absorbed the Fun Palace's cybernetic plans (as well as allusions to the Potteries Think-belt) into his 1969 article, "The Architectural Relevance of Cybernetics," several notions of which make their way into both Price's design of Generator and the Frazers' computer programs for it. Pask and Price would work together again on Magnet in the mid-1990s. Pask also was a close collaborator of Nicholas Negroponte and the Architecture Machine Group. Gordon Pask, "The Architectural Relevance of Cybernetics," *Architectural Design* 39, no. 7 (1969).

115. Ibid., 496.

116. Ibid.

117. John Frazer, Letter to Cedric Price, January 11, 1979. Generator document folio DR1995:0280:65 5/5, CPA. Emphasis Frazer's.

118. DJ Pangburn, "Industrial Robot Reprogrammed to Get Bored and Curious Like a Living Thing," *Creators Project*, January 5, 2017, http://thecreatorsproject.vice.com/blog/industrial-robot -reprogrammed-to-get-bored.

119. Cedric Price, *The Square Book* (London: Architectural Association, 1984), 19.

120. Royston Landau, "An Architecture of Enabling," 7. Italics Landau's.

121. Ibid., 3.

122. Cedric Price, "An History of Wrong Footing—The Immediate Past," undated. Generator document folio DR1995:0280:65, 1/5, CPA.

123. Ibid.

124. Personal correspondence between Price and Gilman outline these circumstances. See Boxes 4 and 5, Generator document folio, DR1995:0280:65, 4/5–5/5, CPA.

125. Letters and proposals exchanged between Price and the Frazers in 1989 show innovative suggestions from John Frazer about how a new Generator project might be funded. See

Autographics letters between Price and Frazer, Generator document folio DR1995:0280:65, 5/5, CPA.

126. Price, "Cedric Price Talks at the AA," 33.

127. N. Katherine Hayles, *How We Became Posthuman* (Chicago: University of Chicago Press, 1999), 13–14.

128. Ibid., 19.

129. Royston Landau, "A Philosophy of Enabling," 11.

130. Vitruvius Pollio, *Vitruvius: Ten Books on Architecture*, 1st pbk. ed. (Cambridge: Cambridge University Press, 2001), 17.

Chapter 6

1. Nicholas Negroponte, "The Architecture Machine," *Computer Aided Design* 7 (1975): 190.

2. Nicholas Negroponte, *The Architecture Machine* (Cambridge, MA: MIT Press, 1970), dedication and "Preface to a Preface."

3. Nicholas Negroponte, *Soft Architecture Machines* (Cambridge, MA: MIT Press, 1975), 5.

4. Negroponte, *The Architecture Machine*, "Preface." He wrote, "I shall consider an evolution aided by a specific class of machines. Warren McCulloch . . . calls them ethical robots; in the context of architecture I shall call them architecture machines."

5. Ibid., 1.

6. In particular, J. C. R. Licklider, Warren McCulloch (a cyberneticist and neurophysiologist), and Warren Brodey (a physician and cyberneticist). The influence is clear: Negroponte's writing style picks up McCulloch's, and the title of *Soft Architecture Machines* is inspired by Brodey's 1967 article "Soft Architecture: The Design of Intelligent Environments," *Landscape* 17 (1967): 8–12.

7. Nicholas Negroponte, interview by Molly Wright Steenson, Princeton, NJ, December 4, 2010.

8. Fred Turner, *From Counterculture to Cyberculture: Stewart Brand, the Whole Earth Network, and the Rise of Digital Utopianism* (Chicago: University of Chicago Press, 2006), 180.

9. Nicholas Negroponte, interview by Molly Wright Steenson, Princeton, NJ, December 4, 2010.

10. Nicholas Negroponte, interview by Molly Wright Steenson, Cambridge, MA, June 28, 2010.

11. Negroponte is still professor of media arts and sciences (on leave) and founder and chairman emeritus of the MIT Media Lab.

12. The Urban Systems Lab was also founded during this time in 1968. Felicity Scott's book *Outlaw Territories: Environments of Insecurity/Architectures of Counterinsurgency*, and in particular

chapter 7, "Discourse, Seek, Interact," offers a thorough account of its founding, as well as other projects covered in this chapter. Scott traces the strategies and funding of the USL. For example, she asks of the Ford Foundation grant that it requires a reading into "what types of technology and scientific research were to be put to work in the city, and of course for whom and to what ends." Felicity Scott, *Outlaw Territories: Environments of Insecurity/Architectures of Counterinsurgency* (New York: Zone Books, 2016), 346.

13. "MIT Report to the President" (Cambridge, MA: MIT, 1968), 3.

14. Ibid., 2.

15. Ibid., 32.

16. Ibid., 31–32. Anderson would seem to borrow from how Christopher Alexander had used computers at MIT five years prior.

17. Scott, *Outlaw Territories*, 339.

18. Ibid.

19. Nicholas Negroponte, "The Computer Simulation of Perception during Motion in the Urban Environment" (master's thesis, MIT, 1966), 150.

20. Ibid., "Preface."

21. Negroponte wrote at length about design process in the thesis and prognosticates about the impact of telecommunications and "instantaneous communication" (ibid., 18). On the future of computer-aided design, he wrote, "It is the year 1970. Perspective transformations are part of a Computer Aided Design system, available to all architects. Graphic Standards, Sweets Catalog and Building Codes are stored information. Computer Aided Design is the best of all possible tools. What can happen?" He envisioned the further development of the Kludge—Project MAC's TV set with manual controls and a teletype—for design applications. Although the time frame for their realization was further afield than 1970, his predictions were more or less correct (ibid., 151).

22. Ibid., 2. (When Negroponte founded the MIT Media Lab in 1985, General Motors was one of the founding sponsors.)

23. Architecture Machine Group, *Computer Aids to Participatory Architecture* (Cambridge, MA: MIT Press, 1971), 71. Note that this number does not include the research efforts by the Department of City Planning, which included the Urban Systems Laboratory.

24. MIT, "MIT Report to the President" (Cambridge, MA: MIT, 1980), 132. The numbers for the total sum of research is not given, and other research in the department is not called out by amount. The 1978–1981 proposal for the Dataspace project alone had a three-year, $400,000 budget. Nicholas Negroponte and Richard A. Bolt, *Data Space Proposal to the Cybernetics Technology Office, Defense Advanced Research Projects Agency* (Cambridge, MA: MIT, 1978), 1.

25. Architecture Machine Group, *Computer Aids*, 66.

26. AMG worked with a variety of students, employing an increasing number of undergraduates through the Undergraduate Research Opportunities Program (UROP) who collaborated with faculty and graduate students on its projects, starting with eight students per semester in 1971 and increasing to fifteen per semester, making for a total of about a hundred AMG "enthusiasts" by 1975. While master's students had more experience, Negroponte noted that it was the UROP students who were willing to work eighty-hour weeks, devoting much of their lives to the lab. It was a gateway for UROP students to continue their studies in conjunction with AMG. Many went on to complete master's degrees, with some joining the lab as full-time faculty and transitioning to the MIT Media Lab when it opened in 1985 (some are still there to this day). Numbers and rosters of lab personnel were not kept as a part of Negroponte's personal papers. Negroponte, "The Architecture Machine," 190; Nicholas Negroponte, interview by Molly Wright Steenson, Princeton, NJ, December 4, 2010.

27. Nicholas Negroponte, interview with Molly Wright Steenson, June 28, 2010.

28. Negroponte, *Soft Architecture Machines*, 191.

29. Ibid. Italics Negroponte's.

30. Ibid. Negroponte differentiated between the exercise at the drawing table and the problem of programming. When a student draws perspectives from a vantage point, she demonstrates her mastery of the concept by showing a few examples of special cases. However, writing a computer program that generates perspective views requires the student to first understand the general concept, model it in code, and then debug it until it runs properly.

31. Nancy Duvergne Smith, "'Deploy or Die'—Media Lab Director's New Motto," *Slice of MIT*, July 29, 2014, https://slice.mit.edu/2014/07/29/deploy-or-die-media-lab-directors-new-motto/.

32. Negroponte and Bolt, *Data Space Proposal*, 7. Italics Negroponte's.

33. Ibid.

34. Ibid., 37.

35. Stewart Brand, *The Media Lab: Inventing the Future at MIT* (New York: Viking, 1987), 15.

36. See J. C. R. Licklider, "Man-Computer Symbiosis," *IRE Transactions on Human Factors in Electronics* HFE-1(1960).

37. Architecture Machine Group, *Computer Aids*, "Preface."

38. Ibid.

39. Boston Architectural Center, *Architecture and the Computer* (Boston: Boston Architectural Center, 1964), 65. For an excellent treatment of Steven Coons and his design philosophy, see Daniel Cardoso Llach's excellent book *Builders of the Vision* (London: Routledge, 2015).

40. Negroponte, *The Architecture Machine*, 13.

41. Brodey and Lindgren wrote the following in a style that Negroponte imitates: "Imagine, if you can or will, a machine that is as responsive to you as our postulated tennis teacher—a

machine that tracks your behavior, that attempts to teach you a new control skill or a new conceptual skill and gives you cues as to what you were doing wrong. Furthermore, the machine gauges how far off your actions are from the program you are trying to learn, and 'knows' the state of your perception, it is able to 'drive' your perception gradually and sensitively, pushing you into unknown territory, into making you feel somewhat absurd and awkward just as you do when you are learning those new tennis movements. Suppose, in fact, this machine could sense factors about you that even a human instructor would miss. . . . If the machine could use these 'sensory' inputs in an intelligent fashion, it could be even more responsive to our needs and problems than the tennis instructor. In other words, this supposed machine would functionally be what we call a 'gifted teacher.' This machine would be behaving, in fact, like a deeply perceptive wise man who can behave in such a manner as to drive us out of our resistances to learning new patterns of behavior. . . . What was mere noise or disorder or distraction before becomes pattern and sense, information has been metabolized out of noise, and obsolete patterns have been discarded. The man who helps us sense our wisdom we call wise." Warren Brodey and Nilo A. Lindgren, "Human Enhancement: Beyond the Machine Age," *IEEE Spectrum* 5 (1968): 94.

42. Ibid., 92.

43. Ibid.

44. Charles Eastman used computer programs for space planning at Carnegie Mellon. Lionel March directed the Centre for Land Use and Built Form Studies (LUBFS). William Porter was a professor of urban planning at MIT and developed DISCOURSE, a system for computer-aided urban design. (The seminar that launched the DISCOURSE project lists M. Christine Boyer as a participant; Boyer was my doctoral advisor.) Avery Johnson was engaged in cybernetic and neurophysiological research at MIT. See Felicity Scott, *Outlaw Territories*, for a thorough treatment of DISCOURSE; Architecture Machine Group, *Computer Aids*, 20–21.

45. I am distinguishing here between first- and second-order cybernetics. Negroponte is interested in the latter in his model that takes the observation of a model into consideration. His idea here precedes Humberto Maturana and Francisco Varela's notion of autopoiesis, although it would seem to draw on the same ideas. Maturana and Varela write: "An autopoietic machine is a machine organized (defined as a unity) as a network of processes of production (transformation and destruction) of components which: (i) through their interactions and transformations continuously regenerate and realize the network of processes (relations) that produced them; and (ii) constitute it (the machine) as a concrete unity in space in which they (the components) exist by specifying the topological domain of its realization as such a network." Humberto R. Maturana and Francisco J. Varela, *Autopoiesis and Cognition: The Realization of the Living* (Boston: D. Reidel Publishing Company, 1980), 78–79.

46. Architecture Machine Group, *Computer Aids*, 7. Italics original.

47. Ibid., 15.

48. Ibid., 49–50.

49. Marvin Minsky and Seymour Papert, *Artificial Intelligence Progress Report* (Cambridge, MA: MIT Artificial Intelligence Lab, 1972), 7. Patrick Winston's dissertation research, referred to by

Minsky and Papert, bridged structural, real world objects and networks of semantic explanation. Patrick Winston, "Learning Structural Descriptions from Examples" (PhD diss., MIT, 1970).

50. Negroponte, *Soft Architecture Machines*, 35. Although Negroponte makes a distinction between the two methods, they are not at odds.

51. Stanford Anderson, "Problem-Solving and Problem-Worrying" (lecture, Architectural Association, London, March 1966 and at the ACSA, Cranbrook, Bloomfield Hills, MI, June 5, 1966), 2.

52. "interface, n." OED Online, September 2013, Oxford University Press, accessed November 16, 2013, http://www.oed.com/view/Entry/97747.

53. Ibid. Branden Hookway's book *Interface* offers his own theory of the interface, using this common point of departure. See Branden Hookway, *Interface* (Cambridge, MA: MIT Press, 2014).

54. Negroponte, *The Architecture Machine*, 101.

55. Ibid.

56. Ibid. Lindgren's notion of "assemblage" comes from Thomas Sheridan and William Ferrell at MIT, who wrote, "We consider a man-machine system to be any assemblage of people and machines which are in significant communication with one another and which are performing a task sufficiently well-defined that independent and dependent variables may be operationally specified." The assemblages represent a set of cybernetic feedback loops in which humans and computers interact with each other, such that they together and both affect one another in the system. Sheridan and Ferrell, unpublished manuscript, in Nilo A. Lindgren, "Human Factors in Engineering, Part I: Man in the Man-Made Environment," *IEEE Spectrum* 3 (1966): 136.

57. Negroponte, *The Architecture Machine*, 111.

58. Negroponte, *Soft Architecture Machines*, 48.

59. Negroponte, *The Architecture Machine,* 27.

60. Negroponte, *Soft Architecture Machines*, 49.

61. Negroponte, *The Architecture Machine*, "Preface."

62. Warren Brodey, "Soft Architecture," 8.

63. Ibid.

64. Ibid., 11.

65. Edwards, *The Closed World*, 47.

66. Licklider started working at BBN when its focus was acoustical engineering (and for which radar technology was developed), and in 1957, he convinced the company to invest in a computer. He joined ARPA as the first director of the Information Processing Techniques Office from 1962 to 1964 and came to MIT, first as the head of the Project MAC time-sharing computing

project, from 1968 to 1970, then as a professor, from 1971 to 1974 and again from 1976 to 1985. In between, in 1974–1975, he completed another stint as director of IPTO.

67. "I was all excited to show him the results. I said, I really want to show you what you funded. And he said, you know, I don't fund a project, I funded you, the person. . . . It was a real interesting lesson, a very interesting lesson. . . . They don't do that anymore. But that was the early days of funding at DARPA as well." To be clear, Negroponte is referring to the general DARPA funding paradigm. Nicholas Negroponte, interview with Molly Wright Steenson, December 4, 2010.

68. Nils Nilsson, *The SRI Artificial Intelligence Center: A Brief History* (Menlo Park, CA: SRI International, 1984), 17.

69. National Research Council (US). Committee on Innovations in Computing and Communications: Lessons from History, *Funding a Revolution: Government Support for Computing Research* (Washington, DC: National Academy Press, 1999), 270.

70. In fact, the ONR had financed Marvin Minsky's graduate studies, and Denicoff's successor continued to support Minsky's research on *Society of Mind*. Marvin Lee Minsky, *The Society of Mind* (New York: Simon and Schuster, 1986), 324.

71. Fields attended MIT as an undergraduate and, after completing a PhD at Rockefeller University, joined DARPA in 1974 as a program manager when Licklider returned to the agency. Over sixteen years, he climbed the agency's ranks, becoming director of DARPA in 1989. Fields had a reputation for aggressively supporting private high-tech research in semiconductor and high-definition television development in Silicon Valley and Research Triangle, something that members of President George Bush's administration opposed. He was demoted from his position as director of DARPA in 1990 and, soon after, moved into the private sector. See John Markoff, "Pentagon's Technology Chief Is Out," *New York Times,* April 21, 1990, http://www.nytimes.com/1990/04/21/business /pentagon-s-technology-chief-is-out.html. A 1990 *New York Times* article states that while the Pentagon called it a routine reassignment, it was related to Fields's attempts to move defense research funds into areas that were not about military buildup, but rather toward electronics. In particular, he had put $30 million into HDTV, and the government reallocated $20 million of this amount to other projects along with his reassignment. The editorial states that the research Fields was interested in funding, "for which the Administration fired him, may be important to the survival of the U.S. electronics industry—which is vital to American military strength, even if HDTV may not be. By one estimate, half the total cost of new Army weapons by the year 2000 will be for electronics." Such R&D programs would support projects with both commercial and military uses, the author argues. "The Administration seems instead to be limiting research support 'solely to technologies with military applications,' as a recent Congressional statement charged." Tom Wicker, "In the Nation: The High-Tech Future," *New York Times,* May 24, 1990, http://www.nytimes.com/1990/05/24/opinion/in-the-nation-the-high-tech-future.html.

72. Blocks worlds were first addressed in Lawrence G. Roberts's 1963 dissertation, "Machine Perception of Three-Dimensional Solids," in which he suggested methods for a computer to parse and display a photograph of a three-dimensional set of blocks into a two-dimensional photograph, and vice versa. It wasn't a matter of displaying a single block, but rather determining

where blocks intersected and drawing them appropriately, and transforming how they are displayed (showing multiple views). Roberts was at the Lincoln Lab at MIT. His work refers to Ivan Sutherland's Sketchpad 2 and Timothy Johnson's Sketchpad 3. Lawrence G. Roberts, "Machine Perception of Three-Dimensional Solids" (PhD diss., MIT, 1963).

73. Ibid., 294.

74. The term GOFAI was popularized by John Haugeland. John Haugeland, *Artificial Intelligence: The Very Idea* (Cambridge, MA: MIT Press, 1985).

75. Edwards, *The Closed World*, 171.

76. Ibid. Edwards refers here to Robert Schank, *The Cognitive Computer*; Joseph Weizenbaum, *Computer Power and Human Reason*; and Hubert Dreyfus, *What Computers Can't Do*.

77. Marvin Minsky and Seymour Papert, *Proposal to ARPA for Research on Artificial Intelligence at MIT, 1970–1971* (Cambridge, MA: MIT Artificial Intelligence Lab, 1970), 34.

78. Ibid.

79. Ibid.

80. Ibid., 5.

81. Ibid.

82. Negroponte, *The Architecture Machine*, 121.

83. My analysis of URBAN2 and URBAN5 is based on Negroponte and AMG's writings of it, as cited here, as are my descriptions and readings of other programs and experiences they developed.

84. URBAN2 and URBAN5 used an IBM 2250 display system running on an IBM System/360 computer, and used both FORTRAN IV (the first version of FORTRAN to support Boolean expressions) and a FORTRAN-based graphics package called GPAK that allowed a user to generate, plot, and manipulate computer images.

85. Negroponte, *The Architecture Machine*, 71.

86. Ibid.

87. Nicholas Negroponte and Leon Groisser, *URBAN2* (Cambridge, MA: IBM Scientific Center, 1967). Hereafter, I refer to URBAN2 only in connection with the course that Negroponte and Groisser taught and otherwise refer to URBAN5.

88. Negroponte, *The Architecture Machine*, 75.

89. Ibid.

90. Ibid., 80.

91. Ibid., 91.

92. Ibid. Some of the information it might seek out includes "rate of interrupts, the sequence of contexts, the time spent per mode, and the relevance of sequential acts." Negroponte, *The Architecture Machine*, 89.

93. ELIZA ran on MIT Project MAC's IBM 7094 computer, one of the computers that Alexander also used. Weizenbaum wrote the program in his own list-programming language called SLIP.

94. Joseph Weizenbaum, "ELIZA—a Computer Program for the Study of Natural Language Communication between Man and Machine," *Communications of the ACM* 9, no. 1 (1966): 37.

95. Ibid., 43.

96. Terry Winograd, "Procedures as a Representation for Data in a Computer Program for Understanding Natural Language" (PhD diss., MIT, 1971), 260.

97. According to interviews with both Negroponte and Winograd. Nicholas Negroponte, interview by Molly Wright Steenson, Princeton, NJ, December 4, 2010; and Terry Winograd, interview by Molly Wright Steenson, Stanford, CA, July 7, 2011.

98. In the "Readme" file for the source code in all caps, Winograd wrote, "SHRDLU is a system for the computer understanding of English. The system answers questions, executes commands, and accepts information in normal English dialog. It uses semantic information and context to understand discourse and to disambiguate sentences. It combines a complete syntactic analysis of each sentence with a 'heuristic understander' which uses different kinds of information about a sentence, other parts of the discourse, and general information about the world in deciding what the sentence means. SHRDLU is based on the belief that a computer cannot deal reasonably with language unless it can 'understand' the subject it is discussing. The program is given a detailed model of the knowledge needed by a simple robot having only a hand and an eye. The user can give it instructions to manipulate toy objects, interrogate it about the scene, and give it information it will use in deduction. In addition to knowing the properties of toy objects, the program has a simple model of its own mentality. It can remember and discuss its plans and actions as well as carry them out. It enters into a dialog with a person, responding to English sentences with actions and English replies, and asking for clarification when its heuristic programs cannot understand a sentence through use of context and physical knowledge." SHRDLU Source Code, Eric Lu, penlu, https://github.com/penlu/cmfwyp/tree/master/shrdlu/code.

99. Winograd, "Procedures as a Representation for Data," 35–60. Winograd presents an elegant dialogue with SHRDLU, illustrated with diagrams, that unfolds over a set of pages.

100. Ibid., 345.

101. Ibid., 350.

102. Negroponte, *The Architecture Machine*, 95.

103. Ibid., 71.

104. Ibid., 93.

105. Ibid., 99. Negroponte refers here to Joseph Weizenbaum, "Contextual Understanding by Computers," *Communications for the Association of Computing Machinery* 10, no. 8 (1967): 36–45.

106. Negroponte, *The Architecture Machine*, 89.

107. Rodney Brooks, "Achieving Artificial Intelligence through Building Robots" (Cambridge, MA: MIT Artificial Intelligence Laboratory, 1986), 2.

108. Negroponte, *The Architecture Machine*, 27.

109. Arthur L. Norberg, "An Interview with Terry Allen Winograd" (Charles Babbage Institute, Center for the History of Information Processing, University of Minnesota, 1991), 14, http://conservancy.umn.edu/bitstream/11299/107717/1/oh237taw.pdf.

110. Aspects of this description appeared in Molly Wright Steenson, "Urban Software: The Long View," in *HABITAR: Bending the Urban Frame*, ed. Fabien Giradin (Gijón, Spain: Laboral, Centro de Arte y Creación Industrial, 2010).

111. Architecture Machine Group, "SEEK, 1969–70," in *Software: Information Technology: Its New Meaning for Art*, ed. Jack Burnham (New York: Jewish Museum, 1970), 23.

112. Nicholas Negroponte, "The Return of the Sunday Painter, or the Computer in the Visual Arts" (manuscript, 1976), 9. Nicholas Negroponte Personal Papers, Cambridge, MA.

113. Architecture Machine Group, *Computer Aids*, 138.

114. Negroponte, *Soft Architecture Machines*, 47.

115. Ibid.

116. Architecture Machine Group, "SEEK, 1969–70," 23.

117. Ibid.

118. Ibid.

119. Negroponte, *The Architecture Machine*, 1.

120. Architecture Machine Group, "SEEK, 1969–70," 23.

121. Jack Burnham, "Notes on Art and Information Processing," in *Software: Information Technology: Its New Meaning for Art*, ed. Jack Burnham (New York: Jewish Museum, 1970), 11.

122. Paul Pangaro, telephone interview with Molly Wright Steenson, November 27, 2006. See also Edward Shanken, "The House That Jack Built: Jack Burnham's Concept of 'Software' as a Metaphor for Art," *Leonardo Electronic Almanac* 6 (1998), http://www.artexetra.com/House.html.

123. Ibid.

124. At that time, the lab's short-term interests were in visual perception and automatic manipulation, and applied mathematics; in the longer term, they sought to simplify, unify, and extend heuristic programming techniques, Marvin Minsky and Seymour Papert wrote in a 1970–1971

report to ARPA. Minsky and Papert, *Proposal to ARPA*. AMG fit into and participated in these experiments. Negroponte wrote, in *The Architecture Machine*, "This device is a homemade sensor/effector built by architecture students. The device has multiple attachments (magnets, photocells, markets, etc.) which it can position in three dimensions under computer control. It is anticipated that the mechanism will pile blocks, carry TV cameras, observe colors and generally act as a peripheral device for student experiments in sensors and effectors that interact with the physical environment." Negroponte, *The Architecture Machine*, 105. The students who worked on SEEK were Randy Rettberg, Mike Titlebaum, Steven Gregory, Steven Peters, and Ernest Vincent. Architecture Machine Group, "SEEK, 1969–70," 23.

125. Minsky and Papert, *Proposal to ARPA*, 1–2.

126. Ibid., 13.

127. Negroponte, *The Architecture Machine*, 107.

128. Ibid., 104.

129. Gordon Pask, "Aspects of Machine Intelligence," in *Soft Architecture Machines*, ed. Nicholas Negroponte (Cambridge, MA: MIT Press, 1975), 7–8.

130. Paul Pangaro, a researcher at AMG, met Gordon Pask through these collaborations. It started a lifelong collaboration and Pangaro became Pask's archivist.

131. Conversation theory had influenced Negroponte's view of "idiosyncratic" computing, and AMG researcher Christopher Herot had already been collaborating with Pask on its application to graphics.

132. Heinz von Foerster, "Cybernetics of Cybernetics," in *Communication and Control*, ed. Klaus Krippendorff (New York: Gordon and Breach, 1979), 8.

133. Architecture Machine Group, *Computer Aids*, 1. "The machine will indeed build a model of the user's new or modified habitat. But it is simultaneously building a model of the user and a model of the user's model of it" (ibid., 7). An early sort of user-friendly interaction, the system they proposed "must not only appear to be a 'competent' architect, but most essentially a sympathetic conversant, a good model builder, graphically dexterous and friendly" (ibid., 1).

134. Nicholas Negroponte, Leon Groisser, and James Taggart, "HUNCH: An Experiment in Sketch Recognition" (1971), 1. Reprint, Nicholas Negroponte Personal Papers, Cambridge, MA.

135. Nicholas Negroponte, "Sketching: A Computational Paradigm for Personalized Searching," *Journal of Architectural Education* 29 (1975): 26. Reprint, Nicholas Negroponte Personal Papers, Cambridge, MA. In *Soft Architecture Machines*, Negroponte wrote that HUNCH "faithfully records wobbly lines and crooked corners in anticipation of drawing high-level inferences about! . . . The goal of HUNCH is to allow a user to be as graphically freewheeling, equivocal, and inaccurate as he would be with a human partner; thus the system is compatible with any degree of formalization of the user's own idea. Unlike the SKETCHPAD paradigm, which is a rubber-band pointing-and-tracking vernacular, HUNCH takes in every nick and bump, storing a voluminous history

of your tracings on both magnetic tape and storage tube. HUNCH is not looking at the sketch as much as it is looking at you sketching; it is dealing with the verb rather than the noun. It behaves like a person watching you sketch, seeing lines grow, and saying nothing until asked or triggered by a conflict recognized at a higher level of application." Negroponte, *Soft Architecture Machines*, 65.

136. James Taggart, "Reading a Sketch by HUNCH" (bachelor's thesis, MIT, 1973), 8.

137. Ibid., 14–15. The role of the observer is what differentiates between first- and second-order cybernetics. First-order cybernetics assumes that a system is itself a discrete thing, unadulterated by the observation of or interaction with it. This model does not consider what lies outside its range of direct interaction. Second-order cybernetics, on the other hand, allows for the idea that any system may be changed in the fact of its observation. Thus, second-order cybernetics is the study of how people construct models of systems, not just how the systems themselves function and learn from themselves. Since people are cybernetic models themselves, their observations are de facto second-order cybernetic. It in effect makes for a cybernetics of cybernetics or, in the case of AMG and HUNCH, a model of a model.

138. The authors wrote, "In the process of discovering the structure of the sketch, massive amounts of data are reduced to a collection of points and relations between points. It performs these operations with uncanny accuracy, using only local information about the dynamics of the line." Horizontal and vertical lines hold structural meaning in architectural drawings, but parallel and perpendicular lines depended more on context. Negroponte, Groisser, and Taggart, "HUNCH," 9.

139. Negroponte, *Soft Architecture Machines*, 65.

140. For example, horizontal and vertical lines hold structural meaning in architectural drawings, but parallel and perpendicular lines depended more on context. Negroponte, Groisser, and Taggart, "HUNCH," 9.

141. Ibid., 2.

142. Ibid., 56.

143. "As a result of these difficulties, it was initially decided to side-step the issue by refusing curves as valid input. This decision can be partially justified on the grounds that, in the assumed architectural context, curves just do not occur that frequently," Taggart wrote in his thesis. "Thus, while ignoring the problem of curves imposed a limitation on HUNCH, the resulting simplification of the goals seemed to get us a long way before it became a problem." Taggart, "Reading a Sketch by HUNCH," 45.

144. Nicholas Negroponte, Leon Groisser, and James Taggart, "HUNCH," 8. Negroponte even extended the attack on curves. In *Soft Architecture Machines,* he wrote, "A myth of computer-aided design has been that computer graphics can liberate architects from the parallel-rule syndrome and hence afford the opportunity to design and live in globular, glandular, freeform habitats. We do not subscribe to this attitude. We believe that orthogonal and planar prevalencies result from much deeper physiological, psychological, and cultural determinants than the T-square.

Partly as a consequence of this posture, the Architecture Machine Group initially and purposely ignored curves, feeling that straight lines and planar geometries could account for most graphical intentions." Nicholas Negroponte, "Recent Advances in Sketch Recognition," *Proceedings of the June 4–8, 1973, National Computer Conference and Exposition* (New York: ACM, 1973): 666–667. No matter that Negroponte was rejecting the architectural work of many modern architects who engaged organic, curved forms, such as Eero Saarinen, Friedrich Kiesler, and even the inflatable, soft structures by his colleague Sean Wellesley-Miller, who contributed the "Intelligent Environments" chapter to *Soft Architecture Machines*. At some point, he loosened his stance, as the system was able to incorporate B-splining methods for curve calculation—appropriate, given Negroponte's mentorship by Steven Coons, whose greatest contribution to computer-aided design is in the calculation of curves and surfaces, in what is called the "Coons Patch," still used today. While HUNCH could not draw curves, Alan Kay's Dynabook could in 1975. Alan Kay, "Personal Computing," in *Meeting on 20 Years of Computer Science* (Pisa, Italy: Istituto di Elaborazione della Informazione, 1975), 15.

145. Taggart, "Reading a Sketch by HUNCH," 14.

146. Negroponte, "Sketching," 4.

147. Senator Mansfield asked Director of Defense Research and Engineering John S. Foster about research in a Senate hearing. "It was abundantly clear in his response that the Pentagon then believed all fields of science and technology were open to it, that it saw no inconsistency in funding basic research in fields already funded by civil agencies, and that all research projects it sponsored were somehow relevant to Defense needs. The Defense Department was adamant in its position that it must continue the full spectrum of research then being undertaken, even though by definition the outcome of much such research can neither be predicted nor its possible relevance to military science known." James L. Penick, *The Politics of American Science, 1939 to the Present*, rev. ed. (Cambridge, MA: MIT Press, 1972), 343, as quoted in Arthur Norberg, Judy O'Neill, and Kerry Freedman, *Transforming Computer Technology: Information Processing for the Pentagon, 1962–1986* (Baltimore: Johns Hopkins University Press, 1996), 36.

148. Mansfield Amendment text quoted in Herbert Laitinen, "Reverberations from the Mansfield Amendment," *Analytical Chemistry* 42, no. 7 (1970): 689.

149. "Members of MIT's AI community were determined, he asserted, to keep IPTO's focus on a particular type of AI research, and did so with their perceptron book, a book published in 1969 by Marvin Minsky and Seymour Papert which purported to prove that neural nets could never fulfill their promise of building models of the human mind. Only computer programs could do this, hence MIT's emphasis in AI." Norberg, O'Neill, and Freedman, *Transforming Computer Technology*, 35.

150. Stewart Brand, *The Media Lab*, 162.

151. Nicholas Negroponte, interview with Molly Wright Steenson, June 28, 2010.

152. Thomas A. Bass, "Being Nicholas," *Wired* 3, no. 11 (1995), http://www.wired.com/wired/archive/3.11/nicholas_pr.html.

153. Brand, *The Media Lab*, 163.

154. Nicholas Negroponte, interview by Molly Wright Steenson, Princeton, NJ, December 4, 2010.

155. MIT had its share of major protests. They grew in number and strength throughout late 1969, and in 1970, the Students for a Democratic Society (SDS) occupied MIT president Howard Johnson's office and riots took place around campus. At issue was government-funded military research in classified labs on campus. Two major laboratories conducted such research: the MIT Instrumentation Laboratory, founded in 1932 and renamed Draper Laboratory in 1970, and the Lincoln Laboratory, founded in 1951, which grew out of MIT's Radiation Laboratory. Draper most famously produced guidance systems for intercontinental ballistic missiles and the Apollo mission to the moon. Lincoln developed the Semi-Automatic Ground Environment (SAGE) after World War II and was known at that time for its electronics in air defense systems, early warning radar, and advances in early digital computing. MIT president Howard Johnson convened a panel to advise the Institute on whether to divest or convert these special laboratories. Ultimately, Johnson and the Pounds Panel spun Draper Lab out into a privately managed entity and kept Lincoln under MIT's umbrella. Johnson considered whether Lincoln and Draper Laboratories could or would want to shift priorities in a new direction: Lincoln could, and thus would remain a part of MIT. Draper would not and could not, and continued its work outside of MIT. There were also organizational issues at stake: Lincoln's management was appointed by MIT, whereas Draper's were not and would therefore be harder to manage.

156. Bass, "Being Nicholas."

157. Wil Haygood, "Ambassador with Big Portfolio: John Negroponte Goes to Baghdad with a Record of Competence, and Controversy," *Washington Post,* June 21, 2004.

158. Numerous sources tell this story. Succinctly, Jonathan Grudin notes these changes in his article on the connection of AI to the field of human–computer interaction (HCI). Jonathan Grudin, "Turing Maturing: The Separation of Artificial Intelligence and Human-Computer Interaction," *interactions* 13, no. 6 (2006): 56. Further, John Johnston wrote that Herbert Simon and Allen Newell engaged in this reduction. John Johnston, *The Allure of Machinic Life: Cybernetics, Artificial Life, and the New AI* (Cambridge, MA: MIT Press, 2008), 61.

159. Although expert systems used the real world as a point of departure, they still presumed that knowledge could be easily categorized and automated—again an aspect of the dominant "closed world" model. Edwards, *The Closed World*, 295.

160. "Lighthill Report Overview," http://www.chilton-computing.org.uk/inf/literature/reports /lighthill_report/overview.htm.

161. Brooks, "Achieving Artificial Intelligence through Building Robots," 2–3.

162. Ibid., 2.

163. Ibid.

164. Minsky and Papert, *Proposal to ARPA*, 34.

165. The Graphical Conversation Theory proposal extended HUNCH and combined it with research into computer graphics, computer-aided design, user modeling, and other areas of research (such as the Architecture-by-Yourself system by Guy Weinzapfel and Negroponte, inspired by and in conjunction with Yona Friedman) into a new research platform. Theodora Vardouli wrote at length about the notion of "participatory architecture" and Architecture-by-Yourself, in her master's thesis at MIT. Theodora Vardouli, "Design-for-Empowerment-for-Design: Computational Structures for Design Democratization" (master's thesis, MIT, 2012).

166. Christopher F. Herot, "Graphical Conversation Theory Proposal (Appendix)," in *Self-Disclosing Trainers: Proposal to the Army Research Office* (Cambridge, MA: MIT Architecture Machine Group, 1977), i.

167. Ibid., 17.

168. Architecture Machine Group, "Graphical Conversation Theory" (Cambridge, MA: MIT, 1976), 1.

169. Nicholas Negroponte, "NSF," *Architecture Machinations* 3, no. 27 (August 2, 1977): 10, Box 2, Folder 3, Institute Archives and Special Collections, MIT Libraries, Cambridge, MA (hereafter IASC-AMG).

170. The proposal was a response to a reorganization at the NSF. With Graphical Conversation Theory, AMG attempted to address both sections by combining AI and computer graphics in one proposal. Previously, AMG was sponsored by a single section, Computer Applications in Research, that funded a number of AMG projects related to computer graphics. These included touch-sensitive displays, vector and raster graphic formats, graphical input techniques, personalized (idiosyncratic) systems, and the Architecture-by-Yourself design system. Nicholas Negroponte, "NSF," 14, Box 2, Folder 3, IASC-AMG.

After the reorganization, AMG's research fell into the interests of two different NSF sections, Computer Graphics (which belonged to Computer Systems) and Intelligent Systems, each headed by a different person. John Lehman led computer graphics; Sally Sedlow led intelligent systems. Nicholas Negroponte, "Washington, 9/29/1976," *Architecture Machinations* 2, no. 40 (October 1, 1976): 21, Box 1, Folder 5, IASC-AMG; and Negroponte, "NSF," 10, Box 2, Folder 3, IASC-AMG.

171. First, the scope of Graphical Conversation Theory was much bigger than what the NSF tended to fund. NSF projects tended to last just over two years; AMG requested five years of funding, and the $1.41 million it asked for would have been the majority of the funding awarded by the NSF Computer Systems group that year. Negroponte wrote, "I will venture an educated guess that (not counting our support) Computer Graphics gets about $400K of support by NSF, nationwide. This is precious little. My guess comes from John Lehmann's comment that he funded $2M out of $8M requests for funds. His office has many other charters." Negroponte, "NSF," 10, Box 2, Folder 3, IASC-AMG. Second, it was not clear to the NSF that the project had enough to do with artificial intelligence. Negroponte argued that the proposal stated its relevance clearly. Yet Gordon Pask's ideas at this stage were esoteric and hard to follow, and although he

was a well-known cybernetician, he was in fact critical of mainstream AI. Paul Pangaro, "Dandy of Cybernetics; Obituary: Gordon Pask," *The Guardian*, April 16, 1996, 16. Third, the computer graphical proposal cover of which AMG was so proud was emblematic of the clash in style between the lab and the NSF. "The graphical quality of our document was immediately read to be PR [public relations] and to be expensive ('an example of poor husbandry of funds'). It is sadder still because it contradicts the very agreement *all* of the reviewers held: graphical augmentations (in computer interactions) are vital." Although one review was positive, the other four were negative. Negroponte wrote that they were "hyperbolic, to say the least. Several were unprofessional, emotional, thoughtless, or factually wrong." Another "was a slam, discrediting the whole peer review process," he stated. Negroponte also suggested that the NSF's filing system must have removed and discarded the glossy cover and the abstract. Negroponte, "NSF," 12, Box 2, Folder 3, IASC-AMG. Fourth, AMG clashed with the NSF's structure and peer-review process and protocol: there was a broader misalignment between peer-review culture at the NSF and the DARPA "closed world" that received and propagated defense research funding. Further confounding to AMG was the fact their previous relationship with the NSF did not seem to count. This ran counter to Negroponte's experience with DARPA and the ONR, where long-standing personal relationships with program directors ensured continuity of funding. In addition, the NSF required proposals be submitted to itself as a whole, not to a specific group: AMG instead addressed the proposal specifically to the "Computer Systems" and "Intelligent Systems" groups. In addition, they did not realize they could have submitted a list of potential reviewers that the NSF could consult, at their discretion. Negroponte, "NSF," 12, Box 2, Folder 3, IASC-AMG. And perhaps a fifth reason should be added: one member of the committee said that the proposal was rejected because of the group's evident hubris, according to Michael Naimark, a researcher at AMG at that time. Molly Wright Steenson, personal conversation with Michael Naimark, San Francisco, November 18, 2015.

172. Paul Pangaro, who had been a research associate at AMG as well as Pask's protégé and eventual archivist wrote, "Negroponte adopted Pask's notion of personalization by means of his own phrase, 'idiosyncratic computers,' a perfectly apt term. On several occasions, he tried to incorporate Pask's ideas into the lab's ideas. The lab worked with Pask to construct a research proposal submitted to the US National Science Foundation. Merging the research lab's interest in computer graphics with the Paskian framework, the proposal was called graphical CT. We submitted perhaps the best graphically designed proposal ever (and were criticized for it). The reviewers were split, one calling it brilliant and important to the future of user interface design; another calling it disorganized and uncertain as to its potential outcome. Both were right, but the Foundation chose against taking any risk, and declined funding." Paul Pangaro, "Thoughtsticker 1986: A Personal History of Conversation Theory in Software, and Its Progenitor Gordon Pask," *Kybernetes* 30, no. 5/6 (2001): 793.

173. Negroponte, "NSF," 12, Box 2, Folder 3, IASC-AMG.

174. Architecture Machine Group, "Graphical Conversation Theory," 293.

175. Nicholas Negroponte, interview with Molly Wright Steenson, June 28, 2010.

176. Nicholas Negroponte, "About This Issue," *Architecture Machinations* 2, no. 15 (April 11, 1976): 2, Box 1, Folder 3, IASC-AMG. Italics Negroponte's.

177. Norberg, O'Neill, and Freedman, *Transforming Computer Technology*, 9.

178. Edwards, *The Closed World*, 271.

179. Norberg, O'Neill, and Freedman, *Transforming Computer Technology*, 13.

180. In particular, the guidelines for the DARPA Information Processing Techniques Office. Ibid., 37.

181. Ibid., 37–38.

182. Stuart Umpleby, "Heinz Von Foerster and the Mansfield Amendment," *Cybernetics and Human Knowing* 10, no. 3/4 (2003): 188.

183. Negroponte and Bolt, *Data Space Proposal*, 11.

184. The Mac proposal just calls it "response compatibility," but the full term is "stimulus-response-compatibility," which relates to how well what someone perceives maps to their intended actions. See "Stimulus Response Compatibility," http://www.usabilityfirst.com/glossary /stimulus-response-compatibility.

185. Negroponte and Bolt, *Data Space Proposal*, 12.

186. Stewart Brand called it "a personal computer with the person inside." He referred to the space as the "Put That There" room (a project I discuss later in this chapter), but it is clear that he means the Media Room. Brand, *The Media Lab*, 152. Nicholas Negroponte, "Books without Pages" (1979), 8. Nicholas Negroponte Personal Papers, Cambridge, MA.

187. William C. Donelson, "Spatial Management of Information," *ACM SIGGRAPH Computer Graphics* 12 (1978): 205.

188. Ibid.

189. Richard A. Bolt, "Put-That-There: Voice and Gesture at the Graphics Interface," *ACM SIG-GRAPH Computer Graphics* 14 (1980): 263.

190. Brand is writing about the MIT Media Lab's early years. He refers to the space as the "Put That There room" (a project I discuss later in this chapter), but it is clear that he means the Media Room. Brand, *The Media Lab*, 152.

191. Richard A. Bolt, *Spatial Data-Management* (Cambridge, MA: MIT, 1979), 9. The work was sponsored by Defense Advanced Research Projects Agency, Office of Cybernetics Technology, Command Systems Cybernetics Program, Contract number: MDA903-77- C-0037 Contract period: 1 October 1976 through 30 September 1978 and ONR N00014–75-c-0460 & DARPA 903–77–0037 & MDA903-78-C-0039. Nicholas Negroponte, *Media Room* (Cambridge, MA: MIT), 6.

192. Nicholas Negroponte, "PLACE," *Architecture Machinations* 2, no. 35 (August 29, 1976): 2, Box 1, Folder 3, IASC-AMG.

193. Ibid.

194. "Information management system whose distinguishing characteristic is that it exploits the user's sense of spatiality for purposes of organizing and retrieving data." Bolt, *Spatial Data-Management*, 9.

195. Architecture Machine Group, "Augmentation of Human Resources in Command and Control through Multiple Man-Machine Interaction: Proposal to ARPA" (Cambridge, MA: MIT Architecture Machine Group), 36.

196. Ibid.

197. Ibid., 31, 36.

198. Yi-Fu Tuan, *Space and Place: The Perspective of Experience* (Minneapolis: University of Minnesota Press, 2001), 5.

199. Ibid., 6.

200. Ibid., 179.

201. Christopher F. Herot and Guy Weinzapfel, "One-Point Touch Input of Vector Information for Computer Displays," *ACM SIGGRAPH Computer Graphics* 12, no. 3 (1977): 210.

202. Architecture Machine Group, "Augmentation of Human Resources," 5.

203. Bolt, *Spatial Data-Management*, 12.

204. Ibid.

205. Alan F. Blackwell, "The Reification of Metaphor as a Design Tool," *ACM Transactions on Computer-Human Interaction* 13, no. 4 (2006): 509.

206. Marek Zalewski's master's thesis with AMG provides the 160-miles-per-hour speed. Marek Zalewski, "Mini-Documentaries" (master's thesis, MIT, 1979), 4.

207. Despite its military applications, the Aspen Movie Map received the Golden Fleece Award by Senator William Proxmire (D-Wisconsin) for spurious research spending. Brand, *The Media Lab*, 141.

208. Andrew Lippman to Michael Naimark, personal email, October 29, 2004, in Michael Naimark, "Aspen the Verb: Musings on Heritage and Virtuality," *Presence* 15, no. 3, http://www.naimark.net/writing/aspen.html. It also receives a mention by Brand, but Brand lists the wrong year of the rescue. See Brand, *The Media Lab*, 141.

The rescue in Entebbe has a more direct link to MIT than might be expected: Benjamin Netanyahu's brother Yonatan, an officer in the Israeli Defense Forces, was killed in the rescue. Benjamin Netanyahu (under the name Ben Nitay) attended MIT from 1972 to 1976, getting a bachelor's in architecture and a master's in management at the Sloan School. Leon Groisser, cofounder of the Architecture Machine Group, told MIT's *The Tech* student newspaper about getting to know the extraordinarily motivated Netanyahu when he came to MIT. His Sloan School of Management master's thesis at MIT would cross over into AMG and Media Lab territory, though he didn't work with the group: its title, "Computerization in the Newspaper Industry." Charles H. Ball, "Professor Recalls Netanyahu's Intense Studies in Three Fields," *The Tech*, June 5, 1996, http://news.mit.edu/1996/netanyahu-0605.

209. Negroponte is writing about undergraduate student Peter Clay's research in an *Architecture Machinations* article about the prototype videodisc player. Negroponte, "MCA Video Disk," *Architecture Machinations* 3, no. 41 (November 2, 1977): 3, Box 1, Folder 4, IASC-AMG.

210. Kevin Lynch, *The Image of the City* (Cambridge, MA: MIT Press, 1960), 6.

211. The group manufactured two discs for use in the system: one of twenty thousand slides of American architecture, with other animations and photos, the other of street views and landmarks in Boston. Bolt, *Spatial Data-Management*, 57.

212. Scott Fisher, "Viewpoint Dependent Imaging: An Interactive Stereoscopic Display" (master's thesis, MIT, 1982), 6.

213. Ivan Sutherland, "The Ultimate Display," in *Multimedia: From Wagner to Virtual Reality*, ed. Randall Packer and Ken Jordan (New York: W. W. Norton & Co., 2001), 256.

214. Robert Mohl, "Cognitive Space in the Interactive Movie Map: An Investigation of Spatial Learning in Virtual Environments" (PhD diss., MIT, 1982), 2.

215. Ibid.

216. Fields funded the "Augmentation of Human Resources in Command and Control through Multiple Man-Machine Interaction" project.

217. Nicholas Negroponte, *Being Digital* (New York: Alfred A. Knopf, 1995), 108–109.

218. Ibid., 109.

219. Bolt, *Spatial Data-Management*, 28. Compare the size to a four-megapixel screen, which by comparison is a low-resolution contemporary digital camera.

220. One of the 7/32 Interdata minicomputers controlled the program and files management for the Spatial Data-Management Systems and the interactions with the other minicomputers. A Control Data 300MB drive stored the information, with the database for it distributed among the other minicomputers. AMG manufactured two videodiscs. One was a disc of travel, architecture, art, and snapshots; another offered six thousand images of MIT for virtual tours. Donelson, "Spatial Management of Information," 206.

221. Bolt, *Spatial Data-Management*.

222. Donelson, "Spatial Management of Information," 205.

223. Bolt, *Spatial Data-Management*, 14.

224. Ibid.

225. Ibid., 29.

226. Some aspects of its development continued with AMG alumnus Christopher Herot, at the Computer Corporation of America (CCA). The Computer Corporation of America was located on Technology Square in Cambridge, Massachusetts. Founded in 1965, the company developed database systems. See Christopher F. Herot et al., "A Prototype Spatial Data Management System," *ACM SIGGRAPH Computer Graphics* 14 (1980): 63–70. The work was supported under DARPA contract no. MDA-903–78-C-0122. The CCA version allowed a user to keep track of a fleet from above: An aerial view showed all of the ships in a fleet, and zooming in to a particular area offered more granular detail about the fleet. These interfaces could also be viewed through a desktop system and not only in the Media Room. Ibid.

227. The Landsat map images in the SDMS booklet show four thousand square miles of the Boston region, and allowed the user to move step by step into higher resolution maps, up to a Boston street map. Once there, the user could view two hundred slides of Boston's attractions and streetscape—an idea that was explored further in the Aspen Movie Map. Bolt, *Spatial Data-Management*, 42. A further level of manipulation of the video would take place, Bolt wrote, through a time-based dial with semantic units (seconds and minutes) and a slider for "scrubbing" video to move slower or faster. Ibid., 36.

228. Ibid., 35.

229. Although AMG claims that it was the progenitor of the desktop computing metaphor, the practice appeared in several institutions at once, suggesting mechanisms of technology transfer within the research community. "There have been occasional differences of opinion about who 'invented' aspects of the modern desktop, but it seems clear that the main elements arose by the research community drawing together and accumulating successful innovations," wrote Alan Blackwell on the role of metaphor in human–computer interaction. Blackwell, "The Reification of Metaphor as a Design Tool," 497.

230. Ted M. Nelson, *Computer Lib/Dream Machines* (Chicago: Theodor H. Nelson, 1974), 48.

231. Donelson, "Spatial Management of Information," 208. Even more challenging, the information model was supposed be a torus, a doughnut-like shape composed of images that were knitted together, meaning that they could be navigated multispatially—a sort of carrousel of content. Ibid., 207.

232. Ibid.

233. Edward Tufte, *Envisioning Information* (Cheshire, CT: Graphics Press, 1990), 12. Italics Tufte's.

234. Chris Schmandt, *Put That There* (Cambridge, MA: MIT, 1979), http://www.youtube.com/watch?v=0Pr2KIPQOKE.

235. Matt Bunn, "Photography Program Cut," *The Tech* (Cambridge, MA), February 25, 1983.

236. Chris Schmandt, *Put That There—Hack* (Cambridge, MA: MIT, 1980), https://www.youtube.com/watch?v=-bFBr11Vq2s.

237. Mark Poster, "Theorizing Virtual Reality: Baudrillard and Derrida," in *The Information Subject*, ed. Mark Poster and Stanley Aronowitz (London: Routledge, 2001), 117.

238. Ibid., 118.

239. Ibid.

240. Andy Lippman to Michael Naimark, personal email, October 29, 2004, in Naimark, "Aspen the Verb." Michael Naimark was vital to the Aspen Movie Map project and carried on making Movie Maps of different kinds for another two decades. I am grateful to Naimark for a happenstance conversation in San Francisco on February 19, 2012, and for sharing many insights about AMG.

241. Architecture Machine Group, "Mapping by Yourself" (Cambridge, MA: MIT), 11.

242. Architecture Machine Group, "Mapping by Yourself," 8.

243. It included four mapping interface projects. Sound Maps would synchronize sound to a user's actions. Fuzzy Maps would explore display mechanisms for uncertainty, thus requiring some intelligence on the system's part. Transparent Maps presented another use of Fuzzy Maps, providing a sense of depth or showing what lay behind or beneath something, such as the subways beneath a street (ibid., 35). Haptically, tracing over a map would provide feedback of the terrain against the finger. Aurally, sound maps would provide alerts or sounds, depending on where the map was oriented, even potentially emitting a subway's rumble when the user focused on a subway line. And cognitively, the maps would represent what was known and not known through "fuzziness" and uncertainty, through the choice of lines, points, and areas as depicted on the map. Furthermore, the different sensory modes could be mixed—images on the screen, for instance, could combine with haptic force feedback from the device as the user took hold of a three-dimensional view (ibid., 5, 17). This was to be accomplished through dynamic parallax mapping methods that looked different depending on the position of the user's head. For example, "A report is received that a unique type of vehicle—a late-model Ferrari—has been sighted at a certain location (X and Y Streets). A credence factor can be assigned to that report. In this instance, we have information which is exact as to location, but which for some reason, perhaps the reporter knows nothing about cars, there is some doubt as to the validity of type," reads the proposal (ibid., 13). The proposal imagined that in the final phases of development, the window would "permit the user to look down on an environment in a conventional map format, then move the window to view it in full 3D, from an aerial perspective, and even to position the screen vertically, so as to see surface features in elevation and subsurface strata in section" (ibid., 17).

244. Ibid., 15.

245. Ibid., 9.

246. The proposal states, "Military relevancy resides not only in the formidable document preparation tasks of the Navy, but in the disparate audiences, ranging through all levels of competence, education and idiosyncrasy." "Idiosyncrasy" was Negroponte's term for personalized computing. Ibid., 60.

247. Ibid., 10.

248. Ibid., 13.

249. Supervised by Negroponte and Bolt. The project was DARPA-supported for the Rome Laboratory, Air Force Material Command.

250. Negroponte and Bolt, *Data Space Proposal*, 3.

251. Ibid., 3.

252. Ibid.

253. Ibid. Italics original.

254. Ibid., 25–26.

255. Ibid., 36.

256. Ibid., 12.

257. Ibid.

258. Ibid., 17.

259. Ibid., 18.

260. John Harwood, *The Interface: IBM and the Transformation of Corporate Design, 1945–1976* (Minneapolis: University of Minnesota Press, 2011), 10.

261. "interface, n." OED Online. December 2016. Oxford University Press, accessed January 8, 2017, http://www.oed.com/view/Entry/97747.

262. Harwood, *The Interface*, 10.

263. Andy Lippman said that the working definition for many years (ostensibly since AMG) had been "mutual and simultaneous activity on the part of both participants, usually working toward some goal but not necessarily." The corollaries were interruptibility, graceful degradation, limited look-ahead/on the fly, and the "impression of an infinite database." Brand, *The Media Lab*, 46–48.

264. Benjamin Bratton, "Logistics of Habitable Circulation," in *Speed and Politics*, ed. Paul Virilio (Los Angeles: Semiotext(e), 2006), 16–17. Italics Bratton's.

265. Ibid., 17.

266. Patrick Crogan, *Gameplay Mode: War, Simulation and Technoculture* (Minneapolis: University of Minnesota Press, 2011), xv.

267. Bratton, "Logistics of Habitable Circulation," 17.

268. Brand, *The Media Lab*, 152.

269. Negroponte, *Soft Architecture Machines*, "Preface."

270. Negroponte, *The Architecture Machine*, "Preface to a Preface."

271. Negroponte, *Soft Architecture Machines*, 5.

272. The Program in Media Arts and Sciences did and still does reside in the School of Architecture and Planning.

273. Nicholas Negroponte to Julian Beinart, John de Monchaux, and Jerome B. Wiesner, February 24, 1982, "Art and Media Technology Blueprint," 2. Nicholas Negroponte Personal Papers, Cambridge, MA.

274. Ibid., 6.

275. Ibid.

276. Nicholas Negroponte, *Dedication Booklet One, Draft* (MIT Media Lab), 2.

277. Muriel Cooper, cofounder of the Visual Language Workshop coined this term. Brand, *The Media Lab*, 10.

278. This later version boiled down a more complicated early idea Negroponte included in a paper he wrote in 1977, with circles titled "Mechanical," "Video/Audio" and "Digital," with sports, robots, "creativity amplifiers," and "non-trivial games" the points of intersection. Nicholas Negroponte, "The Computer in the Home: Scenario for 1985."

279. Ithiel de Sola Pool was founder and chair of MIT's Political Science Department and died in 1984, a year after *Technologies of Freedom* was published. Negroponte refers to him in texts, but I do not know if they otherwise collaborated.

280. Ithiel de Sola Pool, *Technologies of Freedom* (Cambridge, MA: Belknap Press of Harvard University Press, 1983), 23.

281. Ibid., 58.

282. Ibid.

283. Ibid., 24. De Sola Pool, however, was particularly concerned with the ramifications for politics, business practices, and First Amendment rights, which was not the focus of the Media Lab (although it was for other technocentric media organizations, such as the Electronic Frontier Foundation, founded in 1990).

284. Negroponte, "Art and Media Technology Blueprint," 15.

285. The Media Lab's sponsors circa 1987 broke down into the following categories: automotive (GM); broadcasting networks (ABC, NBC, CBS, PBS, HBO); movie studios (Warner Bros, 20th Century Fox, Paramount), news and information companies (*The Washington Post, The Boston Globe, Asahi Shimbun, Time*, Dow Jones, Fukutake); toys (LEGO and Bandai, Japan's largest toy manufacturer); media technology (RCA, 3M, Tektronix, Ampex); computing technology (BBN, IBM, Apple, HP, Digital); photographic/film (Polaroid, Kodak); and Japanese technology and telecommunication (NHK, NEC, Sony, Hitachi, NTT, Sanyo, Fujitsu, Mitsubishi, Matsushita).

286. Brand, *The Media Lab*, 12. The $10 million is referred to in Gina Kolata, "M.I.T. Deal with Japan Stirs Fear on Competition," *New York Times*, December 19, 1990, http://www.nytimes.com /1990/12/19/us/mit-deal-with-japan-stirs-fear-on-competition.html.

287. After much discussion about groups, resources, and competencies, the Media Lab launched with the following groups in 1985. This list comes from Brand, *The Media Lab*. He notes that it is in flux, and indeed, it does not reflect the changes and the decisions that had been made. I summarize it here because it is more comprehensive than other sources. Below, the group name, sponsors, funding amounts, and leadership come from Brand's list. Summaries are my own.

• Electronic Publishing: electronic and personalized books, newspapers, and TV. $1M mostly from IBM, led by Walter Bender (AMG) (ibid., 12).
• Speech: speech recognition and other cues that portended intelligent telephony agents. $500K, DARPA and Nippon Telephone & Telegraph (NHK), led by Chris Schmandt (AMG) (ibid., 50–56). The consortium included PBS, ABC, NBC, CBS (at first), HBO, RCA 3M, Tektronix, Ampex, and Harris (ibid., 12).
• Advanced Television Research Program: establishing standards for HDTV, $1M from a consortium of the major TV and cable networks and communications technology companies, led by William Schreiber (ibid., 72–74).
• Movies of the Future: eventual compression of movies to compact disc (semantic data compression), $1M, Warner Bros, Columbia and Paramount, led by Andy Lippman (AMG) (ibid., 79–81).
• The Visible Language Workshop: computers, graphic design, and interactive media, $250K, Polaroid, IBM, Hell; cofounded by Muriel Cooper (the creator of the iconic MIT Press logo) and Ron MacNeil (ibid., 12).
• Spatial Imaging: holography, $500K from DARPA and GM, led by Stephen Benton (who worked for Edwin Land at Polaroid) (ibid.).
• Computers and Entertainment: entertainment meets artificial intelligence, $300K, including the Vivarium sponsored by Apple, led by Alan Kay with Marvin Minsky (ibid., 12). The Vivarium is the subject of a chapter of Brand's book. It chronicles the relationship between Alan Kay's Dynabook and Xerox PARC, as well as the further life of Atari (which had absorbed aspects of the SDMS project) (ibid., 95–101).
• Animation and Computer Graphics: real-time computer animation, $300K from NHK and Bandai, led by David Zeltzer (ibid., 110–111).
• Computer Music: electronic music and artificial intelligence, and the Experimental Music Facility, $150K, System Development Foundation, led by Barry Vercoe and Tod Machover (ibid., 107–109).
• The School of the Future (Hennigan School): Logo, LEGO Mindstorms and computers in grade school curriculum, $1M, IBM, LEGO, Apple, MacArthur Foundation, NSF, led by Seymour Papert (ibid., 120–125).
• Human–Machine Interface: a continuation of the Media Room and Put That There, $200K from DARPA, NSF, Hughes, led by Richard Bolt (AMG) (ibid., 143).

288. Bolt's book *The Human Interface* packages Mac's command-and-control projects (many of which Schmandt, Lippman, and Christopher Herot led) in such chapters as "Where in the World

Is Information?" "The Uses of Space," and "The Terminal as Milieu" (the insights of which had been published in reports and papers already discussed in this chapter). According to Brand, Negroponte wrote a book under this same title that was published only in Japanese, and the English original was unusually and apparently destroyed. Brand, *The Media Lab*, 168.

289. Steve Huntley and Michiel Bos, "Pei Explains Architecture of Wiesner Building," *The Tech* (Cambridge, MA), October 4, 1985, http://tech.mit.edu/V105/PDF/V105-N39.pdf.

290. Pei Cobb Freed & Partners. Three artists contributed to the Wiesner Building: Richard Fleischner (siteworks), Scott Burton (sculpting the seating both interior and exterior), and Kenneth Noland ("Here-There," a mural in the lobby that extends to the exterior). http://web.archive.org/web/20150323153510/http://www.pcf-p.com/a/p/7829/s.html.

291. Huntley and Bos, "Pei Explains Architecture of Wiesner Building." It seems that Negroponte was not satisfied with some of Pei's design decisions and the progress of construction. In the Art and Media Technology Blueprint Memo addressed to Julian Beinart, John de Monchaux, and Jerome Wiesner, Negroponte wrote, "I am puzzled by the current state of the building, in part (maybe it is only me) because we don't really know the current state and schedules, with the exception that there is an ever growing hole in the ground." He thought that it might be time to "start worrying about some of the architectural issues that are seriously unresolved, nothing to do with the subdivisions. For example, dramatized by the most recent rendering, most of us are horrified by the ugliness of this building, climaxed by an arch that makes little sense in the absence of the theatre that was across the walkway. Negroponte, "Art and Technology Blueprint," 12.

292. Nicholas Negroponte to Cathy Halbreich, Debbie Hoover, Ricky Leacock, William Porter, Harry Portnoy, and Jerome Wiesner, September 4, 1980, "Memorandum: The Building as Medium," title page, Nicholas Negroponte Personal Papers, Cambridge, MA.

293. Negroponte, "Memorandum," 1.

294. Ibid., 1–2.

295. Ibid., 2.

296. Ibid., 2.

297. Brand, *The Media Lab*, image plate 3.

298. Negroponte, "Memorandum," 7.

299. Ibid., 6.

300. Ibid., 2.

301. Ibid.

302. Ibid., 9.

303. Ibid., 5, 11.

304. Ibid., 8.

305. Ibid.

306. Adaptive interaction, personalization, information surround, embodied interaction, and movie media and formats remain central foci of research for the lab; Schmandt and Lippman today run the Speech Recognition and Viral Spaces groups, respectively. Furthermore, the integration of media, information, interface, and the built environment is still essential to the group, apparent from the titles alone in such groups as Changing Places, Fluid Interfaces, Mediated Matter, Object-Based Media, Responsive Environments, Tangible Media, Affective Computing, and Information Ecology.

307. See Timothy Lenoir and Henry Lowood, "Theaters of War: The Military-Entertainment Complex," in *Collection, Laboratory, Theater: Scenes of Knowledge in the 17th Century*, ed. Helmar Schramm, Ludger Schwarte, and Jan Lazardzig (Berlin: Walter de Gruyter, 2005); Crogan, *Gameplay Mode*; and Jordan Crandall, "Operational Media," *CTHEORY*, no. a148 (2005), http://www.ctheory.net/articles.aspx?id=441.

308. Eyal Weizman, *Hollow Land: Israel's Architecture of Occupation* (London: Verso, 2007), 57.

309. De Sola Pool, *Technologies of Freedom*, 58.

310. Ulric Neisser, *Cognitive Psychology*, The Century Psychology Series (New York: Appleton-Century-Crofts, 1967).

311. Ibid., 8.

312. Negroponte, *Soft Architecture Machines*, 5.

Chapter 7

1. World Economic Forum, *Davos 2015—The Future of the Digital Economy*, https://www.youtube.com/watch?v=PjW_GSv_Qm0.

2. Mark Weiser, "The Computer for the 21st Century," *Scientific American* 265 (1991): 94.

3. Rob Kitchin and Martin Dodge, *Code/Space: Software and Everyday Life* (MIT Press, 2011), 16.

4. Ibid., 17.

5. In a blog post, Tesla underscored that Autopilot still requires the driver to be engaged with the vehicle. "When drivers activate Autopilot, the acknowledgment box explains, among other things, that Autopilot 'is an assist feature that requires you to keep your hands on the steering wheel at all times,' and that 'you need to maintain control and responsibility for your vehicle' while using it. Additionally, every time that Autopilot is engaged, the car reminds the driver to 'Always keep your hands on the wheel. Be prepared to take over at any time.' The system also makes frequent checks to ensure that the driver's hands remain on the wheel and provides visual and audible alerts if hands-on is not detected. It then gradually slows down the car until hands-on is detected again." But does that actually meet the driver's expectations of what Autopilot is? The Tesla Team, "A Tragic Loss," Tesla.com, June 30, 2016, https://www.tesla.com/blog/tragic-loss.

6. Thank you to Kaylee White for her insights on the human values versus those of the autonomous vehicle.

7. Antoine Picon, *Smart Cities: A Spatialised Intelligence—AD Primer* (John Wiley & Sons, 2015), 12.

8. Donna Jeanne Haraway, "A Cyborg Manifesto," in *Simians, Cyborgs, and Women: The Reinvention of Nature* (New York: Routledge, 1991), 149.

9. Ibid.

10. A recent study examined the makeup of a dataset of words, word2vec, that derived from Google News texts that was used to train neural networks. These neural networks look for patterns in how words were positioned next to each other. But when researchers at Microsoft Research and Boston University looked at the pairings, they found that it was "blatantly sexist," according to MIT Technology Review. "And they offer plenty of evidence to back up the claim. . . . For example, it is possible to pose the question: 'Paris: France:: Tokyo: x' and it will give you the answer x=Japan. But ask the database 'father: doctor: mother: x' and it will say x=nurse. And the query 'man: computer programmer:: woman: x' gives x=homemaker." The researchers proposed a mathematical reverse warping of the corpus, and worked with ten humans that they involved through the Mechanical Turk crowdsourcing system to confirm whether they found the word pairings to be biased; if more than half of the respondents found it biased, then they marked it as such. Emerging Technology from the arXiv, "How Vector Space Mathematics Reveals the Hidden Sexism in Language," July 27, 2016, https://www.technologyreview.com/s/602025/how-vector-space-mathematics-reveals-the-hidden-sexism-in-language/.

11. Eli Pariser, *The Filter Bubble: What the Internet Is Hiding from You* (New York: Penguin, 2012).

12. Graham Dove, Jodi Forlizzi, Kim Halskov, and John Zimmerman, "UX Design Innovation: Challenges for Working with Machine Learning as a Design Material," in *Proceedings of the SIGCHI Conference on Human Factors in Computing Systems,* CHI '17 (New York: ACM, 2017).

13. "I am optimistic deep learning will become more practical to teach soon, perhaps even before the end of 2016," Gene Kogan wrote. "Machine Learning for Artists," *Medium,* January 3, 2016, https://medium.com/@genekogan/machine-learning-for-artists-e93d20fdb097#.yof9dfwzl. Kogan taught a workshop called "Machine Learning for Interaction Design," http://ciid.dk/education/summer-school/ciid-summer-school-2017-nyc/workshops/machine-learning-for-interaction-design/. Rebecca Fiebrink, a lecturer at Goldsmiths, teaches "Machine Learning for Musicians and Artists," https://www.kadenze.com/courses/machine-learning-for-musicians-and-artists/info.

14. Elizabeth Churchill, Mike Kuniavsky, and Molly Wright Steenson, "Designing the User Experience of Machine Learning Systems," https://mikek-parc.github.io/AAAI-UX-ML/.

15. Malcolm McCullough, *Digital Ground: Architecture, Pervasive Computing, and Environmental Knowing* (Cambridge, MA: MIT Press, 2004), xii.

Selected Bibliography

This book has also benefited from the use of several archives: The Cedric Price Fonds at the Canadian Centre for Architecture in Montreal; MIT's Special Collections in Cambridge, Massachusetts; the Getty Research Institute Special Collections; and Nicholas Negroponte's personal papers.

Alexander, Christopher. *The City as a Mechanism for Sustaining Human Contact*. Berkeley: Center for Planning and Development Research, University of California, 1966.

Alexander, Christopher. "A City Is Not a Tree, Part 1." *Architectural Forum* 122, no. 4 (1965): 58–62.

Alexander, Christopher. "A City Is Not a Tree, Part 2." *Architectural Forum* 122, no. 5 (1965): 58–61.

Alexander, Christopher. *HIDECS 3: Four Computer Programs for the Hierarchical Decomposition of Systems Which Have an Associated Linear Graph*. Cambridge, MA: MIT Press, 1963.

Alexander, Christopher. *Notes on the Synthesis of Form*. Cambridge, MA: Harvard University Press, 1971.

Alexander, Christopher. "The Origins of Pattern Theory: The Future of the Theory, and the Generation of a Living World." *IEEE Software* 16, no. 5 (October 1999): 71–82.

Alexander, Christopher. "Systems Generating Systems." *Architectural Design* 38 (1968): 605–610.

Alexander, Christopher, and Peter Eisenman. "Discord over Harmony in Architecture: The Eisenman/Alexander Debate." *Harvard GSD News* 2 (1983): 12–17.

Alexander, Christopher, Sara Ishikawa, and Murray Silverstein. *A Pattern Language: Towns, Buildings, Construction*. New York: Oxford University Press, 1977.

Alexander, Christopher, Sara Ishikawa, and Murray Silverstein. *Pattern Manual (Draft)*. Berkeley: Center for Environmental Structure, University of California, 1967.

Alexander, Christopher, V. M. King, and Sara Ishikawa. *390 Requirements for the Rapid Transit Station*. Berkeley: Center for Environmental Structure, University of California, 1964.

Alexander, Christopher, and Marvin L. Manheim. *The Design of Highway Interchanges: An Example of a General Method for Analysing Engineering Design Problems.* Cambridge: Department of Civil Engineering, Massachusetts Institute of Technology, 1962.

Alexander, Christopher, and Marvin L. Manheim. *The Use of Diagrams in Highway Route Location: An Experiment.* Cambridge: School of Engineering, Massachusetts Institute of Technology, 1962.

Alexander, Christopher, and Barry Poyner. "Atoms of Environmental Form." Paper presented at the Emerging Methods in Environmental Design and Planning; Proceedings of the Design Methods Group First International Conference, Cambridge, MA, June 1968; Cambridge, MA, 1970.

Alexander, Christopher, and Barry Poyner. *The Atoms of Environmental Structure.* Berkeley: Center for Planning and Development Research, University of California Institute of Urban and Regional Development, 1966.

Anable, Aubrey. "The Architecture Machine Group's Aspen Movie Map: Mediating the Urban Crisis in the 1970s." *Television & New Media* 13, no. 6 (2012): 498–519.

Anderson, Stanford. "Problem-Solving and Problem-Worrying." Lecture at the Architectural Association, London, March 1966; and at the ACSA, Cranbrook, Bloomfield Hills, MI, June 5, 1966.

"An Interview with the Commissioner of Curiosity and Imagination of the City That Could Be." *AIA Journal* 65, no. 4 (1976): 62–63.

Ankerson, Megan Sapnar. "How Coolness Defined the World Wide Web of the 1990s." *Atlantic,* July 15, 2014. http://www.theatlantic.com/technology/archive/2014/07/how-coolness-defined -the-world-wide-web-of-the-1990s/374443/.

Ankerson, M. S. "Writing Web Histories with an Eye on the Analog Past." *New Media & Society* 14, no. 3 (May 1, 2012): 384–400.

Antonelli, Paola. Interview with Pierre Apraxine. In *The Changing of the Avant-Garde: Visionary Architectural Drawings from the Howard Gilman Collection,* edited by Terence Riley, 147–154. New York: Museum of Modern Art, 2002.

Architecture Machine Group. *Augmentation of Human Resources in Command and Control through Multiple Man-Machine Interaction: Proposal to ARPA.* Cambridge, MA: MIT Architecture Machine Group, 1976.

Architecture Machine Group. *Computer Aids to Participatory Architecture.* Cambridge, MA: MIT Press, 1971.

Architecture Machine Group. *Mapping by Yourself.* Cambridge, MA: MIT Press, 1977.

Architecture Machine Group. "Seek, 1969–70." In *Software: Information Technology: Its New Meaning for Art,* edited by Jack Burnham, 20–23. New York: Jewish Museum, 1970.

Ashby, W. Ross. *Design for a Brain: The Origin of Adaptive Behavior.* New York: Wiley, 1960.

Baran, Paul. *On Distributed Communications Networks: I. Introduction to Distributed Communications Networks.* Santa Monica, CA: The RAND Corporation, 1964.

Bass, Thomas. "Being Nicholas." *Wired,* November 1995. https://www.wired.com/1995/11/nicholas/.

Baudrillard, Jean. *Selected Writings.* Translated by M. Poster. Stanford, CA: Stanford University Press, 2001.

Beck, Kent, and Ward Cunningham. "Using Pattern Languages for Object-Oriented Programs," 1987. http://c2.com/doc/oopsla87.html.

Berkeley, Perry, and Richard Saul Wurman. "The Invisible City." *Architectural Forum* 136, no. 5 (May 1972): 41–42.

Binstock, Drew. "Interview with Alan Kay." *Dr. Dobb's,* July 10, 2012. http://www.drdobbs.com/architecture-and-design/interview-with-alan-kay/240003442.

Blackwell, Alan F. "The Reification of Metaphor as a Design Tool." *ACM Transactions on Computer-Human Interaction* 13, no. 4 (2006): 490–530.

Blackwell, Alan F., and Sally Fincher. "PUX: Patterns of User Experience." *Interaction* 17, no. 2 (March 2010): 27–31. doi:10.1145/1699775.1699782.

Bolt, Richard A. "Put-That-There: Voice and Gesture at the Graphics Interface." *ACM SIGGRAPH Computer Graphics* 14 (1980): 262–270.

Bolt, Richard A. *Spatial Data-Management.* Cambridge, MA: MIT Press, 1979.

Boston Architectural Center. *Architecture and the Computer.* Boston: Boston Architectural Center, 1964.

Boullée, Etienne Louis. "Architecture, Essai sur l'Art." In *Boullée and Visionary Architecture: Including Boullée's Architecture, Essay on Art,* edited by Helen Rosenau, 119–143. London; New York: Academy Editions; Harmony Books, 1976.

Bowker, Geof. "How to Be Universal: Some Cybernetic Strategies, 1943–70." *Social Studies of Science* 23 (1993): 107–127.

Boyd, Robin. "Antiarchitecture." *Architectural Forum* 129, no. 4 (1968): 84–85.

Brand, Stewart. *The Media Lab: Inventing the Future at MIT.* New York: Viking, 1987.

Bratton, Benjamin. "Logistics of Habitable Circulation." In *Speed and Politics,* edited by Paul Virilio, 7–24. Los Angeles: Semiotext(e), 2006.

Broadbent, Geoffrey, and Anthony Ward. *Design Methods in Architecture. Architectural Association Paper.* New York: G. Wittenborn, 1969.

Brodey, Warren. "Soft Architecture: The Design of Intelligent Environments." *Landscape* 17 (1967): 8–12.

Brodey, Warren, and Nilo A. Lindgren. "Human Enhancement: Beyond the Machine Age." *IEEE Spectrum* 5 (1968): 79–97.

Brooks, Rodney. *Achieving Artificial Intelligence through Building Robots*. Cambridge, MA: MIT Artificial Intelligence Laboratory, 1986.

Buchholz, Werner, ed. "Architectural Philosophy." In *Planning a Computer System*, 5–15. New York: McGraw-Hill, 1962.

Budds, Diana. "Rem Koolhaas: 'Architecture Has a Serious Problem Today.'" *Fast Company Co.Design*, May 22, 2016. http://www.fastcodesign.com/3060135/innovation-by-design/rem-koolhaas-architecture-has-a-serious-problem-today.

Burnham, Jack. "Notes on Art and Information Processing." In *Software: Information Technology: Its New Meaning for Art*, edited by Jack Burnham, 10–14. New York: Jewish Museum, 1970.

Carse, James P. *Finite and Infinite Games*. New York: Free Press, 1986.

Chermayeff, Serge, and Christopher Alexander. *Community and Privacy: Toward a New Architecture of Humanism*. Garden City, NY: Doubleday, 1963.

Cohill, Andrew. "Information Architecture and the Design Process." In *Taking Software Design Seriously: Practical Techniques for Human-Computer Interaction Design*, edited by John Karat, 95–114. Boston: Academic Press, 1991.

Colomina, Beatriz. "On Architecture, Production and Reproduction." In *Architectureproduction: Revisions 2*. Papers on Architectural Theory and Criticism, 6–23. New York: Princeton Architectural Press, 1988.

Coole, Diana H., and Samantha Frost. *New Materialisms: Ontology, Agency, and Politics*. Durham, NC: Duke University Press, 2010.

Cornberg, Sol. "Creativity and Instructional Technology." *Architectural Design* 38, no. 5 (1968): 214–217.

Crandall, Jordan. "Operational Media." *CTHEORY* a148 (January 6, 2005). http://www.ctheory.net/articles.aspx?id=441.

Crary, Jonathan. *Techniques of the Observer: On Vision and Modernity in the Nineteenth Century*. October Books. Cambridge, MA: MIT Press, 1992.

Crogan, Patrick. *Gameplay Mode: War, Simulation and Technoculture*. Minneapolis: University of Minnesota Press, 2011.

Cunningham, Ward, and Michael W. Mehaffy. "Wiki as Pattern Language." In *Proceedings of the 20th Conference on Pattern Languages of Programs*, 32:1–32:14. PLoP '13. USA: The Hillside Group, 2013.

de Sola Pool, Ithiel. *Technologies of Freedom*. Cambridge, MA: Belknap Press of Harvard University Press, 1983.

Donelson, William C. "Spatial Management of Information." *ACM SIGGRAPH Computer Graphics* 12 (1978): 203–209.

Duffy, Francis, and John Torrey. "A Progress Report on the Pattern Language." Paper presented at the Emerging Methods in Environmental Design and Planning; proceedings of the Design Methods Group first international conference, Cambridge, MA, June 1968.

Edwards, Paul N. *The Closed World: Computers and the Politics of Discourse in Cold War America*. Cambridge, MA: MIT Press, 1996.

Evans, Robin. *Translations from Drawing to Building and Other Essays*. London: Architectural Association, 1997.

Fisher, Scott. "Viewpoint Dependent Imaging: An Interactive Stereoscopic Display." Master's thesis, MIT, 1982.

Furtado, Gonçalo. "Envisioning an Evolving Architecture: The Encounters of Gordon Pask, Cedric Price and John Frazer." PhD diss., University College London, 2008.

Galloway, Alexander R. *Protocol: How Control Exists after Decentralization*. Cambridge, MA: MIT Press, 2004.

Galloway, Alexander R., and Eugene Thacker. *The Exploit: A Theory of Networks*. Minneapolis: University of Minnesota Press, 2007.

Garrett, Jesse James. "Ajax: A New Approach to Web Applications—Adaptive Path," February 18, 2005. http://adaptivepath.org/ideas/ajax-new-approach-web-applications/.

Garrett, Jesse James. "IA Summit 09—Plenary." *Boxes and Arrows*, April 5, 2009. http://boxesandarrows.com/ia-summit-09-plenary/.

Grabow, Stephen. *Christopher Alexander: The Search for a New Paradigm in Architecture. Stocksfield, Northumberland*. Boston: Oriel Press, 1983.

Grudin, Jonathan. "Turing Maturing: The Separation of Artificial Intelligence and Human-Computer Interaction." *interactions* 13, no. 6 (September–October 2006): 54–57.

Harary, Frank, and J. Rockey. "A City Is Not a Semilattice Either." *Environment & Planning A* 8, no. 4 (1976): 375–384.

Haraway, Donna Jeanne. "A Cyborg Manifesto." In *Simians, Cyborgs, and Women: The Reinvention of Nature*, 149–181. New York: Routledge, 1991.

Harwood, John. *The Interface: IBM and the Transformation of Corporate Design, 1945–1976*. Minneapolis: University of Minnesota Press, 2011.

Haugeland, John. *Artificial Intelligence: The Very Idea*. Cambridge, MA: MIT Press, 1985.

Hayles, N. Katherine. *How We Became Posthuman: Virtual Bodies in Cybernetics, Literature, and Informatics*. Chicago: University of Chicago Press, 1999.

Hayles, N. Katherine. *My Mother Was a Computer: Digital Subjects and Literary Texts*. Chicago: University of Chicago Press, 2005.

Herot, Christopher F. "Graphical Conversation Theory Proposal (Appendix)." In *Self-Disclosing Trainers: Proposal to the Army Research Office*, n.p. Cambridge, MA: MIT Architecture Machine Group, 1977.

Herot, Christopher F., Richard Carling, Mark Friedell, and David Kramlich. "A Prototype Spatial Data Management System." *ACM SIGGRAPH Computer Graphics* 14 (1980): 63–70.

Herot, Christopher F., and Guy Weinzapfel. "One-Point Touch Input of Vector Information for Computer Displays." *ACM SIGGRAPH Computer Graphics* 12, no. 3 (1977): 201–216.

Horn, Robert E. "Information Design: The Emergence of a New Profession." In *Information Design*, edited by Robert Jacobson, 15–34. Cambridge, MA: MIT Press, 1999.

Huizinga, Johan. *Homo Ludens: A Study of the Play Element in Culture*. London: Maurice Temple Smith, 1970.

Johnston, John. *The Allure of Machinic Life: Cybernetics, Artificial Life, and the New AI*. Cambridge, MA: MIT Press, 2008.

Karan, Pradyumna Prasad. "The Pattern of Indian Towns: A Study in Urban Morphology." *Journal of the American Institute of Planners* 23, no. 2 (1957): 70–75.

Katz, Barry M. *Make It New: A History of Silicon Valley Design*. Cambridge, MA: MIT Press, 2015.

Kay, Alan. "Personal Computing." In *Meeting on 20 Years of Computer Science*. Pisa, Italy: Istituto di Elaborazione della Informazione, 1975. https://mprove.de/diplom/gui/Kay75.pdf.

Keller, Sean. "Fenland Tech: Architectural Science in Postwar Cambridge." *Grey Room* 23 (2006): 40–65.

Keller, Sean. "Systems Aesthetics: Architectural Theory at the University of Cambridge, 1960–75." PhD diss., Harvard University, 2005.

Kitchin, Rob, and Martin Dodge. *Code/space: Software and Everyday Life*. Cambridge, MA: MIT Press, 2011.

Kittler, Friedrich A. *Optical Media: Berlin Lectures 1999*. Cambridge: Polity, 2010.

Klyn, Dan. "Make Things Be Good: Five Essential Lessons from the Life and Work of Richard Saul Wurman, UX Week 2013." Accessed July 18, 2016. http://2014.uxweek.com/videos/ux-week-2013-dan-klyn-make-things-be-good-five-essential-lessons-from-the-life-and-work-of-richard-saul-wurman.

Koffka, Kurt. *Principles of Gestalt Psychology*. International Library of Psychology, Philosophy and Scientific Method. New York: Harcourt, Brace and Company, 1935.

Landau, Royston. "An Architecture of Enabling—the Work of Cedric Price." *AA Files* 8 (Spring 1985): 3–7.

Landau, Royston. "Methodology of Scientific Research Programmes." In *Changing Design*, edited by Barrie Evans, James Powell, and Reg Talbot, 302–309. New York: Wiley, 1982.

Landau, Royston. *New Directions in British Architecture*. New York: G. Braziller, 1968.

Landau, Royston. "A Philosophy of Enabling." In *The Square Book*, edited by Cedric Price, 9–15. London: Architectural Association, 1984.

Landau, Royston. "Toward a Structure for Architectural Ideas." *Arena: The Architectural Association Journal* 81, no. 893 (June 1965): 7–11.

Lenoir, Timothy, and Henry Lowood. "Theaters of War: The Military-Entertainment Complex." In *Collection, Laboratory, Theater: Scenes of Knowledge in the 17th Century*, edited by Helmar Schramm, Ludger Schwarte, and Jan Lazardzig, 427–456. Berlin: Walter de Gruyter, 2005.

Licklider, J. C. R. "Man-Computer Symbiosis." *IRE Transactions on Human Factors in Electronics* HFE 1 (1960): 4–11.

Lindgren, Nilo A. "Human Factors in Engineering, Part I: Man in the Man-Made Environment." *IEEE Spectrum* 3 (1966): 132–139.

Llach, Daniel Cardoso. *Builders of the Vision: Software and the Imagination of Design*. London: Routledge, 2015.

Lobsinger, Mary Louise. "Cybernetic Theory and the Architecture of Performance: Cedric Price's Fun Palace." In *Anxious Modernisms: Experimentation in Postwar Architectural Culture*, edited by Sarah William Goldhagen and Réjean Legault, 199–140. Cambridge, MA: MIT Press, 2000.

Lobsinger, Mary Louise. "Programming Program: Cedric Price's Inter-Action Center." *werk, bauen+wohnen* 94, no. 12 (2007): 38–45.

Manovich, Lev. *The Language of New Media*. Cambridge, MA: MIT Press, 2002.

March, Lionel. "The Logic of Design and the Question of Value." In *The Architecture of Form*, edited by Lionel March, 1–40. Cambridge: Cambridge University Press, 1976.

Martin, William. *Network Planning for Building Construction*. London: Heinemann, 1969.

Marwick, Alice E. *Status Update: Celebrity, Publicity, and Branding in the Social Media Age*. New Haven, CT: Yale University Press, 2013.

Massanari, Adrienne. "In Context: Information Architects, Politics, and Interdisciplinarity." PhD diss., University of Washington, 2007.

Mathews, Stanley. "An Architecture for the New Britain: The Social Vision of Cedric Price's Fun Palace and Potteries Thinkbelt." PhD diss., Columbia University, 2003.

Mathews, Stanley. "Cedric Price as Anti-Architect." In *Architecture and Authorship*, edited by Tim Anstey, Katja Grillner, and Rolf Hughes, 142–147. London: Black Dog, 2007.

Mathews, Stanley. *From Agit-Prop to Free Space: The Architecture of Cedric Price*. London: Black Dog, 2007.

Mathews, Stanley. "The Fun Palace as Virtual Architecture: Cedric Price and the Practices of Indeterminacy." *Journal of Architectural Education* 59 (2006): 39–48.

Maturana, Humberto R., and Francisco J. Varela. *Autopoiesis and Cognition: The Realization of the Living*. Boston: D. Reidel, 1980.

McCarthy, Anna. "From Screen to Site: Television's Material Culture, and Its Place." *October* 98 (Fall 2001): 93–111.

McColough, C. Peter. "Searching for an Architecture of Information." Paper presented at the New York Society of Security Analysts, New York, March 3, 1970.

McCullough, Malcolm. *Digital Ground: Architecture, Pervasive Computing, and Environmental Knowing*. Cambridge, MA: MIT Press, 2004.

Minsky, Marvin. "Steps toward Artificial Intelligence." *Proceedings of the I.R.E.* 49, no. 1 (1961): 8–30.

Minsky, Marvin, and Seymour Papert. *Artificial Intelligence Progress Report*. Cambridge, MA: MIT Artificial Intelligence Lab, 1972.

Minsky, Marvin, and Seymour Papert. *Proposal to ARPA for Research on Artificial Intelligence at MIT, 1970–1971*. Cambridge, MA: MIT Artificial Intelligence Lab, 1970.

MIT. *Course and Degree Programs*. Cambridge, MA: MIT Press, 1972.

MIT. *Course and Degree Programs*. Cambridge, MA: MIT Press, 1977.

MIT. *MIT Report to the President*. Cambridge, MA: MIT Press, 1968.

MIT. *MIT Report to the President*. Cambridge, MA: MIT Press, 1980.

Moggridge, Bill. *Designing Interactions*. Cambridge, MA: MIT Press, 2007.

Mohl, Robert. "Cognitive Space in the Interactive Movie Map: An Investigation of Spatial Learning in Virtual Environments." PhD diss., MIT, 1981.

Moreno, Jacob. "Sociometry in Relation to Other Social Sciences." *Sociometry* 1, no. 1/2 (1937): 206–219.

My. "Lifeboat #5: Richard Saul Wurman." *Journal of Information Architecture* 3, no. 2. http://journalofia.org/volume3/issue2/02-my/.

My. *What Do We Use for Lifeboats When the Ship Goes Down?* New York: Harper & Row, 1976.

Negroponte, Nicholas. *The Architecture Machine*. Cambridge, MA: MIT Press, 1970.

Negroponte, Nicholas. "The Architecture Machine." *Computer Aided Design* 7 (1975): 190–195.

Negroponte, Nicholas. *Being Digital*. New York: Alfred A. Knopf, 1995.

Negroponte, Nicholas. "Books without Pages." 1979. Nicholas Negroponte Personal Papers, Cambridge, MA.

Negroponte, Nicholas. "The Computer in the Home: Scenario for 1985." Architecture Machine Group, Cambridge, MA: MIT, 1977.

Negroponte, Nicholas. "The Computer Simulation of Perception during Motion in the Urban Environment." Master's thesis, MIT, 1966.

Negroponte, Nicholas. *Dedication Booklet One, Draft*. Cambridge, MA: MIT Media Lab, 1984.

Negroponte, Nicholas. *Media Room*. Cambridge, MA: MIT Press, 1978.

Negroponte, Nicholas. "Recent Advances in Sketch Recognition." *Proceedings of the June 4–8, 1973, National Computer Conference and Exposition*, 663–675. New York: ACM, 1973.

Negroponte, Nicholas. *The Return of the Sunday Painter, or the Computer in the Visual Arts*. Manuscript, 1976. Nicholas Negroponte Personal Papers, Cambridge, MA.

Negroponte, Nicholas. *The Semantics of Architecture Machines*. Architectural Forum 133, no. 3, October 1970, 38–41.

Negroponte, Nicholas. "Sketching: A Computational Paradigm for Personalized Searching." *Journal of Architectural Education* 29 (1975): 26–29. Reprint. Nicholas Negroponte Personal Papers, Cambridge, MA.

Negroponte, Nicholas. *Soft Architecture Machines*. Cambridge, MA: MIT Press, 1975.

Negroponte, Nicholas. "Systems of Urban Growth." Bachelor's thesis, MIT, 1965.

Negroponte, Nicholas, and Richard A. Bolt. *Data Space Proposal to the Cybernetics Technology Office, Defense Advanced Research Projects Agency*. Cambridge, MA: MIT Press, 1978. Nicholas Negroponte Personal Papers, Cambridge, MA

Negroponte, Nicholas, and Leon Groisser. *URBAN2*. Cambridge, MA: IBM Scientific Center, 1967. Nicholas Negroponte Personal Papers, Cambridge, MA.

Negroponte, Nicholas, Leon Groisser, and James Taggart. "HUNCH: An Experiment in Sketch Recognition." 1971. Nicholas Negroponte Personal Papers, Cambridge, MA.

Nelson, Ted M. *Computer Lib/Dream Machines*. Chicago: Theodor H. Nelson, 1974.

Newell, Allen, J. C. Shaw, and Herbert A. Simon. *Report on a General Problem-Solving Program*. Santa Monica, CA: RAND Corporation, 1959.

Norberg, Arthur L. *An Interview with Terry Allen Winograd*. Charles Babbage Institute, Center for the History of Information Processing, University of Minnesota, 1991.

Norberg, Arthur, Judy O'Neill, and Kerry Freedman. *Transforming Computer Technology: Information Processing for the Pentagon, 1962–1986*. Baltimore, MD: Johns Hopkins University Press, 1996.

O'Doherty, Brian. *Object and Idea*. New York: Simon and Schuster, 1967.

Pangaro, Paul. "Thoughtsticker 1986: A Personal History of Conversation Theory in Software, and Its Progenitor Gordon Pask." *Kybernetes* 30, no. 5/6 (2001): 790–805.

Pask, Gordon. "The Architectural Relevance of Cybernetics." *Architectural Design* 39, no. 7 (1969): 494–496.

Pask, Gordon. "Aspects of Machine Intelligence." In *Soft Architecture Machines*, edited by Nicholas Negroponte, 6–31. Cambridge, MA: MIT Press, 1975.

Pask, Gordon. "A Comment, a Case History and a Plan." In *Cybernetics, Art, and Ideas*, edited by Jasia Reichardt, 76–99. Greenwich, CT: New York Graphic Society, 1971.

Passonneau, Joseph R., and Richard Saul Wurman. *Urban Atlas: 20 American Cities, a Communication Study Notating Selected Urban Data at a Scale of 1:48,000.* St. Louis, MO: Western Print and Lithographing, 1966.

Picon, Antoine. "From 'Poetry of Art' to Method: The Theory of Jean-Nicolas-Louis Durand." In *Jean-Nicolas-Louis Durand: Précis of the Lectures on Architecture: With Graphic Portion of the Lectures on Architecture*, 1–68. Los Angeles: Getty Publications, 2000.

Picon, Antoine. *Smart Cities: A Spatialised Intelligence—AD Primer.* John Wiley & Sons, 2015.

Pólya, George. *How to Solve It: A New Aspect of Mathematical Method.* Princeton, NJ: Princeton University Press, 1945.

Portola Institute. *The Last Whole Earth Catalog: Access to Tools.* Menlo Park, CA: Portola Institute, 1971.

Poster, Mark. "Theorizing Virtual Reality: Baudrillard and Derrida." In *The Information Subject*, edited by Mark Poster and Stanley Aronowitz, 117–138. London: Routledge, 2001.

Price, Cedric. "Atom: Design for New Learning for a New Town." *Architectural Design* 5 (May 1968): 232–235.

Price, Cedric. "Cedric Price Supplement #1." *Architectural Design* 40 (October 1970): 507–522.

Price, Cedric. "Cedric Price Supplement #3." *Architectural Design* 41 (June 1971): 353–369.

Price, Cedric. "Cedric Price Talks at the AA." *AA Files* 19 (1990): 27–34.

Price, Cedric. "Potteries Thinkbelt." *New Society* 7, no. 192 (June 1966): 14–17.

Price, Cedric. "Self-Pace Public Skill and Information Hive." *Architectural Design* 38, no. 5 (1968): 237–239.

Price, Cedric. *The Square Book.* London: Architectural Association, 1984.

Price, Cedric, Hans-Ulrich Obrist, Arata Isozaki, Patrick Keiller, and Rem Koolhaas. *Re-CP.* Basel: Birkhäuser, 2003.

Quattlebaum, Patrick. "A Conversation with Dan Klyn: Richard Saul Wurman & IA for UXers—Adaptive Path." http://adaptivepath.org/ideas/a-conversation-with-dan-klyn-richard-saul-wurman-and-ia-for-uxers/.

Resmini, Andrea, and Luca Rosati. "A Brief History of Information Architecture." *Journal of Information Architecture* 3, no. 2 (2012). http://journalofia.org/volume3/issue2/03-resmini/jofia-0302 -03-resmini.pdf.

Romanycia, Marc H. J., and Francis Jeffry Pelletier. "What Is a Heuristic?" *Computational Intelligence* 1 (1985): 47–58.

Rosenfeld, Louis. "Design—Structure and Effectiveness." *Web Review* (Archive.org), November 27, 1996. https://web.archive.org/web/19961127163741/http://webreview.com/95/08/17/design/arch /aug17/index.html.

Rosenfeld, Louis, and Peter Morville. *Information Architecture for the World Wide Web*. 1st ed. Sebastopol, CA: O'Reilly, 1998.

Sanoff, Henry, and Sidney Cohn, and the Environmental Design Research Association. *EDRA 1/1970: Proceedings of the 1st Annual Environmental Design Research Association Conference*. Chapel Hill, NC: EDRA, 1970.

Schmandt, Chris. *Put That There*. Cambridge, MA: MIT Press, 1979.

Shanken, Edward. "The House That Jack Built: Jack Burnham's Concept of 'Software' as a Metaphor for Art." *Leonardo Electronic Almanac* 6 (1998). http://www.artexetra.com/House.html.

Shields, Rob. *The Virtual*. London: Routledge, 2003.

Simon, Herbert A. *The Sciences of the Artificial*. Cambridge, MA: MIT Press, 1996.

Smith, Douglas K., and Robert C. Alexander. *Fumbling the Future: How Xerox Invented, Then Ignored, the First Personal Computer*. New York: W. Morrow, 1988.

Summerson, John. "The Case for a Theory of Modern Architecture." In *Architecture Culture, 1943– 1968: A Documentary Anthology*, edited by Joan Ockman and Edward Eigen, 226–236. New York: Rizzoli, 1993.

Sutherland, Ivan. "The Ultimate Display." In *Multimedia: From Wagner to Virtual Reality*, edited by Randall Packer and Ken Jordan, 253–257. New York: W. W. Norton, 2001.

Taggart, James. "Reading a Sketch by HUNCH." Bachelor's thesis, MIT, 1973.

Thacker, Eugene. "Foreword: Protocol Is as Protocol Does." In *Protocol: How Control Exists after Decentralization*, edited by Alexander R. Galloway, xi–xxii. Cambridge, MA: MIT Press, 2004.

Thompson, D'Arcy Wentworth. *On Growth and Form*. Cambridge: Cambridge University Press, 1917.

Tuan, Yi-Fu. *Space and Place: The Perspective of Experience*. Minneapolis: University of Minnesota Press, 2001.

Tufte, Edward. *Envisioning Information*. Cheshire, CT: Graphics Press, 1990.

Turing, Alan. "Computing Machinery and Intelligence." *Mind* 59 (1950): 433–460.

Turner, Fred. "Why Study New Games?" *Games and Culture* 1, no. 1 (2006): 107–110.

Umpleby, Stuart. "Heinz Von Foerster and the Mansfield Amendment." *Cybernetics & Human Knowing* 10, no. 3/4 (2003): 187–190.

Upitis, Alise. "Nature Normative: The Design Methods Movement, 1944–1967." PhD diss., MIT, 2008.

Vardouli, Theodora. "Design-for-Empowerment-for-Design: Computational Structures for Design Democratization." Master's thesis, MIT, 2012.

Virilio, Paul, and Sylvère Lotringer. *Pure War*. Foreign Agents Series. Los Angeles: Semiotext(e), 2008.

Vismann, Cornelia. *Files: Law and Media Technology*. Stanford, CA: Stanford University Press, 2008.

Wasserman, Stanley, and Katherine Faust. *Social Network Analysis: Methods and Applications*. Structural Analysis in the Social Sciences. Cambridge: Cambridge University Press, 1994.

Weitzman, Louis Murray. "The Architecture of Information: Interpretation and Presentation of Information in Dynamic Environments." PhD diss., MIT, 1995.

Weizenbaum, Joseph. "ELIZA—a Computer Program for the Study of Natural Language Communication between Man and Machine." *Communications of the ACM* 9, no. 1 (1966): 36–45.

Weizman, Eyal. *Hollow Land: Israel's Architecture of Occupation*. London: Verso, 2007.

Wiener, Norbert. *Cybernetics: Or, Control and Communication in the Animal and the Machine*. Cambridge, MA: Technology Press, 1948.

Wiener, Norbert. *Cybernetics: Or, Control and Communication in the Animal and the Machine*. Cambridge, MA: MIT Press, 1961.

Wiener, Norbert. *The Human Use of Human Beings: Cybernetics and Society*. Boston: Houghton Mifflin, 1954.

Wigley, Mark, and Howard Shubert. "Il Fun Palace di Cedric Price=Cedric Price's Fun Palace." *Domus* 866 (2004): 14–23.

Wildes, Karl L., and Nilo Lindgren. *A Century of Electrical Engineering and Computer Science at MIT, 1882–1982*. Cambridge, MA: MIT Press, 1985.

Winograd, Terry. *Bringing Design to Software*. New York; Reading, MA: ACM Press; Addison-Wesley, 1996.

Winograd, Terry. "Procedures as a Representation for Data in a Computer Program for Understanding Natural Language." PhD diss., MIT, 1971.

Winograd, Terry. "What Can We Teach About Human-Computer Interaction? (Plenary Address)." In *Proceedings of the SIGCHI Conference on Human Factors in Computing Systems*, 443–448. CHI '90. New York: ACM, 1990.

Winston, Patrick. "Learning Structural Descriptions from Examples." PhD diss., MIT, 1970.

Wodtke, Christina. "Towards a New Information Architecture: The Rise and Fall and Rise of a Necessary Discipline." *Medium*, February 16, 2014. https://medium.com/goodux-badux/towards-a-new-information-architecture-f38b5cc904c0#.f4gqifdrx.

Wolf, Gary. "The Wurmanizer." *Wired*, February 2002. http://www.wired.com/2000/02/wurman/.

Wurman, Richard Saul. "An American City: The Architecture of Information." Convention brochure. Washington, DC: AIA, 1976.

Wurman, Richard Saul. *Cities—Comparisons of Form and Scale: Models of 50 Significant Towns and Cities to the Scale of 1:43,200 or 1"=3,600'*. Philadelphia: Joshua Press, 1974.

Wurman, Richard Saul. "Hats." *Design Quarterly*, no. 145 (1989). Minneapolis, MN: MIT Press for the Walker Art Center.

Wurman, Richard Saul. *Information Anxiety*. 1st ed. New York: Doubleday, 1989.

Wurman, Richard Saul. *Information Anxiety 2*. Indianapolis: Que, 2001.

Wurman, Richard Saul. *Information Architects*. Edited by P. Bradford. Zurich, Switzerland: Graphis Press, 1996.

Wurman, Richard Saul. "Making the City Observable." *Design Quarterly* 80 (1971): 1–96.

Wurman, Richard Saul. *33: Understanding Change and the Change in Understanding*. 1st ed. Norcross, GA: Greenway Communications, 2009.

Wurman, Richard Saul, and Joel Katz. "Beyond Graphics: The Architecture of Information." *AIA Journal* 64, no. 10 (1975): 45–46.

Wurman, Richard Saul, and Scott W. Killinger. "Visual Information Systems." *Architecture Canada* 44, no. 3 (March 1967): 37–38, 44.

Index

Note: Page numbers in italics indicate figures.